W9-AYY-121

Standards and Public Policy

Technological standards are a cornerstone of the modern information economy, affecting firm strategy, market performance and, by extension, economic growth. While there is general agreement that swift movement to superior technological standards is a worthwhile goal, there is much less agreement on the central policy questions: do markets choose efficient standards? How do standards organizations affect the development of standards? And finally, what constitutes appropriate public policy toward standards? In this volume, leading researchers in public policy on standards, including both academics and industry experts, focus on these key questions. Given the dearth of applied work on standards and public policy, this volume significantly advances the frontier of knowledge in this critical but understudied area. It will be essential reading for academic and industrial researchers as well as policymakers.

SHANE GREENSTEIN is the Elinor and Wendell Hobbs Professor of Management and Strategy at the Kellogg School of Management, Northwestern University.

VICTOR STANGO is an Associate Professor of Economics at the Tuck School of Business at Dartmouth.

Standards and
Public Policy

Edited by

SHANE GREENSTEIN AND VICTOR STANGO

CAMBRIDGE
UNIVERSITY PRESS

CAMBRIDGE UNIVERSITY PRESS
Cambridge, New York, Melbourne, Madrid, Cape Town, Singapore, São Paulo

Cambridge University Press
The Edinburgh Building, Cambridge CB2 2RU, UK

Published in the United States of America by Cambridge University Press, New York

www.cambridge.org
Information on this title: www.cambridge.org/9780521864503

First published 2007

Printed in the United Kingdom at the University Press, Cambridge

A catalogue record for this publication is available from the British Library

ISBN-13 978-0-521-86450-3 hardback
ISBN-10 0-521-86450-X hardback

Contents

Figures

Tables

Contributors

SHERRIE BOLIN	is President and CEO of The Bolin Group.
TIMOTHY BRESNAHAN	is Landau Professor in Technology and the Economy, Stanford University.
LUIS CABRAL	is Professor of Economics and Chair, Department of Economics, Leonard Stern School of Business, New York University.
CARL CARGILL	is Head of Corporate Standards at Sun Microsystems.
JOSEPH FARRELL	is Professor of Economics, University of California at Berkeley.
NEIL GANDAL	is Professor in and Chair of Department of Public Policy, School of Government and Policy, Tel Aviv University.
NATALY GANTMAN	is a Ph.D. Candidate in Economics at Tel Aviv University.
DAVID GENESOVE	is a Professor in the Department of Economics at the Hebrew University of Jerusalem.
SHANE GREENSTEIN	is the Elinor and Wendell Hobbs Professor in the Management and Strategy Department of the Kellogg School of Management at Northwestern University.
TOBIAS KRETSCHMER	is a Lecturer in Strategy and Economics, Interdisciplinary Institute of Management (IIM), London School of Economics.
RICHARD N. LANGLOIS	is Professor of Economics at the University of Connecticut.

JEFFREY MACKIE-MASON	is the Arthur W. Burks Professor of Information and Computer Science, and a Professor of Economics and Public Policy at the University of Michigan.
NORBERT MAIER	is a Ph.D. Candidate in Economics at London Business School.
M. LYNNE MARKUS	is the John W. Poduska, Sr. Professor of Information Management at Bentley College.
GABE MINTON	is a Senior Director of Industry Technology at the Mortgage Bankers Association of America.
JANET NETZ	is a Principal at ApplEcon, LLC.
MARCO OTTAVIANI	is Associate Professor of Economics at the London Business School.
MARC RYSMAN	is Assistant Professor of Economics at Boston University.
TIMOTHY SIMCOE	is Assistant Professor of Strategy, Rotman School of Management, University of Toronto.
VICTOR STANGO	is Associate Professor of Business Administration in the Tuck School of Business at Dartmouth.
CHARLES STEINFIELD	is a Professor in the Department of Telecommmunication, Information Studies, and Media at Michigan State University.
JOEL WEST	is Associate Professor of Technology Management, Department of Organization & Management, College of Business, San José State University.
ROLF WIGAND	is the Maulden-Entergy Chair and Distinguished Professor of Information Science and Management at the University of Arkansas at Little Rock.
PAI-LING YIN	is Assistant Professor of Strategy at Harvard Business School.

Introduction

SHANE GREENSTEIN AND
VICTOR STANGO

T ECHNOLOGICAL standards are a cornerstone of the modern information economy. These standards affect firm strategy, market performance and, by extension, economic growth. While there is general agreement that swift movement to superior technological standards is a worthwhile goal, there is much less agreement on how an economy can attain those goals in specific instances. Sometimes there are even debates about whether appropriate standards arose in past episodes – for example, academics still dispute whether Betamax was a technically superior video cassette recorder (VCR) to VHS. Answers are not transparent because a variety of market and nonmarket processes determines the evolution of standards. By default, decentralized market mechanisms, private firms, and standards development organizations shape the development and diffusion of standards.

In addition, when government actors step in to sponsor a new standard or move the market between standards, as they occasionally do, debates about the interaction of competing market and technical factors are not merely academic, nor are the answers transparent. Government actors can make choices about competing specifications for a standard and often have the power to mandate compliance with the standard. Moreover, rarely are these decisions reversed, and when they are, the events are noted for their rarity. For example, the Federal Communication Commission's decision to alter its prior choice over the color television standard a few years later prevented the country from employing technology that all experts regarded as obsolete. It was clearly the right decision in retrospect, and it raises the troubling question about how many poor choices have been made but not reversed because the mistake was less obvious to decision makers than to the technology insiders.

General agreement about appropriate public policy toward government standard setting does not exist. The most basic questions remain

1

unaddressed. For example, when should policymakers move markets between standards? And when is a government policy favoring compatibility superior to one that fosters – or at least accedes to – competition between incompatible systems?

Despite considerable attention from economic theory, many of these questions remain open. Historically, most research has appropriately attempted to answer questions regarding market competition between competing standards.[1] And, if the reader will allow a bold and sweeping assessment about the received wisdom in the field, despite the existing substantial body of work informed policy values two types of studies that are not yet abundant: (1) empirical studies of standardization that compare and contrast outcomes with and without government intervention and (2) studies identifying the key theoretical trade-offs between the vast variety of mechanisms for determining standards, such as government-based, market-oriented, and the many quasi-market and nonmarket processes.[2]

With that in mind, on May 13 and 14, 2004, the Federal Reserve Bank of Chicago and Northwestern University cosponsored a conference entitled "Standards and Public Policy." The conference brought together roughly forty experts in public policy on standards, including economists from academia, the Federal Reserve System, and industry. We have compiled twelve papers from the conference presentations. Readers will note our emphasis: The volume contains papers focusing on applied questions at the nexus of the pragmatic and puzzling. The goal was to move beyond well-examined settings to less familiar ground.

In this introduction, we briefly place the chapters that follow in context. The early chapters are empirical studies of actual standards competition. Middle chapters focus on committees and standards organizations, while the last section of the book examines governmental approaches to standards policy. We cannot claim that this collection is comprehensive. Indeed, we must admit that certain issues remain nearly as murky as before: Our concluding chapter is a self-admittedly tortuous attempt to go beyond "it depends" in the policy debate, by an

---

[1] We do this literature a disservice by referring to it so casually, but we do so in the interest of brevity.
[2] The earlier collections by Besen and Johnson (1986), Gabel (1987, 1991), and Grindley (1995) are exceptions.

expert who has contributed at least as much as any other researcher in the field. Nonetheless, the consensus of our conference attendees is that (at least) this type of discussion moves our understanding forward, even if ultimate answers are hard to find. We hope our readers reach the same conclusion.

1 The economics of standards competition

There are a host of prominent historical cases involving duels between competing standards. The VHS/Betamax duel in the VCR markets is a well-known case. There are many others, such as GSM (Global System for Mobile Communications) versus CDMA (Code-Division Multiple Access) and TDMA (Time Division Multiple Access) in cell phones, IBM (International Business Machines) versus DEC (Digital Equipment Corporation) in minicomputers, Microsoft Word versus Word Perfect in word processing, and US Robotics versus Rockwell in 56 K modems. Standards wars also commonly arise as subplots to related larger product market duels. For example, various banks may belong to incompatible ATM (automatic teller machine) networks, and United Airlines and American Airlines sponsor competing airline reservation systems.

What happens in one of these classic standards wars has been the subject of much study.[3] A primary concern is whether the market can settle on an inefficient standard or optimal speed of adoption. This has been at issue in many of the historical episodes mentioned. As an example, consider the decision faced by adopters of a new communication standard such as the fax machine. If no consumers have fax machines, then no one consumer will want to adopt the first fax machine, because a fax machine has no stand-alone value if it cannot communicate with other machines. Thus, adoption by none seems a plausible outcome – though most prefer a situation in which many

---

[3] Rather than attempting to be exhaustive in our references, we refer the reader to surveys that highlight the main points of the literature. David and Greenstein (1990) is a comprehensive survey of the literature on standards. See Stango (2004) for a more narrowly focused recent discussion of standards wars. Besen and Farrell (1994) and Katz and Shapiro (1994) are excellent pieces covering the economics of compatibility and standards wars. Gandal (2002) provides a more recent survey of some public policy issues related to compatibility and standardization.

consumers adopt. This is a potentially serious policy concern, especially when society as a whole is worse off with adoption by none
instead of by many.[4]

Another related concern is the possibility that the market can exhibit
lock-in, or what Farrell and Saloner (1985) call *excess inertia*, namely,
the propensity to become trapped on an inferior standard. The intuition Farrell and Saloner describe is a situation in which "[adopters] are
fence-sitters, happy to jump on the bandwagon [of the new standard] if
it gets rolling but insufficiently keen to set it rolling themselves."

Based on this theoretical insight, there is at least a weak consensus in
the literature that market-based movement between standards may be
suboptimal. "Suboptimal relative to what alternative?" is a reasonable
question to ask in response. Networks may not develop at all if most
participants are lukewarm about a new standard due to technical
uncertainty, even though all would collectively benefit from it.
Alternatively, bandwagons may gather speed remarkably quickly
once a network becomes large enough to justify investments by potential adopters – indeed, suggesting that markets may, in fact, move
between standards too quickly in some circumstances. The lack of
any or even partial communication between or among all the potentially affected decision makers can exacerbate such bandwagons.

Despite abundant theoretical thinking on these issues, there have
been only a few empirical studies of the economic determinants of
standards. These studies are enabled by the appearance of data allowing researchers to examine standards issues by using econometric techniques.[5] These studies have focused on understanding the mechanisms
behind market events, not their welfare outcomes. Dranove and
Gandal (2003), for example, study application entry in the DVD/
DivX (digital video disc/digital video express) war. DVD and DivX
were two competing technical formats, and one quickly failed in the
marketplace. Dranove and Gandal find that the "preannouncement" of

---

[4] In fact, in this particular case, it was also a concern that contemporaries did worry
about. The technical specifications that became embedded in the fax machine
underwent several revisions (without widespread use) before finally becoming
widely adopted. See the detailed account in Schmidt and Werle (1998).

[5] This discussion omits mention of the growing empirical literature that focuses on
establishing the existence of either direct or indirect network effects, rather than
on standards per se (see, e.g., Rohlfs [2001] or Farrell and Klemperer [in press] for
a discussion of this literature).

the DivX standard affected the adoption of DVD technology, though they do not attempt to assess whether this outcome was efficient. Gandal et al. (1999) show that the diffusion of the new DOS (disc operating system) standard was affected by the availability of complementary software, but similarly do not attempt to ascertain whether the transition was efficient.

Another example of this line of research is a recent paper by Ohashi (2003), which estimates the importance of network effects in the VHS/Betamax standards battle.[6] An interesting result of Ohashi's analysis is that while it appears that consumers valued the VHS standard early in the battle, he estimates that it would have been possible for Betamax to capture the market if it had used its first-mover advantage to build an installed base through low pricing. Again, this analysis focuses on understanding the results from market mechanisms and process, an understanding that would inform policy choices without presuming what type of actions are optimal.

In this same vein, this volume contains three contributions to the literature dealing with competition between standards. Chapter 1, by Timothy F. Bresnahan, Stanford University, and Pai-Ling Yin, Harvard Business School, adds to our knowledge of empirical circumstances shaping the determination of de facto standards. The authors study both economic and technical forces affecting the diffusion of Web browsers, focusing on why Netscape Navigator eventually lost its lead as a de facto standard to Microsoft Internet Explorer. They draw on the theory of standard setting, especially on the positive economics predictions about market outcomes, such as a tendency to tip and a tendency toward inertia. The basic insights of standard setting theory are borne out in the browser war. They introduce new considerations in their analysis of market conditions, such as the rate of growth of demand and the distribution system. This leads to a complete positive theory of standard setting and a complete theory for explaining the otherwise surprising reversal.

---

[6] This paper is part of a larger recent literature using structural techniques to estimate the importance of network effects. Rysman (2003) is an early paper examining network effects in the Yellow Pages market. Nair et al. (2003) estimate the magnitude of indirect network effects between Personal Digital Assistants (PDAs) and PDA software. Knittel and Stango (2004) estimate the strength of network effects in ATM markets.

Chapter 2, by Richard Langlois, University of Connecticut, examines institutional structure as a competitive force in standards wars. He looks at the US cluster tool industry, which manufactures the equipment used to produce semiconductors. Competition for these tools is divided between a large vertically integrated firm, Applied Materials, which uses its own proprietary specifications, and a fringe of more specialized competitors. The fringe has responded to the competition from Applied Materials by creating a common set of technical interface standards.

Rather than calling this a standards battle, Langlois notes that it is better thought of as a battle of alternative development paths: The closed systemic approach of Applied Materials versus the open modular system of the competitive fringe. He analyzes the trade-off between the benefits of system innovation and internal economies of scale and scope on the one hand and the benefits of modular innovation and external economies of standardization on the other. While this case provides an interesting example of an industry where diverse approaches to standardization may coexist, the industry is starting to undergo change. Langlois observes that the industry may see a transformation to a more common structure, where several larger firms adhere to common standards and become broadly compatible systems integrators that outsource manufacturing to specialized suppliers of subsystems.

Chapter 3, by Joel West, San Jose State University, looks at the meaning of open standards in market competition. West defines a standard as open if the "rights to the standard [are] made available to economic actors other than sponsors." He indicates that this transfer can occur if rights are waived or conceded, licensed to other organizations, or are not protected by force of law, such as a patent. He points out that while open product compatibility standards are often viewed as socially optimal, the reality is that not all open standards are really open. His paper illuminates the different aspects for openness and their implications for adoption, competition, and public policy.

West argues that it is important to determine who has access to the standard, including customers, complementors, and competitors. Next, it is necessary to decipher what rights are made available to those who have access to the standard, such as creating the specification, using the specification, and using an implementation. Overall, access to the standard can be limited through membership requirements on the creator side or use rights on the user side. West suggests that policymakers could address the deficiencies in openness in several ways, including direct regulation, procurement, intellectual property law, and competition policy.

These three chapters deal with different aspects of standards competition. Indeed, they all focus on problems that are highly relevant to the business and user communities, which raise questions about the choices faced by market participants. Such research and exploration is a promising development, as it moves the conversation toward applied issues that policymakers must grapple with in actual circumstances.

2 Standards organizations and firm strategy

Although standardization often occurs through competition, nonmarket processes may also shape outcomes. These processes take a variety of forms. Confronted with an incipient or active standards war, firms may behave cooperatively to settle things through joint ventures, consortia or other alliances. For example, banks have formed shared ATM networks (e.g., Star, Plus, and Cirrus) as joint ventures to internalize the network benefit associated with allowing customers access to any banks' ATM machines, as well as to create a sponsor for the standard. They may also develop standards through explicit industry consensus, usually mediated within a formalized industry process. These formal de jure standards can emerge from a specialized industry standards body, or ratification by a standard setting organization (SSO) such as the American National Standards Institute, or ANSI.[7]

The SSOs play many useful roles in solving network coordination problems, especially those related to lack of communication. They can serve as forums for affected parties to educate each other or settle disputes. Clearly, these groups are most likely to succeed when market participants mutually desire interoperability, need to establish a mechanism for communication, and need a mechanism to develop or

---

[7] An organization that handles standards in the United States, ANSI is a subgroup of the ISO (International Standards Organization), which is an umbrella group containing a host of standards bodies.

choose from one of many technical alternatives. For example, this was the role taken by grocers groups in the development of bar codes for retail products. It is also the role taken by the International Telecommunication Union (ITU) in the development and upgrading of interoperability standards for fax machines and related products that use similar protocols.

Unfortunately, standards organizations are not a perfect solution to coordination problems. They can easily fall prey to some of the same structural impediments that plague standards wars. The development of UNIX standards in the 1980s illustrates these weaknesses. Many firms perceived strategic alliances as tools to further their own economic interests and block unfavorable outcomes. As a result, two different consortia, Open Software Foundation and Unix International, originally sponsored two different UNIX standards; and industry participants lined up behind one or another on the basis of economic self-interest. In the early 1990s, the market was confused yet again as different consortia (and firms) sponsored slightly different forms of UNIX. Only the surprising emergence and widespread adoption of Linux in the latter part of the 1990s moved the situation closer to unification around a single technical specification, reducing costs to the building of complementary tools and applications, as well as reducing the costs of maintenance across installation for system integrators and other information technology consultants.

It is no secret that the specifications underlying most standards are at least partially determined in these nonmarket settings. That raises issues associated with the alliances and standards organizations that foster cooperation among firms. Such cooperation can yield procompetitive benefits, but it also can run afoul of antitrust law. There is tension between the benefits accruing from cooperation and the antitrust issues involved with such cooperative behavior. The recent antitrust cases against Mastercard and Visa illustrate the importance of this issue.[8] The inability to overcome the disagreements in the current high-definition–DVD/Blu-ray standards war illustrates the issues when cooperation does not emerge.

There have been several economic studies of nonmarket nongovernmental processes. For example, in his 1996 work, Farrell studies the performance of standard setting bodies, focusing on the trade-offs

---

[8] See Evans (2003) for a discussion of these issues.

between the delays inherent in achieving consensus and the benefits of avoiding a costly standards war. His key notion is of *vested interests*, which are asymmetries between the payoffs of the "winner" and "loser" after a standard has been adopted (the winner is that whose proposed standard is adopted). These vested interests cause delay and impede consensus. Strategies to reduce vested interests, such as licensing, can therefore improve outcomes. In other work, Farrell (1989, 1995) also discusses a similar point in a less formal way, suggesting that weakening intellectual property protection can help markets settle on standards more quickly.[9]

This book contains several studies of the activities inside SSOs. In Chapter 4 of this volume, Shane Greenstein, Northwestern University, and Marc Rysman, Boston University, focus on the early 56K-modem market to highlight the coordination costs of resolving a standards war. The standards war in the 56K-modem market involved two very similar network technologies. The ITU was apparently helpful in resolving the conflict, by establishing a focal point for the industry. Nevertheless, the development of focal points carries costs – in this case, those of membership, meeting, submission, and negotiation associated with the standard setting process. This combination of explicit and implicit costs can add further complications to reaching an effective consensus. The voting environment also has implications for the resolution process. The ITU uses a consensus voting system. Since all firms in the market are members, each can delay the process if its own concerns are not met. The authors conclude that the ITU acted in a way that produced net benefits. In their view, it is unlikely that the alternatives of regulation or the market would have overcome the social costs of coordination any more easily.

Chapter 5, by Charles Steinfield, Michigan State University; Rolf Wigand, University of Arkansas; M. Lynne Markus, Bentley College; and Gabe Minton, Mortgage Bankers Association of America, is a rich study of vertical information systems standards in the US mortgage industry. These standards may address product identification, data definitions, standardized business documents, and/or business process sequences. The case study identifies three important processes in this

---

[9] The primary focus of his discussion – particularly in the 1989 article – is on compatibility and whether markets achieve efficient levels of adoption rather than on markets' choice between competing standards, but the intuition applies.

environment: (1) the way that the standardization process is structured to facilitate participation and consensus, (2) the approaches used to promote adoption of open standards, and (3) the steps taken to ensure the ongoing maintenance and integrity of the standard. The results emphasize the importance of

- company and individual incentives,
- using formal and informal governance mechanisms to minimize conflict and reach consensus,
- inclusive and proactive policies regarding membership,
- a limited scope of standardization activities,
- explicit intellectual property rights policy, and
- trying to institutionalize the entire standardization process into a formal structure.

Chapter 6, by Neil Gandal, Tel Aviv University, Michigan State University; Nataly Gantman, Tel Aviv University; and David Genesove, Hebrew University, focuses on how firms interact in standards organizations to influence their product market, in this case the modem market. Gandal, Gantman, and Genesove explain that network effects are inherent in the modem market because Internet users and Internet Service Providers benefit as more people adopt compatible technology; furthermore, interoperability is crucial for the seamless transmission of data.

While over 200 companies in this market attended standardization meetings from 1990 to 1999 and around the same number received patents from 1976 to 1999, only 45 firms did both. Firms receiving at least one modem patent were more likely to have attended at least one standardization meeting during these time periods; furthermore, large firms are more likely to attend standardization meetings. These results suggest that large firms are behaving strategically; they may in fact be over-attending meetings. While the results show that attendance at meetings and thus getting patents is beneficial, for smaller firms the benefits may not translate into greater market share.

The chapters above again illustrate areas where theory meets the activities of market-based actors. The SSOs can be valuable institutions (as evinced by their ubiquity). Moreover, their existence induces a real possibility for strategic behavior, some of which contributes to outcomes that benefit both users and producers and some of which does not. More work in this area would certainly improve policy.

3 The structure and performance of standards organizations

The problems inherent in standards organizations have been addressed generally by the public choice literature.[10] Yet, the organizational form of standards bodies has received only occasional attention from academic researchers. There is anecdotal evidence that standards bodies often serve as forums for interest group competition, which suggests there is ample room to extend the "economic theory of regulation" to these organizations.[11] User interests can be nonproportionally represented, since users tend to be diffuse and not technically sophisticated enough to master many issues. In addition, large firms often have an advantage in volunteering resources that influence the outcome, such as trained engineers to serve in the organization – engineers who may write standards in their employers' interests. Finally, insiders have the advantage in manipulating procedural rules, shopping between relevant committees, and lobbying for their long-term interests. This can lead to either extraordinary investment in the process to influence outcomes or to "free-riding" off the activities of the organization.

These themes arise in the next three chapters. Chapter 7, by Jeffrey MacKie-Mason, University of Michigan, and Janet Netz, ApplEcon, LLC, discusses interface standards as an anticompetitive strategy at the component level. While economists often assume that standards reduce barriers to entry, consortia can create entry barriers through a number of avenues, such as delaying publication of the standard to gain a first-mover advantage; manipulating standards to require other firms to use royalty-bearing intellectual property; and creating an extra technology layer, which the authors identify and label as "one-way" standards. The authors discuss the conditions under which one-way standards can be anticompetitive. In this strategy, a consortium creates an extra technology layer, or a *translator*, and publishes the information necessary to manufacture compliant components on only one side of the translator. When the consortium does this, the consortium can move the boundary separating systems away from mix-and-match competition and exclude competition on the private side – while appearing open by enabling component competition on the public side.

[10] Weiss (1993) makes a similar point.
[11] The economic theory of regulation derives from work by Becker (1983), Peltzman (1976), and Stigler (1971).

Chapter 8, by Timothy Simcoe, University of Toronto, examines the time it takes SSOs to reach consensus. He studies the Internet Engineering Task Force (IETF) – the organization that issues the technical standards used to run the Internet. The time period of his analysis, 1992–2000, is interesting because "rapid commercialization of the internet led to some dramatic changes in its size, structure, and demographic composition." Simcoe examines the relationship between the composition of IETF committees and time to consensus. Several factors influence the time to consensus: Specifically, the number of participants on a committee of the underlying technology, its interdependency with other standards, the set of design alternatives available to the committees, the economic significance of the specification, and the rules governing the consensus decision-making process. Simcoe shows that there was a significant slowdown in IETF standard setting between 1992 and 2000. Over this period, the median time from first draft to final specification more than doubled, growing from seven to fifteen months. Cross-sectional variation in size, complexity, and indicators of distributional conflict for individual Working Groups or proposals explains only a small portion of the overall slowdown. The remaining is seemingly attributable to changes in IETF-wide culture and bottlenecks in the later stages of the review process.

Chapter 9, by Carl Cargill, Sun Microsystems, and Sherrie Bolin, The Bolin Group, considers recent trends in the organization and performance of SSOs. Cargill and Bolin note that over the last decade, the standard setting process as embodied by many SSOs has become problematic. This deterioration stems in part from the ease with which private entities can form SSOs and "stack" them with members acting in their interests. Competition follows among SSOs organized by competing interests, which is not much better than market-based competition between standards and may even be worse. The authors also lament the lack of clear jurisdictional and procedural rules for SSOs. Cargill and Bolin's policy remedy for the latter problem in particular is the establishment of clearer and more open rules for membership and participation in SSOs. Such a change could move the process of standard setting back within a smaller number of archetypical SSOs, thereby minimizing the societal costs of competition between SSOs.

These chapters push the analysis of SSOs to a new level, yielding many new insights about strategic behavior inside these organizations. All the papers raise issues about the efficacy and goals of rules and norms inside SSOs, which suggests there is ample motivation for more work to inform policy.

4 Standards and government policy

The final section of our volume concerns government approaches to standard setting. Government policy for standards and SSOs lies in disparate places, attended to by industry experts in federal agencies (e.g., the Federal Communication Commission) or state regulators with local jurisdiction (e.g., state and local regulation of electrical supply). In addition, government bodies may also shape the development of standards or the economic networks that grow up around standards. Secure telecommunication transmission standards were important in hastening innovation in customer premises markets, such as fax machines and modems, and in other markets that interconnected with telephones, such as Internet Service Providers. Indeed, the success of third parties in US communications network comes partly from AT&T's standardizing the technology of its network, as well as the Federal Communication Commission's intervention to standardize interconnection in places where AT&T could have done so, but did not.

Formal examination of government policy in determining standards faces many challenges. History never reruns itself with one action and then another as in a laboratory setting, so researchers must make inferences from comparisons across time or region, if that is possible. There are additional inherent constraints on collecting data, interviewing participants, and gaining wider perspective on the lessons from experience. Studies that overcome these challenges are particularly notable and insightful, such as the rich analyses in Besen and Johnson's (1986) study of FM radio and color television, Neuman et al.'s (1999) study of policy formation for National Information Infrastructure, and Farrell and Shapiro's (1992) study of the US high-definition television standards development process.

This book contains a number of contributions in this area. Chapter 10, by Luis Cabral, New York University, and Tobias Kretschmer, London School of Economics, focuses on a policymaker's choice between competing standards and timing of intervention. The authors observe that policymakers may be impatient or patient – caring solely either about the welfare of current adopters of a standard or exclusively about the welfare of future adopters. According to the model, an impatient policymaker should act promptly and support the leading standard. A patient policymaker should delay intervention and eventually support the lagging standard. The authors note that their model is appropriate only for extreme specifications of policymakers' preferences. Real-world policymakers will fall somewhere between the extremes in the model. Cabral and Kretschmer suggest that policymakers may not always choose the superior standard given their preferences.

Chapter 11, by Norbert Maier and Marco Ottaviani, London Business School, models the public policy issues surrounding the transition from the analog to digital television standards. They investigate the incentives of broadcasters to use subsidies and sunset dates to affect the viewers' decisions to switch from analog to digital television. Policymakers have many policy levers, such as controls on the quality of the signals and the content of public services broadcasters; subsidies to manufacturers, broadcasters, or viewers; or a firm switch-off date for the analog signal. They explore a theoretical model where viewers may or may not have identical preferences for digital television. When their preferences are identical, it is never optimal for the broadcaster to subsidize just a fraction of viewers. When instead viewers place different values on the gain from using digital television, broadcasters might want to induce viewers to switch gradually. They also discuss the implications for welfare and effects of universal service requirements.

The final essay of the book, Chapter 12, by Joseph Farrell, University of California Berkeley, discusses the appropriateness of government policies that force compatibility between competing systems or standards. Such compatibility shifts the level of competition from the "system" to the individual components that comprise the standard. Farrell notes that despite considerable attention devoted to this issue, the overall benefits of shifting compatibility to the component level remain ambiguous. Farrell ultimately concludes that in many cases component competition is more beneficial, in large part because component competition increases consumers' choices. There are, however, countervailing benefits from systems competition: For example, it often induces more aggressive pricing. Nonetheless, Farrell urges that the force of most situations generally moves policymakers towards favoring component competition.

5 Conclusion

The process of standardization in markets with network effects is justifiably receiving greater attention than ever before from academics, industry observers, and policymakers. At this point, the questions are well known: Under what type of circumstances should government actors consider intervening in market processes for selecting standards, if at all? How well do nonmarket mechanisms perform by comparison? What trade-offs do policymakers face when choosing standards or shaping the legal restrictions faced by participations in SSOs?

Answers are less readily forthcoming. Perhaps that should be expected. Theoretical work in network economics has clarified our understanding of the circumstances under which problems can occur. But this literature has also shown that many outcomes are possible. Policy intervention may ameliorate the problems arising in standards wars, but they carry their own set of issues. Only a rich and deep analysis will sort between the possible, the plausible, and the optimal.

This book includes some encouraging recent research – theory, empirical studies, and essays – going to the heart of the debate on standards. Such research provides reason to be optimistic that our understanding of the economics of standardization will improve. As we said previously, we hope readers of this volume reach the same conclusion.

References

Becker, G. S. 1983. "A theory of competition among pressure groups for political influence," *Quarterly Journal of Economics* 98: 371–400.

Besen, S., and J. Farrell 1994. "Choosing how to compete: Strategies and tactics in standardization," *Journal of Economic Perspectives* 8: 117–31.

Besen, S., and L. L. Johnson 1986. "Compatibility standards, competition, and innovation in the broadcasting industry," *Rand Report*: R-3453-NSF, Santa Monica, CA: Rand Corporation, November.

David, P. A., and S. Greenstein 1990. "The economics of compatibility standards: An introduction to recent research," *Economics of Innovation and New Technology* 1: 3–41.

Dranove, D., and N. Gandal 2003. "The DVD vs. DIVX standard war: Empirical evidence of preannouncement effects," *Journal of Economics and Management Strategy* 12: 363–86.

Evans, D. 2003. "The antitrust economics of multi-sided platform markets," *Yale Journal on Regulation* 20: 325–81.

Farrell, J. 1989. "Standardization and intellectual property," *Jurimetrics Journal* 30: 35–50.

 1995. "Arguments for weaker intellectual property protection in network industries," *StandardView* 3: 46–9.

 1996. "Choosing the rules for formal standardization," mimeo, University of California, Berkeley.

Farrell, J., and P. Klemperer, in press. "Coordination and lock-in: Competition with switching costs and network effects," in *Handbook of industrial organization*, Vol. III, Mark Armstrong and Robert Porter (eds.), Amsterdam: Elsevier.

Farrell, J., and G. Saloner 1985. "Standardization, compatibility and innovation," *RAND Journal of Economics* 16: 70–83.

Farrell, J., and C. Shapiro 1992. "Standard setting in high-definition television," *Brookings Papers on Economic Activity: Microeconomics* 1992: 1–93.

Gabel, H. L. 1987. *Product standardization and competitive strategy: Advanced series in management*, Vol. XI. Amsterdam: North-Holland.

 1991. *Competitive strategies for product standards*. New York: McGraw-Hill.

Gandal, N. 2002. "Compatibility, standardization and network effects: Some policy implications," *Oxford Review of Economic Policy* 18: 80–91.

Gandal, N., S. Greenstein, and D. Salant 1999. "Adoptions and orphans in the early microcomputer market," *Journal of Industrial Economics* 47: 87–105.

Grindley, P. 1995. *Standards strategy and policy*. New York: Oxford University Press.

Katz, M. L., and C. Shapiro 1994. "Systems competition and network effects," *Journal of Economic Perspectives* 8: 93–115.

Knittel, Christopher, and Victor Stango 2004. "Incompatibility, product attributes and consumer welfare: Evidence from ATMs," National Bureau of Economic Research Working Paper #10962, Cambridge, MA.

Nair, H., P. Chintagunta, and J. Dube 2003. "Empirical analysis of indirect network effects in the market for personal digital assistants," mimeo, University of Chicago.

Neuman, Russell W., Lee W. McKnight, and Richard Jay Soloman 1999. *The Gordian Knot: Gridlock on the information highway*. Cambridge, MA: MIT Press.

Ohashi, H. 2003. "The role of network effects in the US VCR market, 1978–86," *Journal of Economics and Management Strategy* 12: 447–94.

Peltzman, S. 1976. "Toward a more general theory of regulation," *Journal of Law & Economics*, 19: 211–48.

Rohlfs, Jeffrey 2001. *Bandwagon effects in high technology industries.* Cambridge, MA: MIT Press.

Rysman, M. 2003. "Competition between networks: A study of the market for Yellow Pages," *Review of Economic Studies* 71: 483–512.

Schmidt, S. K. and R. Werle 1998. *Coordinating technology: Studies in international standardization of telecommunications.* Cambridge, MA: MIT Press.

Stango, Victor 2004. "The economics of standards wars," *Review of Network Economics* 3: 1–19.

Stigler, G. 1971. "The theory of economic regulation," *Bell Journal of Economics and Management Science* 2: 3–21.

Weiss, M. B. H. 1993. "The standards development process: A view from political theory," *Standard View* 1: 35–41.

1 | *Standard setting in markets: the browser war*

TIMOTHY F. BRESNAHAN AND
PAI-LING YIN

Abstract

We study de facto standard setting in markets with network effects. We closely examine the "browser war," in which Netscape Navigator at first appeared likely to be a de facto standard, but Microsoft Internet Explorer eventually became the standard. This reversal is a puzzle we seek to explain. We draw on the theory of standard setting, especially on the positive economics predictions about market outcomes, such as a tendency to tip and a tendency toward inertia. The basic insights of standard setting theory are borne out in the browser war. In addition, linking standard setting logic to an analysis of market conditions, such as the rate of growth of demand and the distribution system, leads to a complete positive theory of standard setting. This complete theory explains the otherwise surprising reversal.

1 Introduction

1.1 De facto standard setting

We study de facto standard setting in markets with network effects. In markets for system goods – e.g., a computer and the software that runs on it, a CD player and music, a computer connecting to Internet websites – interface standards are particularly important. Like the other chapters in this book, we define interface standards as technical specifications that determine the compatibility or interoperability of different technologies. In such markets, standard setting is linked to the exploitation of network effects. Which standard is ultimately adopted is a key determinant of the variety of systems available to users, market competition, and

The authors would like to thank participants at the conference on Standards and Public Policy at the Federal Reserve Bank of Chicago for helpful comments, and Shane Greenstein for many valuable discussions.

18

technological progress. This has brought a great deal of attention to standard setting from technologists, economists, and policymakers.

Many standards are embodied in particular products. For example, the standard kind of personal computer (PC) used today is defined by its use of Microsoft Windows and Intel-architecture microprocessors. An entire body of theory has grown up to understand de facto standard setting when standards are embodied in products.[1] In these circumstances, the commercial importance of standards and the market success of products are closely linked. The most popular product will also be the de facto standard, and setting a standard can offer a product a dominant market position. Thus de facto standard setting in these cases is of enormous concern to firms in systems industries and will often be central to their business strategies.[2]

1.2 The standards supporting electronic commerce

To examine the positive economics of standard setting in markets, we undertake a case study: setting standards for mass market online commercial applications such as electronic commerce, online content, blogs and many more.

The standards that connect PCs to large "servers" with web pages, electronic commerce sites, and corporate databases were one of the most valuable technological advances of the late twentieth century.[3]

---

[1] For example, see Farrell and Saloner (1985), Besen and Saloner (1989), Church and Gandal (1992), and Dranove and Gandal (2004). Overviews of the broad standards literature can be found in David and Greenstein (1990), Greenstein (1992), Weiss and Cargill (1992), Besen and Farrell (1994), Katz and Shapiro (1994), David and Shurmer (1996), and Stango (2004).

[2] For treatment of strategic issues, see Cusumano et al. (1992), Besen and Farrell (1994), Shapiro and Varian (1999), Gallagher and Park (2002), Ehrhardt (2004), and Yamada and Kurokawa (2005).

[3] A number of distinct standards were set in order to connect PCs to the Internet. Many of these standards, especially those associated with the "plumbing" of the Internet, were set in standards committees or by other de jure methods. By "plumbing" we mean standards in the lower levels of the network's engineering reference model. The most important such standard for the Internet is TCP/IP, known as the Internet protocol suite. It contains a number of standardized communications protocols, including the transmission control protocol (TCP) and Internet protocol (IP). How standards are set in such contexts is an important topic, but not one we take up.

De jure standard setting is an important topic with a rich and interesting literature (Farrell and Saloner 1988; Weiss and Sirbu 1990; Weiss and Cargill 1992; Anton

Commercialization of the browser ended years of failed attempts to set standards for mass market online commercial applications, enabling an explosion of investment in PCs, servers, telecommunications, networking, and software. Browsers embody standards that define the end-user experience for using the World Wide Web (WWW) and enable online commercial applications.[4] This growth has fostered new markets, such as all the auction, resale and retail markets that have emerged on eBay, and has permitted substantial changes in old ones, such as in the distribution of airline tickets. The WWW enabled both large, complex online applications and simpler ones developed by individual "webmasters" (website developers) to reach the mass market.

As a result, society had a large stake in how the browser standard was set. Standard setting for the browser was a race between two firms, Netscape and Microsoft. Each had a powerful incentive to promote its own browser as the winning standard, since the technical features of its browser would define web page design and the exact way in which users interacted with online applications. This standards race also affected competition in the personal computer industry and on the Internet, leading to intense interest from public policy circles as well.[5]

Our second reason for studying the race to set browser standards is theoretical. This case study will teach us much about the theory of de facto standard setting.

The main agents in the browser standards race closely resemble those in the economic theory of indirect network effects. Webmasters and users gained indirect network effects from using particular standards and the associated products. Developers could program websites to be accessible via Netscape or Microsoft's Internet Explorer (IE) or both

and Yao 1995; Axelrod et al. 1995; Hawkins et al. 1995; von Burg 2001; Simcoe 2003; Augereau et al., in press; Gandal et al., in press; and Lerner and Tirole, in press). While often thought of in purely technical terms, sometimes de jure standard setting can be strategic. For example, see MacKie-Mason and Netz (in press).

[4] Our use of the language here follows the theory. Network effects may be realized through a proprietary standard (e.g., when each brand of word processing software stores files in its own way so that users sharing files must buy the same brand) or an open standard (e.g., when any word processing program can read the files of any other). In the browser case, both brands respected open standards such as basic HTML but provided proprietary technologies for more complex applications and web pages.

The commercially important standards included such areas as security, which was critical to use of credit cards for online purchases.

[5] Evans et al. (2001), Fisher and Rubinfeld (2001), and Gilbert and Katz (2001).

(at some cost). Users would run Netscape or IE or both (at some cost). All else equal, website developers preferred to write for the browser that had the most usage by their customers, and users preferred the browser which gave them access to the most and best websites. These are the classic payoffs of indirect network effects.

Standard setting agents of the browser race corresponded closely to those described in the theory. Netscape and Microsoft each had a proprietary browser which embodied a particular set of interface standards between files and applications on the WWW and the user's PC. The race to establish browser standards was an effort to attain a position where positive feedback between mass market browser usage and web pages seeking a mass audience would reinforce one standard over another.

The final reason to study this race is feasibility. The race is well documented in the internal communications of both firms (much of which has been made public) and in quantitative data.

1.3 Our contributions

In the next section, we lay out the positive economics implications of standard setting theory. A number of these are critical both to the logic of the theory and for understanding the race to establish browser standards. The implications we emphasize that apply to the behavior of users and developers include positive feedback in the decision rules of individual actors; indeterminacy of equilibrium; and inertia around particular standards (installed base effects). The implications we emphasize that apply to standard setting firms include first-mover advantages (barriers to entry) and strategic competition that is intense in the period of establishing a standard, then largely absent after standards are set. We thus emphasize competition for the market rather than competition in the market in standards industries.

We depart from received theory, however, by emphasizing the impact of market conditions on de facto standard setting. This apparently simple change takes us through a series of points which at first seem very closely connected to our application but which ultimately lead us to a conceptual departure from received theory.

To begin, we emphasize demand dynamics and distribution as essential background conditions for standard setting. In the browser wars, we are studying a mass market with a growing number of users, and standard setting theory emphasizes the importance of having a large installed base. Mass market use of a technology involves mass distribution of that technology.

The key role of demand dynamics and distribution permit us to understand the most puzzling event of our case study. After Netscape took an early lead in browser standard setting, Microsoft entered with a series of imitative products. The standards race ultimately tipped to Microsoft despite that firm's failure to leapfrog Netscape in the attractiveness of its browser to users.[6]

Growing demand undercut Netscape's initial standard setting advantage but enhanced the strategic importance of Microsoft's control over distribution channels for new browsers. Market conditions devalued Netscape's first-mover advantage and enhanced Microsoft's advantage as a strong second.

These specific results about the browser war are related to a set of general conclusions.

Complementary markets and pre-existing standards play an important role in understanding standard setting in systems industries with dominant multiproduct firms, such as IBM in mainframes in one era of computing or Microsoft in PC software in another. New technologies in computing are frequently invented by outsiders (as they were in the case of the browser). An existing dominant firm typically has control of existing standards and products complementary to the new technology. The firm's position in complements gives it an asymmetric advantage in influencing the channels of distribution. This asymmetry can influence the identity of the standards winner.

Market conditions do not overturn standard setting logic. On the contrary, our broader conclusion is that there is a fundamental interaction between market conditions and the logic of standards theory. The relative strengths of distribution and first-mover advantages vary over time, leaving at most a finite window of time when a second mover can act strategically to interrupt the network effects that build around a first mover. Second, supply-side factors such as taking control of distribution are not sufficient to win a standards race. They matter far

---

[6] This assertion has been highly controversial in economics but not, as we shall see in this paper, controversial among suppliers of commercial browsers. In Bresnahan and Yin (in press), we provide a complete econometric analysis of the importance of browser product quality. More on the controversy can be found in Davis and Murphy (2000), Schmalensee (2000), Evans et al. (2000, 2001), Fisher and Rubinfeld (2001), and Gilbert and Katz (2001).

more if they coincide with rapid and mass adoption of a technology on the demand side. Interaction effects like this are a general feature of a complete positive theory of de facto standard setting in markets.

Our story of the importance of timing and distribution is novel in its connection to the theory of standards, but it is familiar to the most analytical industry practitioners.[7] It is a cliché of the standards literature that a firm's control of standards can result in a dominant market position. It is far less well understood how market demand and supply conditions and suppliers' pre-existing market positions influence standard setting. This chapter contributes to the standard setting literature by analyzing the *market* conditions behind standard setting.

Our positive-economics emphasis on market conditions finally leads us to a sharp conceptual departure from the theoretical standards literature. To resolve the uncertainty in standard setting, many analysts emphasize agents' *expectations* about the de facto standards outcome and/or coordinating *contracts* among agents. This has led to two competing completions of the theory. One emphasizes efficiency while the other emphasizes inertia.[8] We argue that both the efficiency and inefficiency theories have failed to provide a complete positive-economics theory of standard setting. Our market approach provides just that key element.

The missing element in both efficiency and inefficiency theories lies in their treatment of inertia. Neither treats standards inertia quantitatively. Inefficiency theories write as if inertia were infinitely large, or at least so large as to make inefficient standards persist for generations. Efficiency theories write as if inertia were zero, or at least so small that it can always be overcome by contracts. As a result, neither theory can provide a positive explanation of the occasions on which existing inertial standards are overturned.

2 Standards theory 1: demand side/small actors

The positive implications of the theory are important, if incomplete, for understanding standard setting in markets. We divide the key positive implications into two groups. The first group is related to the behavior of

---

[7] In his first book, Bill Gates summarized the strategic implications of the "positive feedback cycle" in a "growing market" by saying that "Both timing and marketing are key to acceptance with technology markets." (Gates et al. 1995, 135)

[8] For examples of efficiency arguments, see Liebowitz and Margolis (1990, 1994). For examples of inertia, see David (1985) and Arthur (1989).

the small or "non-strategic" individual actors, such as individual users of a system or developers of particular applications for the system.

2.1 Positive feedback

The literature on standards and network effects begins with the utility (or profit) of users and developers who are modeled as non-strategic actors.[9] "Indirect network effects" arise when users' utility depends on the number or variety of developers and developers' profits depend on the number or variety of users.

These assumptions about utility and profit have implications for individual behavior. Individual users will tend to choose systems with the most or best applications provided by developers. Users who have sunk costs of obtaining a system will tend to choose systems based at least in part on their expectations of future applications availability.[10] Of course, any particular user will trade off the number and variety of developer applications on a system against other considerations, such as the price of that system or the difficulty of connecting to it.

Similarly, developers will tend to provide for systems that have the most users (or the most profitable users for their particular application). If developers sink costs into a system (for example, by learning how it works), then they will base their choice at least in part on expectations about demand. If the incremental costs of developing for a second system are positive ("porting costs" in the language of developers), then there will be an incentive to supply first or only to the system with the most or most profitable users. Developers will trade off the number and variety of users against other system features, such as technical quality as a development environment, and will sometimes need to act based on expectations.

2.2 Social scale economies

An alternative normative language for network effects and standards uses the language "social scale economies."[11] This normative language emphasizes the benefits of sharing ("social") the network effects

---

[9] See Farrell and Klemperer (in press).
[10] Although individual user and developer sunk costs are distinct from inertia around an existing standard, sunk costs make expectations more important, which increases the tendency toward tipping and inertia.
[11] See Arthur (1994).

associated with standards, and suggests the value of having only one or a few standards ("scale economies"). This articulation is employed to explain standardization as a solution to the inefficiencies of a market of highly complementary goods that is fragmented into multiple systems.

Some scholars, however, use the normative analysis as a positive theory, assuming that there must be a strong equilibrium tendency toward the socially correct degree of standardization and efficient standards choice. This is an elementary error.[12] Like any other scale economies, social scale economies tend to lead to equilibrium with concentration. In this case, it is concentration of standards. However, the social scale economies in and of themselves guarantee only concentration; they do not guarantee either the optimum degree of standardization or the efficient choice of standards.

2.3 Indeterminacy

There is a fundamental indeterminacy at this static level of analysis. The network effects tell us there will be few standards, but not which ones. If we look only at the (static) Nash game among users, or users and developers, it is indeterminate. Indeed, one equilibrium can be the inferior of the two standards, as parts of the literature have emphasized.[13]

One way the literature has resolved the indeterminacy is to model users and developers as choosing systems sequentially, assuming that choices are irreversible, so that the choices of the early ones condition the choices of the later ones.[14] A strong version leads to determinacy in favor of the standard that first gains market share. More generally, the literature examines sequential models with uncertainty (about the system or about future adopters' preferences) in the early going. Then early choices will tend to persist, even if later information arrives that might suggest reversals. The system tends to converge to a single standard: not necessarily the ex post Pareto-superior one, but rather the one preferred by early choosers.

Another way to resolve the indeterminacy is to assume the existence of a contractual, institutional or entrepreneurial mechanism that arises

---

[12] Normative analysis as positive theory is a familiar error in the economics of regulation. See Joskow and Noll (1981) and Peltzman (1989).

[13] See David (1985) and Arthur (1989).

[14] See Farrell and Klemperer (in press) for an overview.

to coordinate choices. The motivation for this resolution arises from the possibility that uncoordinated choices might lead to a Pareto-inferior outcome.[15] In the case of costless contracting or an effective institution, these theories lead to an efficient, coordinated technology choice. Obviously, costless contracting among users and developers (or a perfect coordinating institution) is a strong assumption. In the case of technology choice played out over time, this implies that late adopters and early adopters contract to change the behavior of early adopters.[16]

A final mechanism to resolve the uncertainty is expectations. If early choosers anticipate that later events will lead to a particular standard, they may choose that standard just as if they were late adopters and a large installed base already existed. As a mechanism for resolving the uncertainty, however, rational expectation is an unsatisfactory approach. When more than one option presents a viable standard, then the absence of unique equilibrium in the static game can also lead to expectation indeterminacy in the dynamic game. If the expectation mechanism tends to track efficiency, then the market outcome is likely to be efficient. If the expectation mechanism has an element of persistence forecasting, however, the market outcome is likely to be inertial.[17]

3 Standards theory 2: supply side/strategic actors

The second set of positive implications concerns the incentives and behavior of strategic actors, such as sellers of products that embody interface standards. The theory models these actors as having a strategic motive to influence standards choice.[18] The literature has studied how firms' preferences over standards outcomes vary with their existing product position.[19] The literature has also brought to the foreground a

[15] In this case, we are dealing with the choice of a standard, but the same argument would arise in connection with standardization in general. There are strong theoretical reasons to believe individual action will lead to too little standardization and too much fragmentation in many contexts.
[16] See David and Greenstein (1990).
[17] This argument is made carefully in the *Handbook* chapter by Farrell and Klemperer (in press).
[18] See Farrell and Klemperer (in press) for an overview.
[19] Firms' existing products may be based on technologies which would make them prefer one technical standard over another. Alternatively, firms whose products embody a popular standard may oppose an open or industry-wide standard (or a

powerful incentive for firms whose products embody standards to win a standards race.[20] Once a standard that is embodied in a particular firm's product is set, that firm enjoys a strong market position as users and developers will have limited ability to substitute away from it.

The theory also has brought forward positive implications that inform firm strategy. When users and developers sink system-specific investments, the network effects are dynamic, offering a role for expectations, for strategy, and for inertia. When strategic actors sponsor system-defining technologies, this situation leads to a very rich set of strategic issues, especially when multiple strategic actors contend for the same leading position. As we shall see, these implications are well known not only to economists and strategy scholars, but also to practical business people.[21] This encourages us in further investigation into their value as a positive analysis.

Sellers of systems that might be the beneficiaries of positive feedback should have high willingness to pay to have their standard adopted. In the early phase of market development, sellers will engage in a momentum race to recruit complementors, to gain market share with users, and to seek to improve the features of their systems products relative to competing offerings in order to gain that momentum.[22] The theory has emphasized the value of strategies such as "penetration pricing," i.e., setting a low price – during the period of standard setting – for products embodying standards. It has also emphasized the value of volume-building strategies, such as price discrimination in favor of marginal users and developers.[23]

converter technology), while firms whose existing products embody an unpopular standard will tend to favor it. See Farrell and Saloner (1988, 1992).

[20] See Farrell and Klemperer (in press) for an overview.

[21] See, for example, the email exchange between the CEO of Microsoft and the Chief Technology Officer (Gates and Myhrvold 1994, DX 386) in which Myhrvold writes, "The strength of the Internet is that it is the beneficiary of the positive feedback cycle – more people get on, which attracts more content (and causes more BBS postings) which makes it more attractive for others to get on," and later, "Connectivity tends to make the market share leader become even stronger at the expense of everything else, because of increased sharing."

The email exchange was documented in the antitrust trial *United States* v. *Microsoft Corporation*, Civil Action No. 98-1232 as Defense Exhibit 386 (DX 386). Henceforth, the notation "GX" will refer to government exhibits (accessible at http://www.usdoj.gov/atr/cases/ms_exhibits.htm) and "DX" will refer to defense exhibits.

[22] See Besen and Farrell (1994) or Shapiro and Varian (1999) for efforts to draw these and related implications about supply formally and as advice to managers.

[23] See Farrell and Klemperer (in press) for an overview.

While the literature has emphasized this pattern in connection with price competition, the same points apply to quality competition. On the user side, systems products can offer better quality features that they deliver directly, such as a better user interface. To encourage developer supply based on a particular standard, systems providers may offer a higher quality development environment.[24] More generally, sellers of a systems product embodying a particular standard have a powerful motive to gain both users and developers during a standards race, and thus an incentive to act in a number of ways to attract them.

A particular point in the literature about developer supply has a great deal of strategic importance. A modular technology encourages development of complementary inputs.[25] Developers will tend toward popular technologies because of network effects and toward modular ones because it lowers their costs and increases their opportunities. Developers who rely on the provider of a systems product, however, will be concerned with ex post opportunism after a standard is set. Finding a mechanism to mitigate these concerns and commit to continued openness and modularity is strategic.[26] The strategy literature has also emphasized the importance of a number of different problems for the firm that arise when outside complementors such as developers are important.[27]

This strategic discussion brings forward two different views of the role of strategy by the sellers of goods that embody a standard. In the first view, the positive feedback loop arises because developers choose a standard not only for its native technological qualities as a development environment, but also for the extent to which it is used, while users choose products that embody the standard not only for their

[24] See Bresnahan and Yin (in press) for work on estimating quality competition and Besen and Farrell (1994) for complementary supply analysis and references.
[25] "Modular" technologies are complex systems comprising smaller components that can be independently designed but are able to connect to other components to function as a system (Baldwin and Clark 2000).
[26] See Henderson and Clark (1990), Baldwin and Clark (1997), Gawer and Cusumano (2002), and Miller (2005).
[27] The management literature discusses the trade-off between complements and system integration, in-house vs. out-of-house production of complements, developing and supporting a select few complements or allowing complements to compete against each other. See Cusumano and Gawer (2002). See Yoffie et al. (2004) for examination of these issues by Palmsource, Inc., and Gawer and Henderson (2005) for complement management at Intel.

stand-alone qualities but also for the degree to which developers enhance it. Firms may not have much of a strategic role in this case to influence coordination around their standard if standards are set by expectations or quality differences. Eventually, the race is won, and positive feedback surrounding a systems product is established. The network effects strengthen around the winner and create barriers to entry for alternative standards. In this later phase of market evolution, momentum and comparison to competitors should be far less important as the winner of the "standards race" enjoys a period of monopoly with entry barriers.

A second view is that competition for the market among suppliers of systems products is the mechanism that resolves the indeterminacy about standard setting. The indeterminacy is removed by a refinement, in this case penetration pricing by a particular seller or technological innovation to obtain industry leadership.

4 Resolutions to the indeterminacy of standards theory

Many network effects theorists, especially those thinking about policy issues, at this stage take a normative stance in order to resolve the indeterminacy of standards theory. The first theoretical line exaggerates inertia and suggests that the indeterminacy of equilibrium is resolved by early, irreversible choices. The second theoretical line assumes that the indeterminacy of equilibrium is resolved by an efficient mechanism, typically implemented by the seller of a network good.

Those extreme views might appear to be caricatures, but they are not. Many economists believe that network theory tells us either that there is an efficient mechanism for choosing equilibrium standards or that standards are characterized in the first instance by extreme inertia.

One view sees the inertial costs of moving to a new standard as near zero; the other sees them as so large as to prevent movement to very valuable new standards. What both views miss is the simple economic point that inertia could be an intermediate cost. In that case, an old standard will prevail if inertia is larger than the forces for change to a new standard. Positive economics has a great deal to say in the case of intermediate levels of inertia.

Network effects inertia is the collective cost for users and developers to move to a new standard. Like any cost, when a larger force comes along, it is overcome. In the case of network effects, the larger force needs to affect a large number of users and developers, because only a collective switch to a new standard will succeed. What market conditions will tend to make inertial costs large? What market conditions will tend to foster large forces for movement to a new standard? When will a second mover be able to tip the market in its favor when network effects inertia should create barriers to entry around the first mover?

4.1 Three forces

The logic of network effects theory suggests a number of forces that shift the relative strengths of inertia and of forces for change. The most obvious of these is the invention of new and superior technologies. That gives users and developers a motive to move to a new standard. As the theory emphasizes, however, there is no necessary relationship between that collective motive and individual incentives to move.

A second force is demand dynamics. Rapid growth in the market can devalue the network effects associated with a technology that has an early lead.[28] Each new user can choose, along with other new users, to gain network effects; if other new users outnumber established users, the inertial forces will be swamped by the forces for change. This rapid growth in the market can lead to changes in market leadership, depending on which standard is able to capture the newest adopters of the technology.

This argument is more than a narrow theoretical point. The diffusion of new technologies is very often described by an S-curve. If a standard is established in the early phase of diffusion, it may have considerable inertia among early adopters of the technology. Once adoption of the technology begins to climb the steep part of the S-curve, however, the group of early adopters will be swamped, in absolute numbers, by the mass market of new adopters. That opens a window for a standards switch whose timing is related to the diffusion of technology.

As a result of these changes in market conditions over time, timing matters for participants in a standards race: although inertia will favor the first mover, there is a finite window of time when a second mover can act to take advantage of rapid growth among a large number of mass market adopters. Inertial costs will make it difficult to cause the installed base of adopters to switch to an alternative standard, but the rapid

---

[28] Farrell and Saloner (1986) model new users, but they do not study the rate of growth of the new users.

growth in demand presents an opportunity for an alternative standard to capture the newest adopters in numbers that swamp the size of the installed base. Once market growth has slowed and the number of new users will no longer swamp the number in the installed base, the positive feedback effects and inertia around the leading standard will begin to strengthen, limiting choices by users and developers.

Another way in which markets for new technologies change over time is in the composition of demand. The early adopters of a technology tend to be different from the mass market adopters. They often have a higher willingness to pay for any given level of technical capability, and they are more informed about standards and technologies that are available in the market. Later adopters tend to have much higher adoption costs and worse information. As a result, later adopters can be more responsive to convenience of adoption than they are to the technical capability of the technology. Early adopters may be comparatively insensitive to the number or quality of products developers have brought to market that work with a particular standard, while later adopters are waiting for complete, ready-to-go systems.

The heterogeneity between early and late adopters affects inertia and the forces for change in a number of ways. Early adopters' superior technical knowledge could make their choice influential on later adopters, for example, which would strengthen inertia. Or heterogeneity could mean that mass market users are distant in interests and tastes from early adopters, outside the communications of early adopters, and so on, which would tend to weaken network effects between early and mass market adopters and thus weaken inertia.

In indirect network effects industries, the emergence of important applications will drive the growth rate of users, and thus determine the strength of inertia and the forces for change. Late-emerging applications that users value highly and that choose to work with a particular standard can swing the networks effect momentum to that standard. Unfortunately, there is far less empirical work about the dynamics of supply of applications compatible with a new standard than about the dynamics of diffusion. The management literature on computing, however, emphasizes the importance of the single very influential application, or "killer app," that moves many users to adopt a new standard and creates momentum for a tip to that standard.[29]

[29] Downes and Mui (1998) and Negroponte (1995).

The final point about demand and developer-supply relates to their influence on the supply of products embodying a standard. If the size of the market is large, then there are greater financial incentives for winning a standards race. If market conditions change over time, then the applicable theory on standard setting is likely to be different at different times.

4.2 Market is part of an industry comprising complementary markets

For analytical clarity, the theory of indirect network effects has been written with only users, developers, and suppliers of products embodying standards. While many systems-good industries have all three elements of that vertical structure, the simple three-layer structure is often an abstraction away from a complex environment of complementary markets. Firms' positions in other complementary markets may affect their *incentives* to participate in a standards race and their preferences over which standard is set or whether a standard is set.

Firms' positions in complementary markets may also give them *strategic opportunities* to influence the outcome of a standards race. Network effects imply a strategic goal of gaining a large market share early. The literature focuses on one particular strategic tool for the firm, penetration pricing, to increase the volume of adopters to a particular standard. A firm which has a strong position in complementary markets may, for example, also have control of distribution channels. If the firms engaged in a standard setting race have asymmetric control over distribution channels, the firm with better control may be able to slow the distribution of a competitor's standard and hasten the distribution of their own standard. These strategies can be used to lengthen the window of opportunity for a second mover to upset an incumbent standard by slowing the adoption and therefore positive feedback for the first mover and accelerating the build-up of positive feedback for itself.

Similar considerations relate to strategic opportunities to influence developers. A firm participating in a standards race with control over other, established, complementary standards may be able to influence the technological choices of developers. One strategy is breaking modularity. Making an existing complementary standard incompatible with one of the competing standards makes the technological system less modular. It will also influence developers' choices. A standard setting firm that has an advantage in existing technologies may thereby take advantage of it to steer developers in a new standards race.

A final point is about uncertainty. If expectations do not form around a standard, tipping to that standard may be delayed. This gives a second mover an incentive to create uncertainty if it can. Uncertainty helps the second mover by slowing the build-up of network effects and tipping to the current market leader.[30]

Clearly there are interactions between these strategic opportunities for the firm and the equilibrium logic of network effects. Control over distribution, like creation of uncertainty or penetration pricing, will be more helpful to a second mover if timing of the strategic move pre-dates a potential tip and if there is rapid and substantial growth in demand.

5 Effort to set standards by Netscape

We now turn to the actual events of the browser war to examine how standards theory applied to this incident and to explore the interaction between standards theory and market analysis.

We begin by examining the browser war through the lens of business managers' decisions about strategy. This is helpful because computer industry managers are actively using a framework for thinking remarkably close to the theory of network effects equilibrium. Managers will be helpful, too, in showing how that theory works in a market context. In a later section we will turn to empirical evidence on market outcomes as well as on managers' ideas in order to nail down the importance of distribution in a market context for standard setting.

Before Netscape was founded, there was an "Internet mania" around the browser in 1993 and 1994. These events were well described by the "small actors" part of network theory. The browser was invented inside the academic Internet by students and staffers at a university. The browser let less-technical users access the Internet. A number of open WWW standards let pre-existing data become "content," and also opened up opportunities for new, easily supplied websites. There was a positive feedback loop between users, whose demand for browsers was fed by freeware products such as Mosaic, and webmasters, who had a

---

[30] See Rysman (2004) for a model of delayed adoption that leads to inefficiency.

larger audience for their content. The early positive feedback loop was powerful, but limited in scope to noncommercial uses.

The Internet mania also drove an explosion in demand for PCs. Access to the Internet made the PC more valuable. Web browsing, email, and instant messaging were among the new and important applications that raised the value of PCs. The overall effect was an increased demand for personal computers, speeding the growth of that market.[31] This growth in demand only increased with the commercialization of the World Wide Web via the introduction of the Netscape browser in 1994.

The entrepreneurial firm Netscape was founded to commercialize the browser. The firm took on aspects both of the open standards of the Internet and of proprietary software companies. Netscape's idea for the browser was to set a commercial standard for online applications, and to have a single interface between all users of online applications and all content and applications. To that end, Netscape's browser was a modular component of an open system rather than integrated into a closed system.[32] Prior use of closed systems had meant that the user could access content and data only from sources sponsored by the system provider. The browser's open systems approach meant the user could access content from any provider who used Internet standards. This was a dramatic improvement in the ease of accessing online materials and of providing them.[33]

Coordination on a single standard would allow many applications to create economies of scale in adoption: once adoption costs are incurred, the adopter then has access to all current and future applications. The fixed cost of adoption now can be spread over all browser applications. Applications developers could benefit from being able to access all customers on any type of PC or browser via this open standard. However, the communication protocol between the Netscape browser and the server where the website was being hosted was still proprietary Netscape technology.

---

[31] Goolsbee and Klenow (2002) examine the impact of Internet use on computer demand, especially the externalities across households in adopting.

[32] See Cusumano and Yoffie (1998) for a discussion of Netscape's "open, but not open" platform strategy.

[33] See Gates et al. (1995) for a contrast between the open systems and earlier, inferior, Microsoft approaches.

The essence of the Netscape strategy was, as founder Marc Andreessen put it, "ubiquity" to set a standard that would then be partially proprietary. He characterized this in an interview as "basically a Microsoft lesson, right? If you get ubiquity ... you can get paid by the product you are ubiquitous on, but you can also get paid on products that benefit as a result."[34]

Netscape practiced the types of penetration pricing that standards theory suggested would be effective for strategic actors on the supply side. The Netscape browser was "free but not free." The browser was free to the end user to encourage adoption of the Netscape browser and thus create a large installed base that would attract webmasters. After a period of time, Netscape also sought to gain some browser revenue from corporations and PC manufacturers; they continued, however, to price discriminate in favor of marginal users with some form of free browser. Also, Netscape charged money for the server-side software that would host the websites. (These are "products that benefit as a result.") Thus, those who would directly profit from the commercial application of the browser would be the ones to fund Netscape's efforts.

Netscape also understood the importance of distributing their product to make adoption as easy as possible for new users. Netscape signed contracts to distribute its browser through Internet Service Providers (ISPs) and along with new PCs. This service and hardware was a strong complement to the browser: a user had to have both in order to access Internet content, along with the browser. Netscape employed these distribution channels to overcome the adoption costs for their browser.

Netscape had substantial early success with these strategies. That is not surprising. The possibility of online applications meant there was a large commercial opportunity. The possibility of setting a standard meant that a firm could earn a large return. By this stage in the history of computing, the basic logic of standards theory was familiar from experience and guided efforts to create a new mass market standard.

6 Entry by Microsoft

At first, Microsoft left the browser market to others. The firm limited its Internet connectivity work to low-level "plumbing."

---

[34] See Cusumano and Yoffie (1998, 22) for this interview.

Microsoft did have a plan in place in 1994 and early 1995 for mass market electronic commerce and online applications. That plan did not rely on the widespread use of the Internet, but instead had a closed, proprietary architecture. After Netscape released its commercial browser in December 1994, Microsoft undertook an internal debate between proponents of a browser and proponents of the closed architecture. By spring, the pro-Internet side won that debate. Microsoft entered the browser standards race in the summer of that year with IE version 1.

For Microsoft, the commercial benefits of the browser in isolation were not the main reason for entry into the browser standards race. Instead, an independent browser posed a threat of entry and competition in the operating systems (OS) market. The OS was a valuable monopoly to Microsoft, with high entry barriers. An independent browser might ultimately lead to "commodification" of the OS, just as an independent OS had earlier led to commodification of the personal computer. Alternatively, an independent browser, combined with new technologies from Sun Microsystems called "Java" might lower entry barriers into the OS business. Microsoft was concerned that something "far cheaper than a PC," such as a network computer, might compete with Windows machines (Gates 1995, GX 20).[35]

Microsoft did not so much object to proprietary control of the browser by Netscape as to outside control in general. Much of the early alarm about the browser was that the WWW was open and outside anyone's control. For example, Paul Maritz, number three in the Microsoft leadership at the time, posed a rhetorical question about important developer standards, "What is worse, an open object model or an alternative non-MS one?" (Maritz 1995, GX 498).

This discussion of Microsoft's decision to enter reveals two important and general connections to standards theory. First, the aspects of the browser which made it a potential threat to Microsoft are closely related to browser standard setting: its mass market appeal to users and its appeal to developers seeking to make new applications. Second, Microsoft's defensive decision to enter the browser race illustrates the

---

[35] The historical analogy, the analysis, the remark about commodification, and the quotation all come from a memo by Gates (1995, GX 20) entitled "The Internet Tidal Wave." This memo was documented in the antitrust trial *United States* v. *Microsoft Corporation*, Civil Action No. 98-1232.

important general principle that an established firm may have incentives to control standards in a new, complementary technology.

6.1 Implementation

Implementation of a Microsoft strategy to deal with the possibility of a Netscape browser standard applied the theory of network effects to the specific industry context, as can be seen in a Microsoft browser marketing plan presentation from summer, 1996 (Maritz 1996a, GX 488).[36] This is approximately a year after Microsoft entered the browser standards race. Microsoft had, by this time, made rapid progress in improving its browser and was beginning to catch up to Netscape in product quality. The browser marketing plan laid out the problem facing Microsoft; market share leader Netscape was becoming a "de facto standard."

In Figure 1.1, we reproduce the slide that addresses the problem of reversing Netscape's leadership under the heading of "turning this around." The slide lays out the positive feedback loop of indirect network effects, closely following the core logic of standards theory. The loop passes through end user demand for IE and through websites where developers might use Microsoft technologies (IE/ActiveX sites/ ActiveX controls).[37] This is the positive feedback loop Microsoft would like to get going to "turn around" the situation in which Netscape technologies, plus Java, were becoming an indirect network effects standard.

The slide alludes to many of the key business strategy implications of network effects theory. First, the goal is "winning the platform API [applications programming interface] battle." To win in the WWW-browser context, "Internet Explorer share is key." To get that share, one needs "critical mass and momentum" with end users on the developer/website side. Getting "critical mass and momentum" leads to the positive feedback cycle graphically shown.

---

[36] Other slides from this presentation show a number of quantitative measures used to buttress the argument.

[37] At this time, "ActiveX controls" were small computer programs that ran inside other larger programs in a browser. They permitted website developers to add such features as displaying complex multimedia and database documents in the user's browser. More generally, ActiveX is a Microsoft brand name variously applied to technologies developers use for media, web, etc.

Turning this around

- Key objective is winning the platform API battle
  - Internet Explorer share is key
- Need critical mass and momentum with:
  - Influentials
  - End users
    - Create demand &
    - Broad distribution
  - Builders of websites
  - Developers
- Retention

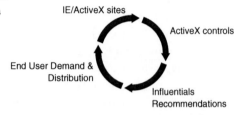

Figure 1.1. Slide from Microsoft marketing presentation (Maritz 1996a, GX 488).

In addition to those familiar theoretical ideas, the slide indicates the importance of distribution as part of building end user demand. This is an example of Microsoft adapting network effects logic to a real world market situation.

The rest of the plan brings forward quantitative evidence for the tip to Netscape and directs a number of employees to induce use of Microsoft technologies by outsiders: users, website builders, developers, and "influentials." The "influentials" (pundits, the trade press, etc.) do not play any role in the theoretical literature, but it is simple to understand their importance in light of the theory. "Influentials" could diminish expectations of end users and developers of a tip to a Netscape standard, leaving time for Microsoft's entry.

The use of network effects theory at Microsoft, as at Netscape, is not limited to a few instances. In other strategic documents not cited here, many analyses leading to management decisions are based on the theory. Managing for de facto standard setting in markets is one of the most important capabilities at Microsoft.

6.2 Individual user switching costs

Individual user switching costs can substantially enhance network effects inertia by increasing the commitment of existing users to the established standard. Microsoft's browser marketing organization set out to measure the importance of individual user switching costs in order to devise strategies for overcoming those costs. We examine reports based on user surveys and on focus groups.

Kumar Mehta (1997, GX 204), responding to the question about whether IE should be tied to Windows 98, summarized "all the IE research we have done" (primarily consumer market research by survey). He wrote, "80% of those who do not use IE say that they have no plans to switch to it, which means that if we take away IE from the o/s most nav [Navigator] users will never switch to us." Mehta's analysis reflects an individual user switching cost model, although some of the reason not to switch may be network effects.[38]

Christian Wildfeuer (1997, GX 202), writing about the results of focus groups of early adopters of Windows 95 (Microsoft's most inframarginal end user customers), summarized the same issue in this way:

Most of our IEUs [individual end users] were Navigator users. They said they would not switch, would not want to download IE 4 to replace their Navigator browser ... To make them switch away from Netscape, we need to make them to upgrade to Memphis [Windows 98] ... We need to strengthen our key asset and our key brand which is Windows to win the internet war on the desktop side ... convert the Navigator installed base and eclipse Netscape's browser market share leadership. But if we rely on IE 4 alone to achieve this, we will fail. (Emphasis in original.)

Microsoft took the advice of these marketing people, avoiding individual end user switching costs by distributing IE to new users and those upgrading to new computers. For these users, the relative cost of switching or adopting IE would be subsumed into the cost they were already incurring to adopt the PC or ISP. Brad Chase (1996a, GX 465) operationalized this by giving higher market share targets to marketing teams in different countries, based on the degree to which Netscape was entrenched.[39]

---

[38] Jonathan Roberts (1997, GX 205) uses the same theoretical frame: "the only real chance IE has of getting them to switch is thru a new pc, an OS upgrade, or a new ISP kit."

[39] This remark led to a standing effort to "out-localize" Navigator and some frustration on Microsoft's part when Netscape effectively produced non-English versions.

However, the only way that capturing new users would help Microsoft gain enough market share to attract webmasters was if the number of new users was substantial relative to the number of users already part of the installed base. As a result, Microsoft had a finite window of time to capture these new users before the Netscape browser diffused throughout the entire population of potential adopters and market growth slowed. Afterward, Microsoft would face the much harder task of overturning switching costs, which would reinforce inertia. Microsoft executives recognized the urgency of their task.

The implementation of Microsoft's strategy, like its strategic plan, draws heavily on standards theory.[40]

6.3 Timing

Microsoft understood the timing challenges it faced against first mover Netscape in a market with network effects. Mr. Maritz (1996b, GX 42) emphasized the importance of timing with his focus on "Near-term browser share." Using the release cycle of browsers as his timing metric, he wrote, "We have to stop the Nav [Navigator]-Web site reinforcement cycle with IE3 and shift it in direction of ActiveX. We thus have to get significant shift BEFORE Nav 4 ships, and in so doing prevent web sites from automatically shifting to exclusively exploit it as they did on Nav 2."

Mr. Maritz was concerned about developers' technical progress in making online applications. As websites became more complex, they would have more features that would involve sinking costs to a particular standard; supplying multiple standards would become too costly. Because of the high share in browser usage enjoyed by Navigator, he forecast that website developers would be tied more and more into Netscape standards (Maritz 1996b, GX 42).

There is an important link to theory here. At the early stage, the second mover's priority is not to gain a leading share but to prevent a tip to the first mover's standard. Microsoft, which controlled the distribution channel, was able to slow down the progress of Netscape. Their early goal, however, was merely to achieve 30 percent market share in twelve months (Chase 1996b, GX 684), not to become the

---

[40] See "How to Get 30% [Browser] Share in 12 Months: Summary Recommendations" (Chase 1996b, GX 684).

market leader. While their market share of the installed base of browser users might be small, it was large enough to be a viable alternative standard in the minds of webmasters. Microsoft referred to this as gaining "mindshare." As long as there was uncertainty about the expected browser standard and high costs to supporting multiple standards, webmasters would delay their decisions about supporting only Netscape. By this strategy, Microsoft delayed the emergence of insurmountable network effects inertia around the Netscape standard and thereby lengthened their window of opportunity to catch up in both installed base and quality.

6.4 Product improvement

Although Microsoft entered the market hastily with an unimpressive clone of Navigator, the firm was one of the best in the world at improving software. It put tremendous resources into rapidly improving the IE browser. Brad Chase (1996b, GX 684) laid out a clear goal of effective imitation: "We must have a plan to clone all the features they [Netscape] have today, plus new ones they will add between now and our next releases."[41] Imitator Microsoft succeeded at closing the gap with innovator Netscape in quality and features.

Given that Microsoft was behind in the standard setting race, a strategy based purely on quality was unlikely to work. Microsoft managers linked this to the theory of indirect network effects. Mr. Chase (1996a, GX 465), in his memo, "Winning the Internet Platform Battle," writes that Microsoft needs a "significant user installed base" to attract developers to either IE or Windows. Without that, "the industry would simply ignore our standards. Few would write Windows apps without the Windows user base."

If both Netscape and IE were being offered via all the same distribution channels, then IE would be at a disadvantage from a network effects perspective, regardless of quality differences. James Allchin (1997, GX 48) wrote:

Pitting browser against browser is hard since Netscape has 80% market-share and we have <20%. I am especially worried that we don't have a long term winning strategy ... Even if we get IE to be totally competitive with

---

[41] Ibid.

Nav/Communicator, why would [it] be chosen? They have 80% market-share. I am convinced we have to use Windows – this is the one thing they don't have.

Because of network effects, simply offering a comparable browser would not be enough to take users from Netscape.

6.5 Distribution

Taking advantage of "Windows ... the one thing they don't have" meant, in practice, using Windows to achieve advantaged distribution for IE.

Why did distribution matter? Microsoft marketing managers identified time and effort to download software over the Internet and the complexity of installing a new piece of software on a computer as costs of adoption.[42] Less sophisticated users could avoid installation hassles by using software that came pre-installed on their computers. Less sophisticated users also tended to be uninformed about new products. They were more likely to adopt whatever came with their PC or ISP.

Distribution through corporate PC purchases ensured distribution of IE to the installed base of Internet users as well, lowering the cost of switching from Netscape. Since information technology managers bought computers en masse, the distribution of IE would be even more rapid.

Given the importance of distribution to capturing these new users, Microsoft contractually obligated computer manufacturers (OEMs) to distribute IE. Starting with the release of Windows 95 in August 1995, OEMs were required to distribute first IE1 and then IE2 with all new Windows 95 computers as a condition to keep their Windows licenses. Consumers who bought Windows 95 without buying a computer, however, would at first find that it had no browser included, and later that it would have IE1 or IE2 included but on a separate disk. Throughout 1995, Microsoft compelled distribution of IE with Windows 95; beginning in early 1996, Microsoft enforced restrictions which compelled display of IE as well, including putting an IE icon on the Windows desktop, under the "Windows Experience" marketing label. Starting with IE3, Microsoft went beyond limitations on OEMs.

---

[42] Over the time period studied, modem speeds grew faster while browsers also grew larger, so the time cost of a download remained roughly constant for the average user.

It was harder for the end user to remove IE from their computer. With IE4, this was even more difficult for consumers. Similarly, Microsoft tightened restrictions on OEMs incrementally over time.

Rapid growth in PC and ISP sales themselves would not necessarily limit distribution of Netscape relative to IE. Indeed, widespread distribution of IE alone would not overcome Netscape's lead. Consumers overwhelmingly preferred Netscape. OEMs protested that there were substantial costs (confusion, support calls, etc.) of distributing the product consumers didn't want next to the product they did.[43]

Microsoft saw that it could create a strong asymmetry between IE and Netscape by contractually blocking distribution of Netscape on PCs and ISPs and enforcing distribution of IE alone. Microsoft blocked OEMs from distribution and display of Netscape Navigator.[44] When technical progress by OEMs tended to make it easier for consumers to choose Netscape over IE, Microsoft banned it.[45] This raised the relative cost of adoption of Netscape dramatically compared to IE. Microsoft could slow down the build-up of network effects around Netscape, thus extending the window of time within which Microsoft could act to gain enough market share to prevent a tip to Netscape.

Why did OEMs agree to these contracts? Microsoft controlled the de facto OS standard for PCs, Windows. The OEMs could not afford *not* to distribute Microsoft Windows and survive commercially. Microsoft's ability to actually control distribution and applications development via the PC and ISPs was a consequence of the existing broader market structure. It was able to use its control of this complement to the browser in order to create an asymmetric advantage in capturing new adopters of browsers. This advantage, combined with a period of rapid growth in new adopters, was able to outweigh the inertial forces and positive feedback that surrounded Netscape.

---

[43] OEMs had designed programs to make it easier for consumers to set up their computer for good "OOB (out-of-box) Experience." When Microsoft banned the practice, a Hewlett-Packard executive wrote, "From a consumer perspective ... [you] are hurting our industry and our customers." (Romano 1997, GX 309)

[44] Compaq executives, for example, had compiled a list of twelve ways in which Microsoft could carry out its threats to punish cooperating with an entrant in a document entitled "Judgment: How Retaliatory Would They Get?" (Thibodeau 1999).

[45] The bans were possible only because Microsoft had a monopoly: "if we had another supplier, I guarantee [that] you would not be our supplier of choice." (Romano 1997, GX 309)

6.6 *Likelihood of contracting alternatives*

Why couldn't developers coordinate and contract between themselves to determine the market outcome or force compatibility between Netscape and IE?

Nathan Myhrvold and Bill Gates of Microsoft considered this question: would users, including content developers, prefer a tip to the IE standard, and if not, could they contract or organize to get the outcome they want? From an email exchange (Gates and Myhrvold 1994, DX 386):

> Content developers will try to remain platform neutral, tool neutral and format neutral, and for the most part they will fail. Once people start to compete they will increasingly become platform and tool specific if there is any advantage in doing so. This includes both the computing platform (i.e. Windows) and also the online service environment ... This will create a new inertia in changing standards.

Mr. Myhrvold thought that only a "large player who can create something significantly new and evangelize it successfully" can lead to a new standard. Efforts of the smaller players to have technologies develop the way they like "for the most part ... will fail." Microsoft executives examined the potential "Coasian" or "price theoretic" limitations of standard standards theory and rejected them. Users would have to act together to defeat the strategy, and that would be prohibitively expensive to coordinate, especially as the more technically aware followers, the developers, are in competition with one another.

7 Evidence from market outcomes

In this section we graphically examine browser usage over time to highlight the role of distribution. We gathered data from a website that has kept logs of browser usage since very early in the browser standard setting race. We tracked the usage shares of five major versions of Netscape Navigator and Microsoft IE over time.[46] The core idea of the graphical analysis is to contrast the browser usage of

---

[46] Our sample is all users using either Netscape or IE to browse a website at the University of Illinois–Urbana Champagne between April 1996 and December 2000. More details on the data can be found in Bresnahan and Yin (in press). Although the sample is likely to overweight users who are tech-savvy and

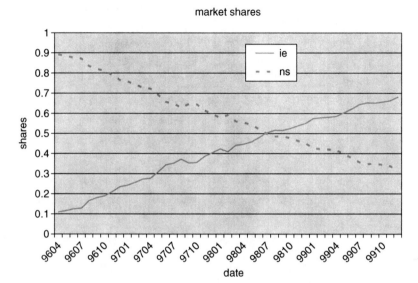

Figure 1.2. Aggregate shares of IE and Netscape browser usage.

observable groups of users. We focus on the gap between groups who are likely to be new users, comparing them to older users, and on groups likely to be particularly influenced by Microsoft's distribution restrictions.

We begin with the aggregate figures. Figure 1.2 shows usage of all versions of IE and Netscape by users of all OSs. Here we see the tipping of the browser market from Netscape to IE.[47]

In addition to knowing what browser they used, we also know what OS users were running on their computer. This lets us distinguish, to some degree, users who had acquired their computer more recently (at the time of usage). Users of Microsoft Windows 98 and Windows 95 obtained their computers during the browser standard setting race, while users of Windows 3.1 (and older versions) did not.

---

prefer Netscape, both of these biases should tend to minimize the impact of distribution.

[47] This graph shows the same pattern as shown in other analyses of the IE versus Netscape shares (including Henderson 2000), with the crossing-point occurring at about the same date.

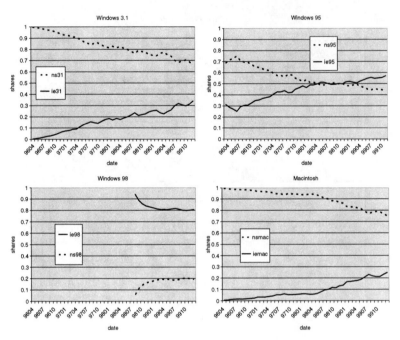

Figure 1.3. Browser brand shares on different operating systems.

Also, users of the more recent Windows versions bought their computers under a more restrictive distribution regime. We also know browser usage by Macintosh computer users; restrictions on the distribution of browsers with new Macs were put in place only part way through our sample.

Figure 1.3 disaggregates by OS, showing the share of each brand of browser on each OS. The tip seen in the previous figure did not occur among the users of each OS; there is a switch from majority usage of NS to majority usage of IE only on Windows 95. There are two patterns on the other OSs. Windows 3.1 users, like Macintosh users, were majority-Netscape throughout the period. Windows 98 users began with a very high share of IE usage, which declines somewhat over time. Much of the change in aggregate shares in which IE came to dominate Netscape in Figure 1.2 merely reflects the higher share of IE on Windows 95 and Windows 98.

The differences across the OSs reflect a number of forces, including differences in the tastes of the users and differences in the availability of browsers. The quality of IE was catching up to NS over time, explaining part of the general tendency toward IE use.[48]

The disaggregated figure immediately casts doubt on a theory in which it was only the increases in IE quality over Netscape quality that explained market tipping to IE. To begin with, the two OSs that finish majority-IE, Windows 98 and Windows 95, are the two on which the distribution advantages for IE were the largest. We can see that the pre-existing users of Windows 3.1 and the largely stable population of Macintosh users were not tipping to IE.[49]

The lack of tipping on Windows 3.1 might be explained by the growing obsolescence of this platform. However, this would not explain the lack of tipping to IE on the Macintosh (Mac). Sales of Macs remained steady during this time. The new users entering the market were not so numerous that they swamped the installed base of Mac users. The figure clearly shows that Netscape users on the Mac were not switching to IE as new and better versions come out.

Similarly, the movement over time toward Netscape browser usage on Windows 98 cannot be explained by IE's growing quality. Every Windows 98 user had a copy of IE distributed with their computer, while almost no Windows 98 users had a copy of Netscape distributed with their computer. Some of the Windows 98 users who preferred Netscape switched to it, taking some time to download and install it (particularly difficult because it was difficult to remove IE).

The importance of distribution and market growth can be seen in Figure 1.4, displaying three kinds of information. In the first pane, we show Windows 98 sales (flow), and in the second pane, the installed base of the four OSs we studied (stock). Both are based on worldwide OS sales over the time period we observed.[50] As can be seen, Windows

---

[48] In Bresnahan and Yin (in press), we provide a fuller econometric analysis of these data, which controls for quality. We also investigate the role of distribution in accelerating the diffusion of new versions of browsers. Our econometric results show a more important role quantitatively for distribution than for quality, both in brand choice and in the diffusion of new versions of the same brand.

[49] Windows 3.1 is unaffected by the distribution restrictions because almost all copies of it were sold before IE was released. It was not until more than halfway through our sample that Macintosh computers came with IE exclusively.

[50] Data derived from Microsoft and IDC resources. IDC, a leading IT market research firm, does not separately report monthly shipments by OS. It reports monthly shipments of all PCs and annual totals by OS (IDC 2000a, 2000b, 2000c, 2000d, 2000e, 2000f, 2000g, and 2000h [additional data from 1996–8

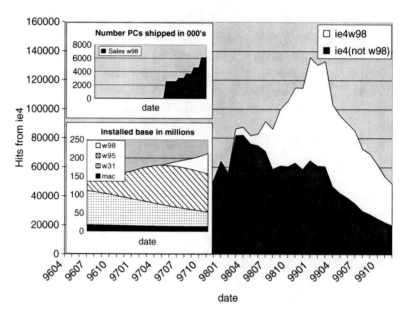

Figure 1.4. Windows 98, OS installed base, and IE4 usage.

98 was a very successful product, but not one that replaced a substantial fraction of the installed base of computers.

In the third pane of Figure 1.4, we show the total usage of IE4 in our data, broken down into two parts. One part is usage of IE4 by Windows 98 users. Overwhelmingly, these are users who got IE but not Netscape with their new computer. The other part is usage of IE4 by all other OS users. While many of the other OS users had obtained IE4 (and not Netscape) with a new computer, some of them were existing computer users who would have to download (or otherwise seek out) IE4 in order to use it.[51] As can be seen from the figure, by the time the usage of IE4

were used]). Fortunately, Microsoft internal documents detail the rate at which new versions of its OS replace old ones in the marketplace. For example, the Microsoft "OEM Sales FY '96 Midyear Review" gives the early history of Windows 95 vs. Windows 3.1 sales (Kempin 1998, GX 421). This forms the basis for our allocation. We follow IDC by assuming 25 percent annual depreciation; lacking the retirements data they keep internally, we use a constant proportional depreciation assumption.

[51] The number of other OS users who had IE4 bundled is substantial. In the average month in the period after IE4 was made available for Windows 95, just over 40% of users had obtained their computer with IE4 bundled to it. The corresponding figure for Macintosh is just under 20%.

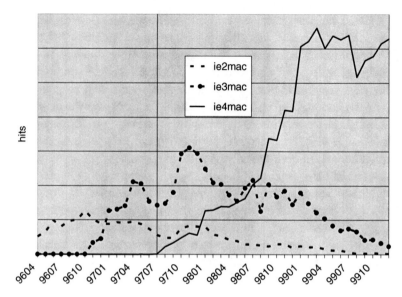

Figure 1.5. Usage of IE browsers by Macintosh users.

peaked, the majority of users were those who obtained it with Windows 98. Thus, the fraction of IE4 users who were using the browser that was distributed with their computer must be even larger.

In Figure 1.5, we highlight the effect of distribution requirements for IE on the Macintosh. Sales of new Macintosh computers were approximately constant over the period, as was the Macintosh installed base. The figure shows usage of three IE browsers on the Macintosh. Two of them, IE2 and IE3, were introduced before the contract between Apple and Microsoft that required distribution of IE with Macs and forbade distribution of NS browsers with them. By contrast, IE4 was released just after that contract took effect. Note that the earlier versions of IE did not exhibit the dramatic growth and high level of usage by Mac users we see for IE4, which was helped by distribution requirements.[52]

---

[52] The figure does not preclude the possibility that this change was caused by a large improvement in IE quality embodied in IE4. Determining whether technical progress or distribution was the larger force in the rapid upswing in IE4 share growth requires regression analysis as conducted in Bresnahan and Yin (in press).

While it is difficult to show graphically, our econometric results show similar impacts for distribution among Windows 95 users (Bresnahan and Yin, in press). New versions of IE were taken up very rapidly by users who obtained them bundled with new computers; other populations did not take up the new versions nearly so rapidly.

The impact of rapid market growth and of control over the distribution of products is dramatic. For a mass market product, tipping involves a large volume of usage. Obtaining that usage is, in a realistic market context, a matter of distribution and marketing as much as of product quality or pricing.

The conditions under which Microsoft was able to overturn Netscape's early lead in the standard setting race can now be seen clearly. Microsoft was able to quickly narrow the gap in quality between IE and Netscape. To create a "strong second" in a short time requires significant financial and intellectual resources, which Microsoft possessed. Microsoft entered not all that long after Netscape, before the market had tipped. Their effort was consistent with the basic timing conclusion of network effects, i.e., that there is more volatility before a tip and more inertia afterwards. They also entered when the market was growing rapidly. Microsoft exercised control over the most important channels of distribution for new PC software to create asymmetric distribution between IE and Netscape. By gaining advantaged distribution for its browser while blocking efficient distribution of Netscape's browser, Microsoft took advantage of the rapid growth in the market to garner a quantitatively large share of browser usage.

There are two important analytical messages here. First, it took an alignment of powerful forces to overcome Netscape's first-mover advantage, including a timely and effective entrant, rapid demand growth, and distribution advantages for the second mover. Second, distribution is key to achieving tipping volume. In a mass market, mass distribution matters. Both of these points arise from connecting the logic of network theory to the market context.

8 Standards theory in markets

Standard setting theory is central to understanding the browser war between Netscape and Microsoft. Many have thought that the second-mover success of IE is a contradiction of the theory in which inertia is infinite and leaped to the conclusion that the zero-inertia version must be correct.

As our empirical examination of the browser war shows, however, the correct completion of the theory arises from linking to market analysis. This section draws from our case study to construct a more complete positive theory of de facto standard setting.

8.1 Inertia can be overcome by new users

The tip to second-mover IE shows that inertia around the first proposed standard need not determine the outcome. Why did developers and users not tip to a Netscape standard?

The first part of the answer lies in the early entry by IE before a standard was set. Netscape Navigator had remarkable success in adoption by users in 1995, and at that stage many websites were developed for Netscape browsers. Nonetheless, two developments remained for the future. The first was the creation of Internet-based markets in online content and e-commerce. As those markets were created, developers would build websites based on advanced, commercial browser features.

The second future development was a large growth in the market for browsers. There were two main sources of growth. Existing PC users adopted the Internet over time. Far more important, however, the demand for PCs expanded rapidly because of the Internet, bringing many new browser customers to the market. As with many technologies, many new browser users were less technically savvy than the early adopters. New users without technical sophistication were particularly influenced by distribution.

At the time of Microsoft's entry only a small portion of the ultimate body of browser users had already chosen the Netscape standard. Advantaged distribution of Microsoft's browser entrant targeted new users. This strategy was effective in the standards war only because it happened early, while demand was still growing rapidly.

Here we have a basic piece of logic of market standard setting. A second mover must arrive "early" in the sense of preceding many decisions. The second mover must be adopted by many users; in the case of IE, this was because of improved distribution. This same logic would also apply to a second mover with a superior product. If it arrives at the market early enough to precede most user and developer decisions, and if it is attractive enough, it may be adopted. Otherwise, positive feedback will lead to inertia around the first mover in setting the standard.

8.2 Complementary markets as source of asymmetry

Analyzing standard setting races without consideration of existing standards in complementary markets can miss important forces. The existence of the de facto standard Windows OS was central to standard setting in browsers. Ignoring complements would lead to a poor model of the incentives for standard setting and of the mechanisms of standard setting.

Pre-existing standards in complements change the incentives of firms that sponsor those standards. In the case of Microsoft, the incentive was to have the browser standard inside its control to avoid competition in the complementary OS market.

Another role of pre-existing standards is to make standard setting strategically asymmetric. In the browser case, the key asymmetry arose in control of distribution channels.

Pre-existing complementary standards can also affect firms' abilities to influence expectations and thereby influence standard setting, as many analysts have noted. More generally, any kind of market power or cost advantage that allows one firm to have differential adoption costs, distribution costs, or means of overcoming inertia than another firm will drive its ability to set the standard.

These strategic asymmetries, however, do not automatically lead to adoption of the advantaged firm's standard. Instead, firm strategy can take advantage of the strategic asymmetries only in a way congruent to industry conditions. The strategic mechanisms of firm influence on standards will, therefore, be highly industry specific. The elements susceptible to general analysis are those linked to large volume and to timing.

There may be a general analysis of "strong seconds" in information technology markets. The second mover will have a greater effect if it implements its strategy before the first inflection point in the S-shaped adoption curve. Similarly, a strong second strategy will have a greater effect before developers have undertaken complex applications. A delay in the arrival of the most important and complex applications and an S-shaped diffusion curve are both characteristic of information technology markets.

Another general point is that prices and contracts are not the only, or even the most important, strategic choice variable in standard setting. Distribution channels and other marketing strategies are equally important. The importance of distribution is a simple and direct extension of the existing positive feedback implications of standards theory. Mass distribution, rapidly achieved, is a step toward positive feedback.

A complete theory of standard setting that links to market analysis implies that there exists a narrow window for strategic action during which a "strong second" can tip the market away from a first mover. The mechanism for doing so will be linked to the volume and timing of demand in the market. New users present an opportunity for a "strong second" to create network effects that can compete with those already established within the installed base of the first mover. Distribution becomes a very important mechanism under this framework for analysis. Complementary markets and pre-existing standards will drive the asymmetries in distribution and incentives that determine the identity of the winner of a standards race. Inertia and network effects around the first mover can be overcome, but only during a finite window of opportunity.

9 Conclusions

By connecting theory to market conditions, we are able to characterize the mechanisms for de facto standard setting in markets. A number of phenomena can be seen both in the logic of standards theory and in the browser market. Positive feedback builds up around a standard, giving markets a tendency toward tipping and toward inertia. This gives standard setting firms an incentive to compete for the market. That incentive is stronger before inertia sets in, and weaker thereafter.

Tipping induces a fundamental indeterminacy in standard setting. Standard setting theory has a variety of normative analyses suggesting mechanisms to resolve the indeterminacy. These range from efficient contracting (which entirely solves the problem of network externalities) to extreme inertia (in which indeterminacy isn't solved at all) or to expectations (which are themselves in general indeterminate).

Our case study of the browser market points to another class of mechanisms, based in markets. It was certainly not the case that efficient contracting among those with an interest in the standard determined the outcome. Instead, the distribution advantages of a large existing firm created a mass of demand which led the tip to a particular browser. It is also certainly not the case that extreme inertia meant that the first mover had an impossible advantage. Instead, a second mover with large distribution advantages, entering while demand was still growing rapidly, was able to reverse the direction of the tip. The positive economic theory of standard setting can be completed by linking it to market analysis.

References

Allchin, James 1997. "IE and Windows," (GX 48), *United States of America* v. *Microsoft Corporation*, Civil Action No. 98-1232. Trial exhibit: email, http://www.usdoj.gov/atr/cases/ms_exhibits.htm.

Anton, J., and D. Yao 1995. "Standard-setting consortia, antitrust, and high-technology industries," *Antitrust Law Journal* 64: 247–65.

Arthur, W. Brian 1989. "Competing technologies, increasing returns, and lock-in by historical events," *Economic Journal* 99: 116–31.

    1994. *Increasing returns and path dependence in the economy*. Ann Arbor, MI: University of Michigan Press.

Augereau, A., Shane Greenstein, and Marc Rysman, in press. "Coordination versus differentiation in a standards war: The adoption of 56 K modems," *RAND Journal of Economics*.

Axelrod, Robert, Will Mitchell, Robert E. Thomas, D. Scott Bennett, and Erhard Bruderer 1995. "Coalition formation in standard-setting alliances," *Management Science* 41: 1493–508.

Baldwin, Carliss Y., and Kim B. Clark 1997. "Managing in an age of modularity," *Harvard Business Review* 75: 84–93.

    2000. *Design rules: The power of modularity, Volume* 1. Cambridge, MA: MIT Press.

Besen, Stanley M., and Joseph Farrell 1994. "Choosing how to compete: Strategies and tactics in standardization," *Journal of Economic Perspectives* 8: 117–31.

Besen, Stanley M., and Garth Saloner 1989. "The economics of telecommunications standards," in *Changing the rules: Technological change, international competition, and regulation in telecommunications*, Robert W. Crandall and Kenneth Flamm, Washington: Brookings Institution, 177–220.

Bresnahan, Timothy, and Pai-Ling Yin, in press. "Economic and technical drivers of technology choice: Browsers," *Annales d'Economie et Statistiques*.

Chase, Brad 1996a. "Winning the Internet platform battle," (GX 465), *United States of America* v. *Microsoft Corporation*, Civil Action

No. 98-1232. Trial exhibit: memo, http://www.usdoj.gov/atr/cases/ ms_exhibits.htm.

1996b. "How to get 30% share in 12 months: Summary recommendations," (GX 684), *United States of America* v. *Microsoft Corporation*, Civil Action No. 98-1232. Trial exhibit: report, http://www.usdoj.gov/ atr/cases/ms_exhibits.htm.

Church, Jeffrey, and Neil Gandal 1992. "Network effects, software provision, and standardization," *Journal of Industrial Economics* 40: 85–103.

Cusumano, Michael A., and Annabelle Gawer 2002. "The elements of platform leadership," *MIT Sloan Management Review* 43: 51–8.

Cusumano, Michael A., Yiorgos Mylonadis, and Richard S. Rosenbloom 1992. "Strategic maneuvering and mass-market dynamics: The triumph of VHS over Beta," *Business History Review* 66, High-Technology Industries: 51–94.

Cusumano, Michael A., and David Yoffie 1998. *Competing on Internet time: Lessons from Netscape and its battle with Microsoft*. New York: Free Press.

David, Paul A. 1985. "Clio and the economics of QWERTY," *American Economic Review, Papers and Proceedings* 75: 332–7.

David, P. A., and S. Greenstein 1990. "The economics of compatibility standards: An introduction to recent research," *Economics of Innovation and New Technology* 1: 3–41.

David, P. A., and M. Shurmer 1996. "Formal standards-setting for global telecommunications and information services – Towards an institutional regime transformation?" *Telecommunications Policy* 20: 789–815.

Davis, Steven J., and Kevin M. Murphy 2000. "A competitive perspective on Internet Explorer," *American Economic Review* 90, Papers and Proceedings of the One Hundred Twelfth Annual Meeting of the American Economic Association: 184–7.

Downes, Larry, and Chunka Mui 1998. *Unleashing the killer app: Digital strategies for market dominance*. Boston: Harvard Business School Press.

Dranove, David, and Neil Gandal 2004. "Surviving a standards war: Lessons learned from the life and death of DIVX," in *Advances in the economics of information systems*, Kerem Tomak (ed.), Hershey, PA: Idea Group Inc., 1–14 (first chapter).

Ehrhardt, Marcus 2004. "Network effects, standardisation and competitive strategy: How companies influence the emergence of dominant designs," *International Journal of Technology Management* 27: 272–94.

false56   *Timothy F. Bresnahan and Pai-Ling Yin*

Evans, David S., Franklin M. Fisher, Daniel L. Rubinfeld, and Richard L.
    Schmalensee 2000. *Did Microsoft harm consumers? Two opposing
    views*. Washington, DC: AEI Press.
Evans, David S., A. L. Nichols, and Richard Schmalensee 2001. "An analysis
    of the government's economic case in *U.S.* v. *Microsoft*," *Antitrust
    Bulletin* 46: 163–242.
Farrell, Joseph, and Paul Klemperer, in press. "Coordination and lock-in:
    Competition with switching costs and network effects," in *Handbook of
    Industrial Organization*, Vol. III, Mark Armstrong and Robert Porter
    (eds.), Amsterdam: Elsevier.
Farrell, Joseph, and Garth Saloner 1985. "Standardization, compatibility,
    and innovation," *RAND Journal of Economics* 16: 70–83.
    1986. "Installed base and compatibility: Innovation, product prean-
    nouncements, and predation," *American Economic Review* 76: 940–55.
    1988. "Coordination through committees and markets," *RAND Journal
    of Economics* 19: 235–52.
    1992. "Converters, compatibility, and the control of interfaces," *Journal
    of Industrial Economics* 40: 9–35.
Fisher, Franklin M., and Daniel Rubinfeld 2001. "*U.S.* v. *Microsoft* – An
    economic analysis," *Antitrust Bulletin* 46: 1–69.
Gallagher, S., and S. H. Park 2002. "Innovation and competition in standard-
    based industries: A historical analysis of the U.S. home video game
    market," *IEEE Transactions on Engineering Management* 49: 67–82.
Gandal, Neil, Nataly Gantman, and David Genesove, in press. "Intellectual
    property and standardization committee participation in the US
    modem industry," in *Standards and public policy*, Shane Greenstein
    and Victor Stango (eds.), Cambridge: Cambridge University Press (this
    volume).
Gates, Bill 1995. "The Internet tidal wave," (GX 20), *United States of
    America* v. *Microsoft Corporation*, Civil Action No. 98-1232. Trial
    exhibit: memo, http://www.usdoj.gov/atr/cases/ms_exhibits.htm.
Gates, Bill, and Nathan Myhrvold 1994. "Internet," (DX 386), *United States
    of America* v. *Microsoft Corporation*, Civil Action No. 98-1232. Trial
    exhibit: email exchange.
Gates, Bill, Nathan Myhrvold, and Peter Rinearson 1995. *The road ahead*.
    New York: Viking.
Gawer, Annabelle, and Michael A. Cusumano 2002. *Platform leadership:
    How Intel, Microsoft, and Cisco drive industry innovation*. Boston:
    Harvard Business School Press.
Gawer, Annabelle, and Rebecca Henderson 2005. "Platform owner entry
    and innovation in complementary markets: Evidence from Intel," NBER
    Working Paper W11852.

Gilbert, Richard, and Michael Katz 2001. "An economist's guide to *U.S.* v. *Microsoft*," *Journal of Economic Perspectives* 15: 25–44.

Goolsbee, Austan, and Peter J. Klenow 2002. "Evidence on learning and network externalities in the diffusion of home computers," *Journal of Law & Economics* 45: 317–43.

Greenstein, Shane M. 1992. "Invisible hands and visible advisors: An economic interpretation of standardization," *Journal of the American Society for Information Science* 43: 538–49.

Hawkins, R., Robin Mansell, and Jim Skea 1995. *Standards, innovation and competitiveness: The politics and economics of standards in natural and technical environments.* Brookfield, VT: Edward Elgar.

Henderson, Rebecca E. 2000. Direct testimony in *United States of America* v. *Microsoft Corporation*, Civil Action No. 98-1232, April 28, 2000.

Henderson, Rebecca, and Kim Clark 1990. "Architectural innovation – The reconfiguration of existing product technologies and the failure of established firms," *Administrative Science Quarterly* 35: 9–30.

IDC 2000a. Client Operating Environments Market Forecast and Analysis, 2000–2004, IDC #22346, June.

2000b. Consumer Internet Service Provider Market Share Update, 1999, IDC #22065, April.

2000c. IDC's Quarterly PC Update: 1Q00 Review/2Q00 Outlook, IDC #22811, August.

2000d. IDC's Quarterly PC Update: 2Q00 Review/3Q00 Outlook, IDC #23224, October.

2000e. IDC's Quarterly PC Update: 4Q99 Review/1Q00 Outlook, IDC #22067, April.

2000f. Internet Service Provider Market Review and Forecast, 1999–2004, IDC #21203, December.

2000g. Network Insider: May 2000, IDC #22379, May.

2000h. Operating Environments Market Forecast and Analysis, 2000–2004, IDC #22597, July.

Joskow, Paul, and Roger Noll 1981. "Regulation in theory and practice: An overview," in *Studies in public regulation*, Gary Fromm (ed.), Cambridge, MA: MIT Press.

Katz, Michael L., and Carl Shapiro 1994. "Systems competition and network effects," *Journal of Economic Perspectives* 8: 93–115.

Kempin, Joachim 1998. "Microsoft OEM sales FY '98 mid-year review," (GX 421), *United States of America* v. *Microsoft Corporation*, Civil Action No. 98-1232. Trial exhibit: report, http://www.usdoj.gov/atr/cases/ms_exhibits.htm.

Lerner, Josh, and Jean Tirole, in press. "A model of forum shopping, with special reference to standard setting organizations," *American Economic Review.*

Liebowitz, S. J., and Stephen E. Margolis 1990. "The fable of the keys," *Journal of Law & Economics* 33: 1–26.

    1994. "Network externality: An uncommon tragedy," *Journal of Economic Perspectives* 8: 133–50.

MacKie-Mason, Jeffrey K., and Janet S. Netz, in press. "Manipulating interface standards as an anticompetitive strategy," in *Standards and public policy*, Shane Greenstein and Victor Stango (eds.), Cambridge: Cambridge University Press (this volume).

Maritz, Paul 1995. "Netscape as netware," (GX 498), *United States of America* v. *Microsoft Corporation*, Civil Action No. 98-1232. Trial exhibit: report, http://www.usdoj.gov/atr/cases/ms_exhibits.htm.

    1996a. "Internet Explorer 3, webmasters, ActiveX: Review of marketing plans," (GX 488), *United States of America* v. *Microsoft Corporation*, Civil Action No. 98-1232. Trial exhibit: presentation, http://www.usdoj. gov/atr/cases/ms_exhibits.htm.

    1996b. "Windows & internet issues," (GX 42), *United States of America* v. *Microsoft Corporation*, Civil Action No. 98-1232. Trial exhibit: email, http://www.usdoj.gov/atr/cases/ms_exhibits.htm.

Mehta, Kumar 1997. "FW: ie data," (GX 204), *United States of America* v. *Microsoft Corporation*, Civil Action No. 98-1232. Trial exhibit: email, http://www.usdoj.gov/atr/cases/ms_exhibits.htm.

Miller, David M. 2005. "Invention under uncertainty and the threat of ex post entry," mimeo, Stanford University.

Negroponte, Nicholas 1995. *Being digital.* New York: Alfred A. Knopf, Inc.

Peltzman, Sam 1989. "The economic theory of regulation after a decade of deregulation," *Brookings Papers on Economic Activity: Microeconomics 1989* (special issue): 1–41.

Roberts, Jonathan 1997. "RE: ie data," (GX 205), *United States of America* v. *Microsoft Corporation*, Civil Action No. 98-1232. Trial exhibit: email, http://www.usdoj.gov/atr/cases/ms_exhibits.htm.

Romano, John 1997. "Letter to Dave Wright, Microsoft Business Manager," (GX 309), *United States of America* v. *Microsoft Corporation*, Civil Action No. 98-1232. Trial exhibit: letter, http://www.usdoj.gov/atr/ cases/ms_exhibits.htm.

Rysman, Marc 2004. "Competition between networks: A study of the market for yellow pages," *Review of Economic Studies* 71: 483–512, http://www.blackwell-synergy.com/doi/abs/10.1111/0034-6527.00512.

Schmalensee, Richard 2000. "Antitrust issues in Schumpeterian industries," *American Economic Review* 90, Papers and Proceedings of the

One Hundred Twelfth Annual Meeting of the American Economic Association: 192–6.

Shapiro, Carl, and Hal R. Varian 1999. "The art of standards war," *California Management Review* 41: 8–32.

Simcoe, T. 2003. "Committees and the creation of technical standards," mimeo, University of California at Berkeley.

Stango, Victor 2004. "The economics of standards wars," *Review of Network Economics* 3: 1–19.

Thibodeau, Patrick 1999. "Compaq witness denies Microsoft bullying," *PCWorld.com*, February 19, 1999, http://www.pcworld.com/news/article/0,aid,9812,00.asp.

von Burg, Urs 2001. *The triumph of Ethernet, technological communities and the battle for the LAN standard.* Stanford, CA: Stanford University Press.

Weiss, Martin, and Carl Cargill 1992. "Consortia in the standards development process," *Journal of the American Society for Information Science* 43: 559–65.

Weiss, Martin B. H., and Marvin Sirbu 1990. "Technological choice in voluntary standards committees: An empirical analysis," *Economics of Innovation and New Technology* 1: 111–33.

Wildfeuer, Christian 1997. "Memphis IEU focus groups report (long mail)," (GX 202), *United States of America* v. *Microsoft Corporation*, Civil Action No. 98-1232. Trial exhibit: email, http://www.usdoj.gov/atr/cases/ms_exhibits.htm.

Yamada, Hideo, and Sam Kurokawa 2005. "How to profit from de facto standard-based competition: Learning from Japanese firms' experiences," *International Journal of Technology Management* 30: 299–326.

Yoffie, David, Pai-Ling Yin, and Christina Darwall 2004. "PalmSource, Inc.," HBS Case No. 704-473. Boston: Harvard Business School Publishing.

2 Competition through institutional form: the case of cluster tool standards

RICHARD N. LANGLOIS

Abstract

Few economists and theorists have thought about the choice of organizational form as a competitive weapon. Here, the author does so by examining the case of cluster tools, which are a type of equipment for manufacturing semiconductors. Within the US industry, competition for these devices is divided between a large vertically integrated firm, Applied Materials, and a large fringe of smaller, more specialized competitors. These latter have responded to the competition by creating a common set of technical interface standards, called the *Modular Equipment Standards Committee standards*. The author analyzes the trade-off between the benefits of systemic innovation and coordination versus those of external economies of scope and modular innovation. Although standards have so far kept the competitive fringe in the ballgame, modularity in the industry may ultimately take a different form, as some of the larger firms adhering to the standards become broadly capable systems integrators that outsource manufacturing to specialized suppliers of subsystems.

1 Introduction

Industrial economists tend to think of competition as occurring between atomic units called *firms*. Theorists of organization tend to think about the choice among various kinds of organizational structures – what Langlois and Robertson (1995) call *business institutions*. But few have

The author would like to thank Shane Greenstein, Robert Leachman, and John Zysman for helpful comments. This paper also benefited from discussions at the conference on Standards and Public Policy, Federal Reserve Bank of Chicago, May 13–14, 2004, and at the summer conference of the Danish Research Unit in Industrial Dynamics, June 15, 2004, Helsingør, Denmark. The author retains responsibility for all remaining errors and obscurities.

thought about the choice of business institution as a competitive weapon.[1]

In this essay I examine, and attempt to learn from, a case in which choice of organizational form is in fact a major element of competition. Cluster tools, a type of equipment for manufacturing semiconductors, are becoming increasingly important as manufacturers attempt to pack more and more circuits on a chip. Within the US industry, competition for these devices is divided between a large vertically integrated firm, Applied Materials, that designs and builds primarily internally according to its own specifications and a large fringe of smaller, more specialized competitors. These latter have responded to the competition from Applied Materials by creating a common set of technical interface standards, called the Modular Equipment Standards Committee (MESC) standards.

Rather than a battle of the standards, the current situation might best be thought of as a battle of alternative development paths: The closed system of Applied Materials, with its significant internal economies of scale and scope, and the open modular system of the competitive fringe, driven by external economies of standardization. At this point, the forces favoring the integrated development path are more-or-less evenly balanced against the forces favoring the path of technical standardization. I analyze these forces in terms of the trade-off between the benefits of systemic innovation and systemic coordination on the one hand and the benefits of external economies of scope and modular innovation. Although standards have so far kept the competitive fringe in the ballgame, modularity in the industry may ultimately take a different, and somewhat more familiar, form, as some of the larger firms adhering to the standards become broadly capable systems integrators who outsource manufacturing to specialized suppliers of subsystems.

2 Background

The integrated circuit (IC) was very much an American invention, developed independently but simultaneously by researchers at Texas Instruments and Fairchild in 1959. As the IC industry grew out of the

---

[1] One exception was Schumpeter (1942, 82), who listed "new forms of industrial organization" as among the sources of the "fundamental impulse that sets and keeps the capitalist engine in motion."

discrete-transistor industry, American firms dominated, both in the fabrication of the chips themselves and in the manufacture of the equipment to make chips. In the early days, semiconductor firms developed much of their own process equipment, often in collaboration with firms in the scientific-equipment industry. Gradually, a distinct semiconductor-equipment industry emerged. In 1980, nine of the top ten firms were American. (See Table 2.1.)

With the rise of Japanese IC fabrication in the 1980s and the loss of American market share in dynamic random-access memories (DRAMs), American dominance in semiconductor equipment also declined. By 1990, only four of the top ten were American, and only Applied Materials remained among the top five. (See Table 2.1.) Between 1980 and 1988, worldwide sales of equipment for lithography, chemical vapor deposition (CVD), and ion implantation quadrupled; during the same period, the American share fell from 75% to 49%, while the Japanese share rose from 18% to 39% (US Department of Commerce 1991). The Japanese success was most pronounced in lithography, automatic test, and assembly and packaging equipment.

The decline in American preeminence in semiconductor equipment generated much the same angst as the better-known decline in American market share in DRAMs. A number of groups, including the National Advisory Committee on Semiconductors (NACS), issued dire warnings (NACS 1990). And Sematech, the government-industry consortium, quickly began defining much of its role as helping reverse the fortunes of the American equipment industry (Robertson 1991). The diagnosis of the equipment industry's problems was similar to that for the semiconductor industry as a whole: the American industry suffered from excess "fragmentation" and insufficient vertical integration. In one of the few contemporary academic examinations of this industry, a study by the Berkeley Roundtable on the International Economy concluded that

with regard to both the generation of learning in production and the appropriation of economic returns from such learning, the US semiconductor equipment and device industries are structurally disadvantaged relative to the Japanese. The Japanese have evolved an industrial model that combines higher levels of concentration of both chip and equipment suppliers with quasi-integration between them, whereas the American industry is characterized by levels of concentration that, by comparison, are too low *and* [by] excessive vertical disintegration (that is, an absence of mechanisms to

Table 2.1. Top ten semiconductor-equipment suppliers, 1980, 1990, and 2000

1980		1990		2000	
Company	Sales	Company	Sales	Company	Sales
Perkin-Elmer (US)	151	Tokyo Electron Ltd (J)	706	Applied Materials (US)	10,410
GCA (US)	116	Nikon (J)	692	Tokyo Electron Ltd (J)	5,142
Applied Materials (US)	115	Applied Materials (US)	572	Nikon (J)	2,432
Fairchild TSG (US)	105	Advantest (J)	423	Teradyne (US)	2,044
Varian (US)	90	Canon (J)	421	ASM Lithography (E)	2,016
Teradyne (US)	83	Hitachi (J)	304	KLA-Tencor (US)	2,003
Eaton (US)	79	General Signal-GCA (US)	286	Advantest (J)	1,865
General Signal (US)	57	Varian (US)	285	Lam Research (US)	1,627
Kulicke and Soffa (US)	47	Teradyne (US)	215	Canon (J)	1,418
Takeda Riken (J)	46	Silicon Valley Group (US)	204	Dainippon Screen (J)	1,390

Notes: Nominal dollars in millions.
US = US firm; J = Japanese; E = European.
Source: VLSI Research.

coordinate their learning and investment processes). (Stowsky 1989, 243, emphasis original)

By 1992, however, the situation had changed markedly, and American firms regained and retained the lead in semiconductor market share.[2] Behind this resurgence lay a number of factors. American firms had increased their attention to manufacturing quality in response to the Japanese challenge. In addition, the decentralized and "fragmented" structure of the industry proved innovative and responsive in a world in which production was becoming international and in which an increasingly modular technology of design permitted efficient vertical specialization. Most important, American manufacturers benefited from a favorable shift in demand away from mass-produced DRAMs and toward design-intensive chips and microprocessors.

The rising tide of the American resurgence and the internationalization of chip production also raised the boats of the American equipment industry.[3] During the nadir of American fortunes in the period 1984–91, Japanese semiconductor companies were responsible for nearly half of all the capital expenditures in the industry. By 1997, however, the Japanese share of those expenditures had fallen to 25 percent, despite an absolute increase in expenditures. This reflected in part an increase in American investment in response to the booming personal computer (PC) market, to which American semiconductor makers (notably Intel) were closely tied. American equipment makers benefited, since, in both the United States and Japan, manufacturers relied heavily on their own indigenous equipment industries.[4] At the same time, manufacturers in other parts of Asia, principally Korea and Taiwan, had doubled their share of capital spending over that period, to a level that together

[2] For a detailed history and analysis of the fall and rise of the American semiconductor industry, on which the remainder of this paragraph draws, see Langlois and Steinmueller (1999).

[3] This paragraph draws on Macher et al. (1999, 266).

[4] In 1997, both the United States and Japan sourced about 75 percent of their equipment from their respective domestic industries, according to data from VLSI Research (cited in Macher et al. 1999, 252 and 266). The link between manufacturers and equipment makers is arguably tighter in Japan, however, where manufacturers often own their own equipment firms (e.g., Hitachi) and where, at least in the view of American industry participants, the relationship of equipment makers to manufacturers is generally more dependent and even "deskilling" of the equipment makers (Langlois 2000). The relative independence of American equipment firms has been an asset in export markets outside Japan.

exceeded Japan's in 1996. This provided a fertile new market for American equipment makers. So-called silicon foundries – firms in the Far East and elsewhere that specialize in the manufacturing stage only – typically produced American-designed products that involved multiple layers with metal interconnections and required sophisticated "mid-process" technology for tasks like CVD and physical vapor deposition (also called *sputtering*). These are areas in which American equipment firms have specialized and excelled.

Indeed, there has arisen something of an international division of labor in the industry, partly by default. We can think of the more than 500 process steps in semiconductor fabrication that can be grouped into three phases akin to the steps in photo developing. The front-end steps involve optical lithography, the process that projects the circuit design onto the silicon wafers in the manner of a darkroom enlarger. The middle steps involve the processing of the wafers in analogy with the business of plunging a photo print into successive chemical baths. And the back-end steps involve testing the finished wafers and packaging them into individual ICs. Just as American manufacturers of DRAMs virtually disappeared during the Japanese ascendancy of the 1980s, so too did American suppliers of lithography equipment – a field that, like DRAMs, Americans had pioneered. In the 1980s, optical giants Nikon and Canon accounted for much of the Japanese market share, and they are joined today by the Dutch firm ASM Lithography. As we saw, test equipment was also an area of Japanese dominance, but that is changing with the ascendancy of American firms like KLA-Tencor, Teradyne, and Agilent (a spin-off from Hewlett-Packard).[5] (See Table 2.2.)

It is in the mid-process stages, however, that American firms have retained and indeed increased their strength. Here a single firm, Applied Materials, accounts for much of that success. By 1992, Applied Materials had overtaken its Japanese rivals to become the largest semiconductor-equipment firm in the world. In the boom year 2000, Applied generated revenues of over $10 billion, almost double those of the next largest firm, Tokyo Electron, an independent concern that is essentially Applied's Japanese counterpart and its principal

---

[5] At the same time, the market for test equipment has shifted toward metrology – real-time monitoring and testing of product and process rather than merely testing of the final product.

Table 2.2. Top fifteen semiconductor-equipment suppliers, 2003

Rank	Company	Sales
1	Applied Materials (US)	4.8
2	Tokyo Electron (J)	3.3
3	ASM Lithography (E)	1.8
4	Nikon (J)	1.3
5	KLA-Tencor (US)	1.3
6	Canon (J)	1.2
7	Advantest (J)	1.1
8	Dainippon Screen (J)	1.0
9	Novellus (US)	0.9
10	Hitachi (J)	0.8
11	Lam Research (US)	0.7
12	Teradyne (US)	0.7
13	Agilent (US)	0.7
14	ASM International (E)	0.6
15	Yokogawa Electric (J)	0.5

Notes: Dollars in millions.
US = US firm; J = Japanese; E = European.
Source: VLSI Research.

international rival.[6] (See Table 2.1.) But Applied is not without American competitors. This single large firm is ringed by an array of smaller, more specialized, less vertically integrated firms led by Novellus and Lam Research. (See Table 2.2.) And herein lies our story. To tell that story properly, however, we need to know more about the mid-process technology of semiconductor fabrication.

3 Single-wafer processing and cluster tools

The traditional approach to the mass production of semiconductors has been batch processing. Silicon wafers, each containing what will become many separate chips, move through the various steps in

---

[6] In fact, however, the product categories in which Applied and TEC compete directly account for only a small fraction of TEC's sales (The Information Network [hereafter InfoNet] 2004a, 4–27).

batches, queuing up when necessary in work-in-process inventories. For example, a large vertical furnace may process more than 200 wafers at a time. Increasingly, however, batch processing is being replaced by single-wafer processing, that is, systems that process one wafer at a time. This is analogous to the continuous-throughput techniques that have largely supplanted batch-processing approaches in the chemical industries.[7] In today's *fabs* – as semiconductor manufacturing facilities are called – about 70 percent of process steps use single-wafer techniques, with batch processing restricted to so-called hot-wall thermal steps (furnaces) and "wet-bench" steps that are literally like plunging a photo print in a chemical bath (The Information Network [hereafter InfoNet] 2004c, 3–5).

Single-wafer techniques are likely to become increasingly significant as semiconductor line widths decrease below 0.25 microns.[8] For reasons that we explore presently, many hot-wall processes are being replaced by single-wafer technologies like rapid thermal processing (RTP), and wet-bench approaches are yielding to "dry" alternatives suitable for single-wafer processing. In principle, a completely single-wafer fab is entirely feasible. By 1993, Texas Instruments's Microelectronics Manufacturing Science and Technology project, funded partially by the US Department of Defense, had demonstrated a small-scale fully single-wafer production line (Doering and Nishi 2001). More recently, Japanese start-up Trecenti Technologies has claimed to have put in production a fully single-wafer 300-mm manufacturing facility (Ikeda et al. 2003). Among the major players, the Taiwanese foundry companies Taiwan Semiconductor Manufacturing and United Microelectronics have apparently moved the farthest in the direction of single-wafer processing (Bass and Christensen 2002).

---

[7] This is an analogy one hears often in this industry. Indeed, it is more than just an analogy, as wafer fabrication involves a series of what are basically chemical-engineering processes.

[8] A micron is a thousandth of a millimeter. Finer line widths allow more dense packing of a chip. Line widths of 20 microns were typical in the early 1970s, falling to 2 to 4 microns in the mid-1980s, and to less than 1 micron today. 4M DRAMS have line widths of around 0.8 microns, 16M DRAMs require line widths of about 0.5 microns, and 64M DRAMs require widths of 0.33 microns or less. Technology now coming on-line will process 300 mm (12-inch) wafers with line widths less than 0.25 microns. Intel's new D1C fab in Oregon produces 300-mm wafers using 0.13-micron technology.

3.1 Single-wafer versus batch processing

The advantages of single-wafer processing are several (Singh et al. 2003). Like most industries, semiconductor fabrication has its share of waggish jargon. One of these is the *milk carton principle*. If you needed to keep a single carton of milk cold, you wouldn't cool down your entire house. But that is in effect what classic batch-processing fabs do. Fabs traditionally store in-process wafers in the ambient air of the facility. This means that, to keep the wafers free of contamination – so critical at such small line widths – fabs must try to keep the entire plant, including the workers who inhabit it, hyper-clean. Quite apart from the cost and difficulties of such cleanliness, even hyper-clean air can cause problems. Since inventories must queue up in ambient air waiting their turn for various batch processes, oxygen can attack and oxidize the wafers, producing a black silicon that can reduce yield.[9] Other process sequences are sensitive to moisture in the atmosphere. The effects of atmospheric degradation become increasingly significant as line widths get smaller. In addition, work-in-progress inventories are subject to other kinds of oxidations, to polymer deformation of resists, and to ordinary dust contamination and handling breakage.

With a single-wafer system, by contrast, one can more easily integrate or cluster together sequential process steps within a controlled atmosphere. In effect, a single-wafer system cools the milk carton in a refrigerator (or a series of refrigerators). This helps eliminate cleaning steps that would otherwise be necessary if the wafers were exposed to air between steps. Moreover, large batch tools, such as diffusion furnaces, cannot maintain uniformity of temperature and other parameters across all the wafers in the batch, a problem that becomes increasingly important as line widths diminish. By processing only one wafer in a chamber at a time, single-wafer tools can achieve much greater process uniformity.[10] Most important, many process

---

[9] Yield – perhaps the most important parameter in semiconductor fabrication – is the fraction of total chips processed that actually work.

[10] Actually, it isn't necessary to process only one wafer in a chamber at a time. So-called semi-batch systems can also achieve high uniformity with a continuous-throughput system that processes several wafers at a time. The Novellus Concept One, for example, is a CVD tool with a lazy Susan holding seven wafers (see Figure 2.2). It is ultimately a single-wafer system, however, as the wafers are fed in and removed one at a time. Each wafer is exposed to one-seventh of the

steps simply require extremely tight atmospheric control. Prominent among these are dielectric planarization, the smoothing of certain layers on the chip, and intermetal connection, the tricky business of making electrical contacts among the various levels of circuitry in a chip.[11] As line widths shrink, however, more and more stages will require the kind of atmospheric control that only a single-wafer system can provide.

A second benefit of single-wafer processing is the ease with which the wafers can be monitored and tested in real time rather than at discrete testing steps. In Shoshana Zuboff's (1988, 126) famous phrase, single-wafer systems are more easily "informated." Monitoring provides a steady stream of data for operators to use in detecting problems quickly and for process engineers to use in uncovering bottlenecks and fine-tuning the system. This includes improved manufacturing-process documentation and more reliable "recipe downloading," the process of programming process steps. Moreover, the real-time aspect of the data makes it possible to engage in closed-loop control, that is, to test and adjust the process as it is happening rather than wait until a step is finished, test, and then adjust subsequent runs. In the long run, the single-wafer approach thus leads more easily to overall factory simulation, including linking to computer-aided design and engineering.

Perhaps the most important benefit of single-wafer processing, however, is reduced cycle time. Cycle time is the time from when the blank wafers enter the production system to when the completed wafers emerge and are ready for assembly and packaging. In a batch system, output rates may be high, but so is cycle time. Instead of thinking about refrigerators, think now about dishwashers, and consider the problem of washing a kitchen-full of dirty dishes. Using a dishwasher is a batch process; washing by hand is a "single-dish" continuous process. Loading the dishwasher may ultimately have a larger throughput, but the first clean plate reaches the cupboard more quickly with washing by hand. Batch semiconductor processing is like running dishes sequentially through many different dishwashers with many different

---

deposition process at each turn of the carousel, which increases uniformity by averaging.

[11] One normally thinks of a simple integrated circuit as a microscopic printed-circuit board of great complexity. In fact, the most complicated modern chips are like several distinct printed-circuit boards sandwiched together and connected in appropriate places by metal plugs. The microprocessors produced at Intel's D1C fab in Oregon require six layers of copper metalization.

capacities. This creates a queuing problem, and the wafers must often sit around in work-in-process inventories waiting to form a batch of the appropriate size for the next process step. By contrast, single-wafer systems push only a single wafer through at a time (putting aside parallel processing steps), but the progress of that single wafer is not slowed as much waiting for other wafers to be ready.[12]

3.2 Cycle time and processing configurations

Faster cycle time means that the first chips get to market more quickly, which can significantly affect ultimate demand by making it more likely that engineers will choose the chip in a systems design. Even for standardized chips like DRAMs, lower cycle time is important because profits are highest earlier in the product life-cycle. But the flexibility of single-wafer processing becomes especially important for specialized and customized chips, production runs of which may not be large enough to justify the set-up costs of batch processing.

Lately, a number of industry observers, including strategy guru Clayton Christensen (Bass and Christensen 2002), have begun predicting the "demise" of Moore's Law. This famous dictum, named after Intel cofounder Gordon Moore, predicts that circuit density will continue to double every eighteen to twenty-four months (Langlois 2002) without increasing production cost, thus yielding an exponential growth in chip performance. Christensen argues that Moore's Law has lately begun to generate such an embarrassment of riches that users are increasingly unable to take advantage of available chip performance. As a result, competition will inevitably move away from the race for higher densities toward customization and speed to market. This in turn will accelerate the transition from batch to single-wafer processing.

---

[12] In addition to reduced queuing time, single-wafer systems can also speed throughput because it simply takes less time to process a single wafer than it does a batch of wafers. This is so for physical reasons: for example, it takes more time to heat up or cool down a large batch than a single wafer. A single-wafer system may also be more easily controlled in a number of respects. This means that the wafer spends less time in the machinery, an important source of lower cycle time. A related benefit of reduced cycle time is the potential for faster learning by doing, since it permits production engineers to see more quickly the full effect on a wafer of all the process steps and allows them to adjust the process for all subsequent wafers (rather than for subsequent *batches* of wafers).

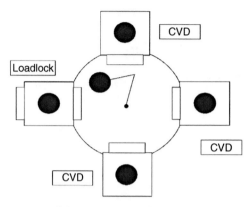

Figure 2.1. A parallel-processing configuration.

Introducing a single-wafer step into a batch fab instantly creates a bottleneck, of course, since throughput of the fab is limited to the throughput of the single-wafer step. The obvious answer is to replicate the bottleneck stage in a parallel-processing configuration. The need for parallel processing was the original motivation for common-platform "cluster" tools. (See Figure 2.1.) Rather than having, say, four separate stand-alone process chambers, each with its own separate facilities for wafer loading and unloading, one could mount the four chambers on a common platform and use a common robotic wafer-handling mechanism to move wafers to and from the various chambers and input-output loadlocks. From the common-platform configuration, however, it becomes an easy step to serial rather than parallel processing. Instead of running the same process in all four chambers, one could instead run different processes, using the wafer handler to move the wafers from one to the other within a controlled atmosphere. This was the genesis of the integrated cluster tool (see Figure 2.2), which represents a genuine move in the direction of single-wafer processing.[13] The parallel configuration offers the benefit of redundancy, and can generate higher throughput when downtime is an issue; but as tools become more reliable, the serial configuration – which boasts superior cycles times – gains the advantage (López and Wood 2003).

[13] In the limit, indeed, independent modules for all fabrication steps could be linked and combined so that, in principle, the wafer never leaves the controlled internal environment of the system. All the modules would be tied together in a computer network, providing a real-time database for monitoring and engineering improvement. This is the ultimate vision of single-wafer processing, what some call the *pipeline fab*.

Richard N. Langlois

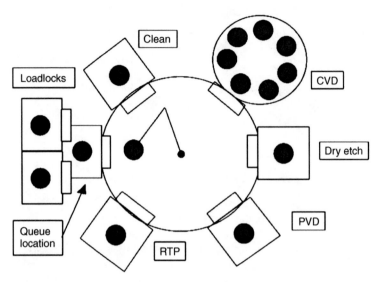

Figure 2.2. A hypothetical modular integrated-processing system (after Burggraaf 1989).

In today's fabs, serial cluster tools typically integrate one major process step (like lithography, etching, deposition, or ion implantation) with related ancillary steps (like cleaning, drying, baking, or coating).[14] The major process steps take place within bays, and wafers typically move in lots of twenty-five among the bays.[15] At least for the present, then, cluster tools are effectively islands of "intrabay" automation within the fab; "interbay" automation is typically the province of automated material-handling systems that shuttle lots among bays. Most prognostications imagine that the future of fab automation will involve a more seamless single-wafer approach, but the exact form this will take remains unclear.

4 Capabilities, organization, and standards

The clustering of modules on a single platform implies the integration of distinct tools, each requiring a distinct set of design and manufacturing capabilities. This is even true of parallel clusters, since making a

[14] This paragraph draws on Robert Leachman's comments on an earlier draft of this paper.

[15] A typical fab might have twenty or thirty process bays, each 50 to 100 feet in length, arrayed perpendicular to a central corridor (InfoNet 2004c, 5–3).

robotic wafer-handler requires capabilities different from those needed for the modules. But the integration of distinct capabilities is especially important in the case of serial clusters. One way to marshal the necessary capabilities is within the boundaries of a single firm large enough to possess and wield all, or at least most of, the capabilities necessary to produce a cluster tool. Another way is somehow to organize and integrate through contract the capabilities of a number of distinct firms. The American semiconductor equipment industry uses both of these approaches simultaneously.

4.1 Applied Materials' capabilities

Applied Materials is of course the preeminent example of a firm that tries to integrate a wide array of capabilities within a single organization. Interestingly, however, Applied's success reflects an initial strategy of *narrowing* its business focus and reducing its portfolio of products.[16] Michael McNeilly founded the company in 1967 to supply equipment to the nascent semiconductor manufacturing industry. Applied went public in 1972, and McNeilly quickly diversified into a variety of ventures that even included the purchase of a maker of silicon wafers.[17] But the recession of 1975 saw profits turn into losses, and Applied's board ousted McNeilly in favor of a venture capitalist called James Morgan. Morgan promptly jettisoned non-core businesses and reoriented the company back to semiconductor process equipment. Applied weathered the Japanese invasion, and even prospered by an aggressive entry into the Japanese and other international markets (Morgan and Morgan 1991).

In the 1980s, Applied placed another major strategic bet. At a time when batch processing ruled semiconductor production, Morgan and his colleagues chose to focus Applied's product development efforts exclusively on single-wafer technology. In 1987, the company

---

[16] This paragraph draws on Kinni (2000, 27–42).

[17] In many respects, the menu of diversification alternatives facing Applied in the 1970s was not unlike that facing the manufacturing sector. Because of the rapid growth of the industry attendant on the development of the planar process and the integrated circuit, American firms enjoyed so many profitable product opportunities that they became vulnerable to a focused attack by the Japanese, who entered with a narrower range of products and strong capabilities in volume production (Langlois and Steinmueller 1999).

introduced its first cluster tool, the Precision 5000, which has been touted as the most successful product introduction in the history of the business. The Precision platform was originally offered as a parallel-processing CVD tool; but within two years, chambers for etch and tungsten processes became available, opening the door to serial configuration. In 1990, the company rolled out another platform, called Endura, built around sputtering processes but later upgraded to include CVD, etch, and RTP modules (InfoNet 2004b, 5–10). Thus, although Applied's capabilities are focused on mid-process cluster tools, the increasing variety of technologies that can be clustered in sequence means that Applied is necessarily widening its technological and product capabilities.

In principle, of course, a maker of cluster tools could contract with outside concerns for the development of some of the modules. Ultimately, a firm could outsource the design of all the modules and simply act as a systems integrator. Applied has quite deliberately chosen the opposite strategy – to develop internally capabilities in all areas of semiconductor fabrication technology. Initially, Applied did contract with firms like Peak Systems for an RTP module and GaSonics (since acquired by Novellus) for a photoresist stripping module, but both of these arrangements generated contractual problems and were abandoned.[18]

The difficulty of using outside suppliers for modules arose in part from the fact that Applied's cluster tool platforms were and are closed proprietary systems. The chambers reside on a central platform, or mainframe, and are linked by a centralized control and communications architecture that uses a closed proprietary standard. This means that the investments that firms like Peak and GaSonics would have had to make in adapting their technology to Applied's mainframe would have been specific to transactions with Applied – the modules, and the knowledge investments they represent, could not be reused in transactions with other buyers.[19]

---

[18] In the case of Peak, the result was a $420,000 judgment against Applied Materials for breach of contract and misappropriation of trade secrets (*Peak Sys., Inc.* v. *Applied Materials, Inc.*, No. 707566 (Cal. Super. Ct. December 1, 1993)).

[19] A follower of Williamson (1985) would be tempted to assert at this point that Applied's strategy of internal development as a whole was no doubt motivated by such problems of contractual hazards and hold-up in the face of

By contrast, modular cluster tools – or simply modular tools – comprise self-contained "smart" modules, each possessing its own computer and its own piping. The modules are tied together not by a central controller but by a set of open interconnect and control standards. The modules conform to a mechanical interface standard, which governs the placement and dimensions of the modules and handlers, and to various communications standards, which govern the way the decentralized computers talk to each other over a network. In the case of cluster tools, such an approach is not hypothetical. Most makers of cluster tools – apart from Applied – adhere in whole or in part to the so-called SEMI/MESC standards, which are promulgated by the Modular Equipment Standards Committee of Semiconductor Equipment and Materials International, the industry trade association.

4.2 The emergence of standards

The process by which standards emerged in the cluster tool industry is rather different from those of well-documented cases like the QWERTY keyboard (David 1985; Liebowitz and Margolis 1990), the VHS videocassette recorder (Cusumano et al. 1992), the IBM-compatible PC (Langlois 1992), the 33-rpm LP record (Robertson and Langlois 1992), or the Ethernet (von Burg and Kenney 2003). In all of those cases, standards emerged through a competition or a "battle of the standards" among alternatives sponsored by a proprietary champion or small consortium. In cluster tools, however, a single standard emerged immediately out of collective action within a fragmented industry.[20]

transaction-specific knowledge and irreversible investments. And, as we will see, the SEMI/MESC cluster tools standards to which Applied's competitors adhere were motivated in part to reduce contractual costs by reducing the transaction specificity of a firm's development of a module. In this case, however, the court agreed with Peak's contention that Applied was secretly developing its own RTP technology all along and was using its contract with Peak to gain knowledge to speed that internal development. Contractual hazards were arguably more the *result* of Applied's strategy than the cause.

[20] A better historical analogy for the MESC standards might be the efforts of the Society of Automotive Engineers, led at first by Howard E. Coffin of the Hudson Motor Car Company, to standardize numerous parts used in the early automobile industry (Epstein 1928, 4–43). Between 1910 and 1920, the Society of Automotive Engineers reduced the number of types of steel tubing from 1,600 to 210 and the number of types of lock washer from 800 to 16. Throughout the

The story begins in 1989.[21] Commercial cluster tools had been on the market for only two or three years, but a number of firms, each considerably smaller than Applied Materials, were either in the market or planning to enter (Burggraaf 1989). In March, a group of representatives from several Bay Area companies congregated at a motel in Fremont to begin what would become a rapid-fire series of meetings. Present at the first meeting were representatives of eleven companies, including the CEOs of four of those companies. In many ways, the cooperation among these firms was a startling change from the individualist go-it-alone culture supposedly characteristic of the industry. From another point of view, however, the cooperation was possible precisely because of the cultural network of Silicon Valley and its web of personal contacts among engineers and marketers in many distinct firms. Clearly, the threat of competition from Applied Materials catalyzed the collective action. Apart from Applied, the cluster tool industry consisted of firms whose capabilities were limited, and not even the largest of these was able to offer a multiple-module tool on its own. In the end, these firms had to rely on coordination across firm boundaries, and standards would help facilitate such coordination.

The ad hoc group called their would-be standard the Modular Equipment Standards Architecture (MESA). They put forward the following mission statement: "Develop technically sound, common, non-proprietary interface standards which the US equipment industry

> initial period of standardization, until the early 1920s, it was the smaller firms that showed the most interest and had the most to gain. The larger firms such as Ford, Studebaker, Dodge, Willys-Overland, and General Motors tended to ignore the Society of Automotive Engineers and relied instead on internally established standards (Thompson 1954, 1–11). In fact, something similar has happened in cluster tools in the wake of standardization. Before the development of standards, all tools used their own idiosyncratic valve designs. Outside suppliers would craft each valve to the user's specifications. The dominant firm in the business is VAT of Liechtenstein, which is noted for the quality of its product. Since the promulgation of standards, however, a standard valve has emerged, making valves more a commodity and less a specialty item. American firms like High Vacuum Apparatus and MDC Vacuum Products have begun to take business away from VAT, and valve prices have fallen dramatically. Another area in which standardization is lowering costs is software. With the development of communications and control standards, an increasing number of aspects of the control software can be handled by standard packages provided by firms like Thesis, GW Systems, Realtime Performance, and Techware Systems.

[21] This discussion of the standard setting process follows my earlier account (Langlois 2000).

can utilize to individually and collectively offer the best available choice of automated, interchangeable, integrated tools" (Benzing 1989). The group worked feverishly over the ensuing weeks to develop a draft standard. The first goal was to standardize the mechanical interface of future cluster tools, that is, the physical connection between the wafer handler and the modules. This included such parameters as the size and shape of the port and the valve flanges, their height above the floor, and the reach of the robot arm. Although invited, Applied Materials did not participate in the standard setting process. Indeed, at one point Applied suggested its own Precision 5000 as an alternative standard, a proposal that was never taken seriously for technical as well as competitive reasons – the Precision 5000 was not a suitably modular design. In the end, however, MESA and Applied were united formally when, at a meeting in September 1989, the MESA group voted to join SEMI, becoming reconstituted as MESC.[22] As a member of SEMI, Applied Materials was effectively a member of MESC and eligible to vote on proposed standards.[23]

4.3 Competing development paths

Rather than a battle of the standards, the current situation might best be thought of as a battle between alternative development paths: the closed system of Applied Materials, with its significant internal economies of scale and scope versus the open modular system of the competitive fringe, driven by external economies of standardization. The latter has grown to be a significant force: The market for modular tools was over $1.5 billion in 2003 (see Figure 2.3), and the two largest SEMI/MESC vendors, Novellus and Lam Research, were the ninth and eleventh largest semiconductor-equipment firms in the world in that year (Table 2.2).[24] This may seem like small potatoes, given that the market for non-modular cluster tools was some $7.8 billion in 2003 (InfoNet 2004b, 9–16). But that figure is somewhat misleading. Much of the lithography stage is now performed using cluster tools, but these

---

[22] Among the principal motivations for joining SEMI was a fear of antitrust litigation, perhaps instigated by Applied (Langlois 2000).

[23] And when the MESC mechanical interface standard eventually came to a vote in June 1990, Applied voted against it (Winkler 1990).

[24] In 2003, Novellus had a 48.5% share of the market for modular tools, and Lam a 33.2% share (InfoNet 2004b, 9–14).

Table 2.3. 2003 Market share in submarkets (percent)

CVD		PVD		Etch		Ion implant		RTP	
Applied	54.5	Applied	84.3	Applied	26.5	Applied	23.9	Applied	45.3
Novellus	31.8	Novellus	7.8	TEL	35.7	Varian	34.5	TEL	29.4
ASM Intl.	8.3	Ulvac	5.9	Lam	29.7	Axcellis	36.1	ASM Intl.	9.3
Others	5.4	Others	2.1	Others	8.0	Nissin	5.5	Others	16.0

Source: The Information Network 2004a.

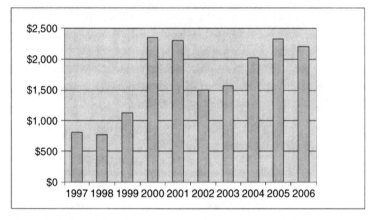

Figure 2.3. Modular cluster tool market, actual and forecast, millions of nominal dollars (source: The Information Network).

are atmospheric tools (that is, tools for processes not involving vacuum or a controlled atmosphere) for which there exist no SEMI/MESC standards. For mid-process technology, Applied is still the clear leader, but the competition seems more real. As Figure 2.4 suggests, if we consider the entire SEMI/MESC network a competitor to Applied Materials, then the modular approach comes in second, ahead of Tokyo Electron. Moreover, if we look at specific submarkets, it appears that much of Applied's overall dominance comes from competing seriously in almost all submarkets, not necessarily from dominating all those submarkets (Table 2.3).

For the moment, then, both development paths seem to be surviving, and neither is obviously driving out the other. Why? Let us pause to think about the basic economics of closed proprietary systems versus

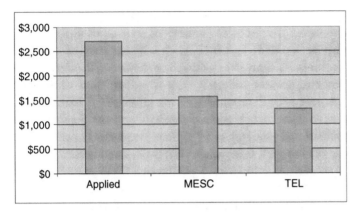

Figure 2.4. Standards adherents as a competitor to Applied Materials, 2003 (cluster tool sales in millions of dollars) (source: The Information Network).

open modular ones. The primary benefits of a closed system lie in the ease of systemic coordination and reorganization. When the nature of the connections among the elements in a system is changing or idiosyncratic to applications, a unified organization can more cheaply coordinate and fine-tune the connections. The value of such systemic coordination depends on both technological and demand factors. In some respects, and in some technologies, the value of idiosyncratic systemic coordination may be exogenous. In the automobile industry, for example, some degree of "integrality" may be inherent in the nature of the product (Helper and MacDuffie 2002, 372). Moreover, as Christensen et al. (2002) have argued, an integrated organization is better able to fine-tune product characteristics to achieve greater functionality in an environment in which users eagerly demand such functionality.

On the other side of the ledger, an open modular system can more effectively direct capabilities toward improving the modules themselves (Langlois and Robertson 1992). Such a system harnesses the division of labor and the division of knowledge, allowing organizational units to focus narrowly and deeply; at the same time, it magnifies the number of potential module innovators, and thus can often take advantage of capabilities well beyond those even a large unitary organization could marshal. In this way, an open modular system "breaks the boundaries of the firm." There are both static and dynamic benefits to an open modular system. At any point in time, a user can mix and match components from a wider variety of sources to fine-tune the system to his or her taste, and thus reach a higher level of utility or tailored functionality than pre-packaged systems could offer. In the semiconductor-equipment industry, this is called "best of breed." A user might mix a CVD module from manufacturer A with an etch module from manufacturer B and a wafer handler from manufacturer C, all assembled and guaranteed by system integrator D, who might add in some off-the-shelf components like valves and controller software. If, however, manufacturer E produces a CVD module that is innovative or otherwise superior in the eyes of the user, that module could replace module A in the package. In this way, the user does not have to rely on the capabilities of any single firm, which may not be on the cutting edge in all technologies.

More important, perhaps, are the dynamic benefits. Over time, an open modular system can lead to rapid trial-and-error learning and thus evolve faster than a closed system. Note that, at least in principle, this effect can counter the functionality benefits Christensen et al. (2002) claim for the closed systems of integrated organizations. It is certainly plausible, if not logically necessary, that a capable integrated producer could achieve greater functionality by tweaking the system architecture than one could have achieved by picking even the best available assortment of modular components within a fixed architecture. But if the components of the open system evolve rapidly enough, an open system can leave yesterday's best-integrated system in the dust. This was certainly the case with PCs. The IBM PC of 1981 was a modular system that contemporary observers considered well below the level of functionality of other (mostly closed) systems. But PC components improved so rapidly that generic PCs eventually began to outperform even special-purpose minicomputers and workstations. The importance of this effect will depend on the number of potential component innovators, which in turn will depend on the extent of the market.

My working hypothesis is that, in cluster-tool world, the forces favoring integrality and those favoring modularity are relatively balanced – for the moment, at least. Applied Materials benefits from a certain degree of integrality inherent in the process of semiconductor fabrication. A fab is a tightly integrated and balanced system, one requiring the integration of knowledge between the manufacturer and the equipment supplier (Weber 2002). In effect, then, the equipment maker must supply not only the equipment itself but also bundled information and guaranteeing functions. A tool must fit in with a user's production line, and it must work properly and consistently. When it fails to work, it must be fixed promptly; moreover, the user must be confident that it will indeed be fixed promptly. And the user and the supplier must communicate information to ensure the continued refinement and improvement of the technology.

A large firm with significant internal capabilities can provide these ancillary services. Such a firm possesses not only the majority of skills necessary to fabricate the machinery it sells, it also possesses complementary capabilities in repair and customer service, including the ability to gather information to improve the product. Reputation is another important complementary asset, since it provides a guarantee to customers that the promised ancillary services, especially on-site repair, will be reliably provided. In this respect, a modular system provided by a network of firms would seem to be at a disadvantage. If the modular approach is to succeed, the role of the system integrator is crucial.

A system integrator is an organization that packages the products of a number of suppliers (chambers, wafer handler, etc.) and provides the necessary ancillary services, including the guaranteeing function. In the absence of standards, the job of the system integrator as coordinator would be more difficult, and working with others would require the sharing of proprietary information in a way that could generate greater transaction costs. With standards, however, much of the necessary coordination is embodied in the standards, and the spillover of proprietary knowledge from one firm to another is minimized. This would increase the chance that the system-integration function could be provided through the market. The integrator would work with the customer to tailor a system; would work with suppliers (itself probably included) to produce the system; and would provide the necessary service guarantees. This means that the integrator would need to have a reputation of value significant enough to act as a hostage (Williamson 1985). In the parlance of the industry, this is called *taking ownership of the system*.

In the SEMI/MESC world, it is often a lead equipment maker that acts as system integrator. And, in practice, this usually means Novellus or Lam. In addition, users – manufacturers themselves – are often effectively the systems integrators. This is especially true of large, highly capable firms like Texas Instruments and IBM. What has not happened, however, is the rise of independent third-party systems integrators, a development some had hoped for early on.[25]

So far, then, the need for close coordination with manufacturers, as well as the often idiosyncratic problems of fine-tuning in the fab, have limited the advantages of standards in cluster tools – relative, at least, to those in, say, PCs or software, where the benefits of modular innovation have wildly outstripped those of systemic integration.

Growth in the extent of the market brings with it experience that can increase internal capabilities, and thus the scope of the firm, in the manner Edith Penrose (1959) suggested. As in the case of the PC (Langlois 1992), industry-wide open standards in cluster tools emerged in a low-capability environment – few firms were capable of producing a complex system without help from others. For example, using very little of its own capabilities and relying on a panoply of vendors, Rochester-based CVC Products (since acquired by Veeco) was one of the early leaders in the use of MESC standards to assemble cluster tools. In 1992, CVC Products announced a MESC-compatible tool integrating components from seven other companies. By 1994, however, the company had done so much internal development in hardware and software that it could offer a tool for which it failed to provide only the wafer-handling robotics and the module controllers (InfoNet 2004b, 3–16). This sort of capability building went on within the larger players like Novellus and Lam as well.

At the same time, however, outsourcing has become the rule in the industry. A startling difference between Applied Materials and MESC-compatible competitors like Novellus and Lam is the extent to which the latter outsource the manufacture of the modules they do produce. In 2001, Lam was an integrated manufacturer with 4,300 employees in thirteen buildings. Today it employs half as many workers in only four buildings (InfoNet 2004a, 4–3). In its 10-K filing for 2003, Novellus puts it this way:

We do all system design, assembly and testing in-house, and outsource the manufacture of major subassemblies. This strategy allows us to minimize our

---

[25] One suggestion in the early days of standard setting was that aerospace firms might take on the role of systems integration (Newboe 1990).

fixed costs and capital expenditures and gives us the flexibility to increase capacity as needed. Outsourcing also allows us to focus on product differentiation through system design and quality control and helps to ensure that our subsystems incorporate the latest third-party technologies in robotics, gas panels and microcomputers.[26]

In part, outsourcing is a strategy to deal with the highly cyclical character of the industry. Applied may be large enough to weather downturns, but smaller firms adapt by transforming fixed into variable costs through outsourcing, which gives flexibility to *decrease* capacity as well as to increase it. Nonetheless, such outsourcing is a general trend in an industry driven by growth in the extent of the market (Langlois 2003). Indeed, it is through this kind of outsourcing that systems integration is emerging in the industry. Independent third parties are not appearing suddenly to coordinate among market participants; instead, integrated firms are retaining – and even deepening – their capabilities in system design, service, and technological coordination, while hiving off manufacturing operations to more specialized firms (Pavitt 2003).

References

Bass, Michael, and Clayton Christensen 2002. "The future of the microprocessor business," *IEEE Spectrum* (April): 3439.

Benzing, Jeffrey C. 1989. Talking paper for the Sematech Workshop on Cluster Tools, May 2, Austin, Texas.

Burggraaf, Peter 1989. "Integrated processing: The 1990s trend," *Semiconductor International* (June): 6569.

Christensen, Clayton M., Matt Verlinden, and George Westerman 2002. "Disruption, disintegration, and the dissipation of differentiability," *Industrial and Corporate Change* 11: 955–93.

Cusumano, Michael, Yiorgios Mylonadis, and Richard Rosenbloom 1992. "Strategic maneuvering and mass-market dynamics: the triumph of VHS over Beta," *Business History Review* 66: 5194.

David, Paul A. 1985. "Clio and the economics of QWERTY," *American Economic Review* 75: 332–7.

Doering, Robert, and Yoshio Nishi 2001. "Limits of integrated-circuit manufacturing," *Proceedings of the IEEE* 89: 375–93.

---

[26] Novellus 2003 10-K filing, 9. See also Lam Research 2003 10-K filing, 6–7.

Epstein, R. C. 1928. *The automobile industry: Its economic and commercial development*. Chicago: A. W. Shaw.

Helper, Susan, and John Paul MacDuffie 2002. "B2B and modes of exchange: Evolutionary and transformative effects," in *The global internet economy*, Bruce Kogut (ed.), Cambridge, MA: MIT Press, 331–80.

Ikeda, Shuji, Kazunori Nemoto, Michimasa Funabashi, Toshiyuki Uchino, Hirohiko Yamamoto, Noriyuki Yabuoshi, Yasushi Sasaki, Kazuhiro Komori, Norio Suzuki, Shinji Nishihara, Shunji Sasabe, and Atsuyoshi Koike 2003. "Process integration of single-wafer technology in a 300-mm fab, realizing drastic cycle time reduction with high yield and excellent reliability," *IEEE Transactions on Semiconductor Manufacturing* 16: 102–10.

The Information Network 2004a. *Applied materials: Competing for world dominance*. New Tripoli, PA: The Information Network.

    2004b. *Cluster tools in IC processing: Technology and market forecasts*. New Tripoli, PA: The Information Network.

    2004c. *Semiconductor factory automation: Technology issues and market forecasts*. New Tripoli, PA: The Information Network.

Kinni, Theodore B. 2000. *Future focus: How 21 companies are capturing 21st century success*. Milford, CT: Capstone Press.

Langlois, Richard N. 1992. "External economies and economic progress: The case of the microcomputer industry," *Business History Review* 66: 1–50.

    2000. "Capabilities and vertical disintegration in process technology: The case of semiconductor fabrication equipment," in *Resources, technology, and strategy*, Nicolai J. Foss and Paul L. Robertson (eds.), London: Routledge, 199–206.

    2002. "Digital technology and economic growth: The history of semiconductors and computers," in *Technological innovation and economic performance*, Benn Steil, David Victor, and Richard R. Nelson (eds.), Princeton: Princeton University Press for the Council on Foreign Relations, 265–84.

    2003. "The vanishing hand: The changing dynamics of industrial capitalism," *Industrial and Corporate Change* 12: 351–85.

Langlois, Richard N., and Paul L. Robertson 1992. "Networks and innovation in a modular system: Lessons from the microcomputer and stereo component industries," *Research Policy* 21: 297–313.

    1995. *Firms, markets, and economic change: A dynamic theory of business institutions*. London: Routledge.

Langlois, Richard N., and W. Edward Steinmueller 1999. "The evolution of competitive advantage in the worldwide semiconductor industry, 1947–1996," in *The sources of industrial leadership*, David C.

Mowery and Richard R. Nelson (eds.), New York: Cambridge University Press, 19–78.

Liebowitz, S. J., and S. E. Margolis 1990. "The fable of the keys," *Journal of Law & Economics* 33: 1–25.

López, Marcel J., and Samuel C. Wood 2003. "Systems of multiple cluster tools: Configuration, reliability, and performance," *IEEE Transactions on Semiconductor Manufacturing* 16: 170–8.

Macher, Jeffery T., David C. Mowery, and D. A. Hodges 1999. "Semiconductors," in *US industry in 2000: Studies in competitive performance*. Washington, DC: National Academy Press, 245–86.

Morgan, James C., and Jeffrey Morgan 1991. *Cracking the Japanese market.* New York: The Free Press.

National Advisory Committee on Semiconductors 1990. *Preserving the vital base: America's semiconductor materials and equipment industry.* Washington, DC: Government Printing Office.

Newboe, Betty 1990. "Cluster tools: A process solution?" *Semiconductor International* (July): 82–8.

Pavitt, Keith 2003. "Specialization and systems integration: Where manufacture and services still meet," in *The business of systems integration*, Andrea Prencipe, Andrew Davies, and Michael Hobday (eds.), Oxford: Oxford University Press, 78–94.

Peak Sys., Inc. v. Applied Materials, Inc. 1993. No. 707566 (Cal. Super. Ct. December 1, 1993).

Penrose, Edith T. 1959. *The theory of the growth of the firm.* Oxford: Basil Blackwell.

Robertson, Jack 1991. "Sematech refocusing for CIM, software?" *Electronic News*, July 29.

Robertson, Paul L., and Richard N. Langlois 1992. "Modularity, innovation, and the firm: The case of audio components," in *Entrepreneurship, technological innovation, and economic growth: International perspectives*, Frederick M. Scherer and Mark Perlman (eds.), Ann Arbor, MI: University of Michigan Press, 321–42.

Schumpeter, Joseph A. 1942. *Capitalism, socialism, and democracy.* New York: Harper and Brothers (Harper Colophon edition, 1976).

Singh, Rajendra, Mohammed Fakhruddin, and Kelvin F. Poole 2003. "The impact of single-wafer processing on semiconductor manufacturing," *IEEE Transactions on Semiconductor Manufacturing* 16: 96–101.

Stowsky, Jay S. 1989. "Weak links, strong bonds: U.S.-Japanese competition in semiconductor production equipment," in *Politics and productivity: The real story of why Japan works*, Chalmers Johnson, Laura Tyson, and John Zysman (eds.), Cambridge: Ballinger, 241–74.

Thompson, G. V. 1954. "Intercompany technical standardization in the early American automobile industry," *Journal of Economic History* 14: 1–20 (Winter).

US Department of Commerce 1991. *National security assessment of the US semiconductor wafer processing equipment industry.* Washington, DC: Office of Industrial Resource Administration, Bureau of Export Administration.

von Burg, Urs, and Martin Kenney 2003. "Sponsors, communities, and standards: Ethernet vs. token ring in the local area networking business," *Industry and Innovation* 10: 351–75.

Weber, Charles 2002. "Knowledge transfer and the limits to profitability: An empirical study of problem-solving practices in semiconductor manufacturing and process development," *IEEE Transactions on Semiconductor Manufacturing* 5: 420–6 (November).

Williamson, Oliver E. 1985. *The economic institutions of capitalism.* New York: The Free Press.

Winkler, Eric 1990. "MESC link for cluster tools approved; Applied votes no," *Electronic News*, June 4: 1.

Zuboff, Shoshana 1988. *In the age of the smart machine.* New York: Basic Books.

3 The economic realities of open standards: black, white, and many shades of gray

JOEL WEST

Abstract

Open standards have long been popular among buyers of goods and services in the information technology sector. Self-interested buyers and sellers, however, have had incentives to overstate (or understate) the openness of various standards. This paper rejects the simplified view that there is a single model of an open standard, as well as the assumption that a fully open solution is always an optimal (or even a feasible) outcome. The author analyzes various economic and techno-logical forces that make standards more or less open and how these economic forces are affected by the policy choices available to firms, standard setting organizations, and regulators. The author uses this analysis to suggest objective measures for standards openness and a typology of common bundles of standards rights; he also notes the practical limits to open standards.

1 Open standards: ideals vs. reality

The concept of "open systems" has become an icon to conveniently express all that is good about computing. It ... has always been held up as the ideal to which computing should subscribe. (Cargill 1994, 3)

As Cargill indicates, "open" for compatibility standards has been promoted as a universally good thing – right up there with motherhood and apple pie. For many corporate and individual users of informa-tion technologies, open standards are the ne plus ultra for external

The author would like to thank Donald Deutsch, Philip Gross, and Andrew Updegrove for sharing their experience and depth of knowledge of standardization processes. The discussions with Ken Krechmer and Timothy Simcoe regarding their own evolving ideas on open standards, and comments on earlier versions by Scott Gallagher and Kai Jakobs were also greatly appreciated. Finally, the author thanks the editors for their invaluable guidance, encouragement, and patience.

technologies.[1] In contrast, for many information technology (IT) vendors, nirvana is having their proprietary standard win a standards battle, which creates switching costs and other lock-ins, thereby providing an ongoing stream of rents to pay shareholders, employees, and of course executive bonuses (e.g., Morris and Ferguson 1993; Shapiro and Varian 1999).

Here, I argue that the many attempts to promote open standards have been at best naïve. Contrasted to these utopian ideals, real world standards are rarely fully open or fully closed: unlike the "Western" movies of fifty years ago, when it comes to standards openness there are no black hats and white hats – only shades of gray. At worst, these unrealizable ideals are economically destructive: producers must be paid somehow, and the cost of developing a standard – and of producing the technology precursors and eventual implementations – must be either directly or indirectly born by the eventual beneficiaries. Thus, economic realism about open standards is a prerequisite to any discussion of open standards, whether firm strategies or public policy.

1.1 The case for open standards

If you ask most buyers today what they prefer about open standards, their answer implies that they believe that open standards assures that multiple vendors will provide competing implementations of that standard, which therefore reduces (or eliminates) the risk of proprietary rent-seeking. More sophisticated users are also aware of the positive feedback mechanism of the adoption of network goods, and they thus hope to share in reduced costs through economies of scale or at least avoid joining (as David 1987 refers to them) the ranks of "angry orphans."

The presumption, then, is that open standards lead to wider knowledge about a technology and more competition, which, in turn, provide wider variety and lower prices for implementations of the standards and the associated complementary products. Meanwhile, lower prices are expected to produce a positive feedback loop, thereby further increasing demand. In Figure 3.1, I summarize a general causal model integrating the implicit arguments advanced by advocates of open

---

[1] For example, a partnership of European standardization bodies has defined an open standard as one "developed and/or affirmed in a transparent process open to all relevant players ...; either free of IPR concerns, or licensable on a (fair), reasonable and non-discriminatory ((F)RAND) basis; driven by stakeholders, and ... publicly available" (ICTSB 2005, 10).

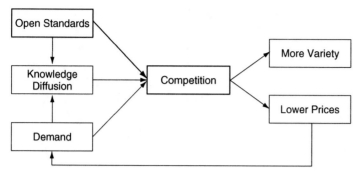

Figure 3.1. Implicit causal model of open standards.

standards – adapted from the West (2005) analysis of similar implicit arguments advocated for Apple Computer.

Beginning with the Open Systems movement of the 1980s, organizational buyers and government regulators have adopted policies formalizing a bias towards open standards, as when the US Government's procurement requirements sustained the POSIX (Portable Operating Systems Interface for UNIX) codification, which was sponsored by the Institute of Electrical and Electronics Engineers (IEEE). At times, the enthusiasm for open standards (particularly among technical users) has approached the fervor of a social movement, as with the "Live Free or Die: UNIX" license plates (Raymond 2003). This ideology of choice and user freedom led directly to the Free Software and Open Source social movements (West and Dedrick 2005).

1.2 Do we know open when we see it?

What is an open standard?[2] Some have argued that Open Source software is the ultimate form of an open standard because implementations are provided freely for all to use (West 2003). Others have argued (at least privately) that Open Source software is merely a single

---

[2] For some standardization experts, the question of an open standard is much simpler, because they claim the word *standard* can only be used for specifications developed (or directly sanctioned) by government agencies or quasi-official bodies such as ANSI, the ISO or ITU. Consistent with the economics literature, this paper uses the broader definition of *standard* to encompass that which provides technical interoperability and comparability, no matter what its origins.

implementation produced by a closed group, without the process fairness of a formal standards development organization (SDO).

One way to define *open standard* would be through inductive theory creation from a series of commonly accepted exemplars. After all, such inductive theory creation is a widely accepted approach in the social sciences and is particularly suitable for reconciling contradictory or paradoxical evidence (Eisenhardt 1989). Therefore, I list four of the best-known IT standards that have been cited by at least some advocates as examples of open standards (Table 3.1), and provide a short history of each standard below:

- *"Wintel" personal computers.* In the 1980s, the IBM PC was hailed as a revolutionary open computing standard – in contrast to the vertically integrated mainframe computer and rival PC standards (Grindley 1995; Grove 1996; West 2005). While competition at the system level was high, it became clear during the 1990s that competition at the processor and operating system level was low, leading to high profits for Microsoft and Intel, and various user attempts to reduce their proprietary rents (Kraemer and Dedrick 1998; West and Dedrick 2001).
- *GSM phones.*[3] The most popular second-generation mobile phone standard was created using formal de jure standardization processes and was fully sanctioned as a government standard (e.g., Haug 2002). Yet, key goals of the standard were to generate patent royalties for participants (estimated at $15 per handset), and thus keep out foreign manufacturers (Iversen 1999; Bekkers 2001; Loomis 2005). Unlike elsewhere, in Europe governments protected GSM from competition through explicit regulations (West 2002).
- *The Open Group.* This group is the steward of the Open Systems movement, promoting UNIX as a multivendor portable operating system. It has rigorous procedures for process fairness and compliance certification, but its high fees limit participation in its standardization efforts to the largest of vendor and user organizations.
- *The Internet Engineering Task Force (IETF).* In contrast to the Open Group, the IETF had no membership fees, open discussions through online mailing lists, and freely distributed standards.

[3] GSM originally stood for *Group Spécial Mobile*, but seeking to shed its Francophone roots while keeping the now-famous acronym, was later changed to Global System for Mobile Communications (Bekkers 2002, 273).

Table 3.1. *Previously cited exemplars for open standards*

Standard	Industry	Sponsor	Open attributes	Closed attributes
"Wintel" (i.e., Windows + Intel)	PCs	Two proprietary component suppliers	Multiple systems vendors Low switching costs between systems More open than proprietary mainframe, rival PC standards	Operating system, microprocessor quasi-monopolies Proprietary rents paid to both suppliers
GSM	Mobile phones	Government-sanctioned SDO	Built on formal standardization best practices True multivendor standard Widespread adoption – world market leader	Excluded all but two non-European firms Patent royalties on all implementations Key Goal: Keep Japanese firms out of European market
Open Group	Workstations	Trade association	Clear process fairness Mission is to be vendor-neutral Objective conformance mechanisms	Membership is $5,000–$500,000 per year
IETF	Internet	Virtual Internet association	No membership requirements Specifications distributed free on Internet	Key standards written by closed group of US Government contractors Fees to participate in standards meetings

Nevertheless, the IETF was supported by high fees for participation in its face-to-face meetings (Gross, personal communication[4]). Also, some of its most successful standards (e.g., SMTP, or Simple Mail Transfer Protocol; TCP/IP, or Transfer Control Protocol/Internet Protocol) were achieved in the organization's early days, when it was an invitation-only group of contractors working for the US Department of Defense. These examples highlight at least two problems with the conventional open versus closed dichotomy. First, a specific producer, user, or policymaker might think, "I know an open standard when I see it," but a consistent classification across all stakeholders seems unlikely.[5] Perhaps in some areas of public policy, an intersubjective definition administered by a small number of privileged individuals is an acceptable solution, but it is problematic in establishing consistent policies for the operation of a complex economy.

Second, just as Gabel (1987) identified multiple dimensions of compatibility, these examples suggest that openness is represented by more than a single dimension. Previous researchers (von Burg 2001, 34; West 2003) have identified multiple intermediate levels of openness between the most proprietary and most open examples of standards.

If different stakeholders have heterogeneous importance ratings for these dimensions and there is perceptual error in rating each standard along a continuum, then attempts to identify the most open standard can easily produce divergent ratings across a range of stakeholders. Thus, we need a more rigorous and consistent way of identifying standard openness. At the same time, we should acknowledge that different stakeholders assign different priorities to the various dimensions of openness, and some stakeholders (e.g., vendors) do not prefer the most open alternative for some of these dimensions.

In the following section, I focus on the role of standards in the IT sector, examine the various economic and technological forces that make standards more or less open, describe the competing interests inherent in open standardization, and introduce a process model for understanding standards adoption. Next, in Section 3, using the

---

[4] Philip Gross, former chairman, Internet Engineering Task Force, interview, August 20, 2004.

[5] In a 1964 Supreme Court opinion, Justice Potter Stewart declined to enact an objective standard for pornography not protected by free speech, famously observing, "perhaps I could never succeed in intelligibly doing so. But I know it when I see it" (*Jacobelis v. Ohio*, 378 US 184).

process model as a foundation, I examine the multiple dimensions of standards openness and discuss what attributes of standards and of the policies used in their creation can increase or decrease their openness. Then, in Section 4, I examine what the practical limits to openness are in privately funded innovation and standardization. Finally, in Section 5, I offer conclusions and directions for further research.

2 Competing interests in open standardization

2.1 Role of standards in the IT sector

Product compatibility standards have been an essential prerequisite for much of the IT sector, which includes computing, software, networking, and telecommunications products. These IT products derive much or all of their utility from the interoperability obtained by implementing compatibility standards. There may be symmetric interoperability between two competing products implementing the same standards, as when one telephone modem, fax machine, or email program talks to another. Or, there may be asymmetric interoperablility across a well-defined interface among two or more classes of products – such as between a computer platform and its applications or a cell phone and its radio base station.

Technical interoperability has economic consequences. Rohlfs (1974) first identified the symmetric case, which we now refer to as a *direct network effect*, where increasing adoption by other users of a given standard increases the utility of that standard to the focal user. Asymmetric compatibility corresponds to what Katz and Shapiro (1985, 424) call "hardware-software paradigm" and what Teece (1986, 289) terms "specialized complementary assets," where the most popular standard attracts a larger supply of complementary products, which in turn increases the attractiveness of the standard. This positive feedback model provides "demand side economies of scale" (Katz and Shapiro 1985; Rohlfs 2001). At the same time, user investments in these specialized assets create switching costs, such that users tend to keep the same standard once procured (Greenstein 1993, 1997).

A final factor in the economics of standards competition is the up-front research and development (R&D) necessary to create both the standard and its implementation. Where such R&D costs are high, they combine with network effects and switching costs to create a barrier

94

Joel West

to potential competitors through increased returns to scale; thus, the most popular standard tends to gain increasing advantage over second-tier rivals (Arthur 1996; Bresnahan and Greenstein 1999). While vendors usually worry about placing second in a standards contest, the "winning" standard in a product category that is never widely adopted may also face dire financial consequences (Grindley 1995).[6]

Given these factors, IT vendors want their respective proprietary standards adopted to provide an ongoing stream of rents. And consequently, IT buyers seek out less proprietary alternatives, as with the UNIX-based open systems.

2.2 Where do standards come from?

Various typologies have classified standards as de jure versus de facto on the basis of whether standards are officially sanctioned by the weight of law.[7] Nevertheless, there is a wide array of possible standard setting organizations (SSOs)[8] ranging from a government agency to a single firm serving its own proprietary interests.[9]

Usually, an SSO defines its scope as translating a particular technology into a completed specification; however, the technical and economic benefits of a standard are delivered by its implementations.

---

[6] This is a necessarily cursory summary of more than twenty years of economic research on the impacts of standards, including research on network effects, switching costs, and their impacts on interfirm competition. For more detailed reviews, see, for example, Shapiro and Varian (1999), West (2000), Sheremata (2004), and Suarez (2004). For discussions of the limits of the network effects theories, see Liebowitz and Margolis (1999) and West (2005).

[7] This bifurcation greatly simplifies prior taxonomies, such as those of Paul David (see David 1987; David and Greenstein 1990; David and Steinmueller 1994). The subsequent discussion of openness skirts the details of these taxonomies, and the reader is referred to the original work for a more complete treatment.

[8] The comparatively recent SSO acronym does not have a formal definition, but in some usages it refers to multivendor organizations – both officially sanctioned and private consortia – and thus implicitly it excludes the case of a single proprietary firm. Here it is used to refer to any organization that creates a compatibility standard.

[9] Other types of SSOs also include an officially accredited SDO (e.g., the ISO); trade or professional associations to which quasi-official authority has been delegated (e.g., the IEEE); trade or professional associations broadly open to all comers (e.g., Consumer Electronics Association); and ad hoc consortia, usually with invitation-only membership, organized to produce a particular group of standards (e.g., the DVD Forum).

Table 3.2. Inputs and outputs in four phases of standards creation and use

Phase	Input	Participant	Policy	Output
Specification	Technology Market demands Participant goals	*any*	Standardization process	Standard specification
Implementation	Specification Existing capabilities Business model	Producer	IP law IP licenses	Product Pricing Use policies
Complement	Specification Implementations	Complementor	Access to standard	Complementary product
Use	Implementations Complements	User	Product licenses	Use benefits

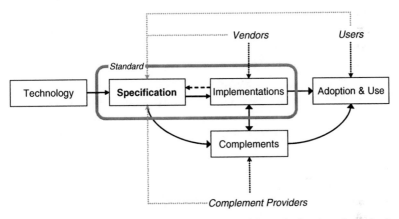

Figure 3.2. Process model for stakeholders in creation and adoption of standards.

Many SSOs thus recognize the role of implementations as a prerequisite to finalizing specifics, as with the Internet Engineering Task Force's (IETF) criterion for "rough consensus and running code" (West and Dedrick 2001). Because of the importance of complementary products, even single-firm standards sponsors often seek feedback from complement providers through large-scale beta pre-release distributions.

This process of creating a specification from a technology, one or more implementations of that specification, complementary products (or complements), and the eventual adoption and use of these products is illustrated by Figure 3.2. The inputs to the standardization process are given in Table 3.2.

2.3 Stakeholders in standardization

The outcome of standardization depends on the SSO's leaders, both in setting its formal policies (if any) and in key early decisions. But who decides who leads? Who is affected by these decisions? There are five classes of potential stakeholders in the standards outcome: (1) technology providers, (2) incumbent vendors, (3) vendor challengers, (4) complement providers, and (5) users.

Technology providers are firms that provide the technology incorporated into the standard, and the outcome of the standard effects how they receive returns on the resources they used for the R&D of their technology. In many cases, these firms are also implementing the eventual standard.

Of the pool of potential implementers, market-leading vendors – or *incumbent vendors* – often seek to use their market power to win acceptance of their own standards, whether they are created within the firm or by a friendly SSO. In either case, the goals are to control direction of the standard implementation and earn a stream of proprietary rents (Morris and Ferguson 1993; Moschella 1997; Shapiro and Varian 1999; West and Dedrick 2000; Gawer and Cusumano 2002).

Many open standards are created by groups of firms united in competing against a proprietary standard to avoid being shut out of the market (Grindley 1995, 31). Such standards alliances by *vendor challengers* often reflect their individual weak market power vis-à-vis the industry leader's. As a leading expert on standards consortia explained, "There was a greater threat of someone getting a monopoly than [there was] the likelihood of themselves getting a monopoly"; the vendor challengers join open standards consortia because "you're not so much gaining an advantage as denying someone else from gaining a proprietary advantage" (Updegrove, personal communication[10]).

For example, vendors in the X/OPEN group sought to win adoption from customers to weaken IBM's market power (Gabel 1987). Conversely, market leaders feel less need to be open, as when IBM (unsuccessfully) sought to promote its Token Ring LAN standard against the IEEE-sanctioned Ethernet standard (von Burg 2001).

---

[10] Andrew Updegrove, partner, Gesmer Updegrove LLP, telephone interview, October 15, 2004.

Whether makers of recorded music (Grindley 1995) or videogames (Gallagher and Park 2002), *complement providers* want one thing: A large market for their respectively complementary products. Like the vendors, they want a high level of adoption, but unlike vendors, they rarely care about the price, and thus generally prefer lower-price, higher-volume implementations of standards. For example, during Apple's brief experiment of licensing Macintosh PC clones, some of the most virulent support for the clones came from the Macintosh trade press and independent software vendors, that would enjoy a larger market if the clone makers increased system sales even slightly. Apple cared whether its profits from licensing clones matched those lost from direct sales, but the complementors did not (West 2005).

Finally, *users* care about the degree to which the standards implementations deliver the promised interoperability. As was previously noted, many also care about the degree to which open specification (or spec-creation process) enables competition between vendors, as well as care about the risk of being orphaned by an abandoned standard. Despite their intended role as the eventual consumer of the standards, users are largely under-represented in IT standardization, which is mostly dominated by IT vendors (Jakobs et al. 2001; de Vries et al. 2003). Many user organizations are happy to leave the details of standardization to their suppliers (Jakobs et al. 1996; Isaak 2006). Nevertheless, monopsony buyers have often played a disproportionate role in determining standards outcomes, as with the influence of government telephone monopolies in Japan and various European countries in setting telecommunications standards (Lyytinen and Fomin 2002), or the role of US cable television operators in forcing the standardization of cable modems (Eisenmann 2004). At the other extreme, highly knowledgeable individual engineers (sometimes referred to as the "geek crowd") loosely organized via the Internet now have a significant influence on standardization policies, particularly as they relate to open source software.

2.4 Cooperative versus competing interests

Vendors, complement providers, and even users may make investments that are specialized to a given standard (Teece 1986). If the standard proves unsuccessful (usually represented by a lack of adoption), that

*Table 3.3. Hypothetical vendor payoff matrix for
joining versus fighting standards coalitions*

Winning standard is ...	Ours	Competitor's
Completely open	+1	−1
Multivendor proprietary	+2 to +5[a]	−11
Single vendor proprietary	+10	−11

Note: [a] Maximum payoff if only one competitor is in the coalition.

investment proves wasted. Thus, all three stakeholder groups share a common interest in seeing the standard widely adopted.

When it comes to proprietary standards, leading vendors and users have conflicting goals. The leading vendors obviously want their own version adopted as the standard – as with, for example, IBM winning mainframes or Qualcomm winning US cell phone adoption. If this does not occur, they would nevertheless prefer that an open standard be adopted than have a rival's proprietary version be adopted. The vendor's worst-case scenario would be to spend resources creating a proprietary standard and then be required to switch to a rival's, such as Sony did with the VHS video recorder standard (Grindley 1995). A stylized version of this payoff matrix is shown in Table 3.3.

Even when facing little or no competition, leading vendors face conflicting goals between sales volume and sales per customer, which West (2003, 1259) identifies as

the essential tension of *de facto* standards creation: that between appropriability and adoption. To recoup the costs of developing a platform, its sponsor must be able to appropriate for itself some portion of the economic benefits of that platform. But to obtain any returns at all, the sponsor must get the platform adopted, which requires sharing the economic returns with buyers and other members of the value chain.

Meanwhile, the vendor challengers might seek to establish an open standard if their own proprietary standard has little chance of adoption.

3 Dimensions of standards openness

Standards have multiple potential dimensions of openness. The practice of standardization thus far suggests that these dimensions are not fully orthogonal, in that openness in some dimensions is correlated to that in others. Still, it is possible to imagine several mutually exclusive and comprehensive systems for mapping the space of standards openness. Here, I organize the classification on the basis of the process model in Figure 3.2.

3.1 Specification rights

The specification creation process converts the basic technology into a set of rules for interoperability between one or more class of goods. The process can range from simple to extremely complex – from a single-firm proprietary standard, where decisions are made within the boundaries of the firm, to a collaboratively developed standard that almost always includes firms creating implementations (vendors), but may also include other stakeholders such as users, complementors, or suppliers of component technologies. For collaborative standards, there will be variance within groups on the basis of differing needs and prior investments. For example, among those standardizing UNIX, only a small number of vendors and users cared about its use in real-time systems such as aircraft (Isaak 2006). Therefore, it matters which stakeholders get a voice and how disagreements are resolved.

Thus, whose interests are served by a specification depends on two factors: The first is what access do outsiders have in the decision process, or who participates – which O'Mahony and West (2005) term "permeability." The second is how the decisions are made by those who do participate.

Who participates?
There are four scenarios under which stakeholders can participate in standards creation or sponsorship.
1. *Fixed group (no new members)*: New entrants are not allowed to participate in the standardization effort, as with most single-firm proprietary standards and most standards fora. In other cases, new firms can join but cannot obtain the same rights as the founding members, as with Intel's USB (universal serial bus) standardization (MacKie-Mason and Netz, this volume).
2. *Members with qualifications (country club)*: Commonly found with standards consortia, here existing members decide which firms can become new members, typically using some combination of

objective and subjectively interpreted criteria. The X/Open consortium fits this pattern (Isaak 2006).

3. *Nondiscretionary membership (fitness club)*: Upon filing a form (and, in most cases, paying dues) nearly all firms can become members. Many trade associations (such as the Telecommunications Industry Association, arbiter of US cell phone standards) use this process.

4. *Nonmember organizations (town meeting)*: There is no membership required to participate, such as the IETF, which prides itself on its openness to participation.[11]

Within these four scenarios, there may be differing levels of accessibility. Qualifications can be interpreted strictly or loosely; the membership dues or participation costs can be a few thousand dollars (allowing small companies to participate), hundreds of thousands of dollars (excluding all but the largest of firms) or proportional to firm size (allowing small firms but maximizing revenues from large firms). There may also be indirect barriers: If a large organization pays to have dozens of engineers become knowledgeable and actively involved, then it may be difficult for competitors to have similar influence without a comparable investment in cash and/or labor.

Specification process

Different SSOs can vary considerably in the openness of the process used to create a specification. Among the most important issues are how decisions are made: For example, a requirement for consensus or a supermajority tends to increase the influence of a small number of participants or, conversely, reduce the ability of a single powerful vendor to dominate the process.

Meanwhile, SDOs are usually held as exemplars of process openness (e.g., Krechmer 2006). Yet, such openness costs time and money; during the 1980s, this proved a disadvantage for formal SDOs, leading to the rise of standards consortia (ConsortiumInfo.org 2005). Such consortia can improve speed and time to market through decreased permeability – either by who may join or by how much influence

---

[11] "The IETF is not a membership organization ... The IETF is a large open international community ... open to any interested individual. The actual technical work of the IETF is done in its working groups. To become a participant in the IETF, one merely becomes active in one or more working groups by asking to be added to the WG's mailing list" (IETF 2004).

smaller firms have, or both. Led by a handful of dominant industry firms, a small consortium with less due process can more quickly complete a specification and begin implementation.[12]

Openness has been a key attribute of both many studies of formal standardization practices (e.g., Cargill 1989; David and Shurmer 1996; Jakobs 2000; Egyedi 2003; Krechmer 2006) and case studies in telecommunications and open systems standardization (e.g., Bekkers 2001; Isaak 2006). The often-studied formal process of openness, however, does not completely predict the actual level of openness. In one of the few studies of the level of openness, Egyedi (2003, 34) concludes that "dominant rhetoric underestimates the openness of most industry consortia and overestimates the democratic process in formal standards committees."

Goals of participation

The decision process and the barriers to participation – whether direct or indirect – have a major impact on whose goals are served in standardization. These goals might include the following:

1. *Matching existing implementations.* One concern is to make standards consistent with existing investments – particularly when standardization is used to codify and harmonize existing implementations. In such post hoc standardization, users and complementors want new standards upwardly compatible with the standards they have already adopted. Vendors want the formal standard to closely match their existing de facto implementations: Sometimes this is achieved through a superset of existing participants, as with POSIX (Isaak 2006). In other cases, it is by "splitting the difference" between two incompatible approaches, as with V.90 standardization of 56 K modems (Gandal et al., this volume).

2. *Patent royalties.* Vendors seek to steer standards to "read on" their patent portfolio, so that they can use the patents to raise the cost to competitors (perhaps to prohibitive levels). Getting patents included in the standards is a crucial part of business models of

---

[12] A membership-only standardization body could be either a standards "consortium" or a "forum", with the former considerably more open than the latter (Andrew Updegrove, partner, Gesmer Updegrove LLP, email communication, August 26, 2005). As current research has not distinguished between the two, for simplicity's sake I generally use the term "consortium" to refer to both in this chapter.

nonintegrated firms that supply technology but not implementations, and thus depend on patent royalties for revenues, as with Rambus and the RDRAM standards.[13]

3. *Alignment of technology.* Beyond patents, potential implementers have varied technological expertise, and thus seek to influence the standard in a direction that will give them a (often transient) competitive advantage in implementation. Such tensions are rarely documented outside the SSO; a rare exception is Bekkers' (2001) account of the French and German goals in GSM standardization.

4. *Pace of standardization.* Participants may wish to control the rate of change in the standard. Proprietary systems and component vendors – whether IBM, DEC (Digital Equipment Corporation), Sun, Intel, or Microsoft – have always used dynamic standards as a source of competitive advantage: The more the standard changes, the harder it is to maintain commercially viable competing implementations, and thus single-firm de facto standards naturally favor a higher rate of change. Isaak (2006) notes that, conversely, successful incumbent vendors often use procedural efforts to slow formal post hoc standardization, which can reduce switching costs and commoditize their respective proprietary implementations.

In addition to trying to change the specification, stakeholders also participate to learn about the nascent standard. The benefits may be transitory, but the value of having early access to an unreleased standard is often enough to attract firms to pay the membership fees that support the standardization effort (Updegrove 2003a). Yet, encouraging firms to pay for such access directly conflicts with providing transparency to nonparticipants. Krechmer (2006) argues that a key measure of openness is the general availability of the specification documents, particularly for work in progress. For some SSOs, this openness first happens during a public comment period – before the standard is formally ratified, but after standards creators have enjoyed early access.

---

[13] The Rambus case is controversial because of questions as to whether its patent claims were finalized before or after the standard was written. Tansey et al. (2005) offer an unusual perspective, presenting many of Rambus' actions as a rational response to implementer efforts to reduce or eliminate intellectual property (IP) royalties.

3.2 Implementation and complementing rights

Specification for a standard will not provide interoperability until an implementation is made available to end users. Vendors involved in creating the standard offer their own individual (or shared) implementations. In some cases, the SSO encourages others also to implement the standard, while in others, competing implementations are not supported or are even actively discouraged. For example, in the open source community multiple implementations are disparaged as "forking."

For symmetric standards, interoperability is directly between implementations, while asymmetric standards require interoperability between implementations and complements. Such complements may be developed by vertically integrated implementers or third-party suppliers of complements. In some cases, customers may be their own complementors, as when management information systems departments create in-house software packages that work with a given platform standard.

Using the specification

Key to implementing or complementing a standard is the availability of a complete specification. This is typically the major focus of a formal SDO, which seeks to create an open, fully documented specification. The policies of consortia vary considerably, with some also publishing formal specifications and others delaying or preventing access by non-member firms. Specifications for creating complements for a standard are generally a proper subset of those necessary for implementing that same standard, allowing a monopoly (or oligopoly) standards creator to encourage complements without providing enough information for rival implementations.

Owners of de facto standards often use a combination of trade secret and copyright law to deter rival implementations, as well as to exclude unlicensed complements. Such methods also help the owners to collect royalties on complements. Nevertheless, statutory and case law in many developed countries have allowed reverse engineering to achieve compatibility to circumvent such barriers – with complements granted more latitude than competing implementations (West 1995).

Incomplete specification and disclosure
Standards differ in their complexity. The specifications for most modern complex systems are incomplete, and divergent interpretations (in implementations and/or complements) reduce actual compatibility until the interpretations are reconciled. For example, omissions from the initial GSM mobile phone standard meant that complementary products from competing vendors could not interoperate for years.

Incomplete specifications may reflect delays in specification, knowledge gaps between specification writers and the actual implementers, or merely the inherent limitation of describing on paper the full behavior of a complex system. Thus, for many software standards (such as UNIX or Linux) it is accepted that the source code for the implementation is more complete and accurate than any written specification – as acknowledged in modern software engineering practices (e.g., Reeves 1992). Hence, source code was incorporated in software engineering practices, such as agile programming and extreme methods (Fowler 2005). In particular, the availability of source code for a reference implementation reduces ambiguity and increases interoperability and openness; a notable example is how the Internet was enabled by the freely available Berkeley UNIX implementation of TCP/IP, which formed the basis for most open and proprietary implementations of the protocol.

Some omissions may be intentional, however. Proprietary firms with high market share may also add nonpublic interfaces to their implementation to provide preferential access to only some providers of complements. For example, a vertically integrated software vendor may seek to link sales of one layer of the software "stack" to another. When the vendor holds monopoly power in one layer, such linking is potentially a violation of national competition laws. This was one of the allegations covered by the 1995 consent decree resolving the first *United States* v. *Microsoft* case (Sheremata 1997). Thus, Krechmer (2006) argues that complete documentation is an essential requirement for an open standard.

Even with full documentation, there are still opportunities for sponsors to gain advantage via tacit information gleaned through the creation of a standard. For example, Sun Microsystems developed and disseminated numerous industry de facto standards that were made available to customers, complementors, and competitors. Yet, much as with a fully proprietary standard such as IBM's MVS operating system or Microsoft Windows, Sun's control and knowledge of the technology gave it the quickest access to specifications and thus a time advantage in creating implementations. Finally, Sun benefited from a pool of tacit knowledge built up through learning by doing (Garud and Kumaraswamy 1993, 360).

3.3 Usage rights

Some rights to implementations are inherent in any standard created to support commercially distributed products. Typically, when a customer purchases a product, he or she purchases the rights to use the standard incorporated in the product and its complements. Many key rights – such as price, terms, or term of usage – are specified by the implementer. In these cases, the openness of the standard itself (e.g., its creation process or formal specification) is germane only to the degree that limited competition might force buyers to accept a single usage model.

Many standards, however, indirectly or directly constrain the rights of buyers to utilize implementations. For example, for many information goods, digital rights management (DRM) limits what users can do with their purchases (Samuelson 2003). In this case, complementors (leading media companies) refuse to provide their information goods for use with a standard unless the standard enforces certain use restrictions. So, from a user perspective, a music file encoded with a file format and DRM system such as Apple's FairPlay or Microsoft's Windows Media is less open than with a file encoded with the (royalty-bearing) MP3 standard which imposes no such usage restrictions.

3.4 Must open be free?

Patents, royalties, and open Standards

Some aspects of a standard can raise costs at any phase of the process. The key emerging cost issue has been the increasing impact of patents and patent royalties (cf. Simcoe, this volume and 2006), primarily due to the success of royalty-based business models for standards such as MP3 and GSM. Other factors have included the case law approval of software patents in the United States, and patent reforms that have made patents easier to enforce without increasing the rigor of the screening process (Graham and Mowery 2003; Updegrove 2003b). Although the royalties are paid in later phases, the impact of IP rights (IPR) on a standard is largely determined by the IPR policies used to create the standard. These policies constrain the ability of sponsors and other interested parties to profit from the incorporation of their own IPR in a standard.

One possible SSO approach to IP, which risks blocking efforts by patent holders, is sheer denial, that is, ignore potential patent issues when writing the standard and let the marketplace sort it out during the implementation phase. A more aggressive approach is mandatory disclosure, that is, requiring standardization participants to disclose any possibly related IP during the specification process. Even this latter policy has limitations: First, in a large corporation, the standardization representative may not be aware of the company's entire IP portfolio. Second (as with other SSO policies), the provisions are not binding on firms that choose not to participate in the SSO effort.

The two most commonly used royalty approaches for standards-related patents are reasonable and nondiscriminatory (RAND) and royalty free. While the RAND approach can be royalty free, in practice it allows a specific subset of standards sponsors (the patent-holders) to create an exclusive club whose members (through cross-licensing) generally have a superior cost structure to nonmembers. Some (e.g., Krechmer 2006) consider RAND to be the minimum acceptable policy for effective open standardization. Meanwhile, the royalty-free approach is strongly preferred by Open Source developers (and others) who consider such that patent royalties – no matter how nondiscriminatory – are not open enough (Festa 2002).

Actual IPR costs go beyond mere policies. Firms within the SSO may seek in good faith to minimize IPR costs, or they may cooperate in creating a patent pool that avoids royalties for participants but increases costs for nonparticipants.

Who pays?

With free standards, there is a real question of where the resources and incentives will come from (1) to create the technology eventually incorporated in a standard (such as a compression algorithm), (2) to include participants in the standardization activity, and (3) to pay for the operation of the SSO itself. Fully proprietary standards such as those from IBM or Microsoft have been cross-subsidized by a vertically integrated standards creator and implementer. Yet, such cross-subsidies then potentially limit innovation to such vertically integrated firms by excluding potential sources of external technology and innovation (West 2006).

Absent such cross-subsidies, revenue models have included four direct methods to offset costs:

1. *Access to specification.* Charging for access to a standard (no matter how nominal) tends to hinder diffusion of the standard and its associated knowledge (Rada and Berg 1995). Specifications may be free from proprietary firms that can assure themselves of revenues from selling an implementation, while nonproprietary SSOs that depend on standardization revenues are more likely to sell their specifications. Outside the IT sphere, important policy questions have been raised about the government-mandated regulations (such as building codes) that require access to commercially sold standards.

2. *Rival implementations.* The patent portfolio of the GSM mobile phone standard was intentionally designed to keep out competitors, such that more than twenty years after deployment of the first GSM system, foreign firms decided that acquiring the patent portfolio of one of the original GSM sponsors was an attractive way to enter the European market (Ramstad and Pringle 2004).

3. *Complementors.* While videogame console makers such as Nintendo encourage third parties to make complementary products (software), a fundamental basis of their business model is that they charge royalties on all third-party products shipped (Gallagher and Park 2002).

4. *Customers.* The MPEG-4 video compression standard was the first audio-visual standard that not only charged royalty fees on encoding and decoding tools (complements), but also sought a royalty for commercial content distributed in the MPEG-4 format (Bier 2002).

In addition to these four direct methods, SSOs potentially institute indirect methods to offset costs. Barriers to rival implementations – including incomplete standardization or withholding of key information from nonparticipants – will increase implementation costs for those nonparticipating firms choosing to implement the standard. Both direct and indirect costs tend to raise user prices, reduce variety of implementations and complements, and reduce adoption of the standard.

4 Distinguishing openness in practice

4.1 *Common bundles of openness*

Firms face a fundamental dilemma in their standardization investment: They need a standard to be open enough to attract adoption but closed enough to be able to appropriate a return on that investment (West 2003). After several decades' worth of experience, there is a range of business models for standards, which fit Gawer and Cusumano's (2002) definition of "open but not open" platforms: Noted below are three basic approaches to these models:

1. *Open to complementors.* In this basic computer industry model – later adopted by the videogame industry – the systems vendor controls platform standards but seeks third-party software vendors to provide essential complements. There are various business models for sponsors gaining direct or indirect revenues from complements, such as the differences between PCs and videogame consoles in the relationship between the implementer and complementors (Takahashi 2002).

2. *Open to the club.* Some standards consortia in computers, communications, and consumer electronics pool the interests of members to gain an advantage over outsiders in terms of tacit knowledge, time to market, or IPR licensing costs.[14] Insiders and outsiders are often separated by a large admission fee, which also provides essential resources.

3. *Open as a public good.* Some combination of industry and public representatives creates a standard that will be shared by all, without discrimination; producers use these infrastructure standards as a basis for their own products.

Other levers are available for opening standards. It is assumed that some variables (price of specifications) have less impact than others (IPR royalties), but absent empirical proof, these present opportunities for further experimentation in the practice of standardization.

In particular, openness of shared implementations offers a new range of possibilities for using open standardization as a means for

---

[14] Updegrove (email communication, August 26, 2005) argues that only a few consortia fit this characterization, and, in fact, most SSOs of this nature are organized as a standards "forum" rather than the more open "consortium."

organizing innovation. The most widespread use of such shared implementations can be found in Open Source software, where West and Gallagher (2006) identify four basic business models, three of which roughly correspond to the three models listed above. In the fourth ("spinout") model, a firm abdicates control and transforms a once private implementation into a public good, in hopes of attracting donated innovations and fueling adoption of the standard.

4.2 Forces to increase or decrease openness

Will a standard become more or less open over time? It is difficult a priori to predict the net effect of the competing forces. There are differing forces at work: Specifically, over time a firm's control over a standard weakens, which increases competition and thus openness. Meanwhile, supply and demand-side economies of scale strengthen the importance of that standard, which thus weakens the threat of competing standards.

Increasing openness

One of the key benefits to being the proprietary sponsor(s) of a platform is gaining transitory competitive advantage over potential rivals, which might be via competing implementations or through providing complementary assets. This is particularly true for computing platforms – processors, operating systems, and middleware – for which vendors continue to add new interfaces to extend their proprietary standard.

Yet, for other types of standards, innovation is episodic: Major changes to cell phone standards have historically happened only once a decade (West 2002); for videogame platforms, once every five years (Gallagher and Park 2002).[15] Thus, for hardware and communications standards, a key goal is to temporarily suspend technological progress for some component of the system in the name of compatibility (cf. Bresnahan and Greenstein 1999). That way, technical interoperability will be assured because products sold over time will interoperate, despite improvements in available technology such as provided through Moore's Law.

---

[15] In this regard, videogame platforms are more like consumer electronics and less like computing platforms.

Ultimately, for standards for which innovation is episodic, implementations tend to become commoditized as tacit knowledge becomes widely dispersed. As such, the competitive advantage of the standard's original specification declines, barriers to entry and imitation decline – resulting in increased competition and openness to implementers. For example, though IBM invented the IBM PC standard, rivals learned how to clone crucial ROM (read-only memory) software, and by 1995 IBM held less than 10 percent of the global PC market (West and Dedrick 2000). Similarly, while Matsushita dominated the VHS standard in the mid-1980s, by 2001 Samsung claimed the top global share in VCR (video cassette recorder) production (Cusumano et al. 1992; *Korea Times* 2001).

Finally, in some cases formal IPR becomes obsolete – either because it is invented around, or because the patent term has expired. RCA once held patents for the 45 rpm record and other key audio technologies, but the patents eventually expired. From 1979 to 1996, the UNIX standard was covered by a patent on Dennis Ritchie's setuid access permission solution (US Patent 4,135,240), but the patent expired just as Linux was beginning to become widely adopted.

Decreasing openness

Other factors tend to decrease openness of a standard by increasing the power of the standards owner relative to implementers, complementors, and users. One common factor increasing the proprietary control of a leading standard is that rivals weaken or disappear through the positive feedback spiral forcing "that which loses advantage to lose further advantage" (Arthur 1996, 100). So, as a once-equal platform contest becomes more unequal, these positive feedback loops mean that the winning platform attracts a wider variety of third-party complements, as has happened in successive generations of videogame consoles (Gallagher and Park 2002; Takahashi 2002).

A related consequence is that an aggressive early battle for complements can dissipate. In other words, the standards victor need not fight for complementors because they will naturally gravitate to the most popular standard. In 1990, Microsoft worked hard to convince independent software vendors (ISVs) not only to invest to upgrade MS-DOS applications, but also to prioritize specializing user interface applications for Windows 3.0 ahead of OS/2 and Macintosh; by 1998, all three alternatives to Windows were declining and major ISVs of necessity made Windows their top priority – decreasing their leverage with Microsoft.

Finally, users often make their own investments in a technological innovation, described as "user innovation" (von Hippel 1988) or "co-invention" (Bresnahan and Greenstein 1996); a common example of this kind of investment among organizational users of information systems has been internal software development (e.g., Baba et al. 1996). If user innovation is specialized to the given standard, then the users' switching costs are raised (Greenstein 1993, 1997). These switching costs may reflect direct economic investments, or "merely" the inconvenience of consumer frustration in the face of obsolete user skills (West 2000). Either type of costs reduces the ability of users to bargain credibly with standards creators or implementers regarding switching to a rival standard.

5 Making sense of open standards

5.1 Realities: the many shades of gray

The goal of this paper has been to dissect an oversimplified and perhaps dangerously naïve view of open standards. Standards have often been characterized as either open or proprietary, but in fact there are many gradations in between. So-called open and closed standards are similar in many ways, such as in the rights for providing complements to or using implementations of the standard. In both cases, those involved in creating a specification gain tacit knowledge that is not available to outsiders.

As with anything else in life, there is no free lunch in IT standardization. The costs to creating standards and firms' responses to them can make standards more or less open. Firms creating a standard hope to gain a payoff through some subsequent competitive advantage, such as creating barriers to imitators. These barriers either directly or indirectly reduce the openness of a standard; and firms will be willing to create open standards only if their business model allows for cross-subsidy of standards creation. In fact, Updegrove (2003a) notes that attempts to make SSOs more open can destroy the revenue model that allows the organization to operate.

Standards have multiple dimensions of openness, with many standards relatively open on one dimension and relatively closed on another. If these dimensions are organized around the phases of standardization – specification, implementation, complements, and use – then different stakeholders will have different priorities, perceptions, and preferences regarding standards openness, depending on what their interest in the standard is. Some of the stakeholder interests will be aligned: Most if not all stakeholders will want to see the standard widely adopted and used. Other stakeholder interests will be divergent, if not contradictory. Users will want many commoditized implementations, while vendors may want a small number of differentiated implementations.

Finally, openness is not a static construct, but instead – as with any artifact of a complex interdependent sociotechnical system – a dynamic one. Some changes tend toward dissipating proprietary advantage and increasing commoditization, particularly for static standards such as those fixed in hardware, where once scarce tacit knowledge of a standard becomes more widely diffused over time through labor mobility, reverse engineering, or rivalrous R&D. The changes in openness may also be structural. The UNIX-related POSIX standards process became less open, as the initial efforts of firms and individuals were supplanted by select members of a vendor consortium (Isaak 2006). Conversely, the initial consortium to create an Open Source ecosystem around the Eclipse tools for Java was originally tightly controlled by IBM, but has since delegated control to a wider group of firms (West and Gallagher 2006).

5.2 *Implications for policymakers*

Openness has direct policy implications. Key aspects of US (and in some cases EU) antitrust lawsuits against IBM, AT&T, Microsoft, Intel, and Rambus, among others, have turned on the openness of standards (e.g., Sheremata 1997; Gilbert and Katz 2001). Public policymakers must define which are the relevant stakeholders in any determination of openness, as reflected in the quasi-experiment of recent antitrust cases related to Microsoft Windows. In the European Union, where rival implementers are relevant to competition policy, regulators forced Microsoft to disclose server application program interfaces (APIs) to enable competing and complementary interoperability; no such order was made in the United States, where injunctive relief must be justified entirely on the basis of user welfare.

The list of relevant stakeholders and their requirements also varies by context, in terms of producers, buyers, and the prevailing business models. For a national telecommunications standard, a monopoly standard is the norm, while a monopoly (or small oligopoly) of service providers is expected but a single hardware vendor would be unacceptable. For videogame consoles, a single hardware provider is an outcome of the business model, as is a requirement that software vendors pay to access the standards' IPRs to support the platform. Hence, competition and buyer choice are provided by competing de facto standards resolved through the marketplace.

Some standardization policy has been defined in terms of the organization form used in standards creation, that is, an accredited SDO such as the ISO. Meanwhile, empirical researchers have shown that some closed standardization fora use processes that are as open as a formal SDO (Egyedi 2003), while nominally public SDOs can be used by participants to close barriers against rivals (Bekkers et al. 2002). Thus, a key implication of this paper is that a requirement for an "open standard" should be defined by the degrees of openness across multiple dimensions rather than the organizational form or even (solely) by the standardization process used. Table 3.4 offers possible examples of such dimensions; Krechmer (2006) offers a partially overlapping typology from a different perspective.

For those involved in multivendor standardization efforts, particularly important is the increasing cost of patent royalties for standards implementations. During the 1980s and early 1990s, a handful of companies created successful business models from designing their IPR into nominally open standards such as GSM, CD-ROM, and MP3. This has prompted hundreds of companies to seek their own patent annuities, raising the IPR costs of succeeding standards. Simcoe (this volume) demonstrates that even the prospect of such bonanzas threatens to grind standardization processes to a halt.

From a policy standpoint, such excesses will self-correct if there is competition between standards; for example, leading W-CDMA cell phone makers sought a cap to patent royalties to reduce the IPR cost disadvantages relative to the rival cdma2000 (West 2006). But the increasing assertion of IPR in standards will force regulators to trade off IPR as an incentive for innovation against other policy goals, as happened in the *Rambus* v. *Infineon* cases (Tansey et al. 2005).

Table 3.4. Dimensions of standards openness

Phase	Stage	Category	Dimension of openness	Open state	Closed state
Creation	policy	access	Access to standardization process	Anyone can participate	Only founding firm(s) can participate
Creation	policy	competition	Control of standardization process	All participants have a vote	Decisions are made arbitrarily by sponsor(s)
Implementation	policy	cost	Cost of standard specification	Free	Expensive
Implementation	policy	access	Access to standard to implement	Any firm can make an implementation	Only sponsor(s) can implement standard
Implementation	policy	access	Access to standard to complement	Any firm can make complements	Complements limited to vertically integrated sponsor(s)
Implementation	policy	cost	Free use of standard IPR	IPR is licensed royalty free	IPR separates firms into "haves" and "have nots"
Implementation	outcome	cost	Ratio of IPR cost to implementation costs	IPR costs are negligible	Implementation costs are dominated by IPR royalties
Implementation	policy	cost, access	Shared reference implementation	A reference implementation reduces implementation costs	Everyone implements from scratch
Implementation	outcome	competition	Competing implementations	Low barriers make implementations a commodity	Only one implementation exists
Implementation, Use	policy	competition, cost, access	Free complete implementation	A shared implementation is available for all to use	Everyone builds their own implementation
Use	policy	access	Access to standard to use	Users have full rights to use the standard	Use is restricted to specific firms
Use	policy	access	Access to standard to use	Users can use the standard for any purpose	Certain types of uses are not allowed (e.g., rival implementations)
Use	policy	cost	Access to standard to use	No further payment is required to use an implementation	Additional payments must be made to standards or IPR owner to use the implementation

But favoring standards competition as a market corrective would go against government policy to explicitly pick a winning open standard – as with US procurement of POSIX systems or European mandates for GSM. If the goal is to promote competition through support of multi-vendor standards, what is a multivendor standard? Is UNIX (with multiple semi-compatible implementations running on proprietary hardware) more competitive than the Wintel standard (with a single processor and operating system supplier but multiple competing systems vendors) (West 2003)? And should goals of openness override other goals of cost or performance? Isaak (2006) notes that despite direct Federal support for UNIX standardization, government procurement eventually bowed to the efficiencies of high-volume commodity PCs that swamped the UNIX-compliant (but low-volume) workstations and minicomputers.

5.3 Further research

Putting aside the simplistic bifurcation between open and proprietary classifications of standards provides a wealth of new research opportunities regarding the antecedents, processes, and consequences of compatibility standards. One opportunity would be to map the variability of openness across technologies, standards, and standardization fora to refine classification of the openness dimensions (or develop new ones) and create repeatable (inter-rater reliable) measures of openness. A parallel example can be seen in Open Source software, where, in considering seventeen Open Source projects, O'Mahony and West (2005) identify three dimensions and measure twelve "design parameters" available for increasing the openness of the projects to other participants. From this, they identify two kinds of openness – transparency and permeability – and conclude that it is much easier for profit-seeking sponsors to provide outsiders with visibility than with some authority over control of the project.[16]

Research could examine the interrelationships between these dimensions and parameters. In practice, there is an assumption that degrees of openness are correlated, but should distinguish between those that are

---

[16] Krechmer (2006) recommends his own list of ten openness criteria, and offers suggestions on how to classify different levels for each. However, his measures are truncated because they omit degrees of "closed"-ness.

causal, from a common antecedent or merely correlational. Are there inverse relationships between specific parameter pairs or is there merely a general constraint to generate revenue somehow? Research should also consider how standardization business models are changing over time, such as how the rise of the Internet increased the expectation of free downloadable standards and reduced the attractiveness of printed (and sold) paper copies.

It is assumed that more-open standards create fewer barriers to imitation and entry. But are some parameters for closing more anticompetitive than others? How do policymakers distinguish between the inherent advantages that accrue to standards creators from anticompetitive behavior creating an illegal cartel? Since some degree of coordination among standards creators (e.g., patent pools) is both exclusionary and reduces implementation transaction costs, where should regulators draw the line? What can be done to encourage forum shopping (e.g., on IP policy or specification openness) that serves user needs rather than vendor needs?

Such studies should also consider the gap in our knowledge of actual (rather than formal) standardization openness. For example, industry veterans talk about how large companies at the hub of business ecosystems mobilize smaller dependent companies to manipulate open standards voting in their own favor, but such manipulations have not been studied.

Conversely, much of the normative advice to firms is about seeking to control proprietary standards (e.g., Morris and Ferguson 1993; Gawer and Cusumano 2002). If even an Intel or a Microsoft cannot unilaterally impose industry standards without alliances with other firms, how much should new proprietary standards sponsors open up enough to win allies, complements, and adoption, without eliminating all proprietary advantage?

More than just a technical specification, a standard defines the interrelationship of products (and thus value propositions and business models) between firms within an ecosystem. Iansiti and Levien (2004) argue that even without formal market power, firms can create durable value and competitive advantage if they can define a unique role in enabling the ecosystem's overall health. Sponsors of standards often have such latitude, particularly if direct rivals can be excluded from the specification process. Elsewhere in this volume, MacKie-Mason and Netz show how Intel has used such exclusion to create two successful multivendor PC industry standards open enough to attract complementors and thus win adoption, but proprietary enough to assure Intel competitive advantage over rival implementations.

Measuring such effects will be problematic, particularly because by its very nature data is most readily available for only a truncated sample of openness. A few researchers (such as Rosenkopf et al. 2001; Simcoe, this volume) have shown how to compile data from those SSOs that have a comparatively high level of specification openness. Studying the increasing number of private, members-only standards consortia depends on to what degree these consortia (to use the classification of O'Mahony and West 2005) provide transparency if not permeability. Rarer still are studies of how standards are created within a single firm, such as the process for resolving the trade-offs of creating or capturing value in standards identified by West (2003). Occasionally, regulators themselves obtain the essential data through litigation discovery process; those rare opportunities have informed our understanding of standards policy (e.g., Fisher et al. 1983) and could potentially fill in some of the gaps in our understanding of open standards.

References

Arthur, W. Brian 1996. "Increasing returns and the new world of business," *Harvard Business Review* 74: 100–9.

Baba, Yasunori, Shinji Takai, and Yuji Mizuta 1996. "The user-driven evolution of the Japanese software industry: The case of customized software for mainframes," in *The international computer software industry: A comparative study of industry evolution and structure*, David Mowery (ed.), Oxford: Oxford University Press, 104–13.

Bekkers, Rudi 2001. *Mobile telecommunications standards: GSM, UMTS, TETRA, and ERMES*. Boston: Artech House.

Bekkers, Rudi, Geert Duysters, and Bart Verspagen 2002. "Intellectual property rights, strategic technology agreements and market structure: The case of GSM," *Research Policy* 31: 1141–61.

Bier, Jeff 2002. "MPEG? Thanks but no thanks," *EE Times*, April 8, http://www.eetimes.com/op/showArticle.jhtml?articleID=16504751.

Bresnahan, Timothy F., and Shane Greenstein 1996. "Technical progress and co-invention in computing and in the uses of computers," *Brookings Papers on Economic Activity: Microeconomics 1996*, 1–77.

 1999. "Technological competition and the structure of the computer industry," *Journal of Industrial Economics* 47: 1–40.

Cargill, Carl F. 1989. *Information technology standardization: Theory, process, and organizations.* Bedford, MA: Digital Press.

——— 1994. "Evolution and revolution in open systems," *ACM StandardView* 2: 3–13.

ConsortiumInfo.org. 2005. "What (and why) is a consortium?" http://www.consortiuminfo.org/what/.

Cusumano, Michael A., Yiorgos Mylonadis, and Richard S. Rosenbloom 1992. "Strategic maneuvering and mass-market dynamics: The triumph of VHS over Beta," *Business History Review* 66: 51–94.

David, Paul A. 1987. "Some new standards for the economics of standardization in the information age," in *Economic policy and technological performance*, Partha Dasgupta and Paul Stoneman (eds.), Cambridge: Cambridge University Press, 207–40.

David, Paul A., and Shane M. Greenstein 1990. "Economics of compatibility standards," *Economics of Innovation and New Technology* 1: 3–41.

David, Paul A., and Mark Shurmer 1996. "Formal standards-setting for global telecommunications and information services," *Telecommunications Policy* 20: 789–815.

David, Paul A., and W. Edward Steinmueller 1994. "Economics of compatibility standards and competition in telecommunication networks," *Information Economics & Policy* 6: 217–41.

de Vries, Henk, Hugo Verheul, and Harmen Willemse 2003. "Stakeholder identification in IT standardization processes," in *Proceedings of the workshop on standard making: A critical research frontier for information systems*, John Leslie King and Kalle Lyytinen (eds.), 92–107, http://www.si.umich.edu/misq-stds/proceedings.

Egyedi, Tineke M. 2003. "Consortium problem redefined: Negotiating 'democracy' in the actor network on standardization," *Journal of IT Standards and Standardization Research* 1: 22–38.

Eisenhardt, Kathleen M. 1989. "Building theories from case study research," *Academy of Management Review* 14: 532–50.

Eisenmann, Thomas 2004. *Scientific-Atlanta, Inc.* Case N2-804-191, Cambridge, MA: Harvard Business School Press.

Festa, Paul 2002. "Patent holders on the ropes," *CNET News.com*, December 2, http://news.com.com/2100-1023-975587.html.

Fisher, Franklin M., John J. McGowan, and Joen E. Greenwood 1983. *Folded, spindled, and mutilated: Economic analysis and US v. IBM.* Cambridge, MA: MIT Press.

Fowler, Martin 2005. "Code as documentation," *MartinFowler.com*, March 22, http://martinfowler.com/bliki/CodeAsDocumentation.html.

FSF 2003. "The free software definition," Free Software Foundation, http://www.gnu.org/philosophy/free-sw.html.

Gabel, H. Landis 1987. "Open standards in computers: The case of X/OPEN," in *Product standardization and competitive strategy*, H. Landis Gabel (ed.), Amsterdam: North-Holland, 91–123.

Gallagher, Scott, and Seung Ho Park 2002. "Innovation and competition in standard-based industries: A historical analysis of the U.S. home video game market," *IEEE Transactions on Engineering Management*, 49: 67–82.

Gandal, Neil, Nataly Gantman, and David Genesove 2007. "Intellectual property and standardization committee participation in the US modem industry," in *Standards and public policy*, Shane Greenstein and Victor Stango (eds.), Cambridge: Cambridge University Press (this volume).

Garud, Raghu, and Arun Kumaraswamy 1993. "Changing competitive dynamics in network industries: An exploration of Sun Microsystems' open systems strategy," *Strategic Management Journal* 14: 351–69.

Gawer, Annabelle, and Michael A. Cusumano 2002. *Platform leadership: How Intel, Microsoft, and Cisco drive industry innovation*. Boston: Harvard Business School Press.

Gilbert, Richard J., and Michael L. Katz 2001. "An economist's guide to US v. Microsoft," *Journal of Economic Perspectives* 15: 25–44.

Graham, Stuart J. H., and David C. Mowery 2003. "Intellectual property protection in the software industry," in *Patents in the knowledge-based economy*, Wesley Cohen and Steven Merrill (eds.), Washington, DC: National Academies Press, 219–58.

Greenstein, Shane M. 1993. "Did installed based give an incumbent any (measurable) advantages in federal computer procurement?" *RAND Journal of Economics* 24: 19–39.

1997. "Lock-in and the costs of switching mainframe computer vendors: What do buyers see?" *Industrial and Corporate Change* 6: 247–74.

Grindley, Peter 1995. *Standards, strategy, and policy: Cases and stories*. Oxford: Oxford University Press.

Grove, Andrew S. 1996. *Only the paranoid survive: How to exploit the crisis points that challenge every company and career*. New York: Doubleday.

Haug, Thomas 2002. "A commentary on standardization practices: Lessons from the NMT and GSM mobile telephone standards histories," *Telecommunications Policy* 26: 101–7.

Iansiti, Marco, and Roy Levien 2004. *The keystone advantage: What the new dynamics of business ecosystems mean for strategy, innovation, and sustainability*. Boston: Harvard Business School Press.

ICTSB 2005. "Critical issues in ICT Standardization," report, Information & Communications Technologies Standards Board, April 25, http://www.ictsb.org/ICTSFG/ICTSFG_report_2005-04-27.pdf.

IETF 2004. "Participating in the efforts of the IETF," Internet Engineering Task Force http://www.ietf.org/join.html.

Isaak, Jim 2006. "The role of individuals and social capital in POSIX stand-ardization," *International Journal of IT Standards & Standardization Research* 4: 1–23.

Jakobs, Kai 2000. *Standardization processes in IT: Impact, problems and benefits of user participation.* Braunschweig, Germany: Vieweg.

Jakobs, Kai, Rob Procter, and Robin Williams 1996. "Users and standardi-zation – worlds apart? The example of electronic mail," *ACM StandardView* 4: 183–91.

    2001. "The making of standards: Looking inside the work groups," *IEEE Communications Magazine* 39: 1–7.

Katz, Michael L., and Carl Shapiro 1985. "Network externalities, competi-tion, and compatibility," *American Economic Review* 75: 424–40.

    1994. "Systems competition and network effects," *Journal of Economic Perspectives* 8: 93–115.

Korea Times 2001. "LG, Samsung boosting world market share for core products," December 12.

Kraemer, Kenneth L., and Jason Dedrick 1998. "Globalization and increas-ing returns: Implications for the U.S. computer industry," *Information Systems Research* 9: 303–22.

Krechmer, Ken 2006. "The meaning of open standards," *International Journal of IT Standards & Standardisation Research* 4: 43–61.

Liebowitz, Stan J., and Stephen E. Margolis 1999. *Winners, losers and Microsoft: Competition and antitrust in high technology.* Oakland, CA: Independent Institute.

Loomis, Tamara 2005. "Cell break," *IP Law & Business* (July), http://www.ipww.com/texts/0705/europhony0705.html.

Lyytinen, Kalle, and Vladislav V. Fomin 2002. "Achieving high momentum in the evolution of wireless infrastructures: The battle over the 1G solutions," *Telecommunications Policy* 26: 149–70.

MacKie-Mason, Jeffrey K., and Janet S. Netz 2007. "Manipulating interface standards as an anticompetitive strategy, in *Standards and public policy*, Shane Greenstein and Victor Stango (eds.), Cambridge: Cambridge University Press (this volume).

Morris, Charles R., and Charles H. Ferguson 1993. "How architecture wins technology wars," *Harvard Business Review* 71: 86–96.

Moschella, David C. 1997. *Waves of power: Dynamics of global technology leadership, 1964–2010.* New York: AMACOM.

O'Mahony, Siobhan, and Joel West 2005. "The participation architecture of online production communities," Working Paper, Cambridge, MA: Harvard Business School.

Rada, Roy, and John Berg 1995. "Standards: Free or sold?" *Communications of the ACM* 38, 2: 23–7.

Ramstad, Evan, and David Pringle 2004. "Alcatel shifts production to China," *Wall Street Journal*, April 27, B5.

Raymond, Eric S. 2003. "Live free or die!" *The new hacker's dictionary*, http://catb.org/~esr/jargon/html/L/Live-Free-Or-Die-.html.

Reeves, Jack M. 1992. "What is software design?" *C++ Journal*, Fall, http://www.developerdotstar.com/mag/articles/reeves_design.html.

Rohlfs, Jeffrey 1974. "A theory of interdependent demand for a communications service," *Bell Journal of Economics* 5: 16–37.

2001. *Bandwagon effects*. Cambridge, MA: MIT Press.

Rosenkopf, Lori, Anca Metiu, and Varghese P. George 2001. "From the bottom up? Technical committee activity and alliance formation," *Administrative Science Quarterly* 46: 748–72.

Samuelson, Pamela 2003. "Digital rights management (and, or, vs.) the law," *Communications of the ACM* 46: 41–5.

Shapiro, Carl, and Hal R. Varian 1999. *Information rules: A strategic guide to the network economy*. Boston, MA: Harvard Business School Press.

Sheremata, Willow A. 1997. "Barriers to innovation: A monopoly, network externalities, and the speed of innovation," *Antitrust Bulletin* 42: 937–72.

2004. "Competing through innovation in network markets: Strategies for challengers," *Academy of Management Review* 29: 359–77.

Simcoe, Timothy 2006. "Open standards and intellectual property rights," in *Open innovation: Researching a new paradigm*, Henry Chesbrough, Wim Vanhaverbeke, and Joel West (eds.), Oxford: Oxford University Press, 161–183.

2007. "Delay and de jure standardization: Exploring the slowdown in Internet standards development," in *Standards and public policy*, Shane Greenstein and Victor Stango (eds.), Cambridge: Cambridge University Press (this volume).

Suarez, Fernando 2004. "Battles for technological dominance: An integrated framework," *Research Policy* 33: 271–86.

Takahashi, Dean 2002. *Opening the XBox: Inside Microsoft's plan to unleash an entertainment revolution*. Roseville, CA: Prima.

Tansey, Richard, Mark Neal, and Ray Carroll 2005. "'Get rich, or die trying': Lessons from Rambus' high-risk predatory litigation in the semiconductor industry," *Industry and Innovation* 12: 93–115.

Teece, David 1986. "Profiting from technological innovation: Implications for integration, collaboration, licensing and public policy," *Research Policy* 15: 285–305.

Updegrove, Andrew 2003a. "What is Congress up to? Watch out for H. R. Bill 1086," *Consortium Standards Bulletin* 2, http://www.consortiuminfo.org/bulletins/apr03.php.

2003b. "Patents: Too easy to get, too hard to challenge?" *Consortium Standards Bulletin* 2, http://www.consortiuminfo.org/bulletins/nov03.php.

von Burg, Urs 2001. *The triumph of Ethernet: Technological communities and the battle for the LAN standard.* Stanford, CA: Stanford University Press.

von Hippel, Eric 1998. *The sources of innovation.* New York: Oxford University Press.

West, Joel 1995. "Software rights and Japan's shift to an information society," *Asian Survey* 35: 1118–39.

2000. "A comparison of PC standard switching decisions by U.S. and Japanese computer users," unpublished Ph.D. dissertation, Irvine, CA: University of California.

2002. "Qualcomm 2000: CDMA technologies," European Case Clearinghouse, Case 302-069-1.

2003. "How open is open enough? Melding proprietary and open source platform strategies," *Research Policy* 32: 1259–85.

2005. "The fall of a Silicon Valley icon: Was Apple really Betamax redux?" in *Strategy in transition*, Richard A. Bettis (ed.), Oxford: Blackwell, 274–301.

2006. "Does appropriability enable or retard open innovation?" in *Open innovation: Researching a new paradigm*, Henry Chesbrough, Wim Vanhaverbeke, and Joel West (eds.), Oxford: Oxford University Press, 109–33.

West, Joel, and Jason Dedrick 2000. "Innovation and control in standards architectures: The rise and fall of Japan's PC-98," *Information Systems Research* 11: 197–216.

2001. "Open source standardization: The rise of Linux in the network era," *Knowledge, Technology & Policy*, 14: 88–112.

2005. "The effect of computerization movements upon organizational adoption of open source," Social Informatics Workshop: Extending the Contributions of Professor Rob Kling to the Analysis of Computerization Movements, March 11, 2005, http://crito.uci.edu/si.

West, Joel, and Scott Gallagher 2006. "Open innovation: The paradox of firm investment in open source software," in *Open innovation: Researching a new paradigm*, Henry Chesbrough, Wim Vanhaverbeke, and Joel West (eds.), Oxford: Oxford University Press.

4 | Coordination costs and standard setting: lessons from 56K modems

SHANE GREENSTEIN AND MARC RYSMAN

Abstract

The authors offer a detailed analysis of the coordination costs behind the standardization of 56K modems. They focus primarily on market events and standard setting activities during early deployment. They argue that the canonical model for a standards war is misleading in the case of 56K. They present alternative questions than the model's and examine different views on how market events during deployment influenced negotiations within the International Telecommunications Union and vice versa.

1 Introduction

We offer a detailed analysis of the coordination costs behind the standardization of 56K modems. Although the canonical model of a standards war could be applied to the case of 56K modems, we argue here that the model is misleading and instead offer up alternative questions for understanding how market events during deployment influenced negotiations and vice versa.

There are three phases to a canonical model of a standards war: First, an economic opportunity arises from a technical upgrade. Second, competition develops between different implementations of that upgrade. Third, resolution of the conflict occurs when one of the implementations wins in a competitive market or a publicly spirited standard setting organization (SSO) becomes involved in resolving the conflict (for a

The authors thank Angelique Augereau, Joseph Farrell, Timothy Feddersen, Alicia Shems, Victor Stango, and many seminar participants for useful remarks on our studies of the 56K modem market. We thank Bill McCarthy, Simoa Campus, Ken Krechmer, Michael Seedman, and Richard Stuart for sharing their observations about events in this market. Rysman acknowledges the support of NSF grant SES-0112527. All errors are ours alone.

review, see e.g., Farrell 1996 or Stango 2004). There are extensive case studies describing a variety of ways for winning a competitive war between fixed specifications. There are also a variety of reasons why an SSO chooses to make a specification a focal point[1] for further development (see, e.g., Chapter 8 of Shapiro and Varian 1999).

On the surface, parallels to the canonical model can be seen in the 56K modem standards war. It did involve a fight between two seemingly symmetric network technologies, each of which provided a possible specification for improving modem speeds beyond 33K. Two large camps of firms formed around each specification, even though service providers and users would have benefited from a single standard from the outset. Eventually, an SSO, the International Telecommunications Union (ITU), intervened with a new standard specification that gained widespread popularity and settled the war. This intervention was useful in that the market appeared to grow rapidly afterwards.

Despite these parallels, we argue that the canonical model is misleading for 56K modems. We support this argument with a detailed study of the standardization process. For the case of the 56K, outsiders have access to adequate, though not excessive, documentation of key events, such as interviews and industry reports in trade magazines, as well as statistical information about deployment prior to the standard's emergence. We exploit this detail by using an eclectic mix of methodologies, weaving together "case study" evidence, interviews with industry participants, interpretations offered by second-hand sources, and novel statistics.

Our methods and data lead us to differentiate the 56K standards war from the canonical model. We highlight four contrasts. First, in a canonical model, each party thinks it can win the standards war. With 56K modems, neither camp of firms thought it could win the war on its own. In actuality, neither one did. Second, in the canonical model the designs sponsored by alternative camps are fixed. With 56K modems an alternative specification became the standard. Third, in the canonical model design and competition occur in sequence. In contrast in 56K modems, design, negotiation, and the market process occurred concurrently and over time rather than in some simple ordering. Finally, the

---

[1] A focal point is a specific option or characteristic that all the major players choose even when there are several other feasible and plausible options.

canonical model treats standards as arbitrary focal points and either does not look at their origins or has a superficial description of their origins. With the case of 56K modems, creating a focal point at the ITU was extremely costly. These fundamental differences in perspective and behavior from the canonical model lead us to pose alternative questions than the model's and, as a result, examine different views on how market events during deployment influenced negotiations with the ITU and vice versa.

We begin by focusing on understanding the factors that shape the costs of coordinating on a new standard – specifically on economic factors that shaped deployment prior to February 1998 when the V.90 standard emerged. The costs of coordination were primarily borne during the early deployment of the 56K modem, a period when users could ostensibly choose between two competing specifications, X2 and Flex. An important feature of the modem market was that consumers signed with an Internet service provider (ISP) only within their local calling area. Hence, competition occurred in distinct local markets, and decision making was fragmented. As a result, we can do statistical analysis normally not available in other examples of technology deployment. Borrowing from our companion paper, Augereau et al. (forthcoming, hereafter AGR), we show that ISPs tended to split across X2 and Flex – not only nationally but also within local markets. While the network features of the product created incentives to coordinate on a single standard, local competition created great pressure to differentiate across the technologies.

We next trace the relationship between early deployment and negotiations within the ITU, for which there are several competing interpretations. We interpret this process as the cost of creating a focal point and pay special attention to the role of intellectual property (IP). To be sure, we could also focus on why the ITU's intervention was beneficial, but as there is little dispute that the benefits were large, that insight is not particularly novel. More interesting, we highlight two common and sharply contrasting views about the relationship between deployment and negotiations. One view emphasizes the way in which market events strongly shape negotiations. The other view argues that decisions were based on engineering choices, not on business incentives. We argue for a middle ground between these two views.

Events of this case illustrate how some aspects of firm participation inside the SSO varied with market circumstances and IP holdings, while other aspects did not. The situation compelled participation and managerial attention of all interested parties, but each came to the SSO with asymmetric negotiating positions. We argue that had positions been different then behavior would also have been different, namely, behavior would have been less urgent or more urgent, and more inclined towards compromise or less inclined.

Our study adds to the comparatively small number of close economic studies of standards wars. (See Stango [2004] for a review of the literature on such wars.) As with other studies in this vein, we identify conundrums for the canon by analyzing important aspects of these events that either fit or do not fit canonical models. Shapiro and Varian (1999, Chapter 8) include a brief summary of announcements by firms in different camps of the 56K modem war as of the end of 1997. We also offer evidence on facets of behavior where previous research is incomplete. We analyze how deployment activity shaped the incentives of parties in negotiations and how the negotiations in the ITU shaped behavior and outcomes. Understanding the parties' asymmetric positions and their relationship to deployment is crucial, we argue, for understanding the behavior and outcomes in this particular standards war, as well as in other standards wars.

We now provide a short literature review of related studies. In the following section, we provide an outline of the industry and setting. We then pose alternative questions and analyses than those to which the canonical model points. In answering these questions and conundrums, we examine different views on how market events shaped negotiations and suggest that each view is incomplete. We then offer an alternative analysis of the case of the 56K standards war.

Our study follows in the spirit of several rich analyses of the role of standards during the diffusion of new communications technology, such as Besen and Johnson's (1986) study of FM radio and color television and Farrell and Shapiro's (1992) rich study of the standards war leading to the specification for HDTV in the United States. Our setting differs because standard setting takes place in an SSO, not under the auspices of a regulator that can mandate standards, such as the Federal Communication Commission (FCC). Standard setting in an SSO requires a different framework, one that understands the factors shaping the negotiation between firms.

Our emphasis also bears resemblance to Von Burg's 2001 study of the multiple implementations of the Ethernet, and Dranove and

Gandal's 2003 study of the DVD/DivX war. There are key differences in our study from the previous ones. In both previous studies, market events determined the choice between alternative specifications, each of which had its commercial sponsors. In Von Burg's study of the Ethernet, three specifications competed in the marketplace and an SSO endorsed all three, whereas in our study we examine how an alternative standard, the V.90, arose at the ITU to replace the two competing specifications, X2 and Flex. In Dranove and Gandal's study, there were two technically different formats competing, as compared to the two similar formats competing in our study; and one of those specifications quickly failed in the marketplace. Also, in the DVD/DivX war, firms tried to bypass the SSO, whereas with X2 and Flex, firms believed that working with the SSO was an inevitable eventuality. Thus, our study of the ways companies worked with SSOs as they competed with each other and the relationship between SSOs and companies is based in different market circumstances. As a result, we highlight a different set of relationships between deployment and negotiations at the SSO. This leads to a very different set of insights about the costs of coordination.

2 Industry and setting[2]

The broad outline of events is not in dispute. Before 1997, the fastest available modem speed was 33K. In early 1997, competing consortiums introduced two types of 56K modems almost simultaneously, X2 and Flex. Although their technical proficiency was identical in that they had the same performance characteristics, they were incompatible. If a consumer chose a different modem than his or her ISP used, then the consumer was reduced to speeds of 33K or worse. These products exhibited network effects in the sense that when more consumers picked a modem, more ISPs would be attracted to it and the ensuing competition would lead to cheaper, better, and more reliable service for the consumer. Nevertheless, sales in the first year went much slower than the two sides had hoped.

In February 1998, ongoing negotiations between the industry participants at the ITU led to the ratification of a new standard, the V.90. It

---

[2] A more in-depth discussion of these issues can be found in Rickard's (1997a, 1997b, 1998) studies.

was incompatible with both of the previous technologies without a proper upgrade of equipment. The V.90 gained almost immediate widespread acceptance, and sales of modems to both ISPs and consumers grew rapidly.

We now explain the details behind the broad outline of events. A modem allows a computer to send and receive data over a telephone line. The speed at which a modem can down- and upload data is measured in bits per second (bps), so a 33.6K modem can send and receive 33.6 kilobits (33,600 bits) of data every second. In the early days of the Internet, modem users typically dialed a telephone number that connected them directly to the computer with which they wanted to exchange data. Modem users could only connect to computers that also maintained modems. Numerous *bulletin boards* sprang up devoted to a wide variety of issues, where readers could post questions and comments. Most exchanges were in "character mode," which used very little memory, so modem speed was not an important issue.

Two changes occurred in the mid-1990s. The first was the rise of ISPs, which allowed users to dial a single number and connect to any computer on the Internet. This meant that only computers associated with ISPs had to maintain modem banks to receive phone calls. Although ISPs charged a fee, consumers often gained because they could access the entire Internet through a local telephone call.[3] Many bulletin board moderators transformed into ISPs as they already had the basic technology (banks of modems) to do so. This led to a very unconcentrated industry. In 1997, about 93 percent of the US population had access to a commercial ISP by a local phone call (Downes and Greenstein 1999). An important feature of concentrating modem usage at ISPs was that ISPs often found it worthwhile to invest in digital connections to the local telephone company switch, which meant that ISPs had fast, high-volume connections to the Internet.

A second change in the mid-1990s was the rise of the World Wide Web. The Web provided a protocol for transferring data over the Internet, which allowed for the widespread use of graphics and digital photographs. This change greatly enhanced both the demand for Internet access and the importance of consumer connection speed.

These two changes made 56K a potentially valuable technology. Up until early 1997, 33.6K modems were the fastest available for use with

---

[3] The ISPs also offered email accounts and access to the World Wide Web.

analog telephone lines. Rockwell Semiconductor was practically a monopolist (over 80 percent market share) in the production of modem chipsets, or the internal hardware of a modem. They licensed their technology to over 100 resellers that produced modems under different names. The most successful of these was US Robotics, with about a 40 percent market share in retail modem sales.

The adoption of digital circuitry between ISPs and the telephone companies allowed for the elimination of one analog-to-digital transformation, which allowed for theoretical modem speeds of up to 56K. US Robotics recognized this possibility first and began work on their X2 modem.[4] Worried that they would be closed from this new market, Rockwell quickly began work on their own 56K modem. After joining with Motorola and Lucent in this endeavor, their product was called K56Flex, or Flex. Due to setbacks at US Robotics and a remarkable production run at Rockwell, both brought their product to market at essentially the same time, February 1997. Some product reviews suggest there were problems with Flex up until July. It is clear from contemporary reports that within six months the two technologies worked equally well, though there could be variability between them depending on local connection characteristics.

The cost of the new modems depended on the purchaser. Modems for consumers were initially priced at around $200, as compared to $100 for 33K modems. For ISPs, the conversion depended on their technology. Since the 1980s, the entire telephone network was being gradually upgraded to a digital system. If an ISP was in an area that had been fully upgraded, it could offer 56K by simply buying a few consumer-grade 56K modems. If an ISP's connection to the telephone network had not been upgraded, it would have to invest in T1 lines or ISDN lines, which represent high-quality digital connections to the Internet.

Because racks of consumer modems had high maintenance and administrative costs, they were an inefficient way to offer 56K to more than a few customers. As a result, ISPs tended to invest in a Remote Access Server, a large server that came equipped with high-quality modems and required T1 lines or ISDN lines. For instance, in March 1997, US Robotics sold the Total Control Network Hub

---

[4] Much of the market was at 28K, which used the same basic technology as 33K, and $56 = 28 \times 2$: Hence the name X2.

that connected forty-eight ports to two T1 lines for $44,126, or $919.29 per port.[5]

The price per port could be driven down to around $500 for larger servers. Digital lines such as T1 lines had installation costs around $2,000. Monthly charges for digital lines were around $50 per port, as opposed to $20 or $30 for analog lines. Note that many ISPs had already invested in Remote Access Servers and T1 or ISDN lines, as they were also an efficient way to handle 33K modems. The ISPs could simply upgrade their server. Doing so cost $50 to $100 per port and was sometimes offered for free as the standards battle intensified. The ability to upgrade depended on the server – US Robotics servers could be upgraded only to X2, most other servers could be upgraded only to Flex. The result was that upgrade costs were much higher for some ISPs than for others.

3 The development of the V.90 standard

Throughout this time period, there were deliberations over standard setting at the Telecommunications Industry Association (TIA) and the ITU. The TIA is an organization of private firms in the United States, and it has representation at the ITU. The ITU is an organization of the United Nations, which sets standards for telecommunication issues under its ITU-T branch. Typically, negotiations on a standard start at the TIA and then are moved to the ITU. Negotiations may simultaneously continue at the TIA, as they did to some extent in this example.

The ITU-T has both government and "sector" members. Sector members are typically private firms. Currently, ITU-T has 189 member states and more than 650 sector members, 128 from the United States. The Department of State, the Department of Commerce and the FCC represent the US Government. A sector membership costs between $20,000 and $50,000 annually and, for US companies, requires approval by the Department of State. All members may participate in any working group, such as Study Group 16, which handled the 56K modems. The negotiation is based on submissions, typically proposals for the potential standard, along with documentation of technical

---

[5] Each connecting consumer requires one port. Because consumers do not all connect at once, ISPs typically required one port for every three or four consumers. The number of ports that a typical ISP maintained at a given point-of-presence ranged from fifty to many thousands.

characteristics and possibly performance data. The ITU requires a consensus vote to approve a standard.

The ITU was holding meetings with industry participants as early as November 1996 and claimed that it would announce a standard for 56K modems about two years after the introduction of the modem. It is important to keep in mind several points when evaluating the progress of the market during ITU negotiations. First, it is not clear how credible the ITU's scheduling claims were. Two years would be very quick relative to previous ITU decisions. Farrell (1996) reports that similar organizations delivered standards in five years, on average. Second, the ITU had no enforcement power in this case; it served only to create a focal point.[6] In theory, if one technology could emerge as the market standard, the ITU's decision might not matter. Therefore, it was crucial that all the major players chose to support and participate in creating the ITU's standard even when other specifications (their own) were available.

Our evidence below suggests that market participants did not believe it was realistic for one of the pre-existing specifications to win in the market. Nevertheless, even two years was considered a long time in this industry, so that may explain why it appears that the technology sponsors seemed to compete as if they were trying to win a standards war, as opposed to waiting for the ITU decision. Certainly, if the ITU decision dragged on for years, as it had with some other standards, then competing vigorously was the only sensible strategy.

As it turned out, 56K modem sales to ISPs went very slowly relative to what the market could have supported.[7] Barely 50 percent of ISPs adopted 56K by October 1997, with almost none of the large ISPs (AOL, AT&T, UUNET, MSN, GTE, Bell-South, EarthLink) adopting. Although there is some evidence that X2 sales were greater than Flex sales, most evidence suggests that sales to consumers were relatively low (we present more evidence of this below). Rockwell and US Robotics felt that the source of these problems was the standards battle.

---

[6] With some technologies, the ITU can compel member governments to use approved technologies in government contracts (but even this relies on the United Nations' enforcement power). But in this industry, the ITU has no enforcement power.

[7] A descriptive article on the ITU website contains quotes from industry experts such as: "The market was drying up ... people had stopped buying 56K modems"; and "A split was there for a short time" (ITU Press and Public Information Service 1998).

With strong industry support, the ITU announced the V.90 standard, an amalgam of X2 and Flex, in February 1998. At the time, this was regarded as the fastest the ITU had ever reached a decision (ITU Press and Public Information Service 1998). Although the V.90 was incompatible with either of the previous two standards, sales were strong and there was widespread adoption by both ISPs and consumers.

In summary, the events of this case appear to have all the elements of a canonical standards war. There was an economic opportunity arising from a technical upgrade of modems, and all parties believed this opportunity would be valuable for users and vendors. There was a conflict between different implementations of that upgrade, but these implementations did not appear to be technically or functionally different from each other. A publicly spirited SSO became involved and promulgated a specification for a new specification as standard, apparently to the benefit of all parties and users. Nevertheless, as we argue in the subsequent section, several questions and conundrums arise that the canonical model does not address. These issues are important for understanding how market events affected negotiations and vice versa.

4 Questions and conundrums

In this section, we use the events surrounding the deployment of the 56K standard to illustrate broad principles about standardization processes. Our analysis stresses why in this instance a canonical model of the standards war is misleading or at least underspecified. We explore different approaches for characterizing standardization processes and stress the role of deployment. We develop quantitative and qualitative evidence about the interaction between deployment and the standardization process at the ITU. Much of this is based on interviews with market participants. Specifically, we discuss the following nine conundrums and questions:

1. Did ISPs have incentives to coordinate?
2. What incentives to coordinate did the modem makers have?
3. Why are focal points with 56K so costly?
4. How do intellectual property conflicts shape the costs of negotiation?
5. How does the voting structure and rules at the SSO shape the costs of coordination?
6. Why do SSOs not encourage the use of side payments?
7. Does standardization lead to technical improvement?

8. How do participants in standard setting processes use all the available information?
9. Are SSOs substitutes for each other?

Our analysis of deployment shows why the product's network features created incentives to coordinate on a single standard, but local competition created great pressure to differentiate across the technologies. In addition, we stress that it is not possible to understand the behavior of market participants without understanding their asymmetric market positions and the negotiation process. The interaction of these asymmetries and negotiations receives the most attention in our study, especially as we identify and characterize different common viewpoints. We ultimately argue that had positions been different, then behavior would also have been different, that is, less urgent or more urgent, and more inclined towards compromise or less inclined.

Readers should keep in mind that our analysis is necessarily speculative, and the methodology must rely on our interpretation of a relatively small number of interviews and articles in the trade press. Most lessons are not "proven" in the sense of statistical analysis or mathematical proof. We also identify places where questions are open because we cannot "test" between differing claims and interpretations for what occurred in the 56K market. With that caveat in mind, we turn to the results from our case study of the 56K modem market.

4.1 Did Internet Service Providers have incentives to coordinate?

The ISPs that adopted 56K modems before the V.90 was available made a choice between one of two existing technologies. Similar to the standard models of network effects, they had an incentive to coordinate on the same technologies as their rivals, which would raise the possibility that they were using the technology that ultimately would become the market standard. However, ISPs had a countervailing incentive. They could adopt the technology that was less popular to take advantage of larger margins available in the admittedly smaller market.

Our companion paper, AGR, explores this issue in detail.[8] Here, however, we provide some simple statistics suggesting that ISPs

---

[8] In this section, we analyze deployment of 56K modem technology as of October 1997 and summarize the more extensive statistical work of AGR. Our primary purpose for showing this data is to emphasize the geographic dispersion of

*Table 4.1. Number and percentage of ISPs adopting
in October 1997 (not weighted by size of ISP)*

Type of specification adopted	Number of ISPs	Percentage of ISPs adopting
None	1,136	50.9%
X2	389	17.4%
Flex	523	23.4%
Both	185	8.3%

preferred differentiation to coordination. In other words, we answer: No, ISPs did not have incentives to coordinate with local competitors. Building on directories of ISPs, we construct a data set on adoption decisions in October 1997, after the products were widely available but before it was clear the ITU would soon reach a decision. For 2233 ISPs, we observe their adoption decision (X2, Flex, both, or neither) as well as a list of telephone numbers that could be used to connect. Merging with a database on local telephone calling areas allows us to determine which consumers could call which ISPs. As consumers almost always sign up with an ISP in their local calling area, we take local calling areas as independent markets.

Several issues arose in construction of the data. First, we observe less than half of the ISPs in existence, though the ones we miss tend to be small and probably would not have adopted in any event. Second, we observe only a single decision for each firm, not what their decision was in each location. Nevertheless, our understanding is that most firms actually did make a single decision for all of their locations simultaneously. Third, some telephone switches may be part of multiple local calling areas. In these circumstances, we arbitrarily assign switches to a single local calling area. Detailed empirical models in AGR suggest that assignments do not affect the results.[9]

In Table 4.1, we show the adoption rates in October. By this time, only about half of the ISPs had deployed. Moreover, the vast majority

deployment and decision making by ISPs in the United States, which were factors in raising coordination costs.

[9] Data came from the Directory, *Boardwatch*. See Augereau et al. (forthcoming) for a more detailed discussion of the data and a more detailed statistical analysis.

Table 4.2. Average adoption rates per local calling area, October 1997

Number of firms (ISPs) per calling area	15.06
Number of adopting firms (ISPs) per calling area	5.98*
X2	2.58
Flex	1.99
Both	0.18

Note: * The sum of rows 3, 4, and 5 do not equal the amount in row 2 because the quantities are averaged.

of non-deploying ISPs were large, so the percentage of customers served by 56K was much lower than a half. About 8 percent of adopters actually adopted both technologies.

Our method creates 2,298 local calling areas. Local calling areas have relatively few firms in each one. The average number of ISPs in a calling area is fifteen with a standard deviation of 20.8. However, there are 738 calling areas with only one ISP and the median number is only three. In Table 4.2 we show average adoption rates by local calling area. Again, there are only a few adopters in each calling area. The average number of adopters in October 1997 is about six ISPs per calling area. Flex leads X2 when tallied by ISP (as in Table 4.1), while X2 leads Flex when tallied by locale (as in Table 4.2).

To discuss local interactions, our approach here is to compare the national adoption rate with the adoption rate in each local calling area. If the rates are close to the same, it suggests that ISPs were differentiating from each other. If local markets are characterized by agglomeration on one standard or the other, it suggests network effects were important.

We look only at ISPs that adopt X2 or Flex and ignore ISPs that adopt neither or both. We look only at the 1,595 markets in which there are at least two such ISPs. Among such firms, 57.7% adopted X2. We are interested in calculating the number of markets in which adoption approximated this rate of 57.7% and term these markets *highly differentiated*. As a point of comparison, we compute what we would have expected if ISPs had made their decisions independently, with a 57.7% chance of adopting X2 and a 42.3% chance of adopting Flex.

Table 4.3. Evidence of differentiation

High differentiation window	High differentiation markets	
	Data	Random
55%–60%	17%	11%
50%–65%	51%	39%
42.5%–72.5%	71%	59%

Notes: "Data" reports the portion of markets with the X2 adoption rate falling into the High Differentiation Window.
"Random" reports number if ISPs adopted randomly with rate 57.7%.

In Table 4.3, we report the percentage of markets for which the adoption rate falls within a given window, where the window roughly brackets the average national adoption rate. For instance, we see in the first row that in 17% of 1,595 markets, the portion of firms adopting X2 fell between 55% and 60%. There are 13,613 separate firm-market combinations. If each one of these had adopted X2 with the probability 57.7%, we would have expected only 11% of markets to fall within this 55–60% window. The results in rows 2 and 3 tell a similar story for larger windows.

The results in Table 4.3 show that the number of differentiated markets is much higher than would be expected if the firms were choosing independently. In other words, contrary to what one would expect, there is no geographic clustering at a local level. In AGR, we establish the statistical significance of this result and account for numerous possible complications, such as that ISPs make only a single choice across markets, that some switches are in multiple local calling plans, that there is an impact from firm characteristics and demographic variables, and that there is possible endogeneity of ISP decision making.

When we brought up our hypothesis that ISPs competitively differentiated from each other in interviews, we received mixed responses, with some subjects finding it believable while others found it implausible. We were struck that the interview subjects with a closer relationship to the smaller ISPs found it plausible, as we believe our result is mostly driven by the smallest ISPs. No subjects provided a convincing alternative explanation for these results.

4.2 What incentives to coordinate did the modem makers have?

There appear to have been ample incentives to coordinate, but for different reasons than one might have expected from studying canonical models of standard setting. It is crucial to understand what issues participants considered open and what issues they considered settled. This case illustrates how participants can be both certain about some aspects of a standard and uncertain about others.

In this instance, everyone had similar expectations about participation: Market participants acted with the belief that an ITU standard eventually would emerge. The open question was when and with what features; and nobody forecast with certainty which specific proposal would emerge. Similarly, that the ITU announced the V.90 in February 1998 was widely regarded as fast by historical norms. Given that this situation was confrontational and many others at the ITU were not, this speed was viewed as sooner than the most optimistic forecast from when the process started two years earlier. Yet, no one ever doubted that such an announcement would arrive eventually.

This raises the related question about what participants expected prior to the ITU standard. Participants acted with the belief that there could be nothing more than a *temporary* de facto standard arising from the market success of one specification or the other. In other words, participants could not forecast how long the market process would continue and how it would proceed, but nobody acted as if this was the *only* possible mode for standard setting. Nor did the market process alone, or in conjunction with the TIA, provide an opportunity for standard setting equivalent to that in the ITU process.

In this light, we can guess why both parties found it in their interest to cooperate with the ITU process even though – after a short period of competition – the X2 standard seems to have had an advantage over Flex in sales and deployment. First, we consider the camp formed around the Flex specification, where the interpretation appears straightforward. The ISPs with server equipment that aligned them with Flex were suffering in the market, and the Rockwell group risked losing them as customers. Hence, the Rockwell group had a clear incentive to agree to a standard that put it on better technical footing.

More surprising, US Robotics never considered ignoring an ITU standard even though it believed it was winning the standards war. The economic incentive for this stance is not transparent in retrospect. Why agree to an ITU standard and allow the Rockwell group to begin marketing substitutable products? Why abandon de facto standardization on X2 through market processes if that provides a lead and adequate profitability?

We can catalogue several related reasons. The first reason was grounded in the history of the market. The Flex group had the most established participants in the industry; Lucent, and particularly Rockwell, were dominant in the previous technology. Despite having the more dominant X2, US Robotics believed that it could not standardize the worldwide market without Rockwell's participation, at least not in a reasonable time. Similarly, Rockwell and Lucent could not act unilaterally and push through their standard without consulting US Robotics. The second reason strengthening the first is that US Robotics believed its advantage in the pre-standard market could be maintained in the post-standard market. For instance, US Robotics established a shelf-space advantage in consumer modems, which it felt had lasting power. Together, these points led US Robotics to believe that the "market-growing" features of an ITU standard outweighed the competitive impact of a public standard.[10] A third reason is one of status. Because Rockwell was historically dominant and US Robotics was regarded as an upstart, agreement between the two represented a symbolic victory for USR because it attained status as a major equipment manufacturer. The ITU standard setting process ratified this status.

These observations motivate an interesting counterfactual question about how the market process shapes the ITU standard. What would have happened if Flex had been dominant in the pre-standard market? Would market participants have treated the ITU standard as inevitable in that case? Given that Rockwell would have been dominant in both

[10] Another explanation for coordination between the US Robotics and Rockwell groups is that they were participating in some sort of repeated game. Note that many features of this market are not conducive to collusion. US Robotics had not produced chipsets in the past and so this was at best the beginning of a repeated game. Also, as new standards appear only once in a few years, there would be a long delay before the "punishment phase." Also, the next technology (broadband) was expected to be extremely different from 56K modems.

the 56K technology and previous technologies, it would seem that it would be in a position to impose a proprietary standard. Our conjecture is that the Rockwell group still would have encouraged an ITU standard, but the open question is whether the standard's specification would have looked different. For example, would Rockwell's negotiators have taken a different stance in the face of IP held by others?

Such counterfactual questions are hard to resolve, by definition. It is especially difficult because the eventual standard was a combination of different specifications, a *compromise* among many. Would the combinations have differed if the market positions had been different? There are generally two views on this hypothetical question, both of which we discuss in further detail below. One conjecture is that the standards process has its own momentum and largely ignores the market position, because other issues, such as resolving conflicts over IP or the technical merits of a proposal, are paramount to the speed of the outcome and the type of specification that results. The other view is that the market position informs the urgency of all parties and contributes to a firm's willingness to compromise in specific ways. Had the market position differed, so too would have behavior at the ITU, which might have affected the eventual speed of decision making and the chosen design.

4.3 Why are focal points with 56K so costly?

In the canonical analysis of standards wars, focal points have a role in settling the standards battle. As options that grab the attention of all the major players, they provide a coordinating device when all parties need one. As the standard emerges, it must combine a bundle of components that must all interoperate. A standard is a public good, providing non-rivalrous information about designs to any manufacturer, resulting in a set of goods that collectively work better together than they would have in the absence of the public good.

In the canonical model of a standards war, it does not matter how focal points arise. They are typically modeled as the outcome of a "sunspot" or a "public coin-flipping." The crucial feature of a focal point is its steadfastness after it emerges. Steadfastness arises from one of several sources: strong and transparent economic incentives from key sponsors; a mandate from a government agency; the presence of difficult-to-change investments by many interested parties; and historical precedent that cannot be erased. In the standards canon, it is not essential whether arriving at that point was costly or not, only that it is difficult to change once there.

On the surface, the deployment of 56K modems fits the canon, because it illustrates why a focal point here had such benefits. Use of a focal point avoids the type of geographic fragmentation that occurs when firms are diffusing competing technological specifications. It also fits the canon in the sense that the ITU had precedent on its side and a promise to follow a predictable process in the future. It had provided industry standards for successive generations of this technology and, as we previously stated, industry participants believed that the ITU would do so again using much the same decision-making process. In addition, other buyers in other countries looked to the ITU standards before purchasing equipment, so the ITU standard potentially had a gate-keeping function as well.

But the ITU is a much more costly mechanism for negotiating a focal point than the low-cost mechanisms typically found in the theoretical models, such as sun-spots or public coin-flipping. In addition to the membership costs previously detailed, participation requires sending delegations to meetings that take place throughout the United States and Canada, and (for other standards) throughout the world. Meetings require submissions with potentially expensive documentation of technical claims. The actual negotiations themselves have their own cost. All participants recalled the pain affiliated with the brokering associated with 56K. All sides involved lawyers, engineers, and marketing executives at many firms. Nobody called this easy.

An obvious reason why this process is so costly is that negotiating an agreement has nontrivial explicit costs. An additional reason is that designing a new technology requires an investment of research and development. A third reason may be some inefficiencies in the ITU system relative to some optimal SSO, but we doubt this is important. Indeed, it can be costly to choose between alternative approaches to a technical problem even when the disagreement is entirely within a single firm. Note that a benefit and a potential reason for the costliness is that once an agreement is reached, market players are less likely to revisit the standard setting process, which raises the likelihood of implementation of any given standard.

This last observation takes on more saliency in light of our next few remarks about negotiations over IP. One of the major negotiating costs in the V.90 involved negotiating through all the parties' IP claims.

4.4 *How do Intellectual Property conflicts shape the cost of negotiation?*

The most naive models of standards wars are portrayed as solely a fight between producer and user surplus. That is, consumers lose when two proprietary implementations for a technical opportunity vie to gain the producer surplus and thereby delay deployment. In this scenario the SSO's only role is to represent the potential for foregone surplus for users and to make vendors act less selfishly. For the case of 56K, the SSO's primary purpose was different.

The ITU serves as a forum for negotiations between parties who choose to participate. This set normally includes the conflicting parties as well as others. If users show up to represent their interests in the negotiations, then they have a voice too, but there is nothing about the negotiations process that guarantees user interests will be central, or even present. Nor is there any compelling law mandating a specific outcome from negotiations. Firm activity is voluntary.

Why do firms use this forum to negotiate? While there were many potential issues to negotiate, the most worrisome in the case of 56K was that a proposed specification might infringe upon IP held by several firms. Resolving IP issues was the primary activity performed during the negotiations. No other factor was as crucial for achieving agreement on the specification of the V.90. Accordingly, protection of IP appears to be the most prominent feature motivating participation.

To a professional manager in communication equipment markets or a consultant familiar with standardization cases, the importance of resolving IP issues is not surprising; however, it is surprising how little attention this topic receives in the canonical framework. We suggest that although there are some well-understood legal issues, there are fewer economic frameworks for analyzing the role for IP at SSOs. More generally, there is no framework for how IP shapes negotiating costs.

One view of how IP shapes negotiation costs is that patents are simply bargaining chips useful for achieving a desirable outcome from the SSO (such as delaying the adoption of the standard). For instance, if one firm holds a patent necessary for solving the technological issue in question, that firm is in a position to negotiate or delay to their advantage.

Of particular importance to our sources was the use of patents to influence standing in the post-standard market. Formally, all firms would have to pay licensing fees to use the patents of other firms covering the standard. But it was widely understood that firms that held patents over the standard would cross-license their patents to each other, thereby ensuring free use of the standard to patent holders. This feature meant that firms prioritized the inclusion of their patents in the final standard.[11]

The second view emphasizes the procedural and cultural momentum that shaped the negotiations. According to this view, business decisions are based on engineering choices, not on the economic incentives of participating organizations. The principal goal is to walk out with the best technical standard according to the evaluators' engineering norms without regard for the impact on private interests directly.

Under this view, negotiation within an SSO is very different from simple bilateral negotiation between parties. For example, the debate over IP was not solely a legal debate, as it might have been if IP lawyers negotiated a bilateral agreement outside the purview of the SSO. Instead, because the debate occurred inside an SSO such as the ITU, it became subject to pre-existing decision-making rules for including or excluding features of a standard. That is, participants closely scrutinized the claims about the functional contribution of a technology covered by a patent and vigorously debated over the technical merits of proposals. The resolution of these disputes was partially tempered by engineering norms of the participants at the ITU subgroups.

Resolving disputes requires appreciation of the minute level of engineering detail and legal nuance embedded in a patent. It is not possible to resolve issues by mechanical means or nondiscretionary decision-making norms. These observations point toward the importance of *formal* and *informal* rules at SSOs for resolving conflicting business interests or conflicting technical claims. As a practical matter, SSOs cannot resolve such matters without a myriad combination – or clash – of views from firm participants, administrative staff, technical talent, and legal expertise.

---

[11] For example, "Companies want a piece of their technology in the standard so that others will have to pay a licensing fee for the use of the technology," said an executive at 3-Com (ITU Press and Public Information Service, 1998).

We take a middle ground between these views – especially as design and negotiation occurred concurrently for the 56K. On the one hand, the role of IP as a negotiating tool was correct because we saw that participants would have opposed a standard that did not include their IP. That IP was important in assuring property-holders' position in the post-standard market was clearly on the minds of many of the people involved. On the other had, there is also more than just a grain of truth to the belief that agreement was dictated by the "best technology" rather than by strategic concerns. It is partly reflected in everyone believing a standard would eventually emerge from the ITU and in the degree of control held by engineers associated with the ITU.

In the case of 56K it is clear (in retrospect) that all firms approached negotiations over IP issues with a sense of urgency about reaching an outcome and a sense of cooperation, or, at a minimum, non-obstructionism to a point. Participants perceived that an ITU standard would help virtually all parties, particularly if done sooner rather than later. As was previously noted, multiple factors, including the market positions of the firms, contributed to those perceptions and, hence, these choices. To be sure, the outcome was ultimately constrained by many of the important technical details that shaped the precise specification, which inevitably resulted in costly negotiations. Without a sense of urgency and cooperation, however, the negotiations would have been even more costly, and would almost certainly have reached resolution at a later date.

4.5 How do the voting structure and rules at the SSO shape the costs of coordination?

Voting structure

Assigning authority for dispute resolution is an important facet of negotiation costs; for example, SSOs in general can resolve disputes via consensus voting or majority voting. We find that market participants have thoughtful and sophisticated assessments of how particular SSOs resolve disputes. Such assessments include views about where an SSO vests authority to resolve disputes and what biases arise as a result of these assignments.

The ITU uses a consensus voting structure and requires nondiscriminatory licensing practices. This structure is important for resolving IP disputes. The open question is whether the specification of a standard is affected by these negotiation rules or whether the outcome would be the same under any set of rules for resolving disputes – both in the case of 56K and in general.

There are two contrasting views about consensus voting, consistent with the two camps we previously identified. One view – consistent with the first camp – stresses the strategic behavior of participants. Firms want their IP in any given standard, and they try to have the standard modified to include their patents. A consensus voting process gives them great leverage to do so. This process might not create the best technology available, but it does create one that all participants will approve. That is, patents may be included just to help the working group achieve a consensus in favor of the proposed standard.

The alternative view – consistent with the second camp – is that technical merit plays an important role in determining inclusion. Through discussion, it is possible to exclude "unimportant" technologies that degrade the functioning of the standard. It is through such a process of review and open debate that a superior hybrid technology emerges. In this view, consensus voting ensures that all participants are heard and ensures that the ITU considers all known options.

Majority voting can have very different implications. In a process based on majority voting, there is much less scope for firms to ensure the consideration of their technology, for better or for worse. We cannot make a blanket statement about the efficiency of majority voting over consensus voting. One of our contacts works with both the IEEE (i.e., Institute of Electrical and Electronics Engineers) and the ITU. The IEEE is based on majority voting, and he reports that outcomes are easily manipulated. When a vote arises that is important for a particular firm, that firm will send a large number of people (e.g., twenty) to the meeting. Most of these attendees do not know what is going on in the meeting, but a group leader signals to them how to vote. One may wonder at the efficiency implications of such a system.

The canonical approach to analyzing a standards war treats the choices as fixed. There is no general framework for thinking about a negotiated specification at an SSO. Hence, the canon does not provide much guidance beyond the conventional wisdom, namely, that consensus procedures lead to better technologies whereas majority voting leads to quicker agreements. Verifying this convention requires evidence about a wide cross-section of cases well beyond the case of 56K and the scope of this article.[12]

Rules

A contrast of views pervades the debate about the comparative relevance of the ITU's requirement that participants agree to license their related patents at a "fair and reasonable rate." Some believe this rule works as intended, whereas others focus on how this rule raises coordination costs. In particular, the ITU requires that any participant holding a patent that may affect a proposed standard must disclose the patent. The participant must also agree to license that patent at a "fair and reasonable rate" and do so in a manner that is nondiscriminatory. This does not imply that licensing is cheap, nor does it mean that patented technology will become widely available at some price. If firms vary from some consensus view of what constitutes a reasonable price they can be sanctioned in other SSO actions, or, at worse, taken to court for violation of a participant's rules.

Lemley (2002) provides an excellent discussion of the various legal issues that arise from this type of requirement and the interaction of SSOs and IP more generally. Lemley stresses the importance of handling IP for the success of an SSO, and one of his central policy recommendations is that SSOs develop clear statements that are similar to the one at the ITU.

The ITU requirement is there to ensure that the ITU is not unknowingly making proprietary technologies into international standards and that a standard can be implemented easily after the ITU has endorsed it. The goal of the ITU requirement is that any firm can make use of the standard whether or not that firm participated in the standards process.

One may question whether this rule accomplishes its stated goal. If the ITU requirement operated as intended, licensing patents associated with a standard would be straightforward. However, if that were the case, firms would not be willing to expend so many resources ensuring that they can cross-license relevant patents after the standard is promulgated.

Assuming that it is difficult to make a standard without infringing on someone's IP, at least in part, we conjecture that there are two possible

---

[12] Indeed, the case of 56K even seems to mildly defy this wisdom, as it was widely regarded as both beneficial and comparatively fast.

outcomes for any negotiating session. One is "unaggressive," that all firms deliberately avoid staking claims over their own IP, volunteer their IP without fuss, and compromise specifications emerge quickly, even when they come close to violating someone's patents. The other norm is "aggressive," that all firms attempt to include their patented technologies in an eventual compromise specification, claim broad importance for them, and achieve a cross-licensing deal to their benefit.

We conjecture that the first norm, unaggressive behavior, cannot survive in the presence of at least one firm acting according to the second norm, aggressive behavior. That is, if one firm tries to include a patented technology and make broad claims about it, then it is in the interest of all firms to do the same. In anticipation of that outcome, it is in every firm's incentive to try to get any advantage they can from making their patented claims earliest.

The ITU rule can be interpreted as an attempt to promote the first norm, where all volunteer the patents freely and without fuss, thereby lowering negotiating costs for everyone. If the second behavioral norm holds, however, the negotiation costs are likely to be high whether or not the rule is present. That is, negotiation costs are high in situations where there are many conflicting claims over IP. In such a case, it is unclear whether the rule about licensing alters behavior or even helps.

In the 56K standard negotiations, participants placed an emphasis on getting their IP included in the standard. On the surface, this appears to be aggressive behavior. For reasons we next explain, we conjecture that this would have arisen under virtually any set of consensus rules and licensing norms. And it made negotiating costs high.

4.6 *Why do SSOs not encourage use of side payments?*

In any basic economic model of negotiations, the objective of negotiations is to identify the set of common solutions that yield net benefits to all parties. It is a common property of such models that all parties can use side payments to enlarge the set of possible outcomes that leave all parties better off.

The negotiations at SSOs, in contrast, typically do not include side payments, and the negotiations at the ITU for 56K modems followed the SSO convention. Why SSOs follow this convention is puzzling, since such a habit drives up costs.

First, we examine *why* costs are raised by the absence of side payments. Consider one naive model of the negotiating process – the joint-surplus maximizing model – which, if side payments were present, would correctly describe negotiating behavior. This model requires side payments for an agreement to arise in any setting where participants have very asymmetric assets. In such a model, participants in a standard setting process always choose the technology that maximizes joint participant surplus. The SSO could simply use side payments to compensate participants who would lose relative to some alternative technology. Firms with inferior technology could be paid to vote with the best technology.

Second, we examine the puzzle of why SSOs do not use side payments, and find that the conundrum is more complex when we highlight the relationship between negotiations and deployment. If side-payments solutions were observed often, then it would not be so important for firms to place their IP in the standard. In practice, it seems that the major form of payment for a vote is to include the voter's IP in the standard, which brings the benefit of allowing the firm to participate in the post-standard market. This is obviously a crude method of payment and its use is puzzling in comparison to side payments, which are much more efficient.

The following observation highlights the relevance of no-side payments. Agreement can be difficult when a firm has relevant IP but does not plan on participating in the post-standard market. In these cases, the IP holder expects licensing payments, which makes the rest of the participants wary of ratifying a particular standard. Our interview subjects noted that a key to the quick agreement on the V.90 was that all the participants who had relevant IP also were producers in the post-standard market. All market players anticipated participating in market processes after the standard was announced and were willing to cross-license their patents, allowing for production without licensing fees.

We conjecture that the absence of side payments here arises for many of the same reasons contracting breaks down between private parties in the face of uncertainty. When the economic value of agreement depends on the resolution of some uncertainty in the future – such as the level of demand – the contract must specify how that future state will be measured and how payoffs between parties relate to that measure. Such state-contingent contracts between bilateral parties are particularly hard to forge when there are different views about the likely value of future events or when discussions about contracts reveal too much about a party's competitive position and strategic plans for the future. It is also hard to enforce such contracts if events cannot be measured in a verifiable manner beyond opportunistic reinterpretation. We conjecture that in a multilateral setting, such as standard setting negotiations at an SSO, such factors greatly interfere with the emergence of written state-contingent contracts.

The absence of written contracts specifying how parties will benefit or lose in the event of certain outcomes does not eliminate the need for some sort of mechanism for paying off parties for resolving their differences. In the absence of a written agreement, we conjecture that parties favor economic payoffs that are contingent on deployment and market success, where each party's market success is a trade secret, by default, and not subjected to reporting biases or other legal disputes about enforcement.

Consistent with our remarks above, there are two views about the relevance of these issues for the case of 56K. One view highlights the technical constraints placed on the outcome and, accordingly, diminishes the importance of side-payment considerations. Another view, and the one to which we are sympathetic, highlights the sense of urgency and cooperation with which parties approached the negotiations as they deployed infrastructure into the marketplace. In that light, firms reaped the benefits from agreement only by accelerating the deployment of 56K and making additional sales. In that sense, lack of side payments heightened incentives to achieve agreement and thus start the selling.

4.7 Does standardization lead to technical improvement?

A standards war determined in the market typically leads to one proprietary technology becoming the standard or to no standardization at all. This simple observation underlies a seeming advantage for SSOs, namely, that they have a greater set of options than a market process. The 56K modem case illustrates the issue concretely. The ITU could (1) endorse one party's specification as standard without change; (2) endorse no specification from any party; (3) endorse a specification that combines elements of standards presently proposed; and (4) endorse a specification that combines elements of present proposals, but add additional elements to make the resulting compromise palatable to all relevant parties. On this basis one might naively conclude that because, unlike markets, SSOs have options 3 and 4 available, they are superior to markets. That is, an SSO may take the best of several proprietary technologies and create a technology superior to any individual firm or consortium would have created on its own.

Such a view is naive because it ignores the negotiation process for reaching a focal point. In this case, even if all parties desire a standard, the consensus system at the ITU essentially excludes options 1 and 2. That is, these first two options were extremely unlikely even given both sides' interest in achieving a standard. Hence, determining standards in an SSO rarely involves a pure expansion of options. Instead, it biases the outcome toward a different type of choice. Is it a better or worse choice? Once again, the canonical framework for a standards war does not consider the trade-off, so we have little prior literature to guide our understanding.

How should one think about the potential costs and advantages of combining technologies? There are two key costs: One involves the short-run costs for designing a standard for the issues under consideration. The second and more subtle cost is of designing a standard in anticipation of what is likely to occur in the near future, as new technical opportunities arise for upgrades. Events in 56K illustrate each of these.

First, there are the costs of simply writing a standard. We were initially surprised that 56K modems did not undergo an enormous improvement at the ITU. While there is some limited evidence that both technologies for 56K modems were improving after their introduction, we came across no declarations in the public press that the V.90 was a noticeable technical improvement over X2 and Flex. Our evidence is weak in that we have no evidence that it was not better, but we are struck by the lack of public discussion of any improvements in the V.90. Clearly, this lesson applies only to 56K modems and does not extrapolate to other technologies.

The second lesson is more transparently illustrated by events here. The V.90 was not the last standard for 56K modems to come from the ITU. There were further upgrades with the V.91 and V.92, which clearly were superior to their predecessor by objective engineering norms – and were widely acknowledged as such. Hence, even if one was unsure about the improvement embedded in the first, there seems little dispute that the first agreement created a unified base specification for building further improvement.

This gives rise to counterfactual questions about what would happen in the absence of agreement or in the presence of a longer delay or a different type of agreement. Would such upgrades have occurred as quickly if a proprietary technology had been the choice for the V.90? Similarly, in the absence of an ITU standard, would de facto market standards advance more quickly, less quickly or at comparable rates? If standards are negotiated by consensus among firms, is it more efficient to have the same partners negotiate with each other? We conjecture that familiarity lowers negotiation costs because participants are familiar with each other's business concerns, IP holdings, and market positions, as well as other factors that shape the costs of negotiations. As noted, the canon does not provide a framework for considering these open questions, both in the case of 56K modems and in general.

4.8 How do participants in a standard setting process use all available information?

Models of negotiations tend to emphasize that disputes arise from the asymmetric positions of the parties and the private information strategically kept from each other. While these behaviors might have been relevant to some parts of the negotiation in the case of 56K, the issues associated with making decisions in the face of market uncertainty and conjectures about the future direction of technology were much more pressing. Participants based their decisions and actions on the best available information, but, despite that, sometimes consensus forecasts about the future turn out to be wrong. Said another way, it is easy to model negotiations as if no uncertainty is present, but doing so is naive and potentially a misleading way to understand the biases inherent to using SSOs to resolve standards wars. It is easy to look back on events with perfect hindsight or with information about how market trends worked out; but this runs the risk of being historically inaccurate.

For 56K modems, part of the impetus for reaching an agreement so quickly stemmed from the belief that 56K modems would be quickly eclipsed by broadband technologies such as digital subscriber lines and cable modems. That is, many participants believed the technical value of upgrading dial-up modems, and the market opportunity for deploying 56K modems as a business, would be short-lived. A lengthy ITU process would risk missing the height of the market opportunity. Of course, within a few years it was obvious that this consensus forecast about the speed of diffusion for the replacement technology was wildly overoptimistic.[13]

In light of the dot-com bust and other overoptimistic forecasts about the rise of the Internet, one may accept a forecasting mistake such as this. This preconception about broadband seems to have been held by every market observer. Yet, as of mid-2004, the technologies are only now beginning to displace the 56K modem in personal computer communications. As Gandal et al. (in press) point out, that still understates the staying power of 56K. ITU standards for 56K modems are still the dominant interface for many technologies such as fax machines and cellular telephones.

More to the point, this case illustrates how forums, such as the ITU, can allow misconceptions to shape outcomes in ways that might not occur in market processes. Markets would arrive at an outcome on the basis of firms' strategies, whether or not they were independently determined, or there was a consensus about the future. In contrast, SSOs magnify the error that arises from a wrong consensus.

This observation complicates comparisons of SSOs to markets. This case illustrates precisely why it is difficult to make blanket assertions. All participants thought the window for the 56K market would be short and, therefore, negotiated with a sense of urgency. This urgency was important in coming to resolution in the face of so many costly negotiating obstacles. In this sense, the mistaken forecast about the near future contributed to reaching resolution, something that might not have occurred if no SSO existed.

We now turn to another example about the role for these forums in settling disagreements about uncertainty. Specifically, even in 2004, we repeatedly encountered the observation that market processes in 1997 were difficult to document, that market information was inherently ambiguous. Even in retrospect some factors are held in dispute. Some participants continue to issue charges about vaporware (mostly about Flex) and express skepticism about publicly stated commitments. While each firm could track its own sales of modems, only one trade magazine, *Boardwatch*, published something resembling a survey of

---

[13] This was a source of great amusement for some of the participants we interviewed.

use among service providers. Different associations provided their members with different viewpoints about actions.[14] In summary, decision making necessarily took place among interpretative confusion built upon factual ambiguity.

In this light, one view of SSOs is as forums offering an opportunity for firms to compare their views, share information, and reduce ambiguity. This information aggregation can be about more than just the technical merits of various approaches to a given problem. It can be about nature of demand and the reconciliation of alternative visions about the path along which the marketplace will develop.

Related, and more understandably, there is disagreement and inherent ambiguity about the consequences of paths not taken. We have found former participants expressing different opinions about what an interim agreement at the TIA might have looked like in the absence of compromise at the ITU. Moreover, we previously highlighted how fragmented the market experience was across the United States, so it is no surprise that, even in retrospect, participants also provide distinct forecasts about whether sales were strong or weak prior to the agreement at the ITU. They also provide different views about whether they would have continued to be strong or weak if the emergence of the standard had been delayed.[15] We speculate that some of these differences are consistent with previously stated positions, and some are simply to save face. To our ears, they will never be resolved.

On the surface, a lack of resolution for such matters is not, per se, of much interest to anyone – with the exception of a market historian or a participant with a stake in how history gets told. But it is interesting for this study because it highlights a trade-off between market processes and negotiated forums. In de facto market standardization processes, such unresolved disagreements are not relevant except in so far as they shape firm strategies that affect market outcomes. In negotiations, however, such disagreements can play a role in shaping consensus outcomes. Hence, in the face of market uncertainty, we perceive a role for such forums in aggregating fragmented information among multiple parties, and we also perceive the possibility that such forums

---

[14] This can be seen, for example, in the wide array of sources quoted by Shapiro and Varian (1999).

[15] For example, contrast the following press release in the ITU Press and Public Information Service's 1998 Plenipotentiary Conference (see www.itu.int/newsarchive/press/PP98/PressRel-Features/Features3.html).

can allow misconceptions to shape outcomes in ways that would not occur in market process.

4.9 Are SSOs substitutes for each other?

Do SSOs compete with one another for jurisdiction? One might view SSOs as arbitrators that compete to have disagreements brought under their purview. In that sense, SSOs choose their structure to attract the most "disputes." For instance, Besen and Farrell (1991) report that the ITU was losing importance relative to regional private SSOs, such as the IEEE, and it responded by dropping the requirement that countries vote before a standard can be approved. Since countries vote only once every four years, bypassing this requirement allowed the ITU to promulgate standards more quickly.

In that light, we can reinterpret some of the events over the 56K modem war. We reinterpret the question about why the Rockwell and US Robotics groups chose to bring their dispute to the ITU. Earlier we asked why they came to the ITU instead of allowing market processes to carry on. In this section we ask why they chose the ITU instead of the IEEE or some other SSO.

We believe this question arises about the canonical model because the canon has an incomplete view of the negotiations process. To illustrate, we have a few potential answers for why the ITU served as SSO and no other forum did. First, as was previously noted, there was precedent. The ITU was the source of all previous modem standards and so had both expertise and infrastructure in its favor.[16] In addition, there were structural advantages at the ITU for modems. The ITU has an international jurisdiction; and an ITU standard meant that producers could immediately begin producing for all areas of the world. Although, because of US influence on technology, the IEEE has a de facto jurisdiction greater than the United States, our sources say that the internationalism of the ITU was perceived as an advantage.

The ITU also was better able to negotiate the regulatory requirements. An FCC cap on the modulation within phone wires limited the new modems to 56K. In fact, speeds greater than 56K could have been achievable in some foreign countries, but those countries were willing

---

[16] This of course raises the question of why modems were ever brought to the ITU in the first place many years earlier, but we leave that aside.

to agree to this standard to achieve an international standard. Presumably, coordinating these issues was easier when done through the ITU, which has a long-standing relationship with both the FCC and international telecommunication regulators, than through the IEEE.

Finally, the status of these institutions in business culture played a role in why the ITU was chosen. Rockwell had a history in defense contracting and was considered an establishment firm. US Robotics was closely associated with ISPs and was considered an upstart. The ITU is the most established SSO in the world. One source claimed the ITU's "establishment credentials" made it an acceptable venue for Rockwell to negotiate with this new competitor. We find it difficult to translate these ideas about credentials into modern economic language, but found them provocative nonetheless. To say the least, this notion is not part of the canonical model of forum shopping during standards wars.

These reasons for using the ITU versus another SSO slightly alter our earlier interpretation of the coordinating advantages from using a negotiated forum. That is, not only will using an SSO help coordinate actors with different interests or who face different geographically independent competitive situations, but it will also help coordinate geographically distinct markets around the globe.

A theoretic model in which SSOs choose their voting rules or other such characteristics and compete for market share in the standards market would be exceptionally interesting (see Lerner and Tirole [forthcoming] for a start), but our research points out important constraints on such models. There exist important asymmetries between existing SSOs in their ability to coordinate otherwise fragmented market actors. Moreover, since there are multiple sources of fragmentation in need of potentially different types of coordination devices, no single forum will be superior for all situations. We conjecture that different forums will possess different comparative advantages, and these advantages cannot be shaped without constraint, nor are these advantages free of an SSO's history and long-standing formal and informal norms for resolving disputes.

5 Conclusion

We provide detailed analysis of a standards war and the costs of coordinating a solution to it. On the surface, this case has the three key elements found in a canonical standards war: an economic opportunity arising from a technical upgrade, a conflict between different implementations of that upgrade, and a resolution to the conflict, this time through the involvement of a publicly spirited SSO. Taking advantage of the detailed information available, we focus on the earliest period of deployment and analyze the interaction of market participants with the behavior of the SSO. Our main point is that this canonical model is misleading or incomplete with regards to the costs of coordination.

Incompleteness arose in several general areas. There is a large difference between a situation in which a regulatory agency intervenes and one in which firms voluntarily negotiate with an SSO. Yet, most previous cases of standards wars involve the FCC, a government agency that can mandate standards. Because regulatory concerns are paramount in understanding the activities of the FCC, the literature on such standards wars provide a set of insights that simply do not carry over to one in which an SSO is involved. The costs of negotiating in an SSO are shaped by a very different set of determinants.

In this case the ITU had no power to mandate a standard. The ITU can issue a specification, which can then act as a focal point. This specification is negotiated and need not have direct correspondence with any specification already for sale. For understanding this outcome it was more essential to understand that the ITU has its own idiosyncratic set of rules and precedents. While different than the concerns of regulators, these rules and sets of procedures give momentum to events and push them in directions that might overlap with – or be orthogonal to – the concerns of users or those with economic interests. Moreover, these activities involve individuals with long-standing professional relationships with each other and with the SSO, factors that also shape the negotiations and outcomes.

The canon is also incomplete in its analysis of the subtle ways in which the costs of coordination vary with firm behavior and market circumstances. Participation is voluntary on some levels and not others. One can see this nuance in three ways. First, all firms in this marketplace were members of this organization. It was inevitable that they would confront each other's claims over IP and marketing goals. Moreover, it was necessary to have an ITU standard to meet international markets. So, no matter how the market progressed, it was necessary for each firm to consider its negotiating position and come to these meetings with a position, whether it was strategic or not. This is not a mandated standard in the sense of a regulatory body mandating involvement of all interested parties and compelling adoption through legal means. Yet, there is a sense in which the situation compelled participation and managerial attention of all interested parties, and the focal point compelled use. We know of no model in the canon that properly captures how economic incentives led to this outcome.

Second, all firms took for granted that an ITU standard was inevitable, though many were uncertain about what it would look like and when it would emerge. The market position of firms then shapes the negotiating position of firms. For many firms, such a standard was valuable for their marketing purposes, and their marketing opportunity had a short window. Those perceptions of the marketing opportunity informed participatory behavior, making some parties less obstructionist than they might have been under different market circumstances. It also made others take a more urgent stance and pressed them to compromise sooner rather than later. Had market positions been different then negotiations could also be different, that is, in the sense of less urgent or more urgent, and more inclined towards compromise or less inclined.

Moreover, market-oriented events help crystallize forecasts. They also show where the market opportunity will move and thus help all parties be more foresighted about which IP is relevant for cross-licensing purposes and which is not, and which factors are relevant for the post-standard market opportunity – a key factor in reaching a compromise. We find it useful to describe this behavior as asymmetric negotiating positions brought about by asymmetric market positions. Again, we know of no model in the canon that captures these features.

Third, once the standards process gets started, the inevitability of the focal point becomes a potential factor in market events. There is a strong possibility that a standards war that ends with another specification simply adds more uncertainty to the marketplace. The uncertainties encompass significant outcomes, such as the speed of announcement, nuances of bargaining position, and the inevitability of a final specification. Even without this process, there were concerns among service providers that their investments would be orphaned. With this process reaching a likely outcome, these investments became contingent on the outcome. For example, it is striking that market participants knew the history of this ITU committee and did not forecast that the process would resolve itself quickly. Yet, once it became more apparent that the ITU committee might defy its own history, then it was in all the parties' interests to wait just a few months more. Yet, once again, no model in the canon places emphasis on how the management of the negotiating process at the SSO feeds back into market events.

From the perspective of economic canon, our close study of the details of events here suggests that the model of the standards war needs modification in several important respects. We conclude that the canon needs to address several open questions: What circumstances lead all firms to be compelled to participate in a voluntary standard setting process and when do circumstances not do so? What factors shape negotiating positions, which can range from being obstructionist to urging compromise? Under what circumstances can the standard-making process produce a feedback from the process into market events, either slowing it down by sowing uncertainty or speeding it up by ending concerns about orphaning? Such questions are essential for analyzing the costs of coordinating in their proper completeness, and for understanding the extent of public benefits that might arise from a delay in emergence of a standard.

From the perspective of policy toward SSOs, our study details important costs in the process for 56K modems. There are explicit costs, such as membership and negotiation costs, and implicit costs, such as a procedure that leads to a suboptimal technology or an inefficient handling of IP rights. However, this analysis should not be seen as a criticism of the ITU or SSOs in general, and particularly not in this instance. Indeed, for the ITU to provide a resolution to a difficult standards problem within eighteen months seems a remarkable accomplishment. Compared to the alternatives of regulation or pure market processes, SSOs may often be a superior coordination mechanism. Moving from a situation where knowledge and technology is dispersed among independent firms to one in which the market is coordinated on a single standard has inevitable costs. Our paper merely details what might be thought of as the "true costs" of coordinating through an SSO in what surely was one of the better circumstances. One can only imagine these costs in circumstances where the outcomes were not as beneficial to so many parties.

We offer these questions with a few caveats in mind. Our conclusions and observations depended on getting accurate information from participants with the good graces to speak with researchers. We have focused the study primarily on the period prior to the issuance of the V.90 standard. It is clear that events did not suddenly stop after this. The market grew and lasted longer than many participants expected. The ITU also upgraded the 56K modem standard several more times. A full appreciation of these later events might generate different insights about what really turned out to matter for later outcomes. Also, and not unrelated, we have largely eschewed welfare analysis in favor of identifying and characterizing the nuances of firm behavior. We identified trade-offs between different types of rules in an SSO and between different types of firm strategies in their negotiating position, but we did not fully develop these observations. A fully specified model would be required to analyze all welfare trade-offs, and we do not attempt to make such an assessment here.

References

Augereau, A., S. Greenstein, and M. Rysman forthcoming (AGR). "Coordination vs. differentiation in a standards war: 56K Modems," *Rand Journal of Economics.*

Besen, S., and J. Farrell 1991. "The role of the ITU in standardization: Pre-eminence, impotence or rubber stamp?" *Telecommunications Policy* 15: 311–21.

Besen, S., and L. Johnson 1986. *Compatibility standards, competition and innovation in the broadcasting industry.* Santa Monica, CA: Rand Corporation.

Downes, T., and S. Greenstein 1999. "Do commercial ISP's provide universal service?" in *Competition, regulation and convergence: Current trends in telecommunications policy research,* S. Gillett and I. Vogelsang (eds.), Mahwah, NJ: Lawrence Erlbaum Associates, 195–212.

Dranove, D., and N. Gandal 2003. "The DVD vs. DIVX standard war: Empirical evidence of network effects and preannouncement effects," *Journal of Economics and Management Science* 12: 363–86.

Ellison, G., and E. Glaeser 1997. "Geographic concentration in U.S. manufacturing industries: A dartboard approach," *Journal of Political Economy* 105: 889–927.

Farrell, J. 1996. "Choosing rules for formal standardization," mimeo, Berkeley, CA: University of California, Berkeley.

Farrell, J., and C. Shapiro 1992. "Standard setting in high-definition television," *Brookings Papers on Economic Activity: Microeconomics* 1–77.

Gandal, N., N. Gantman, and D. Genesove, in press. "Intellectual property and standardization committees in the US modem industry."

ITU Press and Public Information Service 1998, "From competition to cooperation: The road to e-commerce," ITU Plenipotentiary Conference, October 12–November 6, www.itu.int/newsarchive/press/PP98/PressRel-Features/Features3.html.

Lemley, M. 2002. "Intellectual property rights and standard-setting organizations," *California Law Review* 90: 1889.

Lerner, Josh and Jean Tirole, forthcoming. "A model of forum shopping, with special reference to standard setting organizations," *American Economic Review*.

Rickard, J. 1997a. "56K Modems: The battle continues," *Boardwatch*, March.
   1997b. "US Robotics launches the new battle – 56Kbps modems," *Boardwatch*, January.
   1998. "The 56K modem battle," *Boardwatch*, March.

Shapiro, C., and H. Varian 1999. *Information rules: A strategic guide to the network economy*. Cambridge, MA: Harvard Business School Press.

Stango, V. 2004. "The economics of standards wars," *Review of Network Economics* 3: 1–19.

von Burg, U. 2001. *The triumph of Ethernet: Technological communities and the battle for the LAN standard*. Stanford, CA: Stanford University Press.

5 | Promoting e-business through vertical IS standards: lessons from the US home mortgage industry

CHARLES W. STEINFIELD, ROLF T.
WIGAND, M. LYNNE MARKUS,
AND GABE MINTON

Abstract

Vertical information systems (IS) standards are designed to promote communication and coordination among the organizations comprising a particular industry sector. The authors present a case study of the emergence of vertical IS standards in the US home mortgage industry to provide insights into three processes: (1) the way the standardization process is structured to facilitate participation and consensus, (2) the approaches used to promote adoption of open and transparent standards, and (3) the steps taken to ensure the ongoing maintenance and integrity of the standards. Interviews with participants involved with the Mortgage Industry Standards Maintenance Organization, as well as meeting observations, inform the authors' case analysis. The findings emphasize the importance of company and individual incentives to contribute to the process, the formal and informal governance mechanisms used to minimize conflict and develop consensus, and the inclusive and proactive policies regarding membership. Also addressed are the limited scope of standardization activities, an explicit intellectual property rights policy, and efforts to institutionalize the entire standardization process into a formal structure. Discussing implications for theory and practice, the authors pay specific attention to recommendations for policymakers regarding their potential role in the promotion of vertical IS standards development.

This research was funded in part by the National Science Foundation's Digital Society and Technology Program (Award Numbers: 0233634, 0231584, and 0323961). We gratefully acknowledge the support received from the Mortgage Bankers Association of America, the Mortgage Industry Standards Maintenance Organization, the Data Interchange Standards Association, and the unnamed interviewees who provided their insights.

1 Introduction

Information systems (IS) standards – standardized business documents, data definitions, and business processes – have been seen as key to effective interorganizational commerce since the 1980s, when electronic data interchange (EDI) became the technology of choice for business-to-business coordination. Unfortunately, despite much promotion, EDI standards achieved only limited adoption; an estimated 2 percent of the world's businesses (Anonymous 2001b), including just 300,000 US companies (http://www.disa.org), have adopted EDI. Low penetration of electronic interconnection standards, particularly around business semantics (Jain and Zhao 2003), is believed to hinder electronic business and supply-chain integration (Songini 2001).

Recently, the availability of open Internet protocols and technologies, particularly eXtensible Markup Language (XML), has given a boost to both the adoption of EDI (Vollmer 2002) and the development of vertical (that is, industry-specific) XML-based data and process standards (Babcock 2004). Vertical efforts to develop such standards have emerged in electronics (RosettaNet), chemicals (CIDX), insurance (ACORD), petroleum (PIDX), and several other industries. Many observers expect these developments to lower the cost of electronic connection and spur adoption, particularly among smaller firms. Furthermore, many firms view vertical IS standards creation as they would National Public Radio: Larger companies with larger capital bases invest in the creation and maintenance of the standards, while the smaller companies benefit from their adoption.

Despite considerable prior economics research on standards and standardization, many important theoretical and empirical problems remain (Stango 2004). Furthermore, prior literature does not address the aspects of standardization from the perspective of IS research, such as the tendency of companies to modify EDI standards to facilitate doing business with key business partners (Damsgaard and Truex 2000) and the barriers to adoption posed by the companies' legacy IS.

We contribute to the small but important literature on vertical IS standards by presenting a case study of the emergence of electronic interconnection standards in the US home mortgage industry. Owing to the early stage of standards development in that industry, our case focuses on the process of standards development, rather than on the adoption or impacts of standards. Drawing on several streams of theoretical and empirical literature on standard setting processes, we develop a set of research questions to structure our case analysis. We focus on the Mortgage Industry Standards Maintenance Organization (MISMO) and consider questions about (1) how the standardization process is being structured (e.g., what motivates participants, and how are the sometimes competing interests of participants managed?); (2) how adoption of the standard is being promoted (e.g., either through education and training or through changes to preserve participants' competitive positions); and (3) what steps are being taken to ensure the maintenance and integrity of the standard (e.g., formation of a support organization, legal protection, and compliance monitoring).

On the basis of our case analysis, we attempt to draw implications for three different audiences. First, we explore the theoretical implications of our case, highlighting how our findings provide new directions, particularly for IS researchers interested in collective behavior and interorganizational issues. Second, we develop implications for industry practitioners, although these can only be suggestive given our singular focus on the home mortgage industry. To generalize our findings across industries, we draw parallels, particularly to historical cases such as the development of the bar code in the grocery industry. Third and finally, we attempt to draw out implications for the policymaking community by suggesting potential actions that might facilitate broader development and use of interorganizational IS standards that can improve industry performance.

In the following sections, we first define vertical IS standards, review relevant theoretical and empirical literature, and derive a set of research questions to structure the case analysis. After providing an overview of the mortgage industry, MISMO, and the specific vertical IS standards MISMO is developing, we answer our research questions. Lastly, we discuss the implications of our findings for research, practice, and policy.

2 Theoretical background and prior research

Standards are usually defined in the economics literature as "specifications that determine the compatibility of different products" (Stango 2004, 2); an example of such product standards is the Windows operating system. Another type of standard allows adopters to form a communication network (Stango 2004). Here information technology standards can be defined at many levels of abstraction based on the Open System Interconnection model – from the physical connectivity level, through the data link, network, transport, session, and presentation levels, and all the way to the application level. Standards at the presentation and application levels are often referred to as *semantic standards*, while standards below these levels are called *syntactical standards*. The Internet protocol is an example of a syntactical communication network standard; and EDI standards are an example of semantic information systems standards – the type on which we concentrate here. Semantic IS standards can focus on a single industry sector or purport to be applicable across sectors. An example of a cross-industry standard (under development) is electronic business XML (ebXML) (Babcock 2004). Our focus is on industry-specific semantic IS standards, which we refer to as *vertical IS standards*. Vertical IS standards are designed to promote communication and coordination among the organizations comprising a particular industry sector; these standards may address product identification, data definitions, business document layout, and/or business process sequences.

Standards are usually categorized as sponsored (or proprietary) or unsponsored (open) and as de facto or de jure (Stango 2004). Proprietary standards (e.g., Windows) are owned by a company that may license them to others. In contrast, open standards (e.g., MISMO standards) are available to all potential users, usually without fee. In standards research the adoption of open standards is believed to be more problematic than proprietary standards, because the owner of a proprietary standard often has the incentive to subsidize adoption, which is not the case with open standards (Stango 2004). De facto standards achieve adoption through a standards competition (e.g., Windows vs. OS/2); de jure standards achieve adoption through consensus, which is sometimes formally expressed through industry committees or formal standards organizations such as the American National Standards Institute (Stango 2004). De jure standards are rarely proprietary.

These distinctions define the bodies of theory that are relevant to our research. For example, because we are interested in open standards promulgated by industry-wide committees, the sizable economics literature explaining the outcome of standards competitions does not directly apply. In the sections that follow, we briefly review three theoretical perspectives that we believe are relevant to an understanding of the emergence of vertical IS standards: (1) the economics literature on committee-based standardization efforts, (2) the institutional perspective on the process of standardization and (3) the public goods perspective on the standard setting process.

2.1 Committee-based standardization efforts

According to David and Greenstein (1990), standardization occurs through the widespread adoption of four kinds of standards:
1. Standards that exist in the public domain but are not sponsored by an organization with proprietary interest in them (e.g., Linux)
2. Standards that are sponsored by one or more organizations with a proprietary interest (e.g., Windows)
3. Standards that are mandated by government (e.g., the Health Insurance Portability and Accountability Act in the health care industry)
4. Standards that are published by voluntary standard-developing organizations (e.g., the International Standards Organization)

There is reason to believe that standardization through voluntary committees is the most likely route to success for vertical IS standards. As Hills (2000) notes, in the absence of regulation, no standard will actually be adopted unless it fits the needs of the users, and users are in a better position to determine what fits their needs than vendors or outsiders. Because users of vertical IS standards are companies that do business with each other and these companies are of different kinds (e.g., manufacturers and retailers, hospitals and insurance companies), no one user is in a position to design a standard that would meet the needs of all users. Consequently, a voluntary association of industry participants is most likely to succeed in developing an approach to interorganizational coordination that many industry participants would be willing to adopt.

Surprisingly little is known about standardization by committees (David and Greenstein 1990); what research there is generally falls into two categories, namely, how standards committees operate in practice (the structure of decision making, the "rules of engagement" to facilitate reaching agreement) and the strategic behavior of participants attempting to influence the nature of the standard agreed upon. In the specific case of vertical IS standards, the majority of the research has focused on the *adoption* of such standards (e.g., EDI). To our knowledge, only a few case studies (Brown 1997; van Baalen et al. 2000) provide an in-depth look at the processes by which such standards emerge.

2.2 Institutional perspective

In contrast to the economic perspectives, institutional theorists view standards and standards development as institutions or as a form of institution building. Although we may not find a universally accepted definition for the term *institution*, the following description will suffice: "institutions are socially constructed, routine-reproduced (ceteris paribus), program or rule systems. They operate as relative fixtures of constraining environments and are accompanied by taken-for-granted accounts" (Jepperson 1991, 149).

One characteristic of institutions is that they bring order to things. In doing so, they often counter social and organizational uncertainty. They provide context for interorganizational interaction by limiting the available courses of action. According to Jepperson (1991, 146), institutions unify constraint and freedom. In this sense, institutions are reproduced autonomously in that actors (e.g., firms) presume their existence and refer to them. Institutions may influence (indirectly) the actions of actors. Institutional behavioral patterns are perceived as the only way to do things. In time, new institutions replace older institutions. They define the interactions among actors and create the arena or setting in which specific actors meet or make a joint decision about an issue while following certain decision rules (Mayntz and Scharpf 1995).

Vertical IS *standards* can themselves be viewed as institutions that, once adopted, regulate the behavior of industry actors and, possibly, stifle future innovation. But our interest lies in the *process of standardization*, not in the post-adoption impacts of standards. As Mayntz and Scharpf (1995) argue, we believe that the process of vertical IS standardization can be viewed as an institution that guides actors through the uncertain process of collaborating, often with competitors, to fashion a new way of doing business together. For example, rules about who can join the standardization effort and about the handling of intellectual property can be viewed as reducing uncertainty for participants and legitimating standard setting as a normal, taken-for-granted activity.

2.3 Public goods perspective

A third theoretical perspective on vertical IS standards is *public goods theory* (Olson 1965). This theory explains that the inherent character-istic of public goods is such that even if people have not participated in inventing public goods, they cannot be prevented from enjoying them; therefore, public goods are unlikely to be provided. The open source software movement seems to fly in the face of public goods theory; consequently, researchers have begun to explore the collective action literature for clues to why people voluntarily engage in the production of public goods (Markus et al. 2000). For example, recent theoretical and empirical work suggests that public goods theory underestimates the benefits of early contributors to organizational federations such as vertical IS standardization efforts (Monge et al. 1998; Flanagin et al. 2001). Such benefits could come from the opportunity for standards participants to participate in advice networks (Monge et al. 1998; Flanagin et al. 2001).

The relevance of committee-based standardization efforts, the insti-tutional perspective and the public goods perspective on the develop-ment of vertical IS standards is clear in that they are all interconnected. If vertical IS standards are both an institution (which itself is a con-tinually evolving entity) and a public good, then their adoption begs the questions of who joins in this effort at producing standards, how they do it and why. The success of committee-based standardization efforts is problematic because people might lack the motivation to work on developing standards as public goods. Perhaps, however, early contri-butors in vertical IS standards could benefit from the opportunity to use the standard for internal systems integration or as the basis for a new service offering, thus reducing the motivational barriers to participat-ing in standards creation.

2.4 The processes of standards development

A close reading of the empirical literature on vertical IS standard setting processes (Brown 1997; van Baalen et al. 2000) suggests that standards development committees engage in at least three conceptually distinct business processes: (1) *structuring the collaboration*, that is, designing a process that engages participants in the activities of standards crea-tion; (2) *facilitating standards adoption* – for example, educating participants and ensuring that the standard built by the committee has attributes that will favor its adoption; and (3) *maintaining the standard*, that is, providing for the preservation and maintenance of the standard after it is developed. In the sections below, we synthesize the theoretical perspectives of committee-based standards, institutionalism, and public goods to inform our examination of the three standards formation processes.

Structuring the collaboration

Developing a standard that meets the needs of industry participants requires industry players to actually participate in the design of the standard (Xia et al. 2003). Enlisting participation can be difficult because standards have public goods characteristics – companies that do not participate in standards development cannot be prevented from enjoying the benefits of the standard once developed (Olson 1965; Monge et al. 1998; Flanagin et al. 2001). Nor in fact would the committee want to exclude them, since widespread adoption of electronic interconnection standards is essential for significant benefits. Because participation can be quite expensive for organizations in terms of the time spent by key organizational personnel, the risk exists that not enough of the right kinds of organizations and individuals might choose to participate. Thus, it is important to understand what motivates firms and individuals to participate in such efforts.

Additional complications arise when some potential participants in a standardization effort do not participate in a committee-based effort because they believe they will gain greater advantage by going it alone or by developing a proprietary approach they hope will become a de facto standard. Their failure to participate in (or their withdrawal from) a standardization effort can have a chilling effect on the whole cooperative exercise or even cause it to fail (van Baalen et al. 2000).

Even organizations that are willing in principle to participate in standards development may need to be reassured that the effort will be worth their while. Specifically, most organizations would evaluate the costs of participation against the reasonable likelihood that the outcome of the standardization effort would in fact meet the organization's needs, at least in the long run. Therefore, the standardization process would need to be set up in such a way that it could not be easily dominated by a few vested interests.

Promoting standard adoption

The development of a standard does not ensure its adoption, even by the organizations that participate in the process. It is important to note that adopters often face considerable implementation barriers and may fail to implement the standard in ways intended by standards developers. Adopters must know about the standard and have the knowledge and skills they need to adopt it. In many cases, complementary resources must be made available before would-be adopters are in fact able to adopt the standard. In addition, for adoption to be likely, the standard finally agreed upon must meet the adopters' business needs. It must not unduly disadvantage particular companies or segments in their ability to compete. Rather, the standard should provide a level playing field, with adoption creating a common good from which all players benefit. Standard-writing committees must emphasize consensus to ensure broad participation and to satisfy participants' needs, and thus encourage them to adopt (Hills 2000).

But these very strengths can spell some weaknesses. Committees might take longer than markets to arrive at standards, and the standards they produce might be less innovative, in part owing to the committees' need to preserve the competitiveness of industry participants (David and Greenstein 1990). Additionally, although preserving participants' industry positions may promote their adoption of the standard, committees also seem to produce technically more complicated standards (David and Greenstein 1990), perhaps because of the need to preserve backward compatibility with an installed base of technology. Paradoxically, this attribute seems to work *against* widespread adoption of the standard. This line of argument suggests the need to understand the ways in which standards development committees try to ensure that the standard they develop will actually be adopted.

Maintaining the standard

The work of standards developers does not end even when widespread adoption of the standard has been achieved. Although the nature of postadoption processes will vary with circumstances, required activities can include routine administration, updating or extending the standard as technology or needs change, and defending the standard against threats to its existence or success. In this last area, intellectual property threats often come into play, particularly when participating firms attempt to profit from prior patent holdings that were not disclosed during the standards development process. These considerations suggest the need to understand how standards development organizations plan in advance for the ongoing operation and protection of the standard.

2.5 Research questions

The foregoing conceptual framework leads us to the following research questions that we use to structure our case analysis.

1. **How can the process of collaboration on vertical IS standards be structured?**
   a) What motivates organizations and individuals to participate in efforts to create vertical IS standards?
   b) How do governance arrangements in standards development organizations help balance the sometimes competing interests of different industry segments?
2. **How can the adoption of vertical IS standards be promoted?**
   a) What are the actions taken by vertical IS standards development organizations to promote the adoption of the standard?
   b) Does the nature of committee-based vertical IS standards development work to promote adoption by preserving industry structure and participants' competitive positions?
3. **How are vertical IS standards maintained?**
   a) How do vertical IS standards development organizations defend against potential legal threats to the standard?
   b) How do vertical IS standards development organizations defend against the threat of fragmentation or drift caused by participants' reinterpretation of the standard?
   c) What steps do vertical IS standards development organizations take to ensure ongoing governance of the standard?

3 Methods

Evidence to support our case analysis of the standard setting process in the mortgage industry comes from three sources: documents and other archival sources, in-depth interviews, and observation. For the first type of data source, we worked with the primary industry association, the Mortgage Bankers Association of America (MBA), to obtain access to previous internal studies that revealed costs and trends, especially those related to information technology usage, within the mortgage industry. Other data sources for our overview of the mortgage industry include US Census data (US Bureau of the Census 2001) as well as the National Mortgage Association's periodic study results of loan volumes by segment and company. Standards documents, meeting minutes, and other documents available from MISMO further contributed to our case analysis. In addition, we gathered documents at the MBA annual conference on mortgage technology and a trimester meeting of the MISMO Workgroups.

For the second type of source, our primary data collection efforts centered on interviews with key informants involved with mortgage industry standardization activities. We conducted interviews with three people from the MBA (one several times); six additional people active in the standards organization who represented other areas in the residential mortgage value chain – including a government-sponsored enterprise (GSE), a mortgage information and document services provider, a personal mortgage insurer, a mortgage credit reporting company, and two mortgage technology vendors; and three people from the Data Interchange Standards Association (DISA), which served as the secretariat to MISMO and other industries developing vertical IS standards. Interviews were taped and transcribed to facilitate our review and analysis. The names of those interviewed are withheld by mutual consent.

The third critical source of information came from observations and on-site interviews at the two industry meetings we attended: the Mortgage Technology Conference in Orlando, FL (March 2003) and the MISMO Trimester Workgroup Meeting in Dana Point, CA (January 2004). The Technology Conference enabled us to identify key mortgage technology vendors and better understand their role in the standards process. At this meeting we also gained an excellent overview of mortgage industry structure and the importance of information technology in industry participants' strategic positioning. The MISMO Workgroup Meeting allowed us to observe standards activities and governance processes in action, including how the Workgroups made decisions about future standardization efforts.

We hand-coded our interview transcripts for key themes related to our theoretically derived research questions. We also wrote numerous theoretical memos documenting our evolving understanding of key issues. We elaborated our growing understanding through weekly conference calls and periodic face-to-face meetings over the eighteen months we worked on this project. Various versions of this manuscript have been reviewed for factual accuracy by interviewees and other industry experts.

4 Case background

Because every industry is unique, some of the ways in which Internet-related changes play out will vary from industry to industry (Porter 2001). We start with a brief overview of the mortgage industry by highlighting unique structural aspects that may influence the course of the industry's vertical IS standards development process.

4.1 Brief overview of mortgage industry

The US home mortgage industry today is highly fragmented, with thousands of mortgage bankers and brokers, although it is consolidating rapidly. (It is estimated that the top five lenders originate over 50% of residential mortgage loans today and that the top ten firms service over 50% of such loans.) It is also highly vertically disintegrated (Jacobides 2001a), although some analysts claim that it appears to be reintegrating, at least at the top end of the size spectrum (Van Order 2000). Automation and IT-enabled standards appear to be playing an important role in both structural evolutions (Van Order 2000; Jacobides 2001b).

Because of vertical disintegration, most business processes in the mortgage industry require the efforts of more than one organization – a situation that appears to be natural for electronic interchange. But the industry has been slow to adopt technology, and interorganizational standard setting initiatives have made progress only in the last fifteen years. Since the widespread adoption of Internet standards in the past five or so years, the pace of standard setting initiatives and the level of standards adoption in the industry have noticeably increased.

There are two mortgage industry markets: the primary market, where borrowers obtain loans from originators, and the secondary market, where mortgages are sold by originators and bought by investors (Cummings and DiPasquale 1997). The key primary market processes are *origination* (including application and underwriting – which considers the borrowers' credit and property characteristics), *closing and recording* (legal transfer of the property), and *servicing* (receiving payments, managing tax and insurance escrows, monitoring delinquencies, managing foreclosures, and making payments to investors) (Cummings and DiPasquale 1997).

Today, more than half of all mortgages are sold to the secondary market, with the remainder held in portfolio by lending depository institutions (Van Order 2000). There are two paths through which originators sell their loans to the secondary market: (1) directly to investors who hold loans in portfolio and (2) to a conduit who packages and securitizes the loans and sells interests in the securities to investors (Cummings and DiPasquale 1997). Most frequently, the conduits to the secondary market for residential mortgages are GSEs, which are private corporations that are chartered by a federal government mandate to create and grow the secondary mortgage market through securitization (Cummings and DiPasquale 1997). The two prominent GSEs in this market are Fannie Mae and Freddie Mac. The GSEs have grown rapidly into major players: Roughly 50% of the $6.3 trillion (2003 figure) in outstanding US mortgage debt for single-family residences is either held in portfolio by GSEs or is held by investors in the form of mortgage-backed securities guaranteed by GSEs (Cummings and DiPasquale 1997). Both the perceived and real power and privileges of these companies (e.g., they are exempt from Securities and Exchange Commission reporting requirements) generate considerable controversy (McKinnon and Kopecki 2003). The GSEs require their very own oversight body (Office of Federal Housing Enterprise Oversight) and also were recently required to undergo Congressional reviews.

In addition to the GSEs, the MBA has been a major force for standardization in the mortgage lending industry. Founded in 1914, the MBA is the leading industry association for companies in the commercial and residential real estate finance business, the largest segment of the US capital market. Its approximately 3,600 members cover all industry segments, including mortgage lenders, mortgage brokers, thrifts, mortgage insurance companies, and many types of software companies. The MBA represents the industry's legislative and regulatory interests and conducts educational activities and research for its members.

4.2 History of MISMO standardization effort

The origins of MISMO probably lie in the "electronic data initiative" launched by the MBA in the late 1980s to support the automation of interagency mortgage lending processes (Opelka 1994). In 1988, an article in *American Banker* reported that an MBA task force of fifteen member companies had concluded that streamlining mortgage lending could reduce processing time by as much as 50 percent: "Among the changes the report recommends are standardized loan applications and underwriting terms, EDI, uniform appraisal guidelines, and uniform secondary market procedures" (see Trigaux 1988, 3). Since then, the MBA has been working at this agenda one step at a time.

Working with Fannie Mae and Freddie Mac, the MBA's first targets were paper forms such as mortgage applications and appraisal forms (Anonymous 1988; Braitman 1990; Hershkowitz 1992). Next on the agenda was EDI. In 1990,

the MBA mortgage data standards tasks force "submitted three transaction sets for adoption as standard: the residential loan application, the private mortgage insurance application and the request for credit reports. It has been the third party providers of services to the industry that have been among the earliest to see the potential importance of EDI in the industry." (Lebowitz 1990, 83)

EDI standardization efforts proceeded over the next few years (Slesinger 1994). In 1994, the MBA set aside $20,000 for an industry-wide survey of the current and planned use of EDI (Campbell 1994). In the meantime, the GSEs pursued proprietary technology efforts, including automated underwriting systems, electronic partner networks, and other tools: For example, Pizzo (1994, 12) forecast that, "[t]he Fannie Mae financial network will have at its core a group of proprietary software products that virtually hard-wire customers to Fannie's mainframe."

As in many other industries, EDI was adopted by the larger companies in the mortgage industry; smaller companies generally found EDI cost prohibitive and declined to participate. This low level of EDI penetration was especially problematic in the mortgage industry because the industry is so fragmented: Even the largest mortgage lenders deal with many small service providers. The lack of a low-cost technology for interconnection held the industry back, despite its progress toward data standardization.

With the coming of the Internet, the economics of interconnection began to change; XML promised a low-cost solution to the interconnection dilemma. Mortgage industry EDI Workgroups began to discuss the potential of XML. Then, in January 2000, the MBA, in partnership with Fannie Mae, Freddie Mac, and other industry participants, launched MISMO (see http://www.mismo.org), which was established to coordinate the development and maintenance of vendor-neutral XML-based transaction specifications to support data sharing among the many participants in the mortgage lending processes. Pronounced, the acronym MISMO is the Spanish word for *the same* – indeed a fitting name for a standards development organization.

MISMO can be viewed as two standardization efforts in parallel. The first effort concerns data standards for various mortgage transactions related to loan origination, secondary marketing, servicing, and real estate services. Examples of such transactions include application, closing, and underwriting for origination; bulk pool transfer, commitment, and funding for secondary marketing; cash transactions, credit reporting, and default management for servicing; and appraisal, credit, and escrow and settlement for real estate services. This standard setting activity is quite similar to EDI standard setting, although the technology of choice today is XML, which is itself a horizontal standard, similar to TCP/IP.

The third major release of the MISMO data standards is currently under development. Version 1 started from the core concept of an electronic loan package. Data elements from various segments (credit, mortgage insurance, title, appraisal, etc.) were developed separately with the idea that they could then be merged into a loan package. Many participants thought this starting point was limited because it did not specify the actual interorganizational transactions (Bixby and Alvord 2004). Version 2, published in mid-2001, employed the core metaphor of the transaction. But this version has the drawback of not consolidating all the information needed for a single loan. Version 3 is expected to be some blend of the two (Bixby and Alvord 2004). A major achievement of the data standardization effort to date is a data dictionary of over 3,600 elements with business definitions and corresponding XML data element tag names and a reference data model to illustrate the relationships among the data elements in the dictionary. An excerpt from the data dictionary showing several elements from the automated underwriting specifications section is provided in Table 5.1.

The second MISMO standardization effort concerns standards to enable fully electronic mortgages, from initial application, through closing and recording, and then through sale into the secondary market and transfer of mortgage servicing rights. In January 2001, MISMO launched its e-Mortgage Workgroup. The passage of the Uniform Electronic Transactions Act in 1999 and the Electronic Signatures in Global and National Commerce Act in 2000 had made it possible to envision a mortgage-lending process that produces legally binding mortgages entirely without paper. These laws provide that electronic signatures can be used wherever existing law requires a "wet" signature.

To accomplish fully electronic mortgages, the e-Mortgage Workgroup developed "SMART docs," or Secure, Manageable, Archivable, Retrievable, and Transferable documents that lock data and document presentation into a single computerized file by using the underlying data formats of XML (for data transfer) and XHTML (a combination of Hypertext Markup Language – HTML and XML, for document presentation). Standards for SMART docs ensure that information is transferred in a form that is readable both by computers and by humans, thereby enabling the requirements for filing with county recorders' offices to be met along with those of the GSEs and investors.

The SMART doc contains three sections: (1) a header section comprised of metadata indicating the document type, version, and other information about the elements in the document; (2) a data section with the raw data tagged with MISMO's document type definitions, such as the borrower's name and address, as well as tags that format and verify the data elements, as well as link them to the appropriate entries in the view section; and (3) a view section, which is the actual presentation of the document in HTML, Portable Document Format (PDF) or other viewable format (Gudobba 2003). Figures 5.1 and 5.2 provide an illustration of the SMART doc structure.

5 Findings about the mortgage industry's vertical IS standardization process

In this section we discuss the answers to our research questions about each of the three processes that standards development organizations

Table 5.1. Excerpt from MISMO's automated underwriting specifications (AUS) logical data dictionary (LDD)

Processes included in this dictionary: AUS

Name	Description	Source	Context	Processes	Data type
Additional Borrower Assets Considered Indicator	The income or assets of a person other than the borrower (including the borrower's spouse) will be used as a basis for loan qualification.	URLA	Loan Qualification	Underwriting, AUS	Boolean
Additional Borrower Assets Not Considered Indicator	The income or assets of the borrower's spouse will not be used as a basis for loan qualification, but his or her liabilities must be considered because the borrower resides in a community property state, the security property is located in a community property state, or the borrower is relying on other property located in a community property state as a basis for repayment of the loan.	URLA	Loan Qualification	Underwriting, AUS	Boolean
Agency Case Identifier	The FHA-assigned case number for FHA loans or VA-assigned case number for VA loans. The number is used by the FHA or VA to identify a loan. Collected on the URLA in Section I (Agency Case Number).	URLA	Mortgage Terms	Underwriting, AUS	String

| Alimony Child Support Obligation Indicator | Borrower's declaration regarding obligations for alimony, child support, etc. Collected on the URLA in Section VIII line g. | URLA | Declaration | Credit Reporting, Underwriting, AUS | Boolean |

SMART Doc Overview

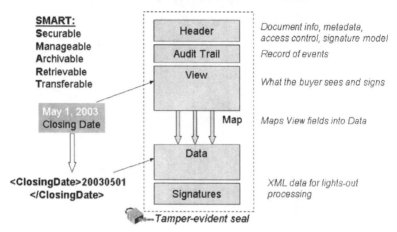

Figure 5.1. SMART doc structure (copyright 2001 Mortgage Bankers Association of America, Inc. Permission to use, copy, modify, and distribute the MISMO LDD and its accompanying documentation for any purpose and without fee is hereby granted in perpetuity, provided that the above copyright notice and this paragraph appear in all copies. The copyright holders make no representation about the suitability of the LDD for any purpose).

engage in: structuring the standardization effort, promoting standards adoption, and planning for standards maintenance.

5.1 Structuring the process

Our concern in this section is with how MISMO structured the process of standards development – how it marshaled the energies of participants and managed the sometimes competing interests of various industry segments.

Harnessing participants' motivations

The motivations of two types of participants are relevant to vertical IS standardization efforts: organizations (including both technology vendors and users) and individuals. We start with the organizations.

HTML View:

Recording Requested By:
Branch One Title

Return To:
William S Grant
65874 Main Street

San Diego California 55558

Prepared By:
Patrick Hartford

6548 Maple Grove
Irvine California90807
——————————— [Space Above This Line For Recording Data] ———————————
DEED OF TRUST

DEFINITIONS
Words used in multiple sections of this document are defined below and other words are defined in Sections
3, 11, 13, 18, 20 and 21. Certain rules regarding the usage of words used in this document are also provided
in Section 16.

(A) **"Security Instrument"** means this document, which is dated 10/07/03, together with all Riders to this
document.
(B) **"Borrower"** is Patrick L. Smith, .

Data View:

XPath	Raw Data	Formatted Data
/LOAN/_APPLICATION/LOAN_PRODUCT_DATA/LOAN_FEATURES/@LoanMaturityDat	20331007	10/07/33
/LOAN/_APPLICATION/MORTGAGE_TERMS/@LenderLoanIdentifier	999-75	999-75
/LOAN/_APPLICATION/MORTGAGE_TERMS/@OriginalLoanAmount	150000.00	150,000.00
/LOAN/_APPLICATION/PROPERTY/@_StreetAddress	18050 15 Mile Road	18050 15 Mile Road
/LOAN/_APPLICATION/PROPERTY/@_City	Fraser	Fraser
/LOAN/_APPLICATION/PROPERTY/@_PostalCode	48026	48026
/LOAN/_APPLICATION/PROPERTY/@AssessorsParcelIdentifier		
/LOAN/_APPLICATION/PROPERTY/_LEGAL_DESCRIPTION/@_TextDescription		
/LOAN/_APPLICATION/PROPERTY/_DETAILS/@RecordingJurisdictionName		
/LOAN/_APPLICATION/PROPERTY/_DETAILS/@RecordingJurisdictionType		
/LOAN/_APPLICATION/BORROWER/@_FirstName	Gary	Gary
/LOAN/_APPLICATION/BORROWER/@_MiddleName	R	R
/LOAN/_APPLICATION/BORROWER/@_LastName	Smith	Smith
/LOAN/_APPLICATION/BORROWER/@_NameSuffix	Sr.	Sr.

XML View:

```
<?xml version="1.0" ?>
- <SMART_DOCUMENT _ID="MD01" MISMOVersionIdentifier="1.0"
    PopulatingSystemDocumentIdentifier="VMP_20031015T171046Z">
  - <HEADER _ID="Head01">
      <DOCUMENT_INFORMATION SMARTDocumentCategoryType="1"
        _FormNumberIdentifier="3005" _Type="SecurityInstrument"
        _StateType="Signable" NegotiableInstrumentIndicator="False"
        MustBeRecordedIndicator="False" _Name="California Deed of Trust" />
    - <SIGNATURE_MODEL>
        <SIGNER SectionIDREF="View01Borrower" AreaIDREF="BorrowerSig1"
```

Figure 5.2. Illustration of the three views of a SMART doc in a "California
Deed of Trust" (source: VMP Mortgage Solutions 2004).

Why companies participate

To some extent, the question of why organizations participate in the development of MISMO standards is unremarkable: Many companies participate in MISMO because they previously participated in the EDI standardization initiatives in their industry segment. But the larger question here is why companies believe it is in their interests to participate in any vertical IS standardization effort. After all, in some industries, companies have declined to participate on the grounds of competitive advantage. For example, Wal-Mart has been reported as being unwilling to join e-business interconnection hubs because its participation would dilute the huge advantage that the company gains from deploying proprietary systems (Laudon and Traver 2003).

In the mortgage industry, the perceived benefits and risks of participating in standard setting vary by segment. Traditional mortgage products are increasingly commodified, so competition is shifting to low prices (for a few particularly efficient producers), the development of innovative products and services, and the creation of distinctive service and relationship advantages. Vertical IS standards enable efficiencies that help companies reduce their costs; at the same time, collaborating on EDI or MISMO data standards does not threaten other bases of competitive advantage. Therefore, barriers to companies' participation in these standard setting efforts are low. As noted by one interviewee from the mortgage insurance sector, collaboration on data standards would help streamline industry business practices since "we all need the same data to do our business and so there's no reason to try to compete on data. [We] compete on service" (M. F., September 16, 2003). In another mortgage industry segment – credit – competition has historically centered on data presentation, such as the unique layout of a bureau's credit reports. According to interviewees, format-centered competition initially formed a barrier to data standardization efforts in that segment. Nevertheless, the credit segment was an early participant in both EDI standards and MISMO. Regardless of sector, the participants we interviewed were unanimous in the belief that the standardization effort works because "we do not compete on data."

The absence of barriers to participation in standard setting efforts is not the same as a positive incentive to participate. And positive incentives do exist. For example, although MISMO standards are expressly intended for interorganizational interconnection, some large companies with diverse lines of business or nonintegrated legacy systems have already benefited from using MISMO standards for *internal* integration, according to an interviewee from MISMO (C. A., October 2, 2003). This is an example of what Liebowitz and Margolis (1998) call autarky (or stand-alone) benefits from a network technology, which can help overcome the critical mass needed for adoption.

Another direct benefit of participation is that "standards tend to be oriented towards the individual companies that contributed their time to developing them" (L. A., September 30, 2003). During MISMO meetings, discussions usually start with a participant volunteering his or her company's business data types as a model from which standard data elements can be identified. Naturally, some of the finalized standards bear a resemblance to those models. Even without serving as a model, participants in discussions can make sure that the standard meets their data needs. For example, an interviewee from one of the GSEs explained that one transaction set contains some XML tags with a designation from his company that represents unique data requirements not shared by the other GSE (C. A., October 2, 2003).

Other interviewees explained that participating in the EDI and MISMO standardization efforts created new business opportunities for their companies. One systems expert we interviewed (L. A., September 30, 2003) noted that his formerly small company benefited greatly from his early and prominent participation in the data standardization effort because it increased his company's visibility in the industry, which resulted in rapid growth. This example is reminiscent of arguments that the opportunity to participate in, advise, or influence networks is a benefit that motivates participation in the creation of public goods (Monge et al. 1998; Flanagin et al. 2001).

Another type of business opportunity was described by an interviewee from a mortgage document preparation company (Q. F., October 2, 2003): The e-Mortgage standards plausibly have the potential to disintermediate document preparation companies. The interviewee, however, claimed to be unworried about that possibility, because constant change in the industry had made his company nimble, and the company was constantly on the lookout for new opportunities – some of which arose during the data standardization effort. The company developed a viewer for e-Mortgage SMART docs (analogous to the Abode Acrobat reader for PDF documents); the reader was given away free to companies in the industry, but a more functional software product was available for sale.

In summary, companies reported receiving a variety of benefits from their participation in data standardization efforts. But the expectation of benefits is only part of the story about why companies participate. In many ways, the more interesting story is why individuals participate, often on their own time.

Why individuals participate

According to MISMO's operating policies, each company is expected to pay the travel expenses for its own MISMO delegates. But company financial support for travel is only part of the cost. It is the individual participants who must travel to meetings and manage MISMO activities in addition to their regular jobs. Consultants who participate in MISMO may not be able to bill clients for the time they spend on MISMO activities. Although there may be an eventual payoff in "business development," in the short term, MISMO participation competes with fee-generating work.

In light of these personal costs, we found it surprising that some participants are heavily involved and have been for years (including the earlier EDI efforts). Industry insiders speak of the "same ten (or twelve) people" who seem to be involved in every activity. Many of the people we interviewed for this study were identified to us as belonging to this group; they serve on multiple work groups and often hold leadership roles. Although they are empathically supportive of MISMO's efforts, they are also quite clear about the personal costs and motives for participating. To illustrate personal costs, one interviewee described the effort as being "like a night job on top of our day job" (K. A., September 30, 2003). Another interviewee revealed the importance of personal motives when he explained, "I was more or less participating on my own time just because it was something I was interested in" (L. A., September 30, 2003). It is clear from these comments that participation in MISMO cannot be fully explained by company motivations. Personal and social factors also play a key role. People may become involved out of personal interest, but they stay involved because they become committed to the cause or to each other. When personal motivations are compatible with organizational goals, all goes well. But sometimes they do not: For example, a key player in the bar code standardization effort devoted so much time to creating the public good that he eventually lost his job (Brown 1997).

Management of competing interests

From the discussion above, it is clear that MISMO (with the help of its participants) has created a structure that is capable of marshaling the efforts of volunteers from various parts of the industry around the design of the standard. But such voluntary efforts are fragile structures, vulnerable to threats from the competing interests of a diverse membership. This raises the question of how MISMO can prevent conflicts of interest and cope with them when they arise. At least three factors can be identified: (1) MISMO's explicit scope of effort, (2) MISMO's formal governance mechanisms, and (3) social give and take.

MISMO's explicit scope

Two key decisions early in MISMO's history have proved critical in limiting divisive conflicts that could cause the process to fail. First, MISMO standardization efforts focused on the data needed for *inter*organizational processes; data needed only for *intra*organizational processes was defined as out of scope. According to a prominent MISMO staff member we interviewed, the rational for this focus was to allow companies to "keep their own proprietary formats ... [and only] invoke the standard when exporting data to other firms" (C. L., May 28, 2003).

Second, MISMO limited its efforts to specifying *data* standards rather than trying to specify *process* standards as well (Markus 2000), as had been done in several other industries, such as electronics and chemicals. Admittedly, there is a fine line between specifying the data needed for a business process and specifying the process itself. In either case, one must start with the process – what needs to be done – to arrive at what data to include. Process standardization begins to encroach upon service, which is the basis for industry competition; so, to avoid this pitfall, MISMO remained scrupulous in its focus on data.

In addition, MISMO focused on data alone because, as one interviewee reported, early attempts to develop a process standard were challenged by one of the participating technology vendors that felt it had a patent covering that particular process (C. A., October 2, 2003). As a result of the threatened patent legislation, two steps were taken to forestall future conflicts. First, MISMO developed its Intellectual Property Rights Policy, which we discuss in detail in a later section. Second, although data standards discussions often start with example processes of participant firms, MISMO determined that the resulting

standard must not delineate a specific firm's protocol. As one inter-
viewee stated, "we just have to be careful that you will never see 'do A,
B, C, D, E, F, G in this order' as a MISMO specification" (C. A.,
October 2, 2003).

MISMO governance
The formal governance of MISMO is a second way to manage potentially conflicting interests. In particular, a key concern is to ensure
participation from all segments of the industry and from both large
and small companies, so that the effort is seen as truly representing the
needs of all industry players. The entire governance structure of
MISMO is set up to fulfill this goal.

Membership in MISMO is voluntary and open to all, regardless of
company size or the specific segment of the mortgage industry value
chain within which a company operates. MISMO is subdivided into a
number of Workgroups reflecting every aspect of the mortgage industry value chain, as well as Workgroups focusing on foundational data
definition standards. Participants in MISMO can join the Workgroups
of their choice and participate in all activities except the leadership
positions, which are filled in annual elections held by subscriber organizations (organizations that pay a membership fee annually to support
MISMO).

To ensure a fair and efficient process, Workgroups are required to
follow published agendas. A code of conduct published on MISMO's
website defines conflicts of interest and acceptable behavior, particularly with regard to potential violations of antitrust regulations.
Members are reminded at each meeting that industry associations
such as MISMO are perfectly legal but that discussions of such things
as rates, terms, prices, and conditions of service are not. Members are
encouraged to raise any concerns they might have about the direction
of discussion in MISMO meetings.

Individual Workgroups go even further to promote open commu-
nication. For example, at the January 30, 2004 MISMO meeting in
Dana Point, CA, the Architecture Workgroup presented and discussed
the following rules to guide their deliberations:
• No issue is over until the final vote
  ○ New facts appear daily
  ○ Interim votes give guidance to the path to be followed
• Will seek consensus, if not possible, then vote as a last resort

- Everyone deserves respect
- Everyone has a contribution
- Freedom to speak your mind
- Seek Nash equilibrium
  ○ Enlightened self interest
  ○ Practical acceptance vs. theoretical purity

The MISMO Governance Committee oversees the organization and gives final authorization for changes in the standards architecture after reviewing the recommendations of the relevant Workgroup. The governance committee reflects a balance between large and small players, as well as the breadth of the mortgage industry value chain. Seats on the governance committee, which is elected by the full membership, are provided to lenders, servicers, GSEs, insurers, credit reporters, and technology vendors representing different industry segments. In addition, the MBA has nonvoting seats on the committee, which reflects its role as neutral facilitator.

MISMO holds three in-person meetings per year and periodic interim meetings. The costs of participation are minimized by limiting the number of in-person meetings; instead, MISMO relies on the use of listservs, teleconferences, and electronic balloting. Hence, smaller firms are not kept out of the process by steep participation costs. Email notifications of upcoming votes are sent out, and electronic balloting ensures that each company can influence election outcomes. MISMO operates on a "one company, one vote" process, both for elections to committee governance positions and for actual standards submissions and change requests. In other words, each member company gets only one vote regardless of the number of representatives from that company. Moreover, the costs of using MISMO standards are minimized by making specifications freely available – even to non-participants – through downloadable documents available on the MISMO website.

Informal give and take
Structures alone cannot bear the full burden of managing potentially conflicting interests. Just as the proof of the pudding is in the eating, the proof of a governance structure lies in how it operates in practice. Interviewees explained that the standardization process was sometimes contentious at two levels: which interorganizational processes were addressed in which order, and which data elements were included

and in which transaction set. Generally, these questions were resolved informally by consensus or by the same commonsense norms of interaction that are useful in any volunteer effort.

Interviewees agreed that the ideal way to resolve conflicts of all types was via consensus. And, with the long-standing social relationships among the same ten people smoothing the way, MISMO participants generally try for consensus. Deciding which data elements belong in a transaction set is fairly easy to resolve by consensus, since, as one interviewee noted, "[I]f somebody needs a piece of data, we're all going to take it" (M. F., September 16, 2003). However, deciding on which transaction to work on next can be a bit more contentious. Here, the solution is different, but inherently simple – rely on volunteers. If enough people indicate their willingness to work on a transaction, then it will be addressed by the group. If not, then the transaction is left out.

Self-determined participation and volunteerism is a great rule for fairly allocating volunteer effort, but it does have drawbacks. First, some people may want to work on a transaction, while others may not believe it is in their interests to standardize that transaction. Second, important processes may not be addressed if participants from those processes are lacking. For example, this appears to have happened in the hazard insurance domain. As one interviewee reported, "[T]he lenders say they want hazard industry data standards, but there hasn't been enough participation from the hazard insurance industry, the people who really know the data" (L. A., September 30, 2003). We will discuss in a later section how these issues work themselves out and their implications for adoption.

Intraorganizational conflict

Intriguingly, there is one area of conflicting interests for which MISMO has no satisfactory answer – conflict over standards *within* the companies participating in standards development. One MISMO insider explained that is common for participants from the same firm to have different interests regarding what the standard should be (C. L., May 28, 2003). In one example, conflicting opinions regarding the structure of data elements surfaced between those in a mortgage-lending firm responsible for loan origination and those who processed loans for sale.

A consequence of such conflict is that a company's participation in standard setting does not ensure that the company will adopt the standard eventually built. Participants in standard setting often must fill the role of internal change agent by selling the standard to their own companies. Because participation in standard setting does not assure adoption, we next consider the role of the standards development organization and the standard itself in facilitating the standard's adoption.

5.2 MISMO and standards adoption

To promote adoption of the standard, MISMO has not only engaged in substantial communication and educational efforts but has also worked behind the scenes to enlist powerful supporters to help over-come barriers to adoption. In the areas of communication and educa-tion, MISMO's efforts are substantial. Sessions are devoted in every MBA national conference and mortgage technology conference to providing updates on MISMO's progress. The MISMO website con-tains much publicly available information as well as protected resources for subscribers. Also, MISMO's efforts are regularly reported in leading industry publications such as *Mortgage Banking* and *Mortgage Technology Magazine*.

In addition to these public efforts, MISMO insiders have worked hard to ensure the commitment of the GSEs, which have long pursued proprietary technology initiatives. In the terms of one interviewee, the MBA built "moral suasion" for the standardization process (C. L., May 28, 2003). Perhaps the biggest boost to the adoption of MISMO standards occurred when the GSEs agreed to support them in July 2001 (Anonymous 2001a). News accounts confirm the significance of GSE support, not only for MISMO's data standards, but also for its e-Mortgage initiatives:

Fannie Mae has opened the door to widespread origination of paperless mortgages with the release of its formal requirements for lenders ... Fannie says its rules will not create dual business processes by mirroring many of today's selling servicing requirements. Further, it said the requirements will conform to the Mortgage Bankers Association of America's Mortgage Industry Standards Maintenance Organization SmartDoc data format. (Anonymous 2002)

Gaining the GSEs' commitment was critical because, had these powerful organizations decided to go their own way with information technology, any industry-wide standardization effort would provide much less benefit to members. And although strong support by the GSEs might smack of undue influence, it also removes a major barrier to the widespread adoption of the standards.

Efforts by MISMO to secure standards adoption have not been limited to moral suasion. Like the committee that developed the bar code, MISMO has had to involve itself in the details of many complementary changes (e.g., in technology or business processes) that would be required for the standard to be successfully adopted. The eNote registry is a prime example. Because many digital copies of an electronic mortgage are likely to exist, uncertainty about who holds the authoritative copy could be a deterrent to adoption. To address this problem, MBA released requirements for an eNote registry in March 2003 that would track the location and the owner or controller of electronically originated and closed mortgage notes (Anonymous 2003).

The goal of committee-based standardization efforts is not just to produce standards but also to ensure that the standards are adopted. Therefore, a large part of the work of standards committees is to select standard characteristics, not just for technical goodness, but also for implementability. Nevertheless, the outcomes of consensus decision-making processes are inherently emergent; as a result, standards may have characteristics that work either for or against eventual adoption. Although it is too early in the MISMO initiative to predict adoption success and impacts, we examine certain standards characteristics that have the potential to either favor or inhibit adoption.

Characteristics that might favor adoption
A key early decision was that the MISMO standards would not merely identify needed data elements, but also define and rationalize them. In previous EDI efforts, the meaning of data elements was often incorrectly assumed to be commonly understood; as a result, pairs of trading partners reinterpreted the terms, which led to standards drift (Damsgaard and Truex 2000). Furthermore, there was no guarantee that proceeding with one transaction set at a time would result in a parsimonious set of business terms. The same data element differently named or similar terms with the same name could be used in several transaction sets, making it very expensive to develop software that supports the standard.

Our interviewees were unanimous that MISMO's greatest achievement to date has been its data dictionary with rigorously defined and standardized terms. When each working group comes forward with a proposed transaction set, the set is scrutinized by MISMO's core data group to enforce consistent naming and avoid unnecessary duplication. Even so, the lexicon is large, containing over 3,600 business terms.

In addition to improving data quality, MISMO's data dictionary reduces developers' cost of implementing the standard in software. One interviewee reported that the consistent naming convention used in the data dictionary made it much easier to write software that integrated across different transactions (Q. F., October 2, 2003). In the mortgage industry, where technology adoption has historically lagged others, the increased availability of low-cost software to support MISMO standards should certainly promote the standard's adoption.

Independently of the payoffs for developers and subsequent adopters, there is enough flexibility in the standard setting process to allow participants to meet their needs in ways that increase the likelihood that they will adopt the standards. For example, one interviewee explained that the GSEs wanted to pursue a certain transaction set – investor reporting – but that the affected software vendors were reluctant to participate for fear that the proposed changes would negatively influence their revenue (I. L., September 16, 2003). The basic concern was that their contract required them to maintain compliance with GSE standards, so if a new transaction were added to the standard, software vendors would be forced to implement it without being able to gain from additional charges. However, participants found a way to put the data needed by the GSEs into another transaction set, addressing both the GSEs' and vendors' interests.

Characteristics that might inhibit adoption

Other aspects of the MISMO standard might have a less positive or even a negative impact on adoption. Consensus-based standard setting processes are hostages to those who participate and devote their time and effort to develop the standards. When key stakeholders do not participate, either an important piece of the standard does not get built, or it gets built in ways that do not meet the needs of the absent group.

We previously mentioned that the failure of hazard insurers to participate in MISMO has delayed the tackling of hazard insurance transactions. Another instance of low participation has led to even less desirable results. Several interviewees commented that mortgage lenders have been underrepresented at MISMO meetings (I. L., September 16, 2003; K. A., September 30, 2003). Several reasonable explanations for their absence were offered. Large lenders were early adopters of EDI and might be satisfied with their existing approaches to interorganizational data exchange. As a group, lenders have been well served by the technology products offered by GSEs and software vendors. They simply might not see the benefit of XML standards, or they might not see the business issues inherent in standardization; accordingly they might be content to allow their interests to be represented by their software vendors.

Interviewees deplored the low participation of the mortgage lenders and argued that their failure to participate has had less-than-optimal results (I. L., September 16, 2003; K. A., September 30, 2003). Their concern was that the resulting standard might not be adopted or might have negative consequences if it were to be adopted. In particular, without heavy influence from lenders who are involved in a variety of different aspects of the mortgage process, the more numerous vendors, who focus on specific transaction subsets, were able to vote to treat each transaction independently. As one interviewee explains, the standard took on a "stovepipe view of the world, where we're not going to have an origination data structure that's broad enough to be used in all different transactions" (I. L., September 16, 2003). Vendors were more interested in having each transaction set fit their own precise needs, even though this was less than optimal from the lenders' perspective. Fortunately, the version of the architecture currently under development is giving the participants the opportunity to revisit that decision.

Even without an absence of participation by a critical stakeholder group, the outcome of standards discussions can be unnecessarily complex and hence unfavorable for adoption, because committee-based standardization efforts tend to preserve the competitive interests of the participants. One interviewee gave the vivid example of the (in his view) unnecessarily complex three-part e-Mortgage SMART doc (see Figures 5.1 and 5.2). One part contains the data, a second part maps the data into the viewable third part and verifies that the data in the view is consistent with the underlying data section, and a third part is the generated viewable document. According to this participant, a simpler and easier-to-implement solution exists but was not adopted because the simpler solution would have worked against the interests of certain industry participants. He had proposed a two-part document structure, with one section being XML data and a second section being an Extensible Stylesheet Language Transformation (XSLT) form that contains the instructions to generate the output. However, his proposal lost support when he said that this would simplify the process by allowing browser software to generate reports rather than the specialized software prepared by document preparation companies. It would have, in effect, eliminated the value added by these companies, and threatened their role in the home mortgage value chain (L. A., September 30, 2003).

Other participants disagreed that the decision was made on the basis of such political considerations. Publications and presentations of the SMART Doc Focus Group argue that because XSLT is a programming language with conditional statements, the potential exists for fraud or error that could creep in without proper validations (e.g., different loan amounts could be computed each time a document is generated).

The MISMO working group needs to resolve how an XSLT stylesheet will be validated and how standard conversions will be performed in XSLT. Validation and consistently generated conversions will ensure that what was seen on the computer screen the first time is immutably the same as those generated at a later date. (MISMO 2004a, 5)

Consequently, the majority of Workgroup members believed that it was simpler to provide an explicit link between the "data" and the "view" parts of the SMART doc (via the third part, the arc map) than to eliminate the redundancy of information in the two parts by using XSLT.

The interviewee who proposed the XSLT solution now believes that change in the industry will eventually occur, it will just take time. He observes, "I'm involved [too]: my livelihood comes from the inefficiencies of the industry. [Eventually, MISMO standards will be a] catalyst for bigger and bigger changes" (L. A., September 30, 2003). In the meantime, however, the concern remains that the complexity of the three-part e-Mortgage standard might hinder adoption, as is evidenced by another interviewee who felt that the SMART doc framework was quite complicated and would have preferred a simpler structure at the start to keep the costs down (K. A., September 30, 2003).

5.3 MISMO standards maintenance

The need for standards development organizations often continues well after widespread adoption of the standard. Especially where vertical IS standards are concerned, numerous "environmental" changes – technology changes, for example – can call for the need to update or revise the standard. For MISMO, plans to explore the future use of Schema in the data domain and of XSL in the e-Mortgage standards is an example of just such a technology change.

Business needs also can change. New mortgage products might be developed that require new data elements to be defined and added to the data dictionary. In addition, the history of the bar code shows that vertical IS standards can be vulnerable to a variety of threats, such as legal challenges or gradual erosion as companies try to customize the standard to their individual needs.

We now examine how MISMO (1) addresses the potential threats of legal challenges, (2) responds to possible threats of fragmentation and (3) plans for its continued existence.

Defense against legal challenges

Although MISMO did not initially have a comprehensive policy for the protection of intellectual property rights (IPR), after a threatened lawsuit (that fortunately never materialized), it was clear IPR was a topic that could no longer be ignored. After MISMO considered and rejected several IPR approaches used by other collaborative ventures (such as the "copyleft" license of the Open Source movement), MISMO opted for a royalty-free license approach to IPR. All companies participating in MISMO activities were bound by an IPR agreement that (1) required each company to pay for its own people's time on the project, (2) required each company to license any contributions to MISMO free of charge, and (3) allowed MISMO to derive products from the companies' contributions and make these products available to others (i.e., to sublicense them) via the Web or other means.

These provisions were expressly designed to prevent companies from pursuing a "submarine patent" approach, whereby participants file for their own business process patents while waiting for the technologies to reach a point at which they can be implemented. Then, once other companies attempt to implement the standard, the opportunistic patent filer can claim royalties on what was supposed to have been an open and freely available standard. Thus, MISMO proactively implemented its IPR approach to prevent undisclosed and submarine patents from surfacing (MISMO 2004b).

Defense against fragmentation

A more frequent threat against MISMO standards is likely to be the risk that companies would modify the standard to fit their own needs, thus diluting the standard. This certainly happened with EDI (Damsgaard and Truex 2000), and it could happen with XML data standards as well. Contributing to the tendency could be the inherent flexibility of XML – the ability to add new data elements without significant rework. As one interviewee noted, a key benefit of XML is that it affords any company the ability to add extra data elements to suit its particular needs in any given transaction (Q. F., October 2, 2003). This can create problems, however, if numerous companies need those same extra fields, and they all add them, but they each call them something else. Although the original data elements would remain standardized, the new ones would not. Like any living language, new terms are occasionally added to industry lexicons, and MISMO needs to provide for standards evolution.

One interviewee explained how the need to respond quickly to business changes without creating burdensome changes for their customers led companies in the mortgage insurance industry to try to tweak the existing standards rather than rewrite them from scratch when business needs change. But as he further noted, simple tweaking may not be enough to meet all needs and other groups may choose to start over completely (I. L., September 16, 2003).

Not only is the maintenance of the MISMO data standards an ongoing activity, but so is the effort required to test products (e.g., new software) for compliance with the standard. Not surprisingly, the question of compliance testing has become an urgent item on the agenda at MISMO meetings. For instance, in the January 2004 meeting of the Origination Workgroup, participants debated various issues such as the following:

- Should compliance be judged in relationship only to required extensions of the standard or also to optional extensions?
- Should compliance be assessed on an annual basis (versus periodic or permanent) or only with respect to specific software versions?
- Should compliance be evaluated at the logical database level, the transaction level, or some other level?
- How much should be charged for compliance testing?
- How compliance should be tested, for example, by a test suite that runs behind the scenes.

A permanent organization

The ongoing needs for standard extension, compliance testing, and protection of the standard against various external threats are a strong argument for the formation of a permanent organization. In the January 2004 MISMO meetings, preliminary plans were unveiled for setting up a permanent 501(c)(6) organization as a wholly owned subsidiary of the MBA.

6 Discussion and implications

Our study of the development of standards in the mortgage industry contributes to the scant literature on the evolution of vertical IS standards. We argue here that there are many similarities between the mortgage industry case and the development of vertical IS standards in other industries, which suggest that our findings should generalize well to other contexts. We then revisit our key findings and discuss how they augment our knowledge about IS standards creation, adoption and maintenance, and offer not only guidance for other standards groups, but also insights for further research and theoretical development. Following these discussions, we continue with the implications of the mortgage industry case study for policymakers, with a particular emphasis on what it might suggest for the role of the government in vertical IS standards development.

6.1 Generalizing the home mortgage case to other industries

How well does the mortgage industry case generalize to other industries? To support this discussion, we refer to the development of the bar code in the grocery industry (Brown 1997), as well as to supplementary interviews conducted with the DISA, an organization that has assisted several industries with vertical IS standard making.

The development of the bar code illustrates the challenges an industry faces in using standardized data formats and information systems across firms, while it also reveals the similarity of strategies across industries that are in the process of developing vertical IS standards (Brown 1997). In the context of structuring the collaboration over standards formation, grocery manufacturers and retailers had long held informal discussions about the need to standardize product identification, but they could not agree on what the standard should be.

Fearful that leading retailers would require them to adopt multiple different labeling conventions, grocery manufacturers finally convinced retailers to join a standards committee by threatening to create their own standard, though they freely acknowledged that this solution would not be best for the industry as a whole. Formation of the committee required exquisite attention to rules governing who would be allowed to participate and vote. Throughout the committee's deliberations, balancing the interests of different industry participants, especially smaller players lacking resources as well as vendors with interests in their own proprietary technology, was a constant consideration. Consultants to the committee expressed amazement when members unanimously voted on a solution that increased costs for manufacturers, because that was the best solution for the industry as a whole.

There are also many interesting parallels between MISMO's standardization efforts and the bar code standardization committee's efforts to spur adoption by firms in the sector by limiting the scope of the effort and engaging in educational and promotional activities. Early on, the committee agreed on an operating principle that undoubtedly contributed to the standards' adoption: "The symbol ... shall not place an undue competitive burden on any segment of industry" (Brown 1997, 59). An additional principle was that symbol selection would be based on in-store performance tests, so that the test results could speak for themselves to skeptical would-be adopters. Because the bar code required complementary resources in printing and scanning innovations, the committee worked tirelessly with vendors to ensure that industry participants would have the wherewithal to adopt. (Vendors did not always cooperate. The leading vendor of scanners withdrew from the market when the committee did not choose the symbol it had proposed and developed.) Committee members conducted endless presentations about their efforts to industry groups and even individual companies. All these decisions and activities helped promote adoption of the standard.

Standards maintenance was not initially a focus of the bar code committee, but it ultimately became an important consideration. The best illustration of the ongoing nature of the standardization committee's work is the ineffective plans of bar code developers to put themselves out of business (Brown 1997). The bar code requires central administration for assigning numbers to manufacturers (who then assign numbers to their products). The bar code developers expected that the job of administration would ultimately diminish until it could be handled by a part-time assistant in an industry association. On the basis of that assumption, they funded the role on a declining basis over five years. Eventually, committee members admitted that the job was actually continuing to grow sharply, and they needed to create a permanent nonprofit organization, the Uniform Code Council, and governance structure for it. They also had to cope with a variety of ongoing issues, such as defending the standard from various legal threats and from encroachment or alteration by other standards groups. Indeed, their experience offered an important lesson about the need to have a very clear intellectual property policy. The bar code was never patented, and some individuals later brought suit, unsuccessfully, claiming patent infringement.

There are a few significant differences between the bar code case and MISMO's standardization effort. First, the bar code standardization effort required the development of hardware for printing and scanning; MISMO data standards do not have hardware requirements to any significant degree. Second, partly as a result of the hardware requirement, adoption of the bar code could not begin until the standard development process was completed. In contrast, development of MISMO standards is occurring in versions, as is common with software-based innovations, and adoption is proceeding in parallel with further development. Third and finally, it is still too early in the mortgage industry IS standardization process to foresee the full range of issues that will arise during adoption and maintenance of the MISMO standards. Despite these differences, the many parallels between the experiences of the grocery industry in developing bar codes and those of the mortgage industry suggest that some generalization is appropriate. At a minimum, both of these cases reveal how important it is to develop an adequate structure for collaboration, emphasize strategies to encourage adoption, and ensure ongoing maintenance of standards.

According to interviews with DISA, many other industries have had some success in developing vertical IS standards by following much the same process as the mortgage industry, including chemicals, travel, insurance, and others. Representatives from DISA highlighted a few of the characteristics they felt differentiated successful from unsuccessful standardization efforts. In keeping with our findings regarding the need to structure collaboration appropriately, it appears that similar governance approaches have been successfully used elsewhere. Indeed, the MISMO governance structure was to some extent inherited from the earlier EDI Accredited Standards Committee (ASC) X12 standardization efforts: DISA served as the secretariat for the earlier EDI effort and also has been assisting MISMO. In many ways, secretariats facilitate the process behind the scenes, including by registering members, collecting dues, providing legal services, maintaining websites, and publishing standards documents. Given that the participants from the industry still must fulfill the obligations of their regular company work in addition to any standards activity, some outside help may be important for any industry.

The scope of standardization efforts was also an important issue in other industries, according to DISA interviewees (e.g., April 14, 2004). They were particularly cautious about efforts in other industries to move beyond data definition standards into business process guidelines (sometimes known as *best practices*), which they felt make it more difficult to gain consensus and adoption.

High costs of participation, technical complexity beyond the level of automation found in an industry, and too great a perceived role for a dominant technology vendor were also associated with difficulties in vertical standardization efforts. In situations where high participation costs and technical complexity are present, DISA found that smaller players were discouraged and that it was difficult to create the critical mass needed for consensus-based standards development. When dominant technology vendors attempted to drive the standards process, DISA found that other vendors viewed these efforts with suspicion and were reluctant to participate.

Collectively, these cross-industry comparisons suggest that the basic logic followed in the MISMO case generalizes to other industries; and those industries that fail to adequately structure participation, keep costs low, and limit the scope of efforts may not succeed.

6.2 Contributions to theory and practice

Having established that the MISMO standards case generalizes to other industries, we next turn to what the findings imply for theory and practice. We continue to employ our tri-part framework and discuss our findings' contributions in relation to (1) structuring the process, (2) promoting standards adoption, and (3) maintaining the standard.

Contributions in the area of structuring the process

Our research questions 1a and 1b focused on the issue of how the standards development process is structured. We previously observed that according to both a public goods theory perspective and David and Greenstein's (1990) analysis of committee-based standards processes, little was known about why companies and individuals participate in standards development given the costs they incur. One finding that emerges from our interviews is that industry characteristics can strongly influence costs of participation in standards development. In particular, that traditional mortgage industry products had become somewhat commodified allowed otherwise competing firms to find a basis for focusing efforts on standards.

In addition, our observations and interviews reveal a number of important incentives that motivate companies, suggesting that the resulting benefits of the public good are not the same for all firms in the industry. That is, participating firms may experience somewhat higher benefits than nonparticipating firms in at least two ways. First, through their participation firms can help ensure that the committee works on standards that will be useful for their business and will fit their needs. Second, firms can use their participation to enhance their own legitimacy as a player in the industry and improve their visibility and reputation – potentially leading to increased future business. This latter benefit suggests the surprising outcome that smaller or lesser-known firms may have a disproportionate incentive to participate – perhaps resulting in an overrepresentation of smaller, less influential firms. Balancing this tendency, however, are the more limited financial and personnel resources of smaller firms. This finding contributes to earlier empirical work showing that public goods theory underestimates the benefits received by early contributors in standard-making efforts (Monge et al. 1998; Flanagin et al. 2001).

Additional theoretical implications derive from our finding that, despite the occasionally significant personal costs not fully reimbursed by company contributions, individuals are motivated for personal, altruistic, and social reasons to participate in the process. Interviewees universally recognized that the core group of ten highly interested people experienced rewards just by being embedded in that group. The strong social bonds between these people not only acted as an incentive for participation, but they were also helpful in defusing conflicts and enabling compromise. Although the importance of personal relationships as a lubricant and governance mechanism in support of electronic transactions has been pointed out in prior literature (Kraut et al. 1999), the role of such relations in the standard setting process has not yet received much attention.

Our analysis of the structure of the standard-making process in the mortgage industry also reveals a number of critical elements that committees can use to help manage competing interests and mitigate conflict. First, the scope of the vertical IS standard setting processes appears to be important in the success of these efforts: MISMO deliberately avoided trying to develop standards for everything, because the attempt to standardize members' internal processes and data structures would likely entail both *inter-* and *intra*organizational conflict. Instead, that MISMO focused only on the data flowing between organizations, as well as on data rather than process standards, limited the potential for conflict. Vertical IS standards often affect multiple stakeholder groups *within* the organizations that participate in standard setting efforts – in the case of the mortgage industry, for example, originating units, servicing units, and legal departments may each view a proposed standard from different points of view. Managing the scope of standard setting processes is a useful tactic for keeping intraorganizational conflict from affecting the successful completion of an interorganizational standard. A potential downside of this approach is that some participants may lack the level of internal systems integration needed to adopt or capture benefits from interorganizational standards (Markus 2000).

Second, the role of governance mechanisms appears to be an important tool for reducing the potential for conflict. Open membership, voluntary participation on particular workgroups, transparency in decision making, fair voting rules, efforts to reduce costs of participation, and a separate governance committee were some of the ways that MISMO increased participation and minimized conflict. These findings support and further inform the prior work on committee-based standards (David and Greenstein 1990; Brown 1997; van Baalen et al. 2000).

Third, attention to informal governance mechanisms generated additional insights. Prior analysis of committee-based standards suggests that, especially among user committees, work often proceeds by consensus (Hills 2000), and MISMO committees were no exception. Our findings reveal some of the informal mechanisms that allow committees to function in this way, such as the importance of the core of the same ten people who helped broker compromises, as well as the method of choosing projects on the basis of simply having a critical mass of people willing to volunteer. However, a cost of choosing projects in this way – that some important standards remain undeveloped due to lack of participation – was also revealed.

Contributions in the area of promoting standards adoption

Our research questions 2a and 2b focused on what standards development organizations can do to help promote adoption of the standard and what consequences such actions might have for industry structure and participants' competitive position. Clearly, many of the structuring factors previously discussed had consequences for the likelihood that firms in the mortgage industry would eventually adopt the standards. The open and inclusive membership and governance mechanisms ensured that participants would not think that any one player had undue influence. Moreover, the active efforts to enlist further participation, educate members, and distribute standards via low-cost Internet channels enhanced the probability of adoption.

Our analysis also emphasizes the critical importance of the development of a data dictionary for vertical IS standards efforts. Interviewees all agreed that this was MISMO's greatest achievement and that it paved the way for all future work done by the organization. The dictionary gave potential adopters confidence that the resulting standards would not fall prey to standards drift caused by different interpretations of the meaning of elements in transactions – with the result that more firms adopted the standards (Damsgaard and Truex 2000). Whether such an approach would work in other industries is an important question for further research.

An open participation process is important, but the MISMO case suggests that standards-development organizations must be more proactive in recruiting participants to promote future adoption of the standard. Many of the interviewees noted how important it was that the GSEs were brought into the process. Because of their dominance as buyers in the secondary market for mortgages, without their agreement no standard would have had much chance of being adopted. Indeed, the GSEs' participation altered the adoption process from being a simple network effect. This result suggests that, depending on industry structure, adoption may depend on the decisions of a few key early adopters who furnish benefits for the remaining population (Olson 1965).

Our case analysis further suggests that not including key stake-holders, coupled with a process whereby the standards projects addressed are dependent on having a critical mass of interested parties present, will hinder adoption. In particular, interviewees observed the relative lack of participation by large mortgage banks, which may have been a function of their desire to leverage prior heavy investment in proprietary EDI systems.

The actions taken to promote adoption did appear to have some observable consequences for the types of standards developed, which in turn might have implications down the road for industry structure and competitiveness. As Hills (2000) predicted, voluntary coalitions, such as MISMO, are more likely to develop standards that preserve members' interests, even if new technology might enable a more efficient solution. The three-part SMART doc standard developed by MISMO that appears to preserve the role of document preparation companies illustrates the applicability of this theoretical expectation to the vertical IS standards arena.

Contributions in the area of maintaining the standard

Our research questions 3a, 3b, and 3c focused on the actions standards development organizations take in order to ensure ongoing maintenance of standards, defense against legal challenges to the standard, and defense against fragmentation and drift. As noted in our review of the bar code case (Brown 1997), vertical IS standards developed by voluntary committees require ongoing maintenance that may not have been anticipated by the initial standards group. As a result, a relatively impermanent organization may not be adequate, and a more formal institutional structure may be required to structure participants' actions and reduce uncertainty (Jepperson 1991; Mayntz and Scharpf 1995). The actions taken by MISMO to create a permanent 501(c)(6) organization responsible for ongoing standards development and maintenance activities support this conclusion.

Our findings further suggest that standards organizations must take steps early on to ward off future legal challenges that may negate any collective benefits from the standards being developed. The IPR policy was expressly designed to reduce the likelihood of such challenges, particularly coming from so-called submarine patents.

Finally, fragmentation and drift caused by reinterpretation of the standards were not only offset by the development of the data dictionary, but also by other strategic choices made early in the process. In particular, our case emphasizes the importance of considering how the standard can evolve as newer technology arrives. In the MISMO case, the choice of XML, and the explicit recognition of how the current standards can migrate to Schema and XSL, will help avoid fragmentation and drift.

6.3 Policy implications

Although our primary focus has been to reveal the underlying dynamics surrounding vertical IS standards development, the case does lend itself to a discussion of policy implications. Governments have an interest in enhancing the efficiency of industries, and can encourage the formation of vertical IS standards in a variety of ways. We now discuss their potential roles as an enabler, a convener, a participant, a funding agent, a promoter, and a user. A critical role for policymakers, especially those with regulatory and/or legislative authority, is that of an *enabler* for the development and use of vertical IS standards. An enabler provides the essential conditions as a foundation upon which electronic transaction standards may be built. For example, in the mortgage industry case study presented here, federal policymakers acted as enablers by passing key legislation that made an all-electronic mortgage possible. As noted earlier, the passage of the Uniform Electronic Transactions Act in 1999 and the Electronic Signatures in Global and National Commerce Act in 2000 made it possible to envision a mortgage lending process that produces legally binding mortgages entirely without paper.

As a *convener*, government agencies might use their considerable influence to bring key players to the table. In this role, they can be viewed as objective facilitators, rather than as potential competitors. Such a role may be especially useful when attempting to stimulate cross-industry IS standards efforts. Many transactions not only take place but are also structurally similar across industries; so a standard that already exists in one industry might benefit or be fruitfully applied to another. Loan data in the home mortgage industry, for example, has relevance for other large purchases, such as automobiles, and therefore might have relevance to the car industry. One project underway at the

National Institute of Standards and Technology is attempting to compile a number of vertical industry standards organizations to try to stimulate what is now being called e-business standards convergence (see http://www.nist.gov/ebsc).

Government agencies also can and should be *active participants*, operating much as other industry participants in committee meetings. Participation by agencies with knowledge of important regulations can help ensure that viable standards emerge from committee efforts. Within MISMO, a somewhat related example is the participation by the GSEs in the process, even though they are essentially private companies with government charter.

In addition, government entities can play the role of *funding agent*. Selective funding may be used to assist smaller firms with the costs associated with membership and active participation. Moreover, the funding of foundational research and development efforts that might not be undertaken by industry members would be another example of this type of role.

As a *promoter*, the government may use financial support to spur adoption of the standard. This may be in the form of grants and other forms of assistance to firms under the condition that developed standards are adopted and used. Tax credits and other incentives may be supplied for firms that participate and adopt industry standards.

The government can also play a role as a *user* of vertical IS standards. As a buyer of goods and services from many industries, it can mandate that sellers use established vertical industry standards in all transactions. Such mandates can have a great effect on standards adoption. Our DISA interviewees, for example, noted that ASC X12 publications "flew off the shelves" when the government mandated use of this standard in the Health Insurance Portability and Accountability Act (April 15, 2004).

One role that the MISMO case suggests is *not* appropriate for the policymaking community is as the sole *developer* of IS standards meant for a particular industry. Rather, the case demonstrates how important it is to have full participation from all segments of the industry, especially from those companies that must use the standard in their daily operations. Moreover, the case emphasizes the need for vertical IS standards to be flexible and to allow for ongoing evolution.

In conclusion, the case of MISMO in the home mortgage industry sheds much needed light on the processes by which vertical IS standards emerge and suggests a number of potential roles for practitioners and policymakers. Although it is limited to one industry with unique characteristics, parallels to previous and contemporary vertical IS standards efforts are noteworthy. Further empirical work is needed to learn if the processes unfold similarly in different industry structures. In addition, further theoretical development and empirical work are important for understanding how the efforts of standards development organizations play out in terms of standards adoption and impacts.

References

Anonymous 1988. "MBA makes 'extraordinary progress' in effort to stream-line lending," *CTS Accounting Software Survey* 12: 25.

2001a. *News release: Common format adopted for automated underwriting.* Washington, DC: MISMO.

2001b. "XML for the world," *Computer Business Review Online*, January 4, 2001, http://www.cbronline.com/content/comp/magazine/archive/000574.asp.

2002. "Fannie Mae releases its requirements for e-mortgages," *Origination News* 11: 2.

2003. *News release: MBA announces release of industry eNote registry requirements.* Washington, DC: Mortgage Bankers Association of America.

Babcock, C. 2004. "What's behind electronic business XML," *Information Week*, March 1, http://www.informationweek.com.

Bixby, M., and G. Alvord 2004. "Data standards and mortgage credit reporting," in *The standards edge: Dynamic tension*, S. Bolin (ed.), Piedmont, CA: Bolin Communications, 331–9.

Braitman, E. 1990. "Coming: A simpler mortgage application," *American Banker* 12: 12.

Brown, S. A. 1997. *Revolution at the checkout counter: The explosion of the bar code.* Cambridge, MA: Harvard University Press.

Campbell, N. S. 1994. "EDI wagon starts to roll," *Real Estate Finance Today* 11: 9–10.

Cummings, J., and D. DiPasquale 1997. *A primer on the secondary mortgage market.* Boston: City Research.

Damsgaard, J., and D. Truex 2000. "Binary trading relations and the limits of EDI standards: The procrustean bed of standards," *European Journal of Information Systems* 9: 142–58.

David, P. A., and S. Greenstein 1990. "The economics of compatibility standards: An introduction to recent research," *Economic Innovation and New Technology* 1: 3–41.

Flanagin, A. J., P. Monge, and J. Fulk 2001. "The value of formative investment in organizational federations," *Human Communication Research* 27: 69–93.

Gudobba, R. 2003. *Smart documents: Forming the foundation of e-mortgages.* Fraser, MI: VMP Mortgage Solutions.

Hershkowitz, B. 1992. "Cover report: Cutting edge solutions," *Mortgage Banking* 52: 32.

Hills, B. 2000. "Common message standards for electronic commerce in wholesale financial markets," *Bank of England Quarterly Bulletin* 40: 274–85.

Jacobides, M. G. 2001a. "Mortgage banking unbundling: Structure, automation and profit," *Mortgage Banking* 61: 28–40.

2001b. "Technology with a vengeance: The new economics of mortgaging," *Mortgage Banking* 62: 118–31.

Jain, H., and H. Zhao 2003. "A conceptual model for comparative analysis of standardization of vertical industry languages," *Proceedings of the workshop on standard making: A critical research frontier for information systems.* Seattle, WA: December 12–14, 210–21.

Jepperson, R. L. 1991. "Institutions, institutional effects, and institutionalism," in *The new institutionalism in organizational analysis*, W. W. Powell and P. J. DiMaggio (eds.), Chicago: University of Chicago Press, 143–63.

Kraut, R., C. Steinfield, A. Chan, B. Butler, and A. Hoag 1999. "Coordination and virtualization: The role of electronic networks and personal relationships," *Organization Science* 10: 722–40.

Laudon, K., and C. Traver 2003. *E-commerce: Business, technology, society*, 2nd edition. Boston: Addison-Wesley.

Lebowitz, J. A. 1990. "Automation," *Mortgage Banking*, 50: 83.

Liebowitz, S., and S. Margolis 1998. "Network effects and externalities," in *The new Palgraves dictionary of economics and the law*, Vol. II, P. Newman (ed.), New York: MacMillan, 671–5.

Markus, M. L. 2000. "Paradigm shifts – e-business and business/systems integration," *Communications of the AIS* 4, http://cais.isworld.org/articles/default.asp?vol=4&art=10.

Markus, M. L., B. Manville, and C. Agres 2000. "What makes a virtual organization work: Lessons from the open source world," *Sloan Management Review* 42: 13–26.

Mayntz, R., and F. W. Scharpf 1995. "Der Ansatz des akteurzentrierten Institutionalinismus," in *Gesellschaftliche Selbstregelung und politische Steuerung*, R. Mayntz and F. W. Scharpf (eds.), Frankfurt: Campus Verlag, 39–72.

206   *Charles W. Steinfield et al.*

McKinnon, J. D., and D. Kopecki 2003. "Fannie Mae, Freddie Mac targeted by republicans to curb taxpayer exposure," *Wall Street Journal Online Edition*, http://www.wsj.com.

Monge, P. R., J. Fulk, M. E. Kalman, A. J. Flanagin, C. Parnassa, and S. Rumsey 1998. "Production of collective action in alliance-based interorganizational communication and information systems," *Organization Science* 9: 411–33.

Mortgage Industry Standards Maintenance Organization 2001. "Automated underwriting specifications," *Logical Data Dictionary*, Version 2.1, http://www.mismo.org/mismo/docs/Full_LDD_090303.htm.

   2002. *SMART document overview: Frequently-asked questions*, Version 1.0 (October 9), http://www.mismo.org/mismo/spec_faq.cfm.

   2004a. *SMART doc technology overview*, Version 1.0 (October 9), http://www.mismo.org/mismo/docs/drftspc/draft/eMortgage_SMART_Doc_TechOverview_v_1-0.pdf.

   2004b. *Intellectual property rights policy of the Mortgage Industry Standards Maintenance Organization, Inc.*, Version 1.2. (May 14), http://www.mismo.org/mismo/pdf/ipr_policy.pdf.

Olson, Mancur 1965. *The Logic of Collective Action: Public Goods and the Theory of Groups*. Boston: Harvard University Press.

Opelka, F. G. 1994. "Toward paperless mortgages," *Savings & Community Banker* 3: 39–40.

Pizzo, S. 1994. "Fannie, Freddie tech plans have lenders worried," *National Mortgage News* 19: 12–13.

Porter, M. E. 2001. "Strategy and the Internet," *Harvard Business Review* 79: 63–78.

Slesinger, P. K. 1994. "Data standardization: Streamlining access to the secondary market," *Mortgage Banking* 54: 107–9.

Songini, M. 2001. "Lack of standards blocks supply-chain automation," *Computerworld* (April 5): http://www.computerworld.com/softwaretopics/erp/story/0,10801,59259,00.html.

Stango, V. 2004. "The economics of standards wars," *Review of Network Economics* 3: 1–19.

Trigaux, R. 1988. "Group lists ways to speed mortgages," *American Banker* September 9, 3.

US Bureau of the Census 2001. *Statistical Abstract of the United States*. Washington, DC.

van Baalen, P., M. van Oosterhout, Y. H. Tan, and E. van Heck 2000. *Dynamics in setting up an EDI community*. Delft, The Netherlands: Eburon Publishers.

Van Order, R. 2000. "The US mortgage market: A model of dueling charters," *Journal of Housing Research* 11: 233–55.

VMP Mortgage Solutions 2004. http://www.vmpmtg.com/.

Vollmer, K. 2002. *Market overview: EDI software and services.* RPA-032002-00008, Cambridge, MA: Giga Information Group, Inc.

Xia, M., K. Zhao, and M. J. Shaw 2003. "Open e-business standard development and adoption: An integrated perspective," *Proceedings of the workshop on standard making: A critical research frontier for information systems*, Seattle, WA: December 12–14, 222–35.

6 Intellectual property and standardization committee participation in the US modem industry

NEIL GANDAL, NATALY GANTMAN,
AND DAVID GENESOVE

Abstract

The authors take a preliminary look at the interaction between patenting and standardization committee participation in the US modem industry. Both involve a much wider set of firms than the downstream modem manufacturers themselves. Not surprisingly, the two activities are highly correlated across firms. Using five-year periods, Granger causality tests show that while patenting is predicted by participation in earlier standardization meetings, meetings participation is not predicted by earlier patenting. The authors interpret these results as reflecting the timing of standard setting relative to innovation.

1 Introduction

The past two decades have witnessed a proliferation of high-tech consumer electronic products which exhibit network effects. Successful diffusion of these products is often contingent on a single product winning a battle of market standards or firms achieving compatibility among competing standards.[1] The benefit to consumers from purchasing a network good depends on the number of other consumers who eventually purchase the same network good, or a compatible one. This

We are especially grateful to Ken Krechmer and thank participants at the Standards & Public Policy Conference, Federal Reserve Bank of Chicago, May 13–14, 2004 for helpful comments. We are grateful to Elaine Baskin, Ken Krechmer, and the Communications Standards Review for providing the Telecommunications Industry Association standardization participation data.

[1] This section draws from Gandal (2002).

situation has two main implications for competition in network markets, with competing standards:

1. Consumers' expectations regarding the future size of a network are critical in the adoption decision. On the one hand, the expectation that one technology will become a standard may be self-fulfilling. On the other hand, fragmented expectations may lead to a battle with no winner. Postrel (1990) partly attributes the failure of quadraphonic sound in the 1970s to competing standards.
2. When network effects are relatively strong, long-term coexistence of competing incompatible standards is unlikely. A small initial advantage will likely influence consumer expectations about the adoption of a particular standard, which, in turn will lead to more consumers adopting the standard. Thus, an early lead can be transformed into an advantage that is difficult to overcome.

Thus, competition in network goods markets without a previously agreed-upon standard will often entail suboptimal demand and high risks for firms. Hence, firms may be willing to have a single standard set "outside" of the marketplace. Broadly speaking, there are three ways that can happen: First, national standards bodies, such as the US Federal Communications Commission (FCC), can impose the standard on the market. Second, officially accredited standards development organizations (SDOs)[2] can agree on which standards to set. An SDO must trace its accreditation to a governmental body, such as the American National Standards Institute (ANSI). In fact, ANSI accredits more than 270 public and private SDOs that follow ANSI policy in developing voluntary (consensus) standards and is the only US representative to both the International Organization for Standardization and the International Electromagnetic Commission. The standards set by SDOs are non-proprietary. Third, industry trade groups, consortia, and other standard setting organizations (SSOs)[3] can jointly develop

---

[2] Examples of SDOs include the International Telecommunications Union (ITU), the oldest international standards body in the world, and the International Electrotechnical Commission. Given the importance of compatibility among international phone networks, the standards set by the ITU are done so by international consensus.
[3] SDOs are a subset of SSOs. See Caplan (2003).

standards. As with standards set by SDOs, these standards are also typically non-proprietary.[4]

There is by now a large body of literature on the economics of compatibility and standardization.[5] Although the literature is primarily theoretical, there is a growing empirical literature as well. Despite the increasing importance of SDOs and SSOs in achieving standards, there is surprisingly little systematic economics research, either theoretical or empirical, on these institutions.

Firms in oligopoly markets interact strategically in many different dimensions. In the case of industries where standardization and compatibility are important, firms meet in standardization organizations in addition to competing in both research and development and the product market. Indeed, firms have come to recognize the strategic importance of participating in standard setting organizations and hence increasingly send senior decision makers in addition to technical staff to these meetings.[6]

There are several reasons why firms participate in standards meetings. As mentioned previously, in industries in which interoperability is important, competing incompatible standards may lead to the market failure of the technology itself. An additional reason to participate in standards meetings is that firms profit from getting their intellectual property into the standard. Most standards committees allow firms to earn "reasonable and non-discriminatory" royalties if their intellectual property is part of the standard. In many cases, this may be the best way for firms to earn revenues from intellectual property. Although economic models of standard setting typically envision two firms with complete and proprietary incompatible technologies, often many firms

---

[4] The DVD (digital video disc) industry provides an example of a jointly developed standard. Throughout the 1990s, video hardware and software manufacturers sought a digital format to replace videocassettes. In order to avoid another Beta/VHS format war, hardware manufacturers led by Sony, Toshiba, and Panasonic, and movie studios, led by Warner and Columbia (a division of Sony), worked together to establish a single standard. The result was the non-proprietary or "open" DVD standard.

[5] We will not provide a detailed survey here. See David and Greenstein (1990) for a comprehensive survey of previous work, and Farrell and Klemperer (in press) for a detailed survey of more recent work. Gilbert (1992), Katz and Shapiro (1994), Gandal (1995), and Matutes and Regibeau (1996) provide selective reviews of the literature. See Gandal (2002) for a discussion of policy issues and Stango (2004) for a survey of the literature on standards wars.

[6] See Cargill (2004).

are involved, and no single one owns a full set of patents covering the essential components of the technology. In such cases, no single firm can credibly threaten to develop its own standard unilaterally.

Another reason for participating in standards committees is that knowledge diffuses through the meeting process. Firms may gain key insights that will contribute to future intellectual property or help improve their competitive position in the product market.

In this paper, we focus on modems. Network effects arise in modem markets because compatible modems are required to transfer data between the sending and receiving parties, for example, between consumers and Internet service providers (ISPs). Consumers benefit from a modem standard because this enables them to change their ISP without having to change modems. Additionally, a standard enables consumers to travel to other geographic areas and connect to the Internet through the local ISPs.

In 1996 there were two competing incompatible technologies in the 56K (kilobit) analog modem market. If a consumer used one standard while his/her ISP used a different standard, the data transmission speed did not approach 56 kilobits per second (kbs), but rather was that of the previous technology – 33 kbs per second.[7] The incompatibility in the market led to confusion among consumers and reduced sales. As one industry analyst wrote somewhat colorfully, "Back in 1996, for example, there was the heated, worldwide standards battle involving 56 kbs analog modem technology that dragged on for a couple of years. Consumer confusion soared, modem sales declined dramatically, and the modem industry in general received a strong punch in the stomach."[8] The standards war featured efforts by both sides to influence the expectations of adopters, with exaggerated claims of dominance. However, the consensus is that, rather than tip the market, the standards war instead caused confusion among consumers and ISPs, which delayed modem adoption.

Here, we empirically examine the interaction between intellectual property and participation in standardization committee meetings. We employ "meeting" data from the Telecommunications Industry Association, the SDO responsible for developing voluntary (consensus) standards in the analog modem market in the United States. We first conclude this section with a literature review. In Section 2, we discuss

---

[7] See Augereau et al. (2003).   [8] See Garen (2000).

the modem market; we chose this market because the product is well defined. In Sections 3 and 4, we present our data on patents and on participation at standardization committee meetings, respectively. We report basic correlations and Granger causality tests in Section 5. Our major finding is that while participation in standards meetings predicts future intellectual property (both unweighted and citation weighted patents), the reverse is not true: patents and citations are not good predictors of future meeting attendance. We interpret these results primarily as reflecting the timing of standard setting relative to innovation, although we also consider the effects of knowledge diffusion at the meetings. In Section 6, we conclude and provide a direction for further research.

In Farrell and Saloner's (1988) seminal theoretical paper about the economics of standards committees, the authors find that standards committees have desirable properties. In their study, each firm has a proprietary (incompatible) standard. There are network effects, so both firms prefer to use the same standard, but each prefers its own standard to that of the rival firm. Farrell and Saloner then examine the incentives for these firms to achieve coordination via standardization committees and they compare committees to (1) a pure market process in which there is no communication among firms and firms can make unilateral standardization choices and (2) a hybrid committee/market process in which firms meet in committees and yet can also make unilateral standardization decisions. They find that committees can better set standards in the sense that committees are more likely than market processes to achieve coordination, that is, standardization (which is efficient in their model). Nevertheless, there is a trade-off here since the committee process will typically take longer than it would if standardization choices were left to the market. Perhaps, not surprisingly, the hybrid process outperforms the other two mechanisms.

Several recent empirical papers are a welcome addition to a small, primarily case study literature. Lemley (2002) examines the intellectual property policies of standardization organizations. Augereau et al. (2003) examine the modem standards war of 1996 through 1998; they claim that the failure to reach standardization in the market was due to ISPs' incentives to differentiate their product. Simcoe (2004) examines the standard setting process of the Internet Engineering Task Force and finds that increased levels of commercial participation are associated with an increase in the time to reach agreements on standards. Meidan (2004) examines a "standard setting race" between two SSOs – an official SDO and a commercial SSO – for the case of cable modems. Using event study methodology and stock market returns, she finds that the commercial consortium's standardization decisions created increased competition in the retail market.

2 Modems

Modems were invented in the 1950s. In 1977, Dennis Hayes invented the first modem for personal computers (PCs). In 1978, he founded Hayes Associates, Inc., and in 1979, he shipped the first PC modem. Hayes became the industry standard, achieving 60 percent of the world's modem market in 1985.[9] Hence many competing vendors marketed their modems as Hayes-compatible. The PC modem changed the industry from one that worked via leased lines to one that worked via dial-up connections.

Early modem speeds were very slow by today's standards. In 1981, modems ran at speeds of 1.200 kbs. In 1983, Hayes released the Smartcom II, which ran at modem speeds of 2.400 kbs. By 1996, the maximum speed had increased to 56 kbs (see Table 6.1).

Early modems were prohibitively expensive as well. In 1981, the average price of a (1.200 kbs) modem was approximately $1,500, that is more than a dollar for each bit per second. By 1997, the price of an (analog) modem with a speed of 56 kbs had fallen to less than $300, or $0.005 for each bit per second.[10] That translates into a more than 30 percent decline in speed-adjusted prices per year for the fifteen-year period from 1981 to 1996.[11] The International Telecommunications Union (ITU) standards shown in Table 6.1 typically were developed before competition developed in the market.[12] Nevertheless, there was a standards war in this industry over the 56K standard. In September 1996, US Robotics (3COM) submitted the first V.90 56K proposed standard to the ITU. In November 1996, Lucent and Rockwell agreed

---

[9] See http://gtalumni.org/StayInformed/magazine/win99/high.html.
[10] Prices in Table 6.1 come from Bob Kenas (1997).
[11] In comparison, quality-adjusted computer prices fell by about 15% in the 1980s and early 1990s and only reached rates of decline of about 30% in the second half of the 1990s. See Gordon (2000) and Oliner et al. (1994).
[12] There often were precursor modems from individual vendors before the ITU standards, but their numbers were low.

214 Neil Gandal, Nataly Gantman, and David Genesove

Table 6.1. Analog modem timeline

Maximum speed (in kbs)	Year	Average price	ITU standard
9.6	1984	1,167	V.32
14.4	1991	653	V.32bis
33.6	1994	505	V.34, V.34+
56.0	1996	350	V.90

to make their chipsets interoperable by using the so-called Kflex standard. However, the Kflex and US Robotics standards were incompatible. Because of the incompatibility, sales to consumers and ISPs were lower than expected. Hence, the industry appealed to standardization agencies to establish a standard.

In April 1997, the ITU set up a special committee to determine a 56K (V.90) standard.[13] In February 1998, the V.90 standard was approved by the ITU. The relatively short time between the first submission and the setting of the standard was apparently a record for the ITU. Following the introduction of the standard, all new Kflex and US Robotics modems were produced according to the V.90 standard and hence were interoperable. Hence, even when a standards war broke out, the standard was eventually resolved through a committee process.

3 Patent data

We obtained all 604 patents issued between 1976 and 1999 with the word *modem* in the title.[14] We then matched the patent numbers using the National Bureau of Economics Research patent data, which is

---

[13] Since the Telecommunications Industry Association (TIA) TR-30 committee was the US technical advisory group to the ITU during this period, it was also actively involved in the process. Indeed, Les Brown, the chairman of the TIA TR-30.1 subcommittee at the time, was listed on the ITU press release announcing the standard. See http://www.itu.int/newsarchive/press_releases/1998/04.html.

[14] Nearly half (44.5%) of these patents are to be found in the three-digit patent class 375 ("Pulse or Digital Communications"). Another 18.5% are in 379 ("Telephonic Communications"), and another 12% in 370 ("Multiplex Communications"). The remaining 25% are to be found in more than thirty other classes.

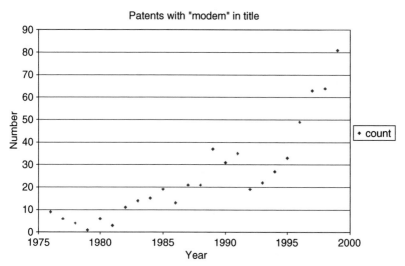

Figure 6.1. Patents with the word *modem* in the title: 1976–99.

publicly available at http://www.nber.org/patents/. From the website, we obtained data on the grant year, the assignee, and the number of citations to each patent. Figure 6.1 shows that until 1982 there were less than 10 patents issued per year with the word *modem* in the title. For 1982–99, the number of modem patents per year increased steadily, reaching 80 in 1999.

One hundred and ninety-four firms received patents with the word *modem* in the title during the 1976–99 time period. In Table 6.2, we show the number of modem patents and citations to these patents by firm for 1976–99, as well as for the subperiods 1976–89 and 1990–9. (The citations are dated by the year of the receiving patent.) Motorola, the leader in cable modems from its introduction in 1997 on, had the most patents overall, as well as the largest number during 1990–9. Hayes, the first and initially dominant firm in the industry, was ranked high during 1976–89, but fell in the rankings during 1990–9. US Robotics, the current market leader in dial-up analog modems, was absent from the top fifteen during 1976–89, and was ranked only twelfth during 1990–9. The list of firms includes not only modem manufacturers, but producers of both modem inputs and complementary products as well, as the fourth column in the table indicates.

Table 6.2. *Patents with the word* modem *in the title*

	Patents granted 1976–99				Patents granted 1976–89			Patents granted 1990–9		
Firm	Patents	Citations	Products[a]		Firm	Patents	Citations	Firm	Patents	Citations
Motorola	27	122	D,U		Paradyne	13	156	Motorola	21	86
Paradyne	24	180	D		Hayes	10	186	IBM	18	74
IBM	23	119	U,I		Univ. Data	9	171	Intel	15	43
Hayes	18	334	D		Codex	8	131	Multi-Tech	13	101
Univ. Data	16	220	D		Racal Milgo	8	122	Fujitsu	13	63
Codex	15	262	D		Hycom	6	103	AT&T	12	166
AT&T	15	199	C		Motorola	6	36	Compaq	12	74
Fujitsu	15	78	C		IBM	5	45	NEC	11	42
NEC	15	77	C		Texas Ins.	5	20	Paradyne	11	24
Intel	15	43	U		Telebit	4	129	Lucent	11	13
Racal Milgo	13	180	D		NCR	4	48	Hayes	8	148
Multi-Tech	13	101	D		NEC	4	35	US Robotics	8	106
Compaq	12	74	C		AMP	4	14	Codex	7	131
Lucent	11	13	I		AT&T	3	15	Univ. Data	7	49
Texas Ins.	10	31	U,I		Philips	3	33	Codex	7	131
Total top 15	232	2,002			Total top 15	89	1,211	Total top 15	167	1,120
Other firms	372	2,893			Other firms	91	1,344	Other firms	257	1,220

Note: [a] Firms products are coded as follows: "downstream" modems (D), upstream inputs into modems (U), infrastructure for modems (I), or complementary products (C).

4 Standardization meetings

In the United States, the Telecommunications Industry Association (TIA) is the primary association that sets voluntary standards in this area. The TIA was formed as the result of a merger of the United States Telecommunications Suppliers Association and the Information and Telecommunications Technologies Group of the Electronic Industries Alliance in 1988.

The TIA is an SDO accredited by the ANSI to develop voluntary telecommunications standards. As such, TIA's intellectual property policy is consistent with that of ANSI: Namely, any essential patent in a US standard must be licensed according to "reasonable and non-discriminatory" terms.

We focus on the TIA TR-30 committee, which is responsible for setting analog standards in data transmission systems and equipment. One of the key responsibilities of the TIA TR-30 committee is to set analog modem standards in the US.[15] The TIA TR-30 committee was also the US technical advisory group to the ITU, the organization that sets international telecommunications standards. This committee has three subcommittees that address three subtopics:

- TR-30.1 – Modems
- TR-30.2 – Data termination equipment–data communication equipment interfaces and protocols
- TR-30.3 – Data communications equipment evaluation and network interfaces

The committee and the subcommittees meet on a regular basis, with approximately five to six meetings per year (see Table 6.3). The committee and subcommittee meetings are typically held jointly. Occasionally a subcommittee will hold an additional separate meeting.

Our data consists of participation records of the 56 TR-30 meetings that took place between 1990 and 1999.[16] The TR-30 subcommittees show that the committee is responsible for more than just modems. However, participation data for the subcommittees is not complete and only available for a few of the years. Nevertheless, the main committee

---

[15] There is a separate standards committee for digital modems, hosted by the Alliance for Telecommunications Industry Solutions.
[16] We do not have attendance data for five of the meetings during 1990–9: specifically, three meetings during 1990–4 and two meetings during 1995–9.

Table 6.3. Summary of meetings data: TR-30 and the subcommittees

	TR-30	TR-30.1	TR-30.2	TR-30.3
Meetings 1990–9	56	57	55	60
Meetings 1990–4	29	26	27	29
Meetings 1995–9	27	31	28	31

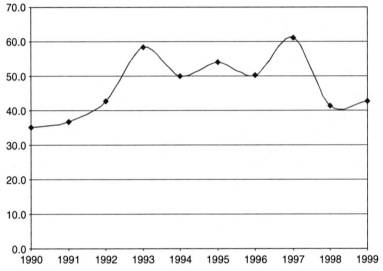

Figure 6.2. Average attendance per TR-30 meeting: 1990–9.

meeting and the subcommittee meetings are held at the same time at the
same location, and most participants who attend the main committee
meetings attend the subcommittee meetings as well. Indeed, there is a
very high correlation (0.92) between participation at TR-30 standardization meetings during the 1993–9 period and participation at TR 30.1
committee meetings during the same period.[17] Hence, it is reasonable
to use TR-30 participation data.

Figure 6.2 shows the average attendance at TR-30 meetings over the
1990–9 period. The figure shows a steady increase from approximately

[17] The 1995 and 1998 participation data is missing for the TR-30.1 subcommittee.
Hence, we use the equivalent data for the full TR-30 committee. This calculation
is made for the forty-five firms that hold patents and attended meetings.

Table 6.4. Participation at TR-30 meetings

Firm	Attendees, 1990–9	Attendees, 1990–4	Attendees, 1995–9	Products[a]
Motorola	209	122	87	D,U
AT&T	190	136	54	C
Rockwell Semiconductor	141	53	88	U
General Datacomm	106	71	35	I
US Robotics	74	37	37	D
Intel	69	39	30	U
Satchell Evaluations	67	44	23	O
Hayes	66	40	26	D
3COM	58	0	58	D,U
Telecom Analysis Systems	55	33	22	O
Racal Milgo	54	38	16	D
Db Consulting	47	25	22	O
Texas Ins.	46	7	39	U,I
IBM	44	15	29	U,C
National Semiconductor	40	24	16	U
Participation, top 15 (1990–9)	1,266	682	584	
Total participation	2,355	1,136	1,219	

Note: [a] Firms products are coded as follows: "downstream" modem (D), upstream inputs into modems (U), infrastructure for modems (I), complementary products (C), or other (O).

35 participants per meeting in 1991 to 58 in 1993. Attendance remains relatively high, peaking in 1997 at 62 participants per meeting during the standards war over the 56K modem. Afterwards, for 1998–9, attendance falls to slightly more than 40 per meeting, perhaps partially due to resolution of the standards war and the advent of the digital modems.

Overall, 177 firms participated in at least one TR-30 meeting during the 1990–9 time period. In Table 6.4, we present the 1990–9 participation data for the top 15 of those firms; we also include data for the sub-time periods of 1990–4 and 1995–9. Four firms – Motorola, AT&T, Rockwell, and General Datacomm – accounted for 25% of the meeting participants for 1990–9, and the top 15 firms accounted for approximately 54% of total participants during that same time period.

Not listed in Table 6.4 are the top 15 firms for each subperiod, which are obviously different than those from the entire 1990–9 period. Our data shows, however, that while the top 15 firms of 1990–4 accounted for more than 66% of the participants, the top 15 firms of 1995–9 accounted for just 51% of the participants. This suggests that an increasing number of firms believe that there are benefits from participating in the meetings.

5 Patenting and meeting participation

Approximately 194 firms received patents with the word modem in the title during the 1976–99 period. Similarly, 177 firms attended TR-30 standardization meetings during the 1990–9 period. The Herfindahl index (HHI) for patents during the 1990–4 period is 378, and 225 during the 1995–9 period. Similarly, the HHI for standardization meetings is 448 for 1990–4 and 262 for 1995–9. Hence both intellectual property and standards meeting "competition" have become less concentrated over time. These concentration figures are extremely low relative to what the modem product market concentration figures are likely to be, but, as we saw, both meeting participants and patentees are drawn from a much wider set of firms. However, the modem patent HHI is not so much greater than the average three-digit patent class HHI of 314, which is striking considering that the average number of assignees in a three-digit class is almost 2,400 – an order of magnitude greater than our set of patent modems.[18]

When we merge the two data sets (by assignee number), we find that only 45 firms both attended TR-30 standardization meetings during the 1990–9 period and held patents with the word modem in the title. (Thus, 326 firms either held one or more patents or attended one or more meetings, but not both.)

---

[18] The average three-digit HHI and number of assignees is calculated on the NBER data for 1976–99 patents only.

Table 6.5a. Patent and citation data summary by meeting participation

	Patents				
	Total	1976–89	1990–4	1995–9	Citations
Attended meetings	281	65	56	160	2,027
Did not attend meetings	323	115	78	130	2,868
TOTAL	604	180	134	290	4,895

Table 6.5b. Meeting summary data by patents

	Attendees		
	Total	1990–4	1995–9
Have patents	1,519	725	794
Do not have patents	836	411	425
TOTAL	2,355	1,136	1,219

Nevertheless (see Table 6.5a), these 45 firms accounted for more than 47% of the total patents issued and 41% of the citations for 1976–99. In addition, 55% of the firms with patents attended standardization committee meetings for 1995–9, up from the 41% for 1990–4. Also (see Table 6.5b), 64% of the attendees at the TR-30 standardization meetings for 1990–9 held relevant modem patents.

An interesting question is whether there are participants who regularly attend standard committee meetings but do not hold patents (or vice versa). Of the fifteen firms with the most participants (see Table 6.4), only three firms did not hold patents. Two of the three, Satchell Evaluations (67 participants) and Telecom Analysis Systems (55 participants), test modems and other telecommunications equipment. The third, Db Consulting (47 participants), provides information on relevant standards to the disabled community. These three firms clearly had no intellectual property, even nascent, to promote in attending these meetings. They attended for informational reasons (and perhaps for user-advocacy reasons in the case of the third firm).

Of the fifteen firms with the most modem patents during the 1976–99 period, only Fujitsu, a major provider of electronics and communications products, did not attend any standardization meetings. Of the fifteen firms with the most patent citations, only three did not attend standardization meetings: Fujitsu, Hycom Data Communications, and ITT Industries. ITT Industries is a global engineering and industrial manufacturing company with important products in communications and networking. Hycom is a Korean firm that integrates data/voice network infrastructures, and it received most of its citations in the 1976–89 period. We do not know why these firms did not participate in the meetings. A reasonable conjecture is that their patents covered either elements of the technology for which there was no competing standard or add-on components that did not require standardization. Regardless of the reason, our informal analysis suggests that nearly all key players in the modem industry both participated in standardization meetings and held relevant patents.

6 Empirical analysis

We now use the merged data set to conduct a more formal analysis. We first define the following variables at the firm level:

Patents: Total number of patents issued during the 1976–99 period

Citations: Total number of citations during the 1976–99 period

Meetings: Total number of meeting participants for the 1990–9 period

Meetings1:   Total number of meeting participants for period 1, 1990–4

Meetings2:   Total number of meeting participants for period 2, 1995–9

Patents1:   Total number of patents issued during period 1, 1990–4

Patents2:   Total number of patents issued during period 2, 1995–9

Citations1:   Total number of citations during period 1, 1990–4

Citations2:   Total number of citations during period 2, 1995–9

Descriptive statistics appear in the appendix. See Tables 6.6a and 6.6b for correlations for the following three variables: (1) total number of patents for the 1976–99 period, (2) total number of citations for the 1976–99 period, and (3) TR-30 meeting participation for the 1990–9 period. We present the data for all 326 firms that have at least one

Table 6.6a. Correlation among variables: all 326 firms

	Patents	Meetings	Citations
Patents	1.00		
Meetings	0.52	1.00	
Citations	0.80	0.39	1.00

Table 6.6b. Correlation among variables: the 45 firms attending meetings and holding patents

	Patents	Meetings	Citations
Patents	1.00		
Meetings	0.55	1.00	
Citations	0.75	0.45	1.00

patent or attended at least one meeting in Table 6.6a; and we present the same summary data for the 45 firms that had patents and attended meetings in Table 6.6b.

These tables show that there is a very high degree of correlation between patents and citations. This, of course, is not surprising. The interesting result is the relatively high degree of correlation between patents and meetings. Also, the correlations are similar for both data sets. See Table 6.7a (full data set) and Table 6.7b (45 firms) for correlations using the period 1 and period 2 variables. We first compare the correlations across periods 1 and 2 for the same variable. The correlation between Meeting1 and Meeting2 is 0.72 for all 326 firms, while it is 0.68 for the smaller data set.

The correlations between patents across periods and between citations across periods are lower than the correlations across meeting attendance. The correlation between Patent1 and Patent2 is 0.35 for the full data set and 0.27 for the smaller data set. Similarly, in the case of citations, the correlation across the two periods is 0.30 for the full data set and 0.22 for the smaller data set.

When we look across different variables and different periods for the full data set, we find that the contemporaneous correlation between

Table 6.7a. Correlations among patents and meetings

	Full data set (326 firms)				
	Meetings1	*Meetings2*	*Patents1*	*Patents2*	*Citations1*
Meetings1	1.00				
Meetings2	0.72	1.00			
Patents1	0.36	0.28	1.00		
Patents2	0.42	0.56	0.35	1.00	
Citations1	0.33	0.27	0.89	0.35	1.00
Citations2	0.60	0.45	0.31	0.60	0.30

Table 6.7b. Correlations among citations and meetings: smaller data set

	The 45 firms attending meetings and holding patents				
	Meetings1	*Meetings2*	*Patents1*	*Patents2*	*Citations1*
Meetings1	1.00				
Meetings2	0.68	1.00			
Patents1	0.46	0.27	1.00		
Patents2	0.39	0.55	0.27	1.00	
Citations1	0.39	0.25	0.90	0.25	1.00
Citations2	0.63	0.41	0.25	0.54	0.22

citations and meetings is higher in period 2 than it is in period 1. Similarly, the correlation between patents and meetings is higher for period 2. Perhaps the most striking result is the relatively high correlation between Citations2 and Meetings1 (0.60 for the full data set and 0.63 for the smaller data set).

The relatively high correlations in Tables 6.7a and 6.7b between intellectual property, which includes patents and citations, and meeting participation data begs the question of whether there is a causal relationship between these variables. That is, does increased participation in standard committee meetings lead to increases in intellectual property, or do increased intellectual property holdings lead to greater participation at standards meetings?

Given the limitations of our data, we can test for causality only in the narrow, technical sense formalized by Granger (1969) and Sims (1980).[19] In this interpretation, a variable X causes Y if lagged values of X are significant in explaining Y in a regression in which lagged values of Y are also explanatory variables. It is, of course, possible that causality can exist in both directions. This test is performed using vector autoregressions. We are not estimating a structural model when performing these tests; nevertheless, we believe that this type of analysis is useful for an initial examination of these variables.

Since it typically takes an average of two to three years to receive a patent, it seems sensible to use two periods that correspond to periods for which we have data on standard committee participation: 1990–4 and 1995–9. Because there is only a single lag for the standard participation data we employ the following specification:

$$Y_t = \beta_0 + \beta_1 Y_{t-1} + \beta_2 X_{t-1}.$$

Formally, X causes Y if X_{t-1} is significant in explaining Y, after controlling for Y_{t-1}. We present results from vector autoregressions of intellectual property on meeting participation and vice versa in Tables 6.8a and 6.8b.

In the case of all the full data set (326 firms), the first column of Table 6.8a shows that early patents predict later ones; every additional early patent is associated with about half of an additional later patent. Even controlling for this effect, early participation in standards meetings predicts later patents. An additional participant at each of the twenty-nine meetings in the first half of the 1990s would predict an additional 1.7 patents in the second half. The second column of Table 6.8a similarly shows that early citations predict later citations. Likewise, after controlling for the lagged dependent variable, early participation in standards meetings explains the later citations as well.

In Table 6.8b, we present results for the smaller data set, namely, for the 45 firms that both patented and attended at least one meeting. Now, the lagged dependent variable has no predictive power in either of the first two columns. Yet participation in the early standards meetings still predicts the late patents and citations.

---

[19] This section draws from Gandal et al. (1999), who conducted a similar type of analysis.

Table 6.8a. Granger causality analysis: all firms
(t-statistics in parentheses)

Full data set N = 326	Dependent variable			
	Patents2	Citations2	Meetings2	Meetings2
Independent variables				
Constant	0.50	0.27	1.68	1.66
	(4.45)	(1.23)	(3.93)	(3.95)
Patents1	0.45		0.24	
	(4.32)		(0.59)	
Citations1		0.08		0.027
		(2.50)		(0.94)
Meetings1	0.057	0.44	0.57	0.56
	(6.48)	(12.02)	(16.99)	(17.12)
Adjusted R-squared	0.22	0.37	0.51	0.51

Table 6.8b. Granger/Sims causality tests: all 45 firms
(t-statistics in parentheses)

Small data set (45 firms) N = 45	Dependent variable			
	Patents2	Citations2	Meetings2	Meetings2
Independent variables				
Constant	2.44	3.37	10.28	9.96
	(3.11)	(0.34)	(3.56)	(3.51)
Patents1	0.26		−0.64	
	(0.73)		(−0.46)	
Citations1		−0.03		−0.02
		(−0.26)		(−0.19)
Meetings1	0.05	0.52	0.51	0.49
	(2.11)	(4.90)	(5.63)	(5.67)
Adjusted R-squared	0.12	0.36	0.45	0.44

The obvious explanation for our finding is that firms with pending but not yet granted patents attend the committee to have the standard incorporate their intellectual property. However, as there is typically a lag of only two to three years between patents applications and patent grants, it is possible that firms lobby to introduce innovations for which they have not yet applied for a patent – although there are obvious risks in doing so. Another possible explanation is that the information garnered at these meetings helps advance firms' intellectual property portfolio. Another type of knowledge diffusion may be relevant to the effect of early meetings on citations; firms may cite patents of other firms attending standards meetings. We hope to discriminate among these various explanations in further research.

The third and fourth columns of Tables 6.8a and 6.8b show that past participation in early standardization meetings is a good predictor of participation in later ones. With our limited data, we cannot hope to discriminate between a heterogeneity explanation for this correlation, and a state-based explanation, that is, that firms that participate in standardization meetings realize the benefits from doing so and continue to participate in the future. More interesting is the finding that neither early patents nor early citations predict participation in the later standardization meetings. This finding indicates that only recent innovations are the subject matter of these meetings. Innovations covered by patents that are four to five years old must either no longer be technology relevant or have had their standardization decision already made – they are either already in or out of the standard.

7 Conclusion

We empirically examined the interaction between patenting and participation in standardization committee meetings. We showed that while many firms obtained modem patents and many firms participated in standardization meetings, only a small subset of firms (45 of 326) both obtained patents and participated in the standardization meetings. These firms accounted for a significant percentage of the patents received and the total number of meeting attendees. For these 45 firms, we find a fairly high correlation among the intellectual property (measured by both patents and citations) and meeting participation data. Using Granger-causality tests, we also find that although participation in standards meetings predicts future intellectual property, early patents or citations do not predict later participation in the meetings. We interpret these results primarily as reflecting the timing of standard setting relative to innovation, although we also consider the effects of knowledge diffusion at the meetings.

Missing from this analysis is a formal consideration of the firms' importance in the product market. This third element is difficult to add not only because there are various modem product markets (dial-up, faxes, etc.), but also because both meeting participants and patentees often are not modem producers at all, but input suppliers or users. Furthermore, market share data is difficult to obtain. Nevertheless, understanding the three-way interaction of meeting participation, patenting, and product market competition is surely essential to a full understanding of the role of standardization committees in the modem market, and in markets more generally. We hope to address this issue in further research.

References

Augereau, A., S. Greenstein, and M. Rysman 2003. "Coordination vs. differentiation in a standards war: 56 K Modems," mimeo, Boston: Boston University.

Caplan, P. 2003. "Patents and open standards," National Information Standards Organization, available at http://www.niso.org/press/whitepapers/Patents_Caplan.pdf.

Cargill, C. 2004. "Standardization, the necessary luxury," available at http://www.geoplace.com/gw/2004/0403/0403ogc1.asp.

David, P., and S. Greenstein 1990. "The economics of compatibility standards: An introduction to recent research," *Economics of Innovation and New Technology* 1: 3–41.

Farrell, J., and P. Klemperer, in press. "Coordination and lock-in: Competition with switching costs and network effects," in *Handbook of industrial organization*, Vol. III, Mark Armstrong and Robert Porter (eds.), Amsterdam: Elsevier.

Farrell, J., and G. Saloner 1988. "Coordination through committees and markets," *RAND Journal of Economics* 19: 235–52.

Gandal, N. 1995. "A selective survey of the literature on indirect network externalities," *Research in Law and Economics* 17: 23–31.

2002. "Compatibility, standardization, and network effects: Some policy implications," *Oxford Review of Economic Policy* 18: 80–91.

Gandal, N., S. Greenstein, and D. Salant 1999. "Adoptions and orphans in the early microcomputer market," *Journal of Industrial Economics* 47: 87–105.

Garen, C. 2000. "Analog modems take center stage: Industry trend or event," *Electronic News*, August 7, http://www.findarticles.com/cf_dls/m0EKF/32_46/65023364/p1/article.jhtml.

Gilbert, R. 1992. "Symposium on compatibility: Incentives and market structure," *Journal of Industrial Economics* 40: 1–8.

Gordon, R. 2000. "Does the new economy measure up to the great inventions of the past?" *Journal of Economic Perspectives* 14: 49–74.

Granger, C. 1969. "Investigating causal relations by econometric models and cross-spectral methods," *Econometrica* 37: 424–38.

International Telecommunication Union 1998. "Agreement reached on 56 K modem standard," available at http://www.itu.int/newsarchive/press_releases/1998/04.html.

Katz, M., and C. Shapiro 1994. "Systems competition and network effects," *Journal of Economic Perspectives* 8: 93–115.

Kenas, B. 1997. "Modems," available at http://www.nric.org/fg/fg2/sc1/fg2-sc1-modems-final.doc. Original sources include the Information Technology Industry Council and the Data Analysis Group.

Lemley, M. 2002. "Intellectual property rights and standard-setting organizations," *California Law Review* 90: 1889.

Matutes, C., and P. Regibeau 1996. "A selective review of the economics of standardization: Entry deterrence, technological progress, and international competition," *European Journal of Political Economy* 12: 183–206.

Meidan, M. 2004. "The effects of the standardization process on competition: An event study of the standardization process in the US cable modem market," mimeo, Stanford, CA: Stanford University.

Merges, R. 1998. "Institutions for intellectual property transactions: The case of patent pools," mimeo, Berkeley, CA: University of California-Berkeley.

Oliner, S. D., D. E. Sichel, J. E. Triplett, and R. J. Gordon 1994. "Computers and output growth revisited: How big is the puzzle?" *Brookings Papers on Economic Activity* 1994: 273–317.

Postrel, S. 1990. "Competing networks and proprietary standards: The case of quadraphonic sounds," *Journal of Industrial Economics* 39: 169–85.

Simcoe, T. 2004. "Committees and the creation of technical standards," mimeo, Berkeley, CA: University of California-Berkeley.

Sims, C. 1980. "Macroeconomics and reality," *Econometrica* 48: 1–48.

Stango, V. 2004. "The economics of standards wars," *Review of Network Economics* 3: 1–19.

Appendix

Table 6.A1. Descriptive statistics: full data set, N = 326

Variable	Mean	Std. dev.	Minimum	Maximum
Meetings	7.22	21.48	0	209
Patents	1.76	3.63	0	27
Citations	14.03	37.00	0	334
Meetings1	3.48	12.87	0	136
Meetings2	3.74	10.30	0	88
Patents1	0.37	1.07	0	8
Patents2	0.87	2.14	0	18
Citations1	4.22	14.61	0	148
Citations2	2.45	10.06	0	132

Table 6.A2. Descriptive statistics: firms with at least one patent and attending at least one meeting, N = 45

Variable	Mean	Std. dev.	Minimum	Maximum
Meetings	33.76	46.83	1	209
Patents	6.24	6.98	1	27
Citations	45.04	70.64	0	334
Meetings1	16.11	29.72	0	136
Meetings2	17.64	21.19	0	88
Patents1	1.24	1.93	0	8
Patents2	3.56	4.32	0	18
Citations1	15.27	27.45	0	148
Citations2	11.31	24.24	0	132

7 Manipulating interface standards as an anticompetitive strategy

JEFFREY K. MACKIE-MASON
AND JANET S. NETZ

Abstract

The creation of interface standards enables competition at the level of components, rather than in complete systems, and consumers often benefit from component competition. Nevertheless, the standard-setting process can be manipulated to achieve anticompetitive ends. The authors consider the conditions under which a standards consortium could impose anticompetitive burdens on the market and examine several strategies such a consortium might employ to achieve anticompetitive objectives. They present a new strategy – one-way interface standards – and discuss the conditions under which it can be anticompetitive.

1 Introduction

Complementary devices in a complex technological system must communicate through interfaces to interoperate successfully. In systems that involve communications and computing functions, interfaces are connections through which signals pass. The devices on both sides of an interface (e.g., the microprocessors and a disk drive, or the PBX [that is, the private branch exchange] and the central office switch) must be designed so that they make the correct physical connection, send the correct signals to each other, and correctly interpret the signals received. We refer to the formal physical and signaling details as the *interface specification.*

Communications and computing functions are featured in a much wider variety of systems than those we think of as primarily telecommunications or computers. For example, automobiles have sophisticated controller systems in which multiple components communicate with each other. Medical devices often perform sophisticated computation. At the least, our analysis applies to any system through which information flows through electrical, photonic, or other electromagnetic signaling. We also expect the general principles to apply to interfaces in other (non-signaling) technologies, though we have not studied such systems.

An interface stands – physically or logically – between two (or more) separate components. Thus, for an interface specification to succeed, it must be adopted by at least one manufacturer of the components on each side of the interface. When an interface specification is published, adopted, and implemented by at least one different firm manufacturing each of the affected components, we refer to it as an *interface standard*.[1]

In this article, we develop three related ideas: (1) technologies can compete as individual components or as complete systems; (2) interface standards are important determinants of component-level competition; and (3) the standard-setting process can be manipulated to distort component competition. Our primary original contribution is to identify a specific strategy – which we call *one-way interface standards* – that standards consortia can use to manipulate a standard-setting process to achieve anticompetitive ends.

Competition and consumers often – but not always – benefit when interface specifications are standardized and openly published. For example, if competing firms can design and manufacture system components that correctly interoperate, then consumers (or systems integrators that then sell to consumers) can mix and match components from different manufacturers to get the set of components that offers the best combination of price and performance. Nevertheless, consumers also may benefit when competition is for complete, incompatible systems, because there may be more incentive for innovation or more efficient adoption and rejection of new technologies.

Most interface specifications are developed by firms participating in the relevant industries. There are several different configurations of industry participants that might work together to create a standard. For example,

- A group may be composed of several manufacturers of each component. In some such cases, a relatively open process is used, in which a membership organization (with or without government sanctioning) accepts any qualified participant that manufactures either (or both)

---

[1] Terms such as "standards" and "open" are used in various ways in the literature. In this article, we use "standard" for a specification that is published, and we use "open" to refer to the public nature of the standard. We specifically do not use "open" to describe the copyright or licensing status of the standard, such as it is often used when discussing open source technologies.

of the complementary components and through a formal process the organization jointly develops the specification. In other cases, membership is limited.

- A group may be composed of firms that manufacture the component on one side of the interface. For example, automobile manufacturers might agree on a specification for attaching tires to wheels without the participation of tire manufacturers.
- A single firm that manufactures products on one or both sides of the interface may specify a standard. For example, once required to do so by the Federal Communications Commission, AT&T announced specifications for attaching customer premises equipment (CPE) to its network.[2] Microsoft also unilaterally announces the specifications of applications programming interfaces (APIs) for software programs to communicate with its operating systems.

It is conventionally assumed that openly published standards lower the barriers to entry in a market because potential entrants can design components that interoperate with existing complements if they adhere to the standard. The standard-setting process, however, can be manipulated to *create or raise* barriers to entry. Just as with a price-setting consortium (that is, a cartel), a standards consortium may be able to harm competition when its membership characteristics satisfy conditions for market power and barriers to entry.[3] There are two conditions sufficient to anticompetitively manipulate a standards process: (1) the consortium must include firms with sufficient market power to ensure industry adoption of the standard, and (2) membership and decision-making control must be restricted in a manner that excludes viable potential competitors.[4]

---

[2] The rules requiring AT&T to permit others to attach CPE to its network and to publish the interface specifications necessary to do so were developed by the courts and the Federal Communications Commission in a series of landmark decisions: *Hush-A-Phone Corp.* v. *United States* (1957); *Use of the Carterfone Device in Message Toll Telephone Service* (1968); *Second Computer Inquiry Decisions* (1980 and 1981); and *Computer & Communications Industry Association* v. *Federal Communications Commission* (1982, 1983, 1984).

[3] The European Commission (1987) recognized these characteristics in *X/Open Group*.

[4] Many standard-setting groups have two levels or groups of membership. One group controls (sets) the standard and the other group has an advisory and/or testing role. For example, the USB 2.0 Implementers Forum has Promoter Members, who are allowed to vote on decisions, and Participant Members, who

When a standards consortium has the potential to exercise market power, various strategies may have anticompetitive consequences. These strategies include delaying publication of the standard to gain a first-mover advantage; creating standards that require other firms to use royalty-bearing intellectual property (e.g., a patent owned by a firm in the standards consortium); and creating one-way interface standards.[5]

To the best of our knowledge, the last strategy – one-way interface standards – has not previously been described in the economics literature. In an industry with complementary system components that interoperate, component manufacturers on *both* sides of the interface require specifications for the physical and/or logical connections that enable the components to interoperate. In general, it is necessary to publish the specification of both sides of the interface protocol for manufacturers on either side to use the standard. However, through creating a blind or a cut-out – in the form of an extra technology layer – a consortium can publish the information necessary to manufacture compliant components on one side of the interface without releasing the information necessary to manufacture components on the other side. We name this strategy one-way interface standards. Such standards facilitate competition for one component, but harm competition for the other, complementary component.

Whether one-way interface standards harm consumers overall turns on the same issues well known in the trade-off between mix-and-match and systems competition. Our contribution is to show how an interface standards consortium can move the boundary that separates systems from mix-and-match competition.

are allowed to participate in the discussions but are not allowed to vote. See the group's bylaws at www.usb.org/data/retail/usbif_bylaws.pdf.

[5] In the penultimate section of this paper, we present three detailed examples of standards consortia that apparently have employed these tactics to use standard-setting processes for anticompetitive gain. One example involves the JEDEC consortium and its creation of a DRAM standard subject to the patents of Rambus, which participated in JEDEC; another is Intel's specification of the Accelerated Graphics Port (AGP) advanced graphics standard; and the third is the development of the Universal Serial Bus (USB) 2.0 and EHCI (Enhanced Host Controller Interface) interface specifications to implement high-speed serial communications with desktop computer peripherals.

2 Benefits and costs of component competition

When interface specifications are standardized and non-proprietary, component competition – that is, competition between multiple manufacturers of a given component in a system – can thrive. However, it is not given that component competition is necessarily superior to systems competition. We briefly describe the benefits and costs of component competition.

2.1 *Benefits from component competition*

Competition on price and performance
When interface specifications are published, more firms can enter the markets for individual components, and the greater entry results in more competition on price, performance, and quality of the component in question (Economides 1988; Matutes and Regibeau 1988). In contrast, when interfaces are not public, competition is between incompatible systems (i.e., combinations of components), rather than between mix-and-match components. Systems competition results in increased product differentiation among components of a particular type: they are compatible with different systems. If there is not much demand for the ensuing variety, it may serve primarily to divide the market. Thus, spurious differentiation can lead to higher prices and may not provide offsetting gain from variety (Farrell and Saloner 1986a). Component competition avoids such spurious product differentiation, and thus can lead to lower prices and higher quality.

Scale efficiencies and lower production costs
By increasing the size of the potential market, public interface standards may enable firms to realize efficient scale and learning economies (Hemenway 1975). This may explain why Apple Macintosh hardware typically costs more than comparably performing PC (personal computer) hardware.[6]

---

[6] Scale economies might explain the price difference for some components that use different interfaces even if the interfaces adhere to published standards. For example, in 2001, PC Connection (a leading component retailer) listed eighty-seven add-in video cards for Intel-based PCs. Mac Connection (owned by the same company) listed only five add-in video cards for Apple Macintosh

Network externalities

For many products, consumers benefit the more other users there are of the same (or a compatible) product. For example, several standards for mobile telephones are in use. Telephone companies in the United States largely adopted TDMA (Time Division Multiple Access) multiplexing, but some adopted CDMA (Code-Division Multiple Access) technology. Europe and most of the rest of the world adopted GSM (Global System for Mobile Communications), which uses TDMA. Consumers with GSM phones benefit from being able to use their phones as they move from country to country.[7] Some US users have started to benefit from this network externality, as providers deploy new GSM networks. To do so, however, customers typically must first purchase more expensive multi-mode phones to make domestic calls outside the rather limited footprint of the GSM networks and then use the different frequencies for GSM that are employed by other nations. If there is a single standard with component competition, then the number of users will be larger and consumers may obtain greater benefits from the network externalities.

More innovation and variety for components

When interfaces between complementary components are standardized, a firm making one component in a system faces a larger potential market than in a market with multiple proprietary interfaces. If interfaces are proprietary, a firm that innovates can only sell its component to the portion of the market that uses the particular system with which its component works. When the potential payoffs are larger, it is worthwhile for small, innovative, new firms to incur the risks and costs of entry, thereby enhancing competition. For example, while maintaining compatibility with the x86 architecture interface standards, firms other than Intel pioneered low-power microprocessors for mobile computers; Cyrix's MediaGX microprocessor spawned

computers. In addition, prices for the PC components were lower. For example, the ATI Tech Radeon 32MB DDR (double data rate) video board for a PC was $166 with an AGP interface. See http://www.pcconnection.com/scripts/productdetail.asp?product_id=214468. The same card for the Macintosh is $209–$240 with an AGP interface. See http://www.macconnection.com/scripts/productdetail.asp?product_id=219741.

[7] One of the authors observed Martin Cave, while in Australia, use his UK phone to call someone with an Australian phone who was sitting in a cubicle 10 feet away.

the sub-$1,000 PC market;[8] AMD (Advanced Micro Devices) and Intel have been leapfrogging each other in a race for the fastest processors; and so forth.

Reduced risk of stranded investments
When interfaces are standardized, consumers will have confidence that they can buy upgraded components that will work with their systems and that these components will continue to work if they purchase a new base system. For example, consumers can add larger and faster hard drives, improved monitors, scanners, and other devices to their base computers (Porter 1985).

2.2 Costs from component competition

There are also some potential costs to consumers from component competition based on open standards. The costs we discuss in this section are not (necessarily) associated with anticompetitive behavior: they can occur in competitive markets. These costs are a consequence of the complementarities inherent in complex technological systems. With complementarities, consumers may be better off with production of systems consisting of components that connect through proprietary interfaces. In such cases, there may be sufficient benefits from competition between systems to outweigh the foregone benefits of component-wise competition.

Reduction in system design variety
Systems competition, with the resulting differentiation between system architectures, may provide benefits by increasing variety. When interfaces are proprietary, a firm that wishes to enter with a new, innovative design in one component may find it necessary to develop an entire system. The result may be an increase in variety of systems. The entry of the NeXT computer in the late 1980s may be an example. NeXT introduced a new operating system that took greater advantage of the

---

[8] The MediaGX combined a microprocessor, memory controller, graphics accelerator, and PCI (peripheral component interconnect) interface on a single chip. At the time, competing offerings would have required at least a processor plus the north bridge of a chipset to match this functionality. *Microprocessor Report* (1997a) attributes the MediaGX's success with driving Intel to finally breach the $106 price floor it had long maintained for its mainstream processors.

object-oriented programming model than did any other desktop operating system. NeXT also produced its own hardware on which to run this operating system, introducing innovations in digital signal processing, raster-oriented (Display Postscript) screen output, mass storage (magneto-optical drives), and other features.[9]

Network externalities
When network externalities are significant, socially undesirable outcomes may occur in a market with open standards and component, rather than systems, competition. For example, when there are already many users of a given standardized system, the incentives to innovate and develop a better system may be insufficient. Even if a firm does develop a better system, consumers may find it too costly to switch (in part because they do not believe that enough other users will switch). In a market with competition among several incompatible systems, entry by a new, innovative system may be easier than in a market with a single common set of standards. This problem, which can lead to sub-optimal innovation, is known as *excess inertia* (Farrell and Saloner 1986a; Katz and Shapiro 1994).

2.3 *Summary: systems versus mix-and-match competition*

Manufacturers of complementary components need to know interface specifications in a system so that their components correctly connect and communicate with the other components. With open interface standards, many firms can make compatible components on both sides of the interface, and thus component competition will be viable. As was previously described, there are both benefits of component competition for consumers and, in some situations, offsetting costs. In some industries, these offsetting costs are sufficient enough that consumers are better served by systems competition, which is marked by proprietary interfaces and components that work only with specific matching complements.

For the most part, the history of the x86-compatible PC industry has been marked by component-based competition; the availability of open

---

[9] The NeXT operating system became the basis for Apple's OS/X operating system, and thus has contributed substantially to Apple's ongoing ability to put some competitive pressure on Microsoft and Intel.

standards has been credited with the high rate of innovation, the variety of low-cost, high-performance products, and the overwhelming success of the PC architecture against closed systems, such as the Apple Macintosh and various RISC-based (Reduced Instruction Set Computer-based) systems. Both systems and component competition have been dominant in different parts of the telecommunications industry.

On the basis of economic theory alone, we cannot conclude that component-based competition and open interface standards are always best for consumers and the economy. Yet, when open standards are preferred, it is usually on the assumption that they benefit component competition. We now identify strategies through which the standard-setting process can be manipulated to harm competition and consumers.

3 Anticompetitive manipulation of interface standards

Collusive agreements between competitors to fix prices or divide markets are generally illegal. Indeed, under the Sherman Antitrust Act, collusion is per se illegal: it is not necessary to prove that the agreement causes harm to consumers; rather, harm is presumed. However, collusive agreements among competitors to establish interface standards are not per se prohibited, and in fact are both common and encouraged by policymakers.

The different stance toward standards agreements follows from the presumption that their effects are primarily pro-competitive. Yet, when there is a combination of firms that together have power in at least one of the markets for components on the two sides of an interface, they may be able to use the process of setting interface standards to increase or maintain market power. Doing so can ultimately harm consumers and society.

To harm competition, a standards consortium must satisfy the two usual conditions. First, it must have market power and be protected by barriers to entry in order to successfully exercise that market power. Thus, for it to be *possible* to harm competition, a consortium needs to include firms with sufficient market power in one or both of the component markets to ensure widespread adoption of the standard. Second, to protect against competitive dilution, the consortium needs to restrict membership and decision-making control in a manner that excludes viable potential competitors. If not – that is, if any competent and interested firm could participate and if the decision process was not biased so that a subset of the members could exert effective control – then it would be hard for the consortium to implement anticompetitive strategies.[10]

The European Union antitrust body discussed precisely these conditions in its *X/Open Group* decision (European Commission 1987). It was concerned with market power because the case involved a standard-setting group of computer firms that were each of considerable size. The Commission also noted that it was possible for the members to exclude competing firms from membership. The Commission concluded that "an appreciable distortion of competition . . . may result from future decisions of the Group" (¶34).

Of course, that a consortium of firms with the *potential* to exclude competition agrees to set standards does not imply that consumers and competition will be harmed. We now describe some strategies with anticompetitive effects that such consortia might employ.

3.1 Charging a toll

One way in which an interface specification consortium can harm component competition is to design royalty-bearing intellectual property into the standard. Suppose one firm in the consortium holds a patent on a technology that is useful but not essential for the interface. That is, the interface could be designed without the patented technology and be equally efficient. The patent holder, however, might induce the consortium to specify that the patented technology be used for the interface and, as a result, would be paid royalties for its use. As an inducement, the patent holder might share the rents by offering consortium members a reduced or zero royalty, ensuring that rivals of the consortium's members will have higher costs than consortium members.

Sometimes a patent holder might be able to deceive a consortium unilaterally into including its patented technology in a specification. Often there are long delays between the date a firm files a claim and the

---

[10] Although restricted voting can enable a consortium to harm competition, it may not be necessary to force democratic participation and fair voting rules to protect competition. It may be sufficient to require that all information shared by consortium members be made simultaneously available to all other competent and interested firms.

grant of the patent. The consortium may not realize that a technology written into a specification is covered by such a "submarine" patent.[11] If the patent is granted after the specification is released and adopted as a standard by the industry, the patent holder may successfully raise its rivals' costs through the royalties it demands. Later, we will discuss the Rambus cases, in which its rivals claimed Rambus employed this strategy.

3.2 Withholding or delaying information

A second strategy through which an interface specification consortium can harm component competition is by withholding necessary interface information from potential rivals for a short or long period, thereby rendering a so-called open standard effectively proprietary (Farrell and Saloner 1992). Withholding necessary information raises rivals' costs (thus raising the prices to end users) and may deter entry (or hasten exit) altogether (Matutes and Regibeau 1996). In particular, if crucial interface information is withheld for long enough, a potential rival will be forced to develop a complete system, in which it controls the interfaces, and then to compete on a systems basis. Thus, the consortium may have colluded to exclude component competition. The creation of the Universal Serial Bus (USB) 2.0 standard, which we describe below, is a possible example of this strategy.

3.3 One-way interface standards

Another potentially anticompetitive strategy is for a consortium to design a standard to facilitate competition in components on one side of an interface while restricting competition in components on the

---

[11] There are many cases in which patent claimants exploited Patent Office rules to intentionally delay the granting and publication of their patents. The Lemelson machine vision patents are a well-known example, in which delays were created by filing a series of continuation and divisional patent applications that claim priority from the initial patent application. The Federal Circuit recently ruled that a patent may be unenforceable if the patent applicant unreasonably delays prosecuting the patent (*Symbol Technologies Inc.* v. *Lemelson Medical, Educational & Research Foundation* 2002).

US patent law was recently amended by the American Inventors Protection Act of 1999 to limit submarine patents. Claims filed after November 29, 2000 will automatically be published eighteen months after they are filed, even if the review process is not complete.

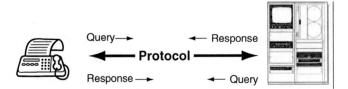

Figure 7.1. Telecom interface protocol.

other side of the interface. We call this a *one-way interface standard*. As we noted earlier, we have not seen this strategy previously identified in the literature.

Implementing a one-way interface standard is not straightforward. Since a standard specifies both sides of an interface, it might seem that the consortium need merely withhold the specification information for one side of the interface. In fact, it is the nature of interface standards that manufacturers of components on both sides need all of the information about both sides of the interface. To understand this requires a bit more detail about interface standards.

Consider a simple interface (see Figure 7.1). We have illustrated the communications part of an interface standard, known as the *protocol*. An enormous variety of technologies (including any system that employs communications or computing) depends on interfaces that send signals between components. The protocol specifies the language for the signaling, including a syntax and vocabulary. In Figure 7.1 we show a piece of CPE and a communications switch. The CPE sends queries and directives to the switch; the switch responds. Likewise, the switch queries the CPE, which in turn responds. The protocol specifies the permissible queries and the responses that can be generated to each query. If the CPE complies with the specification, it knows what messages it can send and what responses the switch can give. If the CPE did not know the responses the switch could give, then it could not be programmed to make use of those responses. Likewise, a compliant CPE knows what queries it can receive and what responses it is expected to give.

From the example, it should be evident that the components on both sides of the interface must know the full specification. The CPE must know not only its own permissible queries and responses to the switch, but also the switch's permissible responses and queries. It is not

Figure 7.2. Telecom interface with translator.

possible to publish only one side of the specification and design components on that side.

How, then, can a standards consortium design a one-way interface standard? The basic idea is to create a "cut-out" or a "blind" – to insert an additional structure between the two components. We call this structure a *translator*. Now the interface specification between one component and the translator can be published, but the interface specification between the translator and the other component is treated as proprietary and is not published. Manufacturers on the open side can manufacture compliant components that communicate with the translator, but non-member manufacturers on the other side cannot make their components communicate with the translator.

To illustrate, consider the following example of how the protocol in Figure 7.1 would break down if both sides were not published. Imagine that the CPE is programmed to communicate in English. However, the switch is programmed to communicate in another language, and the CPE does not know what language the switch is using, nor how to speak it. Clearly, the CPE and the switch cannot interoperate successfully.

Now introduce a translator (Figure 7.2). The interface protocol between the CPE and the translator can specify that they speak English to each other. The language spoken between the translator and the switch can be kept secret. Anyone can manufacture compliant CPE, but only those consortium members who know the secret language spoken by the translator can manufacture switches.

There is a simple and reasonably familiar way to implement a one-way interface standard, at least conceptually. The standard could specify that the two components communicate via public key cryptography (PKC). In PKC communications, keys are created in pairs, one called "public" and the other "private." A message encrypted with the public key can only be decrypted with the private key; likewise, a message encrypted with the private key can only be decrypted with the public key.[12]

The following example illustrates how PKC can be used to implement one-way interface standards. The standard would publish a public key and an algorithm that components on the public side could use to encrypt messages sent to the private side, and to decrypt messages arriving from the private side. Components on the private side would need the corresponding private key to decrypt messages encrypted with the public key and to encrypt messages that could be decrypted with the public key. As long as the component manufacturers on the protected side of the interface kept the private key secret, no other manufacturer could make a component that could communicate with the public side components.[13]

The effect of a one-way interface standard is to extend the boundary of systems competition. Continuing with the example, the switch in Figure 7.1 is a system. That is, the switch is a set of complementary components that communicate with each other to collectively perform services for users. To compete in switches, manufacturers need to implement all of the features that switch users expect – in particular, the ability to communicate with external components through specified interfaces. Thus, there is systems competition in switches. Suppose that when a one-way interface standard is imposed, as in Figure 7.2, the switch is on the proprietary side. Now, a potential competitor that previously would have designed complete switch systems to compete must design both the switch and the translator. That is, since the specification between the CPE and the translator is public, potential switch competitors can connect to CPE if they develop their own translators that conform to the public CPE-translator standard. The system boundary has expanded to include the translator device.[14]

---

[12] Diffie and Hellman (1976) first proposed the PKC; the most widely used implementation is the RSA algorithm (Rivest et al. 1978).

[13] It is unlikely that PKC would actually be used for this purpose for at least two reasons. First, the private key would need to be hard-coded into the physical components, and then it would likely be a straightforward matter for competing firms to discover it. Second, PKC imposes substantial computational overhead, and hence would not be practical for the many very fast, very short messages that communications and computing devices exchange.

[14] Notice that this strategy is similar to tying as a foreclosure strategy: a firm with monopoly power over Good A requires consumers to purchase Good B if they

Expanding the system boundary is a variation on raising rivals' costs. It may be possible to design and market expanded systems (that include proprietary translators), but it takes time and money to do so. If the translator design is sufficiently costly or time-consuming, or if it is protected by intellectual property, then firms excluded from the standards consortium may find it very difficult to compete effectively.

3.4 Timing is critical

Timing is a crucial element in the above strategies. In the communications and computing industries, technological innovation is so constant and rapid that significant delays in time to market can mean the difference between vibrant, successful competition and a persistent pattern of dominance with minor fringe competition. Thus, none of the strategies needs to be leak-proof or permanent. If the dominant firm can impose the competitive disadvantages for as little as a few months or a year, the effects on competition can be devastating. This is particularly so because the ongoing cycle of innovation gives the dominant firm the opportunity to put its competitors "on the treadmill." For example, with one-way interface standards, a dominant firm could introduce one translator after another, for each new or revised interface that arises. Potential competitors would bear an ongoing stream of higher costs and delays in getting to market.

The US Federal Trade Commission (hereafter, FTC 1999) makes this point quite forcefully in its analysis of Intel's conduct published along with the consent decree entered into by Intel and the FTC:

The computer industry is characterized by short, dynamic product cycles, which are generally measured in months. Time to market is crucial. Indeed, the denial of advance product information is virtually tantamount to a denial of actual parts, because an OEM [original equipment manufacturer] customer lacking such information simply cannot design new computer systems on a competitive schedule with other OEMs. An OEM who [sic] suffers denial of such information over a period of months will lose much of the profits it

---

want to get Good A. If demand is sufficient for Good A, this may harm competition in the market for Good B. For a Good B producer to effectively compete, it may have to develop its own version of Good A so that it can offer consumers a complete package of Goods A and B.

might otherwise have earned even from a successful new computer model. Continued denial of advance technical information to an OEM by a dominant supplier can make a customer's very existence as an OEM untenable.

The European Commission (1987, ¶32) noted the same concern in the context of a standards consortium:

In an industry where lead time can be a factor of considerable importance, membership of the group may thus confer an appreciable competitive advantage on the members vis-à-vis their hardware and software competitors ... this advantage in lead time directly affects the market entry possibilities of non-members.

That is, it is not necessary for a standard-setting consortium to withhold the interface specification standard forever for competition to be harmed. If the member firms have advance knowledge of the standard, they can bring compliant products to market before non-members, and even a few months of lead-time can spell the difference between market success and failure.

4 Examples of possible anticompetitive interface specifications

In this section, we examine three examples of possibly anticompetitive interface standards in the computer industry. In one example, the consortium incorporated patented information in a memory standard; in another, a monopolist established a one-way interface standard for graphics processors; and in the third, a consortium imposed a one-way interface standard and gained competitive advantage by delaying the release of necessary specification details for a peripheral standard.

Before discussing the examples of standards consortia in the computer industry, we briefly describe some relevant technological and economic characteristics of microprocessors. By themselves, microprocessors have little or no value to end users. Microprocessors can process computational instructions, but they need software to deliver the instructions. They also need a variety of other devices that assist in performing the tasks that end users desire. For example, microprocessors need memory to hold data and instructions (which end users demand in a variety of configurations, e.g., DRAM [dynamic random access memory], hard disks, floppy disks, CD-ROM [compact disc-read-only memory], etc.). Microprocessors need input and output devices (keyboards, scanners, microphones, cameras, printers, monitors, voice and data network lines, etc.). For all of the above, the microprocessors need communications pathways and devices that manage the vast variety of complex and extremely fast high-speed signals flowing among all of the various devices. In short, end users demand computer *systems*, of which microprocessors are but one component. The systems, in turn, are comprised of numerous components. Between these components are a variety of interfaces.

In the microprocessor industry, many consortia exist to create standards for the interfaces between hardware devices that connect to a PC's microprocessor or to the microprocessor's associated chipset. Many of these consortia have closed membership, and the members of the consortia both control the details of the interface standards and have advance knowledge of the interface details, which provides consortia members substantial lead-time in developing compatible products.

Both systems and component competition occur in the computer industry. When standards are proprietary, competition must take place on a systems basis. An example is the current technology for microprocessors and chipsets. In the mid-1990s Intel made the bus that connects its microprocessor to chipsets proprietary. Since then, Intel-compatible microprocessors and chipsets compete as a system against AMD-compatible microprocessors and chipsets.[15]

When interface specifications are open and standardized, it is possible for multiple firms to compete for the manufacture of a given component for use in the same system. This is known as component competition. An example is the competition among Maxtor, Seagate, IBM, Fujitsu, and others to make and sell hard drives that are used in PCs manufactured by Dell, Compaq, Vobis, Groupe Bull, and others.

---

[15] Intel making the bus proprietary and thus expanding the boundary of its microprocessor system to include chipsets is an example of a one-way interface standard. While the specifications to connect to the chipset from components other than the microprocessor are publicly available, the specifications to connect the chipset to the microprocessor are not publicly available (and are also protected by intellectual property subject to restrictive licensing).

4.1 Inserting patents in standards: JEDEC and Rambus[16]

A possible example of using standard setting for anticompetitive gain concerns standards for computer memory.[17] The parties include:

- JEDEC Solid State Technology Association, a standard-setting organization. Membership is open to any company that manufactures products or provides services related to electronics. One of its subcommittees, JC-42.3, the Subcommittee on RAM Devices, develops standards related to RAM. It published standards in November 1993 and again in 1999 (Alban 2004).

- Rambus, a designer/developer of "high-speed chip-connection technology." This chip-connection technology is incorporated in memory chips. Rambus licenses technology; it does not manufacture memory chips.

- Manufacturers of computer memory, including Hitachi, Hynix, Infineon, Micron Technology, Samsung, and Toshiba.

The actions of Rambus, described in some detail below, have led to many lawsuits. Rambus has been accused by the FTC of unreasonably restraining trade, attempting to monopolize, monopolizing, and engaging in unfair methods of competition in the market for SDRAM technology in violation of Section 5 of the FTC Act.[18] Memory manufacturers have sued Rambus, with allegations of fraud and antitrust violations (Miles and Shankland 2000). Rambus has filed suits against most of the major memory makers alleging patent infringement (Infineon, Micron, and Hyundai, which is now Hynix). A group of standard-setting bodies filed an amicus brief in support of Infineon, arguing that Rambus concealed its intellectual property (Kanellos 2003a). Many of the cases are still active, but the most recent rulings have tended to be in Rambus' favor, interpreting the JEDEC bylaws as

---

[16] The information in this section is primarily from the complaint filed by the FTC in 2002, Fried 2001, Kanellos 2001, and Miles and Shankland 2000.

[17] In particular, this incident involves the move from asynchronous DRAM (dynamic random access memory) to synchronous DRAM (often called SDRAM) that occurred during the 1990s. Some form of SDRAM is the most common memory in computers today. RDRAM (or Rambus DRAM) and DDR DRAM (or double data rate DRAM) are both forms of SDRAM.

[18] In February 2004, an FTC administrative law judge dismissed the case; the FTC is appealing the case (FTC 2004).

not requiring disclosure on Rambus' part.[19] Of course, whether or not JEDEC bylaws specifically required disclosure is immaterial to whether Rambus actually concealed information in the standard-setting process with anticompetitive effects.

The allegations against Rambus are that they used participation in the standard-setting process to write their patents in such a way as to ensure that the JEDEC-adopted SDRAM standards infringed on Rambus' patents. Rambus filed its first patent April 18, 1990. It attended its first JEDEC meeting in December 1991, and joined JEDEC in February 1992. Business documents show that as early as 1992, Rambus believed that SDRAMs infringed on its patents (Alban 2004). The JEDEC bylaws call for all participants "to inform the meeting [of the standards-setting committee] of any knowledge they may have of any patents, or pending patents, that might be involved in the work they are undertaking" (JEDEC 2002, 18). When asked by JEDEC representatives if Rambus had disclosures to make, in one instance Rambus declined to make any such disclosures and in another made limited disclosures regarding a single patent relating to a clocking technology that differed from anything JEDEC was considering.[20]

Rambus stopped attending JC-42.3 meetings in December 1995, and formally left the organization in June 1996. The letter formally withdrawing its membership included a list of Rambus' patents. Infineon accused Rambus of using "informants" after Rambus withdrew from JEDEC to learn of discussions of DRAM standards in order to rewrite its patents to cover JEDEC standards (Kanellos 2001). Rambus filed amended patent applications in 1997 to cover SDRAM technology; these patents were awarded in 1999 and 2000. At that point, Rambus began enforcing its patent rights against memory manufacturers.

In the Rambus cases, the standard-setting group had open membership to anyone involved commercially in the industry. Although restricted membership is sufficient for the potential to manipulate, this condition is not necessary to enable anticompetitive behavior.

---

[19] In particular, the Administrative Law Judge dismissed the FTC case against Rambus (FTC 2004) and the Federal Circuit ruled largely in Rambus' favor in *Rambus* v. *Infineon* (Alban 2004).

[20] In its defense, "Rambus has maintained that competitors knew about its patents and product plans while SDRAM-related standards talks were going on at JEDEC" (Kawamoto 2004).

In the Rambus situation, the seller of the technology allegedly withheld vital information about its intellectual property throughout the standard-setting process, adjusted its patent filings to reflect the standards adopted by the group, and then enforced its patents against the buyers of the technology once they had adopted the standards that Rambus claimed infringed on its patents.[21] Open membership may not protect the standards process if one firm can successfully deceive the other members about crucial property rights.

4.2 One-way interface standards: Accelerated Graphics Port

The Accelerated Graphics Port (AGP) is an example of a one-way interface standard.[22] The AGP has electrical specifications on one side, between the AGP and the peripherals, and software specifications on the other side, between the AGP and the chipset.

The AGP specification[23] was developed by Intel with input from various industry participants, including ATI Technologies (a leading

---

[21] It is possible that, even had JEDEC known about Rambus' intellectual property, it would have adopted the same standards. However, JEDEC does have as one of its goals to avoid using patented technology.

JEDEC standards . . . that require the use of patented items should be considered with great care. (For the purpose of this policy, the term 'patented items' includes items and processes for which a patent has been applied.) While there is no restriction against drafting a proposed standard in terms that include the use of a patented item if technical reasons justify the inclusion, committees should avoid standardization that refers to a product on which there is a known patent unless all the relevant technical information covered by the patent is known to the formulating committee, subcommittee, or task group.

If the committee member indicates that the standard requires the use of patented items, then the committee chairperson must receive a written assurance from the organization holding rights to such patents that a license will be made available to applicants desiring to implement the standard either without compensation or under reasonable terms and conditions that are demonstrably free of any unfair discrimination. (JEDEC 2002, Section 8)

[22] The AGP Forum web page, which is no longer available, describes the AGP interface as "a new platform bus specification that enables high performance graphics capabilities especially 3D, on PCs at mainstream price points" (http://www.agpforum.org/, accessed September 1, 2002).

[23] The information and quotations in this paragraph are from the AGP Forum's website, at http://www.agpforum.org/. The AGP Forum existed until at least late 2002. As of today, the AGP forum web page is no longer available, and a search of Intel's web page does not find anything on the forum. We do not know the exact date between late 2002 and mid-2004 when the forum became defunct.

developer and manufacturer of graphics chips) and Cirrus Logic ("a premier supplier of high-performance analog, digital signal processing [DSP] and mixed-signal chip solutions for consumer electronics"). In May 1996, Intel created "an open industry group," the Accelerated Graphics Port Implementors Forum. The goal of the forum was to "foster design and production of graphics hardware products and PC systems" which comply with the AGP interface specification. Firms could become members for $2,500 a year, with the benefits of "participation in events and technical support subject to availability." Intel had the right to limit the number of participants or to discontinue the program altogether and maintained unilateral control over the standard. As far as we could determine, no microprocessor or chipset manufacturer other than Intel was part of the forum. This is a case in which the standards consortium that implemented the one-way interface standard is essentially a single firm (with input from others).

Intel made the electrical specifications public, which means that firms can manufacture peripherals that will interoperate with AGP.[24] "[T]he AGP 1.0 specification consists of the necessary electrical and signal information that will enable graphics hardware developers and system OEMs to both design and use graphics controllers on the graphics port" (Intel 1996). AGP-compliant PCs and graphics hardware products were available by March 1997. Competition for these products has been vital, in large part because the specification was freely available.[25]

Innovation and competition on the chipset/chip interface side of AGP (i.e., the interface that was not published) has not been so dynamic. Intel, the owner of the specification, had AGP-capable chipsets out in mid-1997 that were compatible with Pentium II processors. Other chip and chipset makers could not immediately manufacture on their side of the standard because the software specifications were not public. Instead, they had to invent around the software specifications.

Although it appeared that parties other than Intel were offering AGP-compliant chipsets within about six months of Intel's introduction

[24] The AGP V3.0 Interface Specification, revision 1.0, September 2002, contains a chapter on the physical layer specification, but not the software layer. See http://developer.intel.com/technology/agp/downloads/agp30_final_10.pdf (accessed May 11, 2004).
[25] More precisely, "[t]he AGP specification will be licensed on a royalty-free, reciprocal basis" (Intel 1996).

of an AGP-compliant chipset, the appearances were deceiving. First, the chipsets offered by third parties were not compatible with Pentium II chips, which at the time were the high-end microprocessors and were introduced in May 1997. Second, the chipsets did not work properly. VIA Technologies and ALI offered chipsets that were compatible with Socket 7 Pentium chips by late 1997 or early 1998; these chipsets were not compatible with Pentium Pro, Pentium II, and beyond. VIA's first supposedly AGP-compliant chipset crashed with Cyrix microprocessors and the AGP 2x mode did not work (Tom's Hardware 1997).

As late as May 1999, HardwareCentral, an online news source "for in-depth computer hardware info,"[26] reported that to use AGP required a "motherboard with Intel's 440LX PCI/AGP chipset," a chipset for Pentium II microprocessors (Risley 1999a). It was expected that the 440LX chipset would be made available for non-Intel processors, and it was reported that Socket 7 motherboards that offer AGP support using the VIA Apollo VP3 and the ALI Aladdin V chipsets were "beginning" to appear. HardwareCentral also reported in May 1999 that AGP was "on the road to becoming non-exclusive to the Intel Pentium II and 440LS chipset" and that Cyrix was "working on the MXi, which will ... support AGP" (Risley 1999b). Not long after that, however, Cyrix indefinitely postponed development of the MXi (Slater 1999).

AMD offered an AGP-compliant chipset in August 1999 (AMD 1999), and VIA Technologies offered Pentium II-compatible chipsets that were AGP compatible about the same time (Shimpi 1999). Thus, Intel was the only supplier of AGP-compatible and Pentium II-compatible chipsets for over two years after the AGP standard was published. Transmeta x86-compatible microprocessor chips did not support AGP until October 2003, and the chips were not marketed in the United States until April 2004 (Sharma 2004), over seven years after the AGP interface was developed. This lack of functionality was something that "prevented the company from getting into the mainstream notebook market" (Kanellos 2003b).[27] In addition,

---

[26] See www.hardwarecentral.com.
[27] Nvidia produced the chipsets for Transmeta's Efficeon processor (Kanellos 2003a).

Transmeta's ability to support AGP came at a time when AGP was beginning to be replaced by PCI Express.

By implementing a one-way interface standard, Intel had a significant time-to-market advantage. For over two years, it was the only company offering chipsets that were AGP-compatible and Pentium II-compatible, and the supposedly AGP-compliant and Socket 7-compatible chipsets that were offered by third parties had essentially no impact on the market. On the other side of the interface, competition was vibrant and immediate, with AGP-compatible products becoming available in the market by March 1997, just a few months after the standard was published. In this example, standard setting encouraged component competition on just one side of the interface.

4.3 One-way interface standards and publication delay: USB 2.0[28]

In this last example, we describe a consortium that has behaved in a way that is consistent with two of our anticompetitive strategies: implementing a one-way interface standard and delaying the release of information about the standard.

The USB is a standard for the microprocessor to communicate with slow- and medium-speed peripherals such as mice, keyboards, printers, scanners, and digital cameras. It defines an interface between a host controller and the peripherals. The host controller, which can be an independent physical device or be integrated onto the chipset, speaks with the system software via the host controller interface. Thus, there are two interfaces working together: the USB interface between the peripherals and the host controller, and the host controller interface between the host controller and the system software. As was previously described, this is a situation with two devices – the peripherals and the microprocessor (and system software) – separated by a "translator," the host controller (see Figure 7.2).

USB 1.1 was originally developed in 1995. Two host controller interfaces, OHCI (Open Host Controller Interface) and UHCI (Universal Host Controller Interface), work with USB 1.1. UHCI is Intel's proprietary interface and is available via a royalty-free, reciprocal license for adopters of USB. Jointly developed by Compaq,

[28] USB 2.0 is also marketed as Hi-Speed USB (see *CNET News.com* Staff 2001).

Microsoft, and National Semiconductor, OHCI is an open standard, available for download at http://www.compaq.com/productinfo/ development/openhci.html (Compaq 1997).

USB 2.0, which increases the speed of the peripheral-to-PC connection by forty times relative to USB 1.1, was completed in April 2000.[29] USB 2.0 is compatible only with a new host controller interface, EHCI (Enhanced Host Controller Interface), which is proprietary to Intel. Version 0.95 of the EHCI was made public in November 2000, but Version 1.0 was not released until April 2002, a full two years after the USB 2.0 specification was published. The EHCI interface is not freely available: Intel licenses it only in exchange for the grant of a royalty-free license to Intel on the licensee's related intellectual property.

A one-way interface standard was implemented because the host controller interface, EHCI, is proprietary to Intel, while the USB 2.0 interface is an open interface. Peripheral manufacturers have the information they need to produce USB 2.0-compliant peripherals and consortium members have the information they need to produce USB 2.0-compliant chipsets and stand-alone host controllers. That is, the consortium released the specification information necessary for makers of complementary peripherals to implement their side of the USB 2.0 interfaces. The EHCI is required to implement the chipset/motherboard side of the USB 2.0 interface. Only non-member chipset and microprocessor firms are denied the information necessary to design their products to meet the USB 2.0 interface specification.

The consortium has the characteristics that allow it to develop standards with an anticompetitive impact. The USB Implementers Forum has two membership classes: Promoter Members, who have voting rights, and Participant Members, who do not.[30] Promoter Members must be engaged in research and development of the USB specifications. The Board of Directors, made up of employees of Promoter Members, has sole discretion to accept or reject applications from other firms to become a voting member.[31] To become a Promoter Member, one must receive *unanimous* approval of the Promoter

---

[29] A beta version was published in October 1999.

[30] The USB Implementers Forum was incorporated as a non-profit organization on January 18, 1999.

[31] Jeff Ravencraft of Intel currently serves as Chairman and President of the Board of Directors of the USB Implementers Forum; before him, the Chairman was Jason Ziller, also Intel's technology initiatives manager. Email communication

Members; any individual Promoter Member has veto power over a Promoter Membership application. Thus, the consortium satisfies one of the criteria that enable a consortium to behave anticompetitively: membership is limited and current members control which firms can become a member.

The voting members of the consortium are Intel, Compaq, Hewlett-Packard, Lucent, Microsoft, NEC Technologies, and Philips.[32] These members created and controlled the interface specification standard for USB 2.0.[33] The consortium does not include any firms that produce chipsets or microprocessors except for Intel. Intel has an opportunity, then, to manipulate the standard-setting process in such a way as to advantage itself against other microprocessor firms (chiefly AMD) and other chipset firms (e.g., VIA Technologies). The second criterion for a standards consortium to have the potential to manipulate a standard anticompetitively is that it must include firms with sufficient influence to ensure that the standard is adopted. In this case, Intel and Microsoft together have the ability to ensure industry-wide adoption of a standard.

In addition to the one-way nature of the interface standard, consortium members had a competitive advantage through early access to the USB 2.0 and EHCI specifications. That is, any firm has been able to build a peripheral that is USB 2.0-compliant, but only consortium members have been able to build the system-side hardware. For example, NEC Technologies announced that it had developed the world's first USB 2.0 and EHCI-compliant host controller on April 12, 2000, fifteen days *before* the USB 2.0 interface was released and six months before the preliminary version of the EHCI interface was released. In August 2000, Lucent announced a host controller[34] and in May 2001, Philips announced a host controller. Until May 2002, implementation of USB 2.0 required the use of a host controller, a separate add-on piece to the chipset. In May 2002, the first chipsets with integrated host

to the authors from Traci Donnell, USB-IF Administration, dated June 2, 2004, and Intel 2002a.

[32] The formation of the USB 2.0 Promoter Group was announced at the Intel Developer Forum in Spring 1999. For USB 2.0, Hewlett-Packard, Lucent, and Philips joined the original core firms behind USB 1.1 – Compaq, Intel, Microsoft, and NEC Technologies.

[33] The bylaws are available from http://www.usb.org/data/retail/usbif_bylaws.pdf.

[34] We believe that Lucent did not succeed in manufacturing this host controller until at least May 2001.

controllers were announced. It was at this point that a non-member of the consortium announced implementation of a USB 2.0 compliant chipset or host controller.[35]

5 Conclusion

We have described the circumstances under which firms can use the standard-setting process in an anticompetitive manner. Anticompetitive strategies include manipulating standards to include a firm's patented intellectual property; using information gained from within the consortium to gain a time-to-market advantage; and creating one-way interface standards. We believe our discussion of one-way interface standards is new to the literature.

Each of these strategies can have the effect of reducing component-based competition, and thus has the potential to harm consumer welfare. Since systems competition can in some circumstances be better for social welfare than component competition, it generally would be prudent to examine the specific facts and economic conditions relevant to a particular interface standard before concluding that the use of these strategies by a standards consortium is harmful. Nevertheless, recognizing the availability of these strategies to consortia demonstrates that standard setting does not guarantee vital component-based competition.

References

Alban, David 2004. "*Rambus* v. *Infineon*: Patent disclosures in standard-setting organizations," *Berkeley Technology Law Journal* 19: 309–31.
AMD 1999. "AMD-750 Chipset overview," August, http://www.amd.com/us-en/assets/content_type/white_papers_and_tech_docs/23016.pdf.
CNET News.com Staff 2001. "Microsoft and XP Give USB 2.0 a break," May 14, http://news.com.com/2102-1001_3-257619.html?tag=st.util.print.
Compaq 1997. "USB and the difference between OHCI and UHCI," September 17, http://www.compaq.com/support/techpubs/whitepapers/ecg0480997.html.
Computer & Communications Industry Association v. *Federal Communications Commission*, 693 F.2d 198 (DC Cir. 1982).

---

[35] In May 2002, VIA announced a chipset that integrated a USB 2.0 host controller. Intel, however, challenged VIA's legal right to produce a Pentium 4 chipset.

Certiorari denied, 461 US 938 (Sup. Ct. 1983).

On second further reconsideration, FCC 84–190 (released May 4, 1984).

Diffie, W., and M. Hellman 1976. "New directions in cryptography," *IEEE Transactions on Information Theory* IT-22: 644–54.

Economides, Nicholas 1988. "Desirability of compatibility in the absence of network externalities," *American Economic Review* 79: 1165–81.

European Commission 1987. "87/69/EEC: Commission decision of 15 December 1986 relating to a proceeding under Article 85 of the EEC Treaty (IV/31.458 – X/Open Group)," *Official Journal of the European Union* 35: 36–43.

Farrell, Joseph, and Garth Saloner 1986a. "Economic issues in standardization," in *Telecommunications and equity: Policy research issues*, J. Miller (ed.), Amsterdam: North-Holland, 165–78.

1986b. "Installed base and compatibility: Innovation, product preannouncements, and predation," *American Economic Review* 76: 940–55.

1992. "Converters, compatibility and control of interfaces," *Journal of Industrial Economics* 40: 9–35.

Federal Trade Commission 1999. "Analysis of proposed consent order to aid public comment," *FTC v. Intel*, Docket No. 9288, available from http://www.ftc.gov/os/1999/9903/d09288intelanalysis.htm.

2002. "Complaint," *In the Matter of Rambus Incorporated*, Docket No. 9302, June 19.

2004. "Initial Decision," *In the Matter of Rambus, Inc.*, Docket 9302, February 24, http://www.ftc.gov/opa/2004/02/rambusid.htm.

Fried, Ian 2001. "Judge scraps Rambus suit against Infineon," *CNET News.com*, May 4, http://news.com.com/2100-1001_3-257065.html?tag=st_rn.

Hemenway, D. 1975. *Industrywide voluntary product standards*. Lexington, MA: Ballinger.

Hush-A-Phone Corp. v. United States. 238 F.2d 266, 268 (DC Cir. 1956). On remand, 22 FCC 112 (DC Cir. 1957).

Intel 1996. "Intel announces accelerated Graphics Port 1.0 specification," August 5, http://www.intel.com/pressroom/archive/releases/agp1spec.htm.

2002a. "Intel releases USB 2.0 Enhanced Host Controller Interface 1.0 Specification, EHCI Compliance-Testing Program," April 17, http://www.intel.com/pressroom/archive/releases/20020417dev.htm.

JEDEC Solid States Technology Association 2002. *JEDEC manual of organization and procedure: JM21-L*. Arlington, VA: JEDEC.

Kanellos, Michael 2001. "Hot-button Rambus-Infineon trial delayed," *CNET News.com*, April 6, http://news.com.com/2100-1001-255473.html.

2002. "Rambus target of FTC antitrust suit," *CNET News.com*, June 19, http://news.com.com/2100-1001-937449.html.

2003a. "Standards bodies file brief in Rambus case," *CNET News.com*, August 13, http://news.com.com/2110-1006_3-5063505.html.

2003b. "Transmeta shows the fine print on Efficeon," *CNET News.com*, October 14, http://news.com.com/2102-1006_3-5090755.html.

2004. "HyperTransport Group ups data transfer speeds," *CNET News.com*, February 9, http://news.com.com/2102-1006)3-5154963.html.

Katz, Michael, and Carl Shapiro 1994. "Systems competition and network effects," *Journal of Economic Perspectives* 8: 93–115.

Kawamoto, Dawn 2004. "Rambus wins major round in FTC Case," *CNET News.com*, February 18, http://news.com.com/2100-1004-5160694.html?tag=nl.

Matutes, Carmen, and Pierre Regibeau 1988. "Mix and match: Product compatibility without network externalities," *RAND Journal of Economics* 19 (Summer): 221–34.

1996. "A selective review of the economics of standardization: Entry deterrence, technological progress and international competition," *European Journal of Political Economy* 12: 183–209.

Micron Technology, Inc. v. Rambus Inc. 189 F. Supp. 2d 201 (US Dist. 2002).

Microprocessor Report 1997a. "MediaGX targets low-cost PCs," March 10.

1997b. "Intel fumbles MMX Transition," July 14.

Miles, Stephanie, and Stephen Shankland 2000. "Micron sues Rambus, says patents invalid," *CNET News.com*, August 29, http://news.com.com/2102-1001_3-245068.html?tag=st.util.print.

Porter, Michael 1985. *Competitive strategy*. New York: Free Press.

Rambus, Inc. v. Infineon Technologies AG. 304 F. Supp. 2d 812, 817 (ED Va. 2004).

Risley, David 1999a. "AGP," May 29, http://www.hardwarecentral.com/hardwarecentral/tutorials/62/1.

1999b. "Latest CPU News," May 31, http://www.hardwarecentral.com/hardwarecentral/reports/17/1.

Rivest, R., A. Shamir, and L. Adleman 1978. "A method for obtaining digital signatures and public-key cryptosystems," *Communications of the ACM* 21: 120–6.

Second Computer Inquiry. 77 FCC 2d 384 (FCC 1980).

On reconsideration, 84 FCC 2d 50 (FCC 1980).

On further reconsideration, 88 FCC 2d 512 (FCC 1981), aff'd sub nom.

Sharma, Dinesh C. 2004. "Transmeta's new chip takes a sharp turn," *CNET News.com*, March 15, http://news.com.com/2110-1044_305173160.html?tag=st.util.print.

Shimpi, Anand Lal 1999. "VIA Apollo Pro 133 A & VCSDRAM," *AnandTech*, October 18, http://www.anandtech.com/cpuchipsets/showdoc.aspx?i=1061.

Slater, Michael 1999. "Microprocessor watch," *MicroDesign Resources*, June 2, http://www.mdronline.com/publications/mpw/issues/mpw001.html.

Symbol Technologies Inc. v. *Lemelson Medical, Education & Research Foundation*. 2002. 277 F.3d 1361 (Fed. Cir. 2002).

Tom's Hardware 1997. "Review of Socket 7 AGP Motherboard FIC PA-2012 Revision 1.1," November 2, http://216.92.8.170/mainboard/97q4/971102/.

Use of the Carterfone Device in Message Toll Telephone Service. 13 FCC 2d 420 (FCC 1968).

On reconsideration, 14 FCC 2d 571 (FCC 1968).

Part 68 Rules (47 CFR § 68.1-.506).

8 | Delay and de jure standardization: exploring the slowdown in Internet standards development

TIMOTHY SIMCOE

Abstract

While the welfare implications of de jure standardization is an extremely complex question, economic theorists and standards practitioners alike have suggested that *speed* is an important dimension of performance for non-market Standard Setting Organizations (SSOs). A variety of factors may influence the timeliness of SSOs, including the complexity of the underlying technology; the commercial significance of the proposed standard; and the rules governing the consensus decision-making process. This chapter uses data from the Internet Engineering Task Force (IETF) to take a preliminary look at the relationship between the size, scope, and composition of SSO committees and the time required for those groups to reach a consensus. In particular, it documents a significant slowdown in IETF standard setting that coincides with the commercialization of the Internet during the 1990s. The chapter concludes by discussing several open questions related to the political economy of voluntary standards creation and suggesting that the increased availability of archival data – from institutions such as the IETF – makes this a promising area for empirical research.

1 Introduction

In 1986, twenty-one people attended the first meeting of the Internet Engineering Task Force (IETF) – the organization that creates and maintains the technical standards used to run the Internet. Over the next fifteen years, the rapid growth and commercialization of the Internet helped make the IETF an important Standard Setting Organization (SSO) for the rapidly converging fields of computing and communications. By 2001, its meetings regularly drew more than 2,000 participants. At the same time, the Internet's success transformed the IETF from a small research-oriented community of engineers and computer scientists into a forum for high-stakes technical decision making. This paper examines how changes in the size, scope, and composition of the IETF influenced the performance of its standard setting process.

In studying the performance of the IETF, I focus on the time required for individual committees or Working Groups (WGs) to reach a consensus. We know that speed is an important dimension of SSO performance because participants frequently complain about excessive delays. For example, a survey by the National Research Council in 1991 asked practitioners to rank "issues in the US standards developing process that need to be resolved." The top response was that "the adoption process [was] too slow" (National Research Council 1990). Farrell (1996) reports a number of estimates from the Institute of Electrical and Electronics Engineers, the International Electrotechnical Commission, and the International Organization for Standardization of the time required to create a new consensus specification. These estimates range from five to seven years – a long time when compared to product cycles in most information technology markets. Papers by Farrell (1996) and Farrell and Saloner (1988) use formal models to explain the long delays in formal standardization. Their theory suggests that delays are the cost of bargaining over competing designs when SSO participants have divergent preferences and/or incomplete information.[1] In this setup, the delays are clearly inefficient. In fact, when the distributional stakes of choosing a design are particularly high, the delays can even dissipate all of the coordination benefits from adopting a common standard.

In practice, while speed certainly matters, reaching a quick decision is not the only priority for most SSOs. The cost of delay is usually weighed against the goals of creating a high-quality specification and promoting its widespread adoption. Given the potential trade-offs, many factors could influence the time required to reach a consensus on new technical standards. These issues include the number of participants on a committee and the diversity of their viewpoints; the complexity of

---

[1] Both models are based on a hold-out game, or "War of Attrition." Farrell and Saloner (1988) study the trade-off between delays and the probability of coordination in a game with complete information, while Farrell (1996) focuses on the trade-off between delay and quality in a version with incomplete information.

the underlying technology and its dependence with other standards; the set of design alternatives available to the committee; the technical or economic significance of the specification; and the rules governing the consensus decision-making process. A serious challenge for any empirical study of nonmarket standard setting is to sort out the impact of these various issues. What makes this difficult is that we never observe the true counterfactual situation – what kind of standard, if any, would have emerged from a faster process? Would it have been adopted?

In this paper I examine the issue of delays in the IETF's de jure standard setting process. I begin by describing the evolution of the IETF between 1992 and 2000 – a period when the rapid commercialization of the Internet led to some dramatic changes in its size, structure, and demographic composition. Then I examine the slowdown in IETF standard setting that took place over the same time period, and its relationship to observable changes in the size, structure, and composition of the organization. Before concluding, I discuss some of the methodological challenges associated with the study of nonmarket SSOs and their decision-making process.

I should emphasize that this examination of IETF standard setting is primarily a descriptive exercise, rather than an effort to uncover the "true" causes of the slowdown in Internet standardization. I do present several regressions that illustrate the correlation between delays and some observable characteristics of IETF WGs and their proposals. These regressions, however, are not an attempt to choose among a set of competing explanations for the observed delays. To preview the results of this exercise, I find that there was a significant slowdown in IETF standard setting – between 1992 and 2000 the median time from first draft to final specification grew from seven to fifteen months. I also find significant variation in the size and complexity of individual IETF WGs and the proposals they produced. Finally, I show that several measures of technical complexity, committee structure, and distributional conflict are correlated with the duration of the IETF standard setting process.

Although this paper does not provide a definitive explanation for the slowdown in IETF standard setting, it does provide several insights into three broad and important questions.[2] First, what was the size and

---

[2] In a related paper (Simcoe 2004), I develop an econometric model that employs a different identification strategy. There, I examine *differences* in the correlation

timing of the slowdown in Internet standard setting? Second, how did the IETF change over this time period? Third and finally, what are the prospects for explaining some or all of the observed increases in average duration? I also discuss several conceptual and methodological issues associated with the empirical analysis of committee performance, particularly the difficulties associated with distinguishing rent-seeking, or distributional conflict from increases in technological complexity, or the impact of an increasing workload. I refer several times to Simcoe (2004), which, using data on the IETF, takes a novel approach to these problems and finds evidence of a link between distributional conflict and delays.

The remainder of the paper is divided into four sections. In the following section, I describe the IETF's standard setting process, its history, and some of the changes that took place during the 1990s. In Section 3, I take a closer look at the slowdown in IETF standards production. I consider a number of potential explanations for this phenomenon, including changes in technology (e.g., increasingly complex specifications), changes in the organization of the IETF (e.g., size or membership composition), and increases in the distributional conflicts inherent in the standardization of Internet-related technologies. In Section 4, I describe some of the methodological issues associated with studies of standard setting committees and their performance. Finally, in Section 5, I suggest that the IETF's experience holds some lessons for researchers, standards developers, and policymakers.

2 The evolution of the Internet Engineering Task Force

This section provides a brief overview of the IETF, describes the IETF standard setting process, and discusses the impact of Internet growth and commercialization on IETF standard setting.

2.1 An overview

The IETF is the primary forum for Internet standards development, and the scope of its activity includes "all protocols, procedures, and conventions that are used in or by the Internet" (Bradner 1996, 2). Standards developed by the IETF, such as TCP/IP (Transmission

between speed and committee characteristics across different classes of standards developed by the IETF.

Control Protocol/Internet Protocol, which is used to route data between computers), the Domain Name System (used to find other computers on a network), and the conventions for formatting email messages are a critical part of the Internet's technical infrastructure. While many IETF standards are ultimately embedded in hardware (e.g., routers, switches, or network cards) they are usually designed as software, and most IETF participants think of themselves as software developers.

The origins of the IETF date back to the ARPANET project, which was initially funded by the US Department of Defense in 1969. ARPANET spawned a small community of computer networking pioneers that included university-based computer scientists, defense contractors, and employees from large corporate research and development labs. After a number of organizational permutations, the core of this community became leaders within the IETF, whose first official meeting was held in January 1986. By the early 1990s, an examination of about 100 participants at one IETF meeting found that "about 1/3 were from vendors, about 1/3 from government (DoD [Department of Defense] and civilian agencies), and over 1/4 from universities and regional network operators" (IETF 1990, 5).

During the late 1980s and early 1990s, the IETF maintained a focus on scientific and engineering research while managing the growth of NSFNET – the successor to ARPANET. The lack of a strong commercial influence was partly due to the National Science Foundation's (NSF) Acceptable Use Policy, which prohibited any commercial use of the network. Nevertheless, when the protocols used by NSFNET and managed by the IETF began to emerge as a significant de facto networking standard, the task of network management was gradually shifted to private companies. When the NSF abandoned its Acceptable Use Policy in 1991 and the protocols used by the World Wide Web were developed a few years later, the growth and commercialization of the Internet accelerated sharply.

The commercialization of the Internet led to major changes in the size, scope, and composition of the IETF. Figure 8.1 shows the dramatic increase in average attendance at IETF meetings between 1986 and 2003. Although these numbers highlight the IETF's growing significance, they may not be a good measure of its size, because anyone who is sufficiently interested can become a "member" of the IETF simply by participating in one of its WGs. Much of the WGs' work actually takes place on email discussion lists, where participants discuss

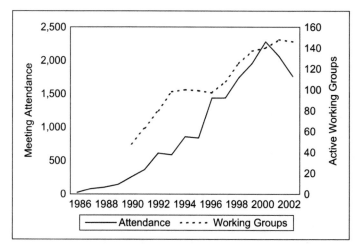

Figure 8.1. Size and scope of the IETF.

proposals that are circulated by email and posted to online repositories. Figure 8.1 also shows the number of active WGs – a rough measure of the scope of the IETF.[3] Between 1990 and 2002, 20 to 30 new WGs were formed each year, and the number of active WGs grew from 65 to more than 140. Figure 8.2 shows the increasing output of IETF WGs between 1988 and 2002. This output is measured in terms of official documents, which are called *Requests for Comments* (RFCs). Compatibility standards (i.e., the actual technical specifications) form a subset of RFCs, called *Proposed Standards*.

The rapid growth of the IETF reflects its transition from a quasi-academic networking community to a high-stakes forum for technical decision making, along with its increasing international significance. These shifts are reflected in the changing demographics of IETF membership. Figure 8.3 uses the email addresses of registered attendees at IETF meetings to illustrate these trends. Between 1988 and 2000, participants with a "commercial" email address (i.e., having a top-level domain of .net or .com) grew from 26% of the membership to 66%. Meanwhile "noncommercial" participants (.edu, .gov, .org, and .mil) fell

---

[3] New WGs are created through a "bottom-up" process that I describe in further detail subsequently.

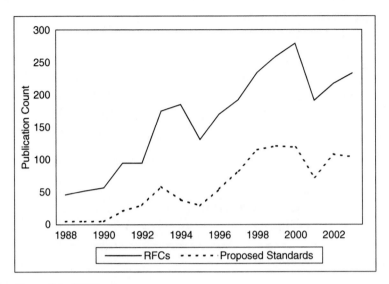

Figure 8.2. IETF output.

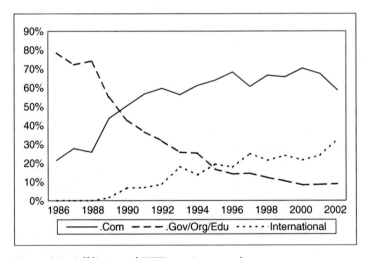

Figure 8.3. Affiliation of IETF meeting attendees.

from 76% to 10%. Participants with international domain names grew from 0% to 33%.

These dramatic changes in the size, scope, and demographic composition of the IETF are largely a measure of the organization's early success at developing and deploying a network that scaled remarkably well throughout the 1990s. Because of this success, the IETF is widely viewed as a leading example of effective de jure standard setting (e.g., Rutkowski 1995, 597). Within the IETF, however, rapid growth and commercialization have created a number of challenges. In Subsection 2.3, I consider these issues in greater detail. First, however, I offer a detailed look at the IETF's standard setting process.

2.2 The formal standard setting process

Within the IETF are various technical areas;[4] each area is supported by one or two area directors who provide guidance to the various WGs and who sit on a steering committee called the Internet Engineering Steering Group (IESG). The IESG is composed of the IETF chair, the area directors, and a small number of other members. In practice, these individuals are longtime members of the Internet community with a strong interest in the integrity of the IETF and its processes. WGs are formed on an ongoing basis to address new technical issues. While the IESG evaluates any proposal to create a new WG, its loose criteria for acceptance are that sufficient interest has been expressed and that the work does not duplicate any other efforts within the IETF. When a new WG is created, it is assigned to a particular technical area.

The "bottom-up" nature of the IETF standard setting process ensures that the scope of the organization is largely determined by the tastes of individual participants. This process begins with the formation of a WG. Interested participants gather at IETF meetings and circulate documents called *Internet Drafts* to the WG email list. These drafts outline the basic parameters of a new standard and serve as the basis for debate.[5] Internet Drafts generally go through a series of revisions until the chair of the WG decides there is a rough consensus on all of the major technical issues. Most drafts go through several rounds of edits, and significant proposals may go through twenty or more, taking several years to complete. Once a draft is completed, there is a last call for comments from the entire IETF, and the document is submitted

---

[4] The current areas are Applications, General, Internet, Routing, Transport, Security, Operations and Management, and Sub-IP.
[5] While an individual may also submit an Internet draft, these drafts are usually absorbed by the relevant WG when they are considered serious proposals.

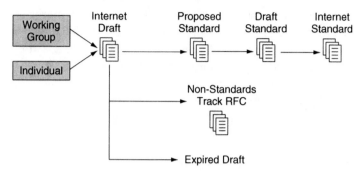

Figure 8.4. The IETF standard setting process.

to the IESG. If the IESG approves a document, it is published as an RFC with the formal designation of Proposed Standard.[6] If the specification outlined in a proposed standard proves successful in practice, the IESG may decide to advance it to the status of *Draft Standard* or *Internet Standard*. Figure 8.4 provides a simple depiction of the process.

The IETF's unofficial motto is "rough consensus and running code." This slogan reflects that the IETF relies on a combination of de facto and de jure standard setting. In the first (de jure) stage of IETF standardization, WG participants seek a rough consensus on the major design issues for a new standard. In principle, the publication of a Proposed Standard marks the start of the second (de facto) stage, which is a lengthy period of prototyping, testing, implementation, and deployment that provides the IETF with evidence of running code before a protocol is advanced to the elevated status of Draft Standard or Internet Standard. In practice, however, very few Proposed Standards reach the later stages of the process – partly because vendors have been increasingly quick to market products based on Proposed Standards.

The open and informal nature of the IETF standard setting process is suggested by the guidelines for promoting an Internet Draft to Proposed Standard. According to the Internet standards process described in RFC 2026 (see Bradner 1996, 11), a Proposed Standard should meet the following criteria: "[T]he specification is generally

---

[6] WGs may also produce "nonstandards track" RFCs that describe procedures, best practices, or particular implementations. These RFCs have a separate set of formal designations, such as *Informational* or *Experimental*.

stable, has resolved known design choices, is believed to be well-understood, has received significant community review, and appears to enjoy enough community interest to be considered valuable."

In practice, however, there is no clear definition of "rough consensus," and it is the job of the WG chair to decide whether one exists. There are no ballots;[7] yet, the strong emphasis on resolving technical disputes before submitting a draft to the IESG ensures that Proposed Standards have majority support within a WG. The last-call process exists to prevent any abuses of the overall process.[8] In addition, the IESG reviews all RFCs before they are published. As was previously mentioned, after publication as a Proposed Standard, specifications enter the de facto phase of the IETF standard setting process. To reach the status of Draft Standard, the IETF requires some evidence of running code, in the form of at least two independent and interoperable implementations. To become an Internet Standard, the IETF must determine that a specification has achieved, "significant implementation and successful operational experience" (Bradner 1996, 13). While the IETF has occasionally organized "connect-a-thons" for interoperability testing, it does not provide any formal development support. Critics have suggested that few Proposed Standards reach the later stages of the IETF process because vendors are more concerned with the actual de facto standardization process than with whether a specification receives additional recognition from the IETF. In fact, the IETF has a WG that addresses its perceived problems; this WG concluded that "the IETF currently has a one-step standards process that ... compresses the process that previously allowed specifications to mature as experience was gained with actual implementations" (see Davies 2004, 10).

The importance of rough consensus relative to running code at the IETF raises questions about the role of SSOs in high-stakes de facto standard setting. On the one hand, advocates suggest that SSOs can play an important role in the market by providing marketing, implementation advice, certification, compatibility testing, and other services that promote coordination on a common standard. The SSOs that

---

[7] One practice that has emerged as a proxy for voting is "taking a hum" at IETF meetings. The practice, which involves a voice vote in which participants hum rather than shout, was adopted because of the concern that louder members might be over-represented in a traditional voice vote.

[8] In the history of the IETF, only a handful of formal appeals have been made.

focus on these activities seem more likely to encounter free-riding problems than organizations focused on developing commercially significant specifications. On the other hand, coordinating the collaborative development of commercially significant technology brings its own set of challenges. For example, I find evidence that the IETF's consensus-building process has become less effective (or at least slower) in recent years. To understand why this happened, it is useful to examine the impact of Internet commercialization on the IETF during the 1990s.

2.3 *Internet commercialization and the IETF*

One of the first signs that the IETF would struggle with the challenges of Internet commercialization was the decision by Tim Berners-Lee (one of the creators of the World Wide Web) to set up a separate SSO. Initially, Berners-Lee had used the IETF as a forum to standardize some components of the Web, such as the syntax for Uniform Resource Locators (URLs). While he admired the IETF's open and informal process, Berners-Lee also worried about the "endless philosophical rat holes down which technical conversations would disappear" (Berners-Lee and Fischetti 1999, 68). By 1995, he realized that it would be challenging for any SSO to keep up with the rapid pace of technical developments related to the Web. In response, Berners-Lee began to develop a standard setting "consortium" that he believed might be better suited to this task.

The World Wide Web Consortium can move faster than the IETF because it requires formal membership (which can be accompanied by formal demands) and places more authority in the hands of a few directors. In his memoir about the Web, Berners-Lee wrote, "I wanted the [World Wide Web Consortium] to run on an open process like the IETF's, but one that was quicker and more efficient, because we would have to move fast" (Berners-Lee and Fischetti 1999, 98).

During the second half of the 1990s, there were several occasions when IETF participants clearly had conflicting commercial interests. Sometimes this happened because the Internet, and consequently the IETF's standards-developing efforts, began to encroach upon the vendors' established products. At other times, the development and commercial application of Internet technologies simply outpaced the IETF's consensus decision-making process. For example, the IETF's

Calendaring and Scheduling WG created a common standard for sharing calendar data across applications. Their efforts progressed slowly, in large part because incumbents with proprietary calendaring applications (e.g., Microsoft Outlook, Lotus Organizer, and Netscape Communicator) raised objections to a variety of features that might threaten the security of their large installed base (Higgins 1997). The Instant Messaging WG provides another example. As this committee was working to create a standard for instant messaging applications, Microsoft and AOL were in the midst of a heated standards war over the compatibility of their proprietary protocols. Both Microsoft and AOL participated in the deliberations, though neither was quick to move to an open messaging standard in the marketplace.

Another sign of Internet commercialization was the growing importance of intellectual property issues within the IETF. The IETF's policy towards intellectual property is a slight variation on the reasonable and non-discriminatory (RND) licensing rule used by many SSOs.[9] While participants are required to disclose any known property rights in a technology that is being evaluated, individual WGs are free to adopt their own rules about the use of proprietary technology in a standard.[10] While most WGs have been predisposed to select alternatives that are either unprotected or available on a royalty-free basis, there is a fair amount of variation. Some WGs have refused to evaluate any technology encumbered by patents, while others have adopted standards containing proprietary technology. In at least one case, a WG found that all of the available solutions were protected in some way or another.

Intellectual property rights in IETF proposals did not emerge as a serious issue until 1995, when Motorola disclosed two patents covering

[9] Lemley (2002) documents a variety of different intellectual property rules adopted by SSOs. The most common policy is based on the idea of RND licensing. Under this rule, proposals may contain proprietary technology, as long as the owner agrees to make the technology available to all prospective licensees on a RND basis.

[10] In principle, the RND requirement is enforced through the operation of the standard setting process. When a proposed standard is known to contain intellectual property, the IESG will only consider implementations by third-party developers – not the patent-holder – when deciding whether to advance the RFC to the status of draft standard. Yet, in evaluating these implementations, the IETF will not actually make a determination of reasonableness on the basis of the terms of a technology license. Rather, the organization treats any independent exercise of the licensing process as a confirmation that this condition has been met.

technology in the Compression and Encryption Control Protocols. Since then, there have been 246 intellectual property disclosures to the IETF. Roughly 66% of the intellectual property disclosures referred to work in progress (i.e., Internet drafts), while 20% covered completed specifications (the remainder did not specify). Fifty-six of these disclosures, or 23%, either promised not to prosecute any patents or to license them free of royalties.[11] In addition, 31% of the disclosures (76) provided a specific patent or patent application number, with the remaining 69% (or 140) referring to unpublished applications. The findings of a WG chartered to evaluate the IETF's intellectual property policy suggest that the growth in disclosures has caused a fair amount of confusion, controversy, and delay in the standard setting process (see Brim 2004).

In late 2002, a WG was formed to discuss potential problems with the IETF standard setting process. This Problem WG identified a variety of symptoms, from a breakdown of the three-stage standard setting process, to free-riding and a failure to consistently use effective engineering practices. They also described several root cause problems. In particular, they suggest that the rapid growth of the Internet led to increases in the scale, scope, and complexity of the IETF. At the same time, the commercial stakes of many IETF decisions had increased dramatically, and the convergence of data and telecommunications markets led to "an influx of experienced participants with a different culture and industry perspective" (Davies and Hofmann 2004, 4). All of these changes placed strains on an IETF management style that emphasized open participation and rough consensus – much of it based on loose interpersonal relationships. The qualitative evidence produced by this WG links the commercialization of the Internet to the overall effectiveness of the IETF. In the next section, I examine data on the duration of the standard setting process to quantify the slowdown in IETF standards production, and I consider a number of potentially contributing factors.

3 The slowdown in Internet standard setting

In this section, I examine the relationship between the size, scope, and composition of IETF WGs and the average duration of the standard setting process. Section 3.1 presents evidence of a slowdown in Internet

---

[11] The other 78% indicated that they would license the technology on a RND basis.

standard setting during the 1990s. Sections 3.2 through 3.4 consider several different explanations for the observed slowdown, including an increase in technical complexity or interdependency among specifications; an increase in the size of the IETF, which created bottlenecks in the standard setting process; and the possibility that Internet commercialization led to an increase in the potential for distributional conflicts among WG participants.

3.1 The slowdown in IETF standard setting

The analysis in this section will focus on Internet Drafts that were eventually published as a Proposed Standard. These documents are the set of Internet Drafts that represent the actual compatibility standards produced by the IETF. Between 1992 and 2000, IETF WGs published 4,032 Internet Drafts.[12] These drafts eventually produced 1,243 RFCs. I exclude from my analysis specifications published after 2000 and those that required more than three years to reach the status of Proposed Standard to avoid biasing the results by sampling on a right-censored variable. The resulting data set contains 571 Proposed Standards. All of the data on these specifications and the WGs that produced them was collected from the IETF's publicly accessible online archives. The publication dates were obtained primarily by analyzing messages sent to the IETF-announce mailing list, which notifies recipients any time a new or updated Internet Draft is published.

I consider two measures of the overall speed of the IETF standard setting process. The first measure (DUR1) is the elapsed time between publication of the initial and final versions of an Internet Draft. (By final version, I mean the last iteration of the editing process prior to the announcement of an IESG protocol action signaling that the draft will become a Proposed Standard.) This is a measure of the length of time required to complete the pre-consensus process, including all of the revisions that take place after a last call and IESG review. The second (DUR2) measure begins with publication of an Internet Draft and concludes when the document is published as an RFC. This variable captures the additional delays in the publication process that occur in

---

[12] The sample begins in 1992 because it was the first year with reliable data on Internet Draft publication.

Table 8.1. Duration of the IETF standard setting process (in days)

	Mean	Standard Deviation	Minimum	Maximum	N
Last Draft (DUR1)	431.0	273.4	9	1,089	571
RFC Publication (DUR2)	549.2	298.6	37	1,456	571

the RFC editing process. Both variables are measured in days.[13] In Table 8.1, I provide some summary statistics.

Figure 8.5 illustrates the slowdown in IETF standards development during the 1990s. The two lines show the trend in median development time for cohorts of Internet Drafts whose first version was published in a given year. Between 1992 and 2000, the median elapsed time from initial publication to final draft grew from 198 days to 549 days – an increase of 177%. The median time from initial publication to RFC publication grew from 335 days to 772 days, an increase of 115%. This represents a substantial slowdown in both absolute and percentage terms. While it is hard to quantify the economic impact of these delays, the opportunity cost of an additional year in development for computer networking firms was presumably high – particularly during a period when these companies were running on "Internet time."

Figure 8.6 shows the distribution of completion times – based on publication of the last draft – for all of the Proposed Standards produced by the IETF between 1992 and 2003. Although the vast majority of IETF standards were completed within a two- to three-year period, a few specifications took substantially longer to produce.

In the remainder of this section, I examine three potential explanations for the slowdown observed in Figure 8.5: (1) increasing technical complexity, (2) the growth of the IETF, and (3) a rise in intracommittee conflicts created by the commercialization of Internet-related technology. While I consider each hypothesis separately, I continually refer back to the results of a common set of simple cross-sectional regressions. These regressions provide estimates of the relationship between the duration measures presented in Table 8.1 and several observable

---

[13] RFC publication dates are only available by month, so I normalize to the 15th day.

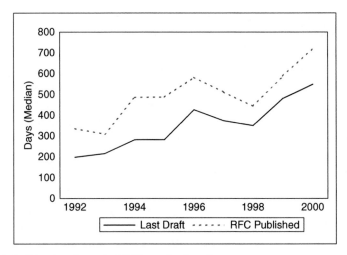

Figure 8.5. The slowdown in IETF standard setting.

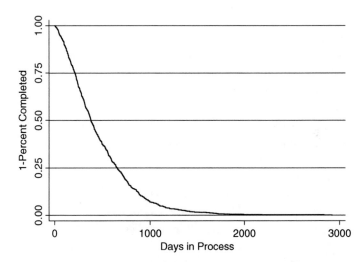

Figure 8.6. Distribution of completion times for proposed standards (1992–2003).

characteristics of the IETF, its WGs, and the specifications they produce. All of the variable definitions, summary statistics, and regression results are presented in the appendix in Tables 8.A1 through 8.A3. In the next subsections, I introduce each of the measures used in this analysis and discuss their interpretation.

I present two basic specifications in Tables 8.A3 and 8.A4. The results in Table 8.A3 are from a least squares regression of proposal duration (measured in days) on a set of variables described subsequently. The results are easy to interpret, since each coefficient can be read as the average number of additional days required to produce a standard following a one-unit change in the associated independent variable. This specification, however, places a number of strong restrictions on the underlying stopping process of IETF proposals.[14] In Table 8.A4, I present the results from a hazard model of the proposal process that relaxes some of these restrictions.[15] I report the coefficients as hazard ratios, or multipliers of the average stopping probability. (In other words, if the coefficient on an independent variable is 0.8, then a one-unit change in that variable leads to a 20 percent reduction in the average probability that a proposal will stop at any given time.)

3.2 Technical complexity

Between 1992 and 2000, the number of Internet users grew at an exponential rate, and new applications of the network appeared on a regular basis. This rapid growth placed many demands on the IETF, which was responsible for designing, maintaining, and upgrading the network infrastructure. These demands ranged from finding efficient ways to allocate the network's limited 64-bit address space to creating entirely new protocols for applications like voice-over-Internet protocol or instant messaging, which placed novel demands on the network. In many cases, the solutions were more complicated than the original protocols and required developers to take a more-systemic view of the underlying network. This increase in complexity and interdependence was summed up by the IETF's Problem Working Group (Davies 2004, 8): "The IETF has historically been most successful when dealing with tightly focused problems that have few interactions with other parts of the total problem solution. Given that the Internet has become more complex, such tightly focused problems are becoming the exception."

---

[14] In particular, this specification assumes there is no duration dependence, or relationship between the elapsed time since publication of the first draft and the probability of conclusion.

[15] I estimate a Weibull hazard model with time-invariant covariates and no frailty.

Table 8.2. Measures of technical complexity (mean by publication year)

	Authors	Pages	Log(Pages)	Cites	Log(Cites + 1)	Versions
1992	2.26	28.28	3.08	5.65	1.72	3.75
1993	2.30	27.13	3.02	5.07	1.64	4.69
1994	2.42	32.09	2.98	7.00	1.59	4.07
1995	2.15	31.76	3.05	7.38	1.83	5.59
1996	2.17	28.88	3.00	7.83	1.93	5.52
1997	2.52	24.09	2.89	7.51	1.98	5.54
1998	2.53	27.19	2.99	9.72	2.14	5.29
1999	2.90	33.49	3.09	9.74	2.08	5.52
2000	2.47	25.13	2.86	9.34	2.13	5.63

Unfortunately, it is not easy to measure the technical complexity or design interdependence of a particular protocol. I consider four indirect measures that serve as rough proxies for the overall complexity of a given specification, namely, the number of authors (author count), the length of the document (page length), the number of citations to other RFCs (outward citations), and the number of versions or revisions of the proposed standard. The relationship between complexity and the number of authors or length of an RFC is straightforward. When a solution is more complex, it usually takes longer to express it and frequently reflects more points of view. I interpret outward citations as a measure of how much a given protocol interacts with and builds upon the work of others. On the basis of this intuitive relationship, I use these citations as a proxy for the design interdependencies of a Proposed Standard. Finally, the number of versions or revisions that a Proposed Standard goes through is likely to reflect the complexity of the underlying technology.

In Table 8.2, I show how each of these measures of complexity evolved over time. Between 1999 and 2002, the average author count for a Proposed Standard grew slightly. Comparing three-year averages for 1992–4 to 1998–2000 there was a 13% increase in the average number of authors per document. There is no apparent trend in the page length of Proposed Standards, particularly when the effect of outliers is reduced using a log transformation. Yet, there does appear to be an increasing tendency for Proposed Standards to cite other RFCs.

Averaging over the same three-year periods, outward citations increased by 63% during the sample.[16] There is also an increase of 50% in the number of revisions that an Internet Draft goes through prior to publication as a Proposed Standard; most of this increase appears to take place during the period between 1992 and 1995.

We can now turn to the regressions in Table 8.A3 to see whether changes in complexity can explain the lengthening duration of the IETF standard setting process. The coefficients on author counts are small and statistically insignificant, suggesting that the slight increase in joint authorship was not a significant factor in the overall slowdown. The regression results consistently suggest that the length of a Proposed Standard is correlated with delay – a one-unit change in log of page length generally leads to an additional two months in the pipeline. Nevertheless, given the lack of any increase in average page length, this does not appear to be an important explanation for the slowdown. There is some evidence that outward citations – a proxy for the interdependence of IETF protocols – played a small role in the lengthening delays. The estimated coefficients in Table 8.A3 imply that a one-unit increase in log of outward citations is correlated with an additional forty to fifty days in average duration. Given the half-unit increase in outward cites observed over this time period, the variable explains between three and four weeks of the slowdown, or between 11% and 15%. Although the number of versions is highly correlated with proposal duration, I did not include it in these regressions, since the variable is quite likely to reflect that other factors may have caused an increase in duration (e.g., if conflicting interests lead the WG to put out a new compromise proposal). In summary, while there is evidence of a relationship between two observable measures of complexity and the time required to produce a new specification, this relationship can explain only a small portion of the overall change in IETF standard setting.

3.3 Growth and committee size

There are two types of organizational growth that might contribute to delays in the standard setting process. The first is the growing scope of

---

[16] The increase in outward citations is not merely a reflection of the growing number of RFCs, since there were a substantial number of standards published prior to 1992.

the IETF, which can be measured in terms of the number of active WGs, or total documents published. Aggregate growth might be associated with high-level coordination failures or the development of bottlenecks in the publication process (e.g., at the IESG). The second type occurs within individual WGs. There are a number of potential links between the size of these committees and the duration of the standard setting process. In smaller groups with frequent repeated interactions, it is easier to develop personal connections that are helpful in bargaining or dispute resolution. As more individuals join a committee, participants come to represent an increasingly diverse set of perspectives, which often leads to an increase in the amount of time required for communication. Large groups often take longer to make decisions simply because there are more participants who feel a need to express their own opinions. Finally, as more participants join a committee, there is an increasing chance that one or more members will delay because they prefer the status quo to any alternative put forward by the group.

I consider three measures of aggregate size, and two that vary across WGs. The number of active WGs, the number of Internet Drafts published by the IETF, and the number of RFCs published by the IETF are all good measures of the organization's overall growth. The first measure I use as a proxy for WG size is the number of Internet Drafts published by a WG in a given year. The second proxy for WG size is the monthly volume of email messages sent to WG discussion lists, which also captures the participation rate. Table 8.3 shows a clear and dramatic increase in the size of the IETF according to each of these measures. Between 1992 and 2000, the number of active WGs more than doubled. The average number of Internet Drafts published by an IETF WG (including expired and nonstandards track drafts) more than doubled from about three per year to more than six. The volume of email sent to the average WG's email discussion list grew by a factor of three. Total RFC publication increased by about 80 percent. Finally, the number of Internet Drafts published grew by a factor of seven.

Unfortunately, it is not possible to use longitudinal data on IETF-wide changes to separate the impact of the IETF's aggregate growth from the influence of other (perhaps unobserved) broad institutional changes. Nevertheless, for illustrative purposes, Table 8.A3 reports one set of results that includes the aggregate growth in WGs, RFCs, and Internet Drafts as independent variables, and a separate set that

Table 8.3. Measures of IETF and working group size

	Number of WGs	IDs/WG	Email messages/ Month	Total number of RFCs	Total number of IDs
1992	50	3.22	17.51	118	161
1993	67	2.49	15.69	111	167
1994	68	3.40	23.73	141	231
1995	71	4.11	33.59	144	292
1996	97	3.80	32.13	202	369
1997	107	5.71	45.22	271	611
1998	108	4.54	36.14	193	490
1999	111	6.64	40.51	241	737
2000	121	7.82	46.11	245	946

absorbs all of these measures into a full set of publication-year fixed effects. When the aggregate growth measures are included, the number of active WGs is most closely correlated with increasing duration. In fact, given the net increase of seventy WGs, the coefficient on this variable suggests that it explains more than two-thirds of the total slowdown. But it is important to reiterate that this is not an appropriate conclusion, given the potential correlation between this variable and other broad shifts in the IETF's process and culture during this time period. After the proposal-year fixed effects are included to control for these changes, the between-WG variation in size does not appear to explain much of the observed slowdown in standardization. The coefficient on Internet Draft production is statistically indistinguishable from zero. The monthly volume of email is also insignificant, and at the observed magnitude would account for a little less than a month of additional delay. In summary, there is little evidence that growth in the size of individual WGs played a significant role in the overall slowdown. While the aggregate growth of the IETF may have played a major role, we do not have the data to adequately demonstrate that this was the case.

3.4 Distributional conflicts

Distributional conflicts in the formal standard setting process are usually tied to switching costs created by investments in competing designs or platforms. These include the expense of product redesigns, the opportunity costs of progressing down production learning curves, and the cost of migrating customers onto a new platform. When platform-specific investments precede the creation of a consensus standard – usually because vendors hope to be first to market – standardization comes to resemble a process of "picking winners." When the costs of losing are large relative to the benefits of coordination, distributional conflicts can lead to delay, because participants are willing to engage in protracted arguments over the choice of a particular technology.

Distributional conflicts are often hard to observe. Participants rarely publicize them, and the explicit goal of most SSOs is to find a compromise solution. I use four measures to look for evidence of a relationship between Internet commercialization, distributional conflict, and delays. Two of these variables are indirect proxies for hard-to-observe conflicts. The first is simply a measure of WG composition. I use contributions to WG email discussion lists to construct a commercialization ratio that measures the proportion of WG messages originating from private-sector institutions.[17] This commercialization measure is not meant to indicate that private-sector participation per se is a leading cause of delays. Rather, I believe it is a proxy for market proximity and the probability that firms are investing in preferred designs before a consensus is reached. The second indirect measure of distributional conflict is the Internet Draft failure rate, or the proportion of Internet Drafts published by a WG that do not become RFCs. This measure is a proxy for the presence of competing design alternatives within a given WG.

I also create two measures of distributional conflict on the basis of intellectual property disclosures. Participants with intellectual property in a technology have additional incentives to push for the selection of that design – particularly if they believe it might generate substantial licensing revenues. At the same time, firms may use intellectual property disclosures strategically to slow the standards development process or push the consensus design in a different direction. The first measure of intellectual property issues is simply a variable that indicates whether anyone has disclosed intellectual property rights for a given Proposed Standard (or IPR disclosure). At a broader level, the

---

[17] I have also measured this ratio using the percentage of commercially affiliated *individuals* or *organizations* in a WG. The three measures are all correlated above 0.9.

Table 8.4. Measures of distributional conflict

	Failure rate (%)	Commercialization (.com %)	IPR dummy	Total IPR disclosure	WG IPR disclosure per RFC
1992	46.79	0.46	0.000	0	0.040
1993	42.43	0.52	0.038	0	0.051
1994	46.52	0.57	0.032	0	0.019
1995	53.98	0.67	0.000	1	0.028
1996	56.88	0.72	0.016	4	0.027
1997	63.40	0.78	0.092	4	0.099
1998	57.70	0.81	0.028	10	0.031
1999	69.06	0.81	0.025	19	0.057
2000	69.91	0.80	0.032	31	0.075

presence of these disclosures may be a reflection of distributional conflicts that exist within the WG. Consequently, the second measure is a count of the disclosures that take place within a particular WG, normalized by its overall output of RFCs (or WG IPR disclosures per RFC).

In Table 8.4, I show the annual means for these measures of distributional conflict along with the total number of annual intellectual property disclosures. There were sizable increases in both of the indirect measures. As measured by the commercialization ratio, private-sector participation increased by 34% between 1992 and 2002. The Internet Draft failure rate grew by about 23%, from just about every other document in 1992 to almost three out of four by 2000. In spite of the rapid increase in the total volume of IPR disclosure, only 19% of the Proposed Standards in our sample had actually been named in a disclosure, and there is no apparent trend in the dummy for IPR disclosure. It is also hard to pick up any strong trend in the amount of WG IPR disclosure per RFC.

Turning to the regressions in Table 8.A3, we find that two of the measures of distributional conflict – the commercialization ratio and the IPR disclosure dummy – had no measurable relationship to the average duration of the standard setting process. The Internet Draft failure rate did have a statistically significant impact on duration, which suggests that WGs took more time to reach a conclusion when they had more proposals to evaluate. Given the 23% increase in failures between 1992 and 2000, this variable can explain between thirty and forty days of the entire slowdown, or roughly 10%. Hence, while the results for the Internet Draft failure rate provide some evidence of a relationship between distributional conflicts and delay, they do not explain much of the total slowdown in IETF standard setting between 1992 and 2000. Finally, note that the level of WG IPR disclosure per RFC is consistently significant, yet has the opposite of the predicted sign. While the magnitude of this effect is small, I interpret this – along with the negative coefficient on inward citations – as evidence that more-important drafts received priority in the publication process.

To summarize, I have just examined the slowdown in IETF standard setting that occurred during the 1990s following the rapid growth and commercialization of the Internet. During this period, the average time required to move a specification through the IETF's publication process increased by about a year, roughly doubling. Using data on individual standards and the WGs that produced them, I found evidence that increasing technical complexity (outward citations) and distributional conflicts (Internet Draft failure rates) were correlated with longer delays. Despite this, even if I assume that these correlations represent the direct effect of observable changes in the IETF standard setting process, these factors can only explain about 20% of the overall slowdown.

4 Identifying the causes of committee performance

The regressions described in the previous section establish that there is a relationship between the size, structure, and composition of IETF WGs and the performance of these technical committees. Yet, it is far from clear that these are causal relationships whereby the observed characteristics directly affect the average committee's performance. Here, I briefly consider some of the difficulties that confront a researcher trying to establish a causal link between the structure and performance of technical committees. I consider two basic types of problem. First, it is often difficult to measure many of the variables in which a researcher is interested – often because committee members have an interest in preserving a certain level of ambiguity. Second, many of the features of the technical committees that the researcher can observe are strongly influenced by the participants' choices. As a result, it is important to consider how these choices are made when interpreting the observed relationships between committee character-istics and performance.[18]

To begin, imagine that, using data from a large sample of commit-tees, we are studying the impact of committee characteristics on the collective decision-making process. For example, we might be inter-ested in how changes in committee size or voting rules influence the average length of deliberations. In the previous section, I approached this problem by developing a set of proxy variables for various com-mittee characteristics, and I used some simple regressions to establish a relationship (i.e., correlation) between these variables and committee performance.

While this approach has the virtue of being straightforward, it is not always clear how well a given proxy variable will capture the relation-ship being examined. For example, I used the Internet Draft failure rate within a committee to measure distributional conflicts; however, since failure rates are generally higher in committees that consider more proposals, this variable may also capture the effect of congestion, or attention overload.

In some cases, we cannot directly observe the variables that we are interested in because the committee benefits from a certain level of ambiguity. This is the case with voting at the IETF. While it would be easier to study the IETF's decision-making process if the participants conducted a series of votes on each proposal, many participants recog-nize that public voting could create a more adversarial atmosphere within the organization. These participants prefer to maintain the much looser process of decision making by rough consensus, because they feel it promotes a more collegial atmosphere.

Another problem with the use of indirect proxies for a hard-to-measure construct such as distributional conflict is that these variables are likely to be correlated with other unobserved committee character-istics. These spurious correlations may be the cause of any observed relationship between the proxy variable and SSO delays. For example, if more-complex technologies take longer to discuss in IETF commit-tees but are also more likely to be patented, some of the correlation between patent disclosure and delays will have nothing to do with

---

[18] In Simcoe (2004), I exploit differences across proposal-types at the IETF to study the impact of distributional conflict on delays. This approach may be useful in studying other committee decision-making processes.

intellectual property conflicts. Rather, the delays will be a reflection of the long discussions generated by complex proposals. In another scenario, proposals that contain particularly high (unmeasured) levels of distributional conflict may draw a large crowd of interested participants, leading to a correlation between committee size and duration that does not reflect the direct impact of size on performance.

The example of committee size varying with the distributional stakes of a standard highlights a *selection problem* with empirical work on committees. For example, the committee characteristics in which we are interested often reflect the decisions of individual participants. As a result, it is hard to know whether observed correlations – such as the relationship between intellectual property disclosure and the delays found above – are caused by an observed attribute of the committee or merely reflect the unobserved conditions that led participants to make a particular choice.

The selection problem can be particularly acute when dealing with characteristics that are influenced by committee members' participation decisions, which occur on several different levels. At the highest level, there is a selection process that determines whether a given technology is standardized in the market or through an SSO. In particular, we might think that when a given standard engenders severe conflicts of interest, it is more likely to be resolved in the market rather than in a technical committee. At another level, participants select between different committees, or between WGs inside the IETF (see Lerner and Tirole 2004). If these alternative venues are equally legitimate and have similar rules and procedures, we might expect this "forum shopping" to lead to more homogeneous preferences within committees and presumably faster decision making. Finally, there is a selection process that determines whether individual participants or potential members decide whether to participate in the standard setting process. These individual joining decisions will be influenced by a number of issues, including the costs of participation, the salience of distributional issues, the ability to contribute to a technical solution, and beliefs about the ex post influence of a committee's recommendation. The empirical approach used in the previous section is likely to attribute the impact of these complex processes to simple observable variables such as committee size.

The preceding discussion suggests a number of difficulties associated with empirical research on nonmarket standardization and, more

generally, with committee decision making. This is not surprising, since
voluntary collaborative committees are complex organizations; however, the problems of selection and unobserved heterogeneity have been
studied in a host of settings, and there are a number of approaches
widely used for dealing with them. One solution that is frequently
prescribed within economics is to find instrumental variables that
influence a particular committee characteristic but are independent of
the many complicating factors described above. For example, the IETF
has recently adopted a lottery system to determine the members of the
IESG from a pool of eligible candidates. If we were interested in how
the composition of the IESG influenced WG performance, we could use
the results of the lottery as an instrumental variable. Unfortunately, it
can be difficult to find plausible candidate instrumental variables. Even
when they exist, the available instruments are frequently unrelated to
the particular problem in which we are interested. Consequently, while
the IESG lottery provides an opportunity to study the impact of IESG
composition on committee decision making, it can tell us little about
the impact of distributional problems.

In Simcoe (2004), I used a different approach to the problems
described above. Instead of searching for instrumental variables,
I used differences in the types of proposal developed within individual
WGs to study how committee characteristics influence delays. At the
IETF, and many other technical SSOs, there are different classes of
proposal. For example, Figure 8.4 shows that IETF WGs create both
standards track and nonstandards track proposals. Because these different types of proposal are produced by the same committees, it is
possible to circumvent many of the problems described by examining
differences between proposal-types *within* a given committee.

Of course, this is only interesting when the substantive differences
between types of proposal correspond to an issue in which we are
interested. In the case of the IETF, I argue that nonstandards track
proposals are substantively similar to those on the standards track. Yet,
because they are only meant to convey information (rather than serve
as an official IETF endorsement of a compatibility standard) nonstandards track proposals produce much less distributional conflict. Since
nonstandards track proposals have these lower distributional stakes,
I use them as a control sample for studying the impact of distributional
issues on proposal durations. In particular, I find that the *difference* in
the length of time required to produce a nonstandards track RFC, as

opposed to a Proposed Standard, is correlated with the percentage of commercially affiliated committee participants and their co-authoring behaviors. While the results in Simcoe (2004) do not explain any more of the variation in committee performance than the regressions presented here, they do a much better job of establishing a link between distributional issues and delay. Since many standard setting organizations recognize the distinction between protocol actions and the informational resolutions that I exploit in the case of the IETF, this approach may be useful in addressing otherwise intractable questions of causation in the study of committee performance.

5 Conclusions

In their survey of compatibility standards, David and Greenstein (1990, 4) conclude, "Much more must be learned about the actual extent of the resources committed to 'anticipatory' standards-writing projects, and the consequences of the particular administrative policies and procedures adopted by these organizations." It has been over a decade since their survey was published, and only a handful of papers have responded to the call for empirical research on de jure standard setting. Here, I have endeavored to clarify some of the reasons behind the slow progress made in tackling these issues, as well as suggest some potential approaches to the problems. Given the influence of non-market institutions in the standard setting process, developing a better understanding of de jure standard setting is an important task. Moreover, it will open the door to research on the *interaction* between market (de facto) and nonmarket (de jure) processes.

In practice, many technologies emerge from a hybrid process that combines both de facto and de jure standardization. Still, scant research explicitly asks when or why some standards are ultimately established in the marketplace while others are developed by nonmarket SSOs. There is a long list of potentially important factors. On the nonmarket side, these factors include the perceived commercial importance of the technology and the possibility of conflicting interests within an SSO; the legitimacy of particular SSOs and the opportunity to forum-shop; the choice of intellectual property rules and strategies; the presence of dominant-firm sponsors; and a variety of characteristics of alternative technical solutions. For markets, issues to consider are the presence of a dominant firm or existing standard; the ability of competing vendors to sow fear, uncertainty, and doubt; the incentives of adopters (who may be different from consumers); and the expected timing of adoption benefits.[19] A goal for research – particularly empirical research – in the next decade should be to assess the relative importance of these various factors on the selection process that determines whether compatibility standards ultimately emerge from a market or a committee. Perhaps the growth of open-source software development will provide an opportunity to collect data on a host of different standardization efforts that will help sort out these issues.

The story of the IETF also holds several lessons for standards developers and policymakers. One lesson from the IETF's early success is the importance of implementation experience in de jure standardization. While the gains from collaborative technology development are presumably a major benefit, SSO participants frequently complained of irrelevant or "over-architected" designs. When asked, their explanations ranged from the perils of design-by-committee (i.e., everyone's pet idea has to be included), to distributional politics, to the nature of the engineering culture.[20] By emphasizing the production of rough consensus and running code, the IETF encouraged participants to do the minimally sufficient amount of specification before trying to implement a new piece of software. This made it easier to gather data for resolving disputes and harder to block implementations that worked.[21] The existence of running code also accelerated the adoption process (particularly when combined with the decision to make much of the technology available for free). Finally, it allowed the government to be involved through the funding of various development initiatives – which was accomplished in a decentralized way – rather than through

---

[19] A number of papers presented at the Standards and Public Policy Conference in Chicago, May 13–14, 2004 consider potential "failures" of both markets (e.g., Cabral and Kretschmer; Greenstein and Rysman) and committees (e.g., Lerner and Tirole; this paper).

[20] Simcoe (2004) develops a simple model of collaborative development where endogenous over-design is the result of conflicting committee interests. The SSOs set too-high standards as a way of resolving distributional conflicts.

[21] The International Organization for Standardization networking model provides an interesting comparison. While their model remains influential as a reference standard, there have been few implementations – primarily because ISO was less concerned with running code than the IETF.

a coordinated effort to establish a national standard (Mowery and Simcoe 2002).

A second lesson that emerges from the IETF's story is that successful SSOs eventually face a predictable set of challenges. After the incredible success of the Internet, some observers speculated that the IETF had invented a better de jure standard setting process. Perhaps they did. Nevertheless, as the IETF grew in size, scope, and legitimacy, it began to experience many of the same problems as its predecessors. Over time, it became harder for the IETF to produce rough consensus in a timely fashion. At the same time, many vendors became so anxious to produce running code that the IETF effectively lost control of a technology once it became a Proposed Standard. In this paper, I have explored some of the underlying causes, which include larger committees, more complex technical problems, and distributional conflicts over specifications with serious commercial implications.

When it comes to solving these problems, it is harder to draw any clearly generalizable lessons from the IETF experience. It is tempting to conclude that the main lesson is to focus on standards and technologies that are truly "anticipatory" – that is, so far from the market that many difficult issues, such as "picking winners" or the constraints imposed by existing specifications, do not arise. Unfortunately, this offers little guidance to existing SSOs. The World Wide Web Consortium's approach was to have SSO members cede more authority to a central coordinating body. Alternatively, SSOs can focus on activities other than collaborative technology development. While economists naturally focus on standardization as a choice problem, many SSOs simply take de facto standards as given and work to promote coordination by reducing the costs of implementation and adoption. These organizations focus on marketing activities, certification programs, compatibility testing, and user groups. Although this approach avoids the difficult choices associated with collaborative design altogether, it may be a reasonable solution when many of the problems explored above loom particularly large.

Finally, I conclude by stressing what a remarkable institution the IETF is. While this paper may have seemed quite pessimistic, given its focus on the slowdown in IETF standardization and the challenges caused by Internet growth and commercialization, it is important to note that many of these challenges are the result of the IETF's extraordinary success. It is amazing that an almost completely voluntary organization with no formal membership or requirements, whose agenda is formulated from the bottom up by interested participants, could develop one of the most significant technologies in recent memory. The IETF's WGs continue to both develop a wide variety of influential standards in areas such as wireless and optical networking and make much of the underlying technology freely available. It will be interesting to observe how this remarkable institution responds to the challenges created by its own success in the future.

References

Berners-Lee, Tim, and Mark Fischetti 1999. *Weaving the web*. San Francisco, CA: HarperSanFrancisco.

Besen, S. M., and J. Farrell 1994. "Choosing how to compete: Strategies and tactics in standardization," *Journal of Economic Perspectives* 8: 117–31.

Bradner, S. 1996. "RFC 2026: The Internet standards process – Revision 3," Network Working Group, Internet Engineering Task Force, http://www.ietf.org/rfc/rfc2026.txt?number=2026.

2003. "An alternative for the IETF standards track," http://www.watersprings.org/pub/id/draft-bradner-ietf-stds-trk-00.txt.

Brim, S. 2004. *RFC 3669*: "Guidelines for working groups on intellectual property issues," Network Working Group, Internet Engineering Task Force, http://www.ietf.org/rfc/rfc3669.txt?number=3669.

Cargill, Carl F. 1989. *Information technology standardization: Theory, process, and organizations*. Bedford, MA: Digital Press.

David, P. A., and S. Greenstein 1990. "The economics of compatibility standards: An introduction to recent research," *Economics of Innovation and New Technology* 1: 3–42.

Davies, Elwyn B. 2004. "RFC 3774: IETF Problem Statement," Network Working Group, Internet Engineering Task Force, http://www.ietf.org/rfc/rfc3774.txt?number=3774.

Davies, Elwyn B., and J. Hofmann (eds.) 2004. "RFC3844: IETF Problem Resolution Process." Networking Group, Internet Engineering Task Force, http://rfc3844.x42.com/.

Farrell, J. 1996. "Choosing the rules for formal standardization," unpublished manuscript, http://emlab.berkeley.edu/users/farrell/ftp/choosing.pdf.

Farrell, J., and G. Saloner 1988. "Coordination through committees and markets," *RAND Journal of Economics* 19: 235–52.

Foray, D. 1995. "Coalitions and committees: How users get involved in information technology standardization," in *Standards, innovation and competitiveness*, R. Hawkins, R. Mansell, and J. Skea (eds.), Northampton, MA: Edward Elgar, 192–212.

Higgins, K. J. 1997. "The squeeze is on at IETF," *Internet Week*, November.

IETF (Internet Engineering Task Force), June 1990. *Internet Monthly Report*. Internet Engineering Task Force, http://sunsite.utk.edu/ftp/usr-218-2/internet-monthly-reports/imr9006.txt.

Lemley, M. 2002. "Intellectual property rights and standard setting organizations," *California Law Review* 90: 1889–981.

Lerner, J., and J. Tirole 2004. "A model of forum shopping with special reference to standard setting organizations," National Bureau of Economic Research Working Paper No. 10664.

Mowery, D. C., and T. Simcoe 2002. "Is the Internet a US invention? An economic and technological history of computer networking," *Research Policy* 31: 1369–87.

National Research Council 1990. *Crossroads of Information Technology Standards*. Washington, DC: National Academy Press.

Rutkowski, A. 1995. "Today's cooperative competitive standards environment and the Internet standards-making model," in *Standards policy for information infrastructure*, Brian Kahin and Janet Abbate (eds.), Cambridge, MA: MIT Press, 594–653.

Simcoe, T. 2004. "Committees and the creation of technical standards," unpublished manuscript, http://groups.haas.berkeley.edu/imio/simcoe012204.pdf.

Appendix

Table 8.A1. Variable definitions

Name	Description	Variation
DUR1	Duration (days) from first to last draft publication	RFC
DUR2	Duration (days) from first draft to RFC publication	RFC
AUTHCNT	Number of authors on RFC	RFC
LOGPG	log(RFC Pages + 1)	RFC
LOGOCT	log(RFC Out Citations + 1)	RFC
LOGICT	log(RFC In Citations + 1)	RFC
TTLRFCS	Count of RFCs published per year by all IETF WGs	IETF
TTLIDS	Count of IDs published per year by all IETF WGs	IETF
TTLWGS	Count of WGs publishing at least one ID in a given year	IETF
IDCNT	Count of IDs published per year by a given IETF WG	WG
MSPM	Messages per month on WG email discussion list	WG
FAILRT	Percent of WG's Internet Drafts not published as an RFC	WG
COM	Percent of "commercial affiliated" emails on WG discussion	WG
IPRDUM	IPR Disclosure for an Internet Draft (dummy)	WG
IPRFC	Count of WG IPR Disclosures per published RFC	WG
RFCCNT	Count of RFC published per year by IETF WG	WG

Table 8.A2. Means, standard deviations, and simple correlations

	MMEAN	S.D.	DDUR1	DDUR2	AAUTHCNT	LLOGPG	LLOGOCT	LLOGICT	TTTLRFCS	TTTLIDS	TTTLWGS	IIDCNT	MMSPM	FFAILRT	CCOM	IIPRDUM	IIPRFC
DUR1	424.70	273.17	1.00														
DUR2	543.98	299.62	0.93	1.00													
AUTHCNT	2.45	1.68	0.13	0.09	1.00												
LOGPG	2.99	0.85	0.18	0.15	0.34	1.00											
LOGOCT	1.96	0.74	0.19	0.16	0.13	0.53	1.00										
LOGICT	1.25	0.98	-0.13	-0.16	0.21	0.33	0.12	1.00									
TTLRFCS	203.45	55.81	0.29	0.26	0.11	-0.04	0.16	-0.21	1.00								
TTLIDS	524.71	262.89	0.31	0.29	0.10	-0.04	0.18	-0.30	0.84	1.00							
TTLWGS	95.76	23.52	0.33	0.30	0.11	-0.05	0.19	-0.24	0.90	0.90	1.00						
IDCNT	72.16	161.92	-0.03	0.00	-0.06	-0.23	-0.20	-0.06	0.02	0.00	0.00	1.00					
MSPS	61.03	72.98	0.20	0.21	0.23	0.06	-0.03	0.09	0.22	0.32	0.27	0.24	1.00				
FAILRT	62.09	23.40	0.25	0.23	0.15	0.04	-0.03	0.02	0.31	0.35	0.31	0.13	0.53	1.00			
COM	0.77	0.15	0.07	0.04	0.11	0.15	0.26	-0.01	0.14	0.11	0.19	-0.01	0.14	0.09	1.00		
IPRDUM	0.04	0.19	0.05	0.05	0.19	0.14	0.01	0.11	0.11	0.05	0.07	0.09	0.16	0.11	0.08	1.00	
IPRFC	0.05	0.13	0.01	0.00	0.18	-0.01	-0.02	-0.02	0.14	0.12	0.10	0.16	0.23	0.26	0.13	0.44	1.00

Table 8.A3. Duration regressions (ordinary least-squares)[a]

	DUR1	DUR1	DUR2	DUR2
AUTHCNT	6.882	9.107	3.404	5.605
	(7.215)	(7.132)	(7.529)	(7.411)
LOGPG	63.262	62.077	69.931	67.950
	(19.175) ***	(19.219) ***	(20.459) ***	(20.550)
LOGOCT	38.372	39.495	45.375	47.140
	(20.873) *	(21.301) *	(21.298) **	(21.741)
LOGICT	−54.171	−61.180	−70.694	−77.628
	(13.107) ***	(13.153) ***	(13.885) ***	(13.955)
TTLRFCS	−0.229		−0.452	
	(0.462)		(0.521)	
TTLIDS	−0.071		−0.023	
	(0.107)		(0.114)	
TTLWGS	3.758		3.305	
	(1.243) ***		(1.366) **	
IDCNT	−0.890	−1.203	−0.012	−0.209
	(1.245)	(1.277)	(1.314)	(1.362)
MSPM	0.284	0.337	0.324	0.369
	(0.218)	(0.227)	(0.235)	(0.242)
FAILRT	1.839	1.694	1.411	1.277
	(0.561) ***	(0.559) ***	(0.616) **	(0.604) *
COM	−34.457	−9.998	−52.024	−36.128
	(80.923)	(80.595)	(89.209)	(88.016)
IPRDUM	34.147	41.793	67.039	75.382
	(65.696)	(64.386)	(82.431)	(81.266)
IPRFC	−210.621	−210.488	−253.641	−252.542
	(75.126) ***	(74.998) ***	(86.004) ***	(86.074)
CONSTANT	−268.742	−143.346	−49.458	−0.867
	(109.375) **	(110.249)	(117.784)	(116.843
Area dummies	Y ***	Y ***	Y ***	Y ***
Year dummies	N	Y ***	N	Y ***
Observations	532	532	532	532
R-squared	0.21	0.25	0.21	0.24

Notes:
[a] Robust standard errors in parentheses
* Significant at 10%
** Significant at 5%
*** Significant at 1%
These estimates are from an ordinary least-squares regression. The dependent variable
number of days from first draft to publication as an RFC. Because of right-censoring
the sample is restricted to RFCs published before January 1, 2001 and taking less th
three years to complete.

Table 8.A4. Duration regressions (hazard model)[a]

	DUR1	DUR1	DUR2	DUR2
AUTHCNT	0.964	0.966	0.978	0.980
	(0.029)	(0.026)	(0.030)	(0.027)
LOGPG	0.644	0.623	0.666	0.650
	(0.059) ***	(0.057) ***	(0.058) ***	(0.056) ***
LOGOCT	0.813	0.874	0.779	0.834
	(0.071) **	(0.079)	(0.066) ***	(0.076) **
LOGICT	1.338	1.371	1.405	1.433
	(0.074) ***	(0.073) ***	(0.079) ***	(0.079) ***
TTLRFCS	1.001		1.001	
	(0.002)		(0.002)	
TTLIDS	1.001		1.001	
	(0.000) **		(0.000) **	
TTLWGS	0.982		0.988	
	(0.006) **		(0.007) *	
RFCCNT	1.002	0.999	1.003	1.007
	(0.003)	(0.004)	(0.004)	(0.005)
MSPM	1.001	1.001	1.000	0.999
	(0.001)	(0.001)	(0.001)	(0.001)
FAILRT	0.988	0.989	0.990	0.991
	(0.003) ***	(0.003) ***	(0.003) ***	(0.003) ***
COM	1.382	1.379	1.363	1.814
	(0.497)	(0.502)	(0.495)	(0.670)
IPRDUM	0.934	0.988	0.731	0.777
	(0.258)	(0.254)	(0.198)	(0.202)
IPRFC	2.450	2.390	2.964	2.933
	(0.639) ***	(0.644) ***	(0.906) ***	(0.926) ***
Area dummies	Y ***	Y ***	Y ***	Y ***
Year dummies	N	Y ***	N	Y ***
Observations	569	569	569	569

Notes:
[a] Robust standard errors in parentheses
* Significant at 10%
** Significant at 5%
*** Significant at 1%
These estimates are from a hazard model of proposal duration. The dependent variable is number of days from first draft to publication as an RFC. The sample is restricted to RFCs published before January 1, 2001.

9 | Standardization: a failing paradigm

CARL CARGILL AND SHERRIE BOLIN

Abstract

Standards, like the poor, have always been with us.

Also, like the poor, there have been well-intentioned attempts to create programs that will make them whole (or at least better). The authors present a proposal for one of these programs on the basis of the beliefs that (1) standardization is failing to serve the interests of the sponsoring organizations, the public, the industry, and the nation and (2) the failure of standardization (as a useful management tool) will have complex and far-reaching consequences for all of the participants. The authors primarily consider voluntary standards, namely, standards that do not have regulatory standing. They focus on and draw their sources from the Information and Communications Technology (ICT) industry. Their article is based on experiential data gained from constant and substantial activity within the standard setting organizations of the ICT industry. Both authors have extensive experience as embedded, empowered, and occasionally neutral *(and, for at least one author, bitter) participants in ICT standardization.*

1 Introduction

Standardization is basically a management technique used to reduce risk and, since 1980, it has moved from being viewed as a technical discipline to being viewed as a "cool" marketing tool within the Information and Communication Technology (ICT) industry. This statement is probably an overly dramatic assertion of what has happened in the market, but we believe that it is generally defensible given our perspective of the events over the past twenty-five years. We believe that there are numerous proof points (but no rigorous studies) to

296

support this contention.[1] Absent these rigorous studies, and using our experience and knowledge of the ICT industry and its standard setting organizations (SSOs),[2] we briefly examine some of what we believe were the major turning points over the past twenty-five years that have made standardization a marketing handmaiden rather than a technical discipline. Much of this explanation will be based upon material contained in the following section, where the changes in the business environment, which funds a huge majority of voluntary standardization, drove the changes that occurred. We primarily consider voluntary standardization – that is, standards that do not have regulatory standing. The moment a specification becomes required by legislation, it passes out of the voluntary arena and out of the purview of our paper.

While standardization should respond to changing business requirements and needs, we believe that some of these changes – namely the excessive proliferation of specifications and SSOs – are undermining the very value of standards and the markets that they serve. Since standardization is an impure public good (one that is developed by the private sector but that has public benefits), government has an interest in and a responsibility to ensure that the system is effective and responsive to public needs. When the private sector fails to successfully manage an impure public good, as we believe they have in standardization, government may intervene. In this paper, we provide suggestions on how government can help to strengthen the standardization system through minimal intervention. We also discuss how the private sector can build upon this intervention to avoid more extensive government intervention and to reform the standardization system so that it more successfully meets the goals of all involved.

---

[1] There are very few rigorous studies in the field of practical standardization – the area where the actual standards are created and used by the sponsoring organizations. We have found little rigorous study of the utility of standards in the ICT industry in which simple questions such as "Are standards beneficial to a company in its product decisions?" or "Is the use of standards increasing or decreasing?" or "Is open source a form of standardization or is it something else?" appear not to have been considered by the academic community.

[2] We use the term SSO to designate any organization engaging in standardization activities. It avoids the conflicts between the formalists who insist that only a standards-developing organization (SDO) can develop standards (and all the rest, mere specifications) and the generalists who insist that all generally used specifications, from formal standards to proprietary software in wide use, are, in fact, standards. This distinction has always appeared to us a specious argument, as we have determined that, in fact, 333 standardized specifications can dance on the head of a pin (with apologies to medievalists).

1.1 A brief, but necessary, history of standardization

Standardization is an essential element to the growth of the computer
industry. Most new ICT industry initiatives center on the concept of
interoperability, one of the fundamental goals of ICT standardization
(and most standardization, for that matter). There are no more homogeneous islands of computing that marked the late 1980s; today's
environment is worldwide, fast paced, and completely heterogeneous.
The impact of this changing environment on business, society, and
culture cannot be overstated. Just as the common gauge for railroads
changed the face of the United States in the last half of the 1800s, the
creation and growth of the standards-based digital economy will have
a profound effect on the nature and future of life in the United States.
More than a decade ago, *The Economist* (Anonymous 1993, February
23, 62) published the following statement in its Survey of Information
Technology:

The noisiest of those competitive battles (between suppliers) will be about
standards. The eyes of most sane people tend to glaze over at the very
mention of technical standards. But in the computer industry, new standards
can be the source of enormous wealth, or the death of corporate empires.
With so much at stake, standards arouse violent passions.

This statement, echoed in one form or another in most literature on
the subject of standardization, is even more applicable today in the ICT
industry. With the advent of the Internet and the World Wide Web,
open standards[3] are becoming more and more a part of the *infratechnologies*[4] that "provide the technical basis for industry standards"
(Leech et al. 1998, ES-8). As Libicki and others (2000, xi) of the Rand
Corporation note, "[W]ith each passing month, the digital economy
grows stronger and more attractive. Much, perhaps most, of this
economy rests upon the Internet and its World Wide Web. They, in

---

[3] An *open standard* is one that is not under the control of a single vendor and is
easily available to those who need it to make products or services.
[4] *Infratechnologies* is a term the National Institute of Standards and Technology
uses to describe a superset of technologies (the technological infrastructure) that
"provide the technical basis for industry standards." Today, Internet and Web
infratechnologies serve as the basis of standards upon which e-business,
e-commerce, and all of the other "e-" activities are being built.

turn, rest upon information technology standards." This fundamental change in the focus of ICT standardization (from one of homogeneous computing to one of interoperable information sharing) has had a significant impact on the way standardization is done.

We now briefly review specifics of how the changes in the ICT standardization process have occurred and provide some history and background on these changes as they relate to the unique aspects of ICT standardization. There are five basic variants of SSOs within the industry: (1) trade associations; (2) formal SDOs; (3) consortia; (4) alliances; and (5) the open source software movement.

We link trade associations and SDOs because they both belong to the formal school of standards – that is, a standards process that is heavily focused on maintaining due process, openness of participation, and a comprehensive appeals process. We link consortia and alliances because both are collections of like-minded organizations and/or individuals who come together to act as advocates for a particular change. Each of the five variants has a place; there is no single optimal choice for developing standards for the entire industry.

1.2 Trade associations and standards-developing organizations

The process that trade associations and SDOs have created within the United States is a result of legal challenges to their work and is absolutely necessary for the regulatory arena or similar arenas, where there is an implied legitimacy ascribed to a specification labeled as an official standard. Of the five forms of standardization activity, the trade association activity has the place of pride for being the oldest, dating from the late 1800s. Generally, the associations were gatherings of professional men who were experts in a particular field (e.g., boilers, fire prevention, mechanical engineering). They set up these groups to create a professional discipline and to preserve this discipline by creating specifications embodying their wisdom for the sake of their colleagues. Hence, societies like the American Society of Mechanical Engineers, the Institute of Electrical and Electronics Engineers (IEEE), and the American Society for Testing and Materials (ASTM) came into being. In most cases, the primary mission of these groups was the education of members in their professional discipline, with standards as a secondary activity to fulfill some of the training requirements.[5] These groups were directly responsible for technical practices that could affect public safety, and they needed to ensure that their specifications were correct. Peer review was not only desirable, it was necessary and expected.

In many cases, the specifications developed by the trade organizations have become the basis for codes and statutes and have acquired a regulatory patina that permits them to be used as defense in liability cases. By definition, if you follow the specifications published by the National Fire Protection Code, you are using techniques and practices that have been tested, tried, and proven to be safe. This makes trade associations an excellent source for codifying successful past practices – things that are stable, structured, and time insensitive. In the ICT industry, however, in areas that do not touch upon, for example, safety issues, looking to past practices for future guidance is usually a prescription for failure.[6]

To understand the formal standardization processes of SDOs in the United States, it is necessary to discuss the American National Standards Institute (ANSI). The US government has not created a national standards body, but the formal process for developing standards in the United States is created, maintained, and administered by ANSI,[7] which is the "first among equals," the rule setter, the interface to the International Organization for Standardization (ISO) and the International Electrotechnical Commission (IEC), and currently the

---

[5] The ASTM seems to have completely morphed into a standardization organization, and, while it maintains a yellow-page listing of consultants and expert witnesses, it does not seem to be educating testing experts. The mission statement of the ASTM (2005) (see http://www.astm.org/NEWS/Mission2.html) reads, "To be the foremost developer and provider of voluntary consensus standards, related technical information, and services having internationally recognized quality and applicability." With a complete yearly set of ASTM standards costing nearly $7,000, and with ASTM standards being cited in legislation, one can understand why the ASTM has moved entirely to standardization activities.

[6] It is necessary to note that the regulatory use of standardization has another and darker side. In two Supreme Court cases, *American Society of Mechanical Engineers* v. *Hydrolevel* (1982) and in *Allied Tube and Conduit* v. *Indian Head* (1988), the standards bodies were found to have abused their ability to affect the market. While the cases varied with respect to details, the economic power of the organization was cited as a major point of contention. In both cases, there were process violations on the part of the organization.

[7] The concept of sectorial approach in standardization is presented in ANSI's (2000) "National standards strategy for the United States," Section V (http://www.ansi.org/public/nss.html).

only organization that can give the imprimatur of an American National Standard to the specifications produced by most US standards organizations. The formal national bodies under the auspices of ANSI in the United States and the international bodies under the ISO and the IEC are referred to as SDOs. More than 170 organizations have sought ANSI accreditation. In fact, ANSI is the primary stakeholder for the United States for all formal organizations (national or international) that currently are the primary providers of specifications used in procurement in the United States. Nevertheless, ANSI does not create standards. It has no expertise in the subject matter of standards; it has expertise only in the maintenance of its process. (For more on ANSI, please see the appendix.)

In the Information Technology (IT) field, the initial standardization organizations were those that operated under ANSI's rules and organizational constricts; and these standardization organizations followed in the footsteps of all the other industrial standardization activities in the United States. We use the term IT deliberately here (and subsequently), as the IT industry and the Communications industry, in fact, did not begin to merge until the late 1980s – a period after ANSI's hegemony in IT standardization had begun to fail. For the Communications industry, the International Telecommunications Union (ITU) was the dominant player, and the ITU was not associated with the voluntary standardization processes of either ANSI or the ISO.

During this initial period of standardization, much of the fundamental hardware standardization activities were occurring – from common interconnections for the keyboard and mouse to printers and storage systems within the IT industry.[8] The negotiations that created these standards – which were complex and confined to a relative handful of providers – were usually under the aegis of one or two standardization

---

[8] A significant difference between the IT sector and other sectors is that within the IT industry, we are, in the main, speaking of voluntary market-driven standards, which are left to the discretion of the provider to supply. It is important to note that the majority of unique IT sector standards are interface standards describing a particular systems interface. They do *not* deal with safety or environmental activities. They are optional in a product – depending upon the business model of the vendor. Standards of this type are (and will continue to be) one of the costs of doing business, just as is translation of instruction manuals into a native language.

committees in the United States.[9] They usually dealt with things that would stay standardized for a long time.

In contrast to European nations at this time, the United States chose to encourage the private sector to enter into standards partnerships. This allowed the trade associations to continue to act as standards associations, while encouraging the formation of new organizations devoted only to standardization – such as the Accredited Standards Committees X3, X9, and X12, each of which deals with IT, Banking, and Electronic Data Interchange (EDI), respectively. (See the appendix for a more lengthy discussion of the international and national standards developing scene.)

1.3 Consortia and alliances

In the late-1980s, a different form of standardization activity appeared, beginning with an organization called X/Open.[10] Providers began to move technology standardization away from the formal ANSI- and ISO-recognized SDOs to those of consortia, which did not have the intricate processes of the SDOs. Consortia initially were created to deal with the "clarity and time to market" problem that was seen as a major obstacle in the formal arena. Much of the problem in the formal arena lay with its arcane rules for openness and review; several of the formal review process steps required six months and could expand to even more time. The consortia, responding to the pressure of time being money, especially since the product life cycle was shrinking, wanted a faster system.

The processes at consortia were unlike the time-consuming and often Byzantine formal processes that the SDOs needed because

---

[9] The two ANSI-accredited standards committees were Accredited Standards Committee X3, which dealt with IT, and Accredited Organization IEEE, which dealt with computer systems. Approximately 85 percent of the key standards were created in X3, including storage interconnect, languages, and so on. The IEEE dealt with physical interconnects (such as local area networks) and eventually moved into software interfaces.

[10] In 1996, X/Open was merged with the Open Software Foundation to create The Open Group. X/Open was originally created in Europe to embrace and extend UNIX ® to limit the spread of US companies into the European IT arena. After ten years of existence, and before its merger, X/Open was largely dominated by major American IT providers, with Siemens as its sole surviving European member.

"[m]ost delegates represent[ed] personal, professional, national, disciplinary, and industry goals" (Cargill 1989, 117) and managing this vast and sometimes contradictory set of expectations forced the SDOs to create intricate rules to ensure that all voices were heard.

The proponents and opponents of consortia have focused on this speed issue, not realizing that increased speed was achieved in a consortium by changing the process. The argument has never been about speed; it has been about the process required to achieve the speed necessary to satisfy the market needs of the members of the organization.

Because consortia usually consisted of groups of like-minded participants (either for technical or market reasons), they did not need to have the lengthy discussions over the mission and intent of the proposed standardization activity – an organization's presence was, in many cases, proof of a general agreement. These organizations and/or individuals came together to act as advocates for a particular change, whether it was for a new specification, a new way of approaching a problem, or a new research and development activity. Consequently, consortia were also often more visible within a company than were formal organizations, because consortia were directly tied to the product success of a company. In other words, a company joined a consortium to promote the creation of a specification that it needed for market reasons – there was an imperative behind the consortia's creation. The same imperative was not necessarily found in formal organizations.

This shift to consortia was amplified by the introduction and ensuing popularity of the World Wide Web in the early 1990s. The establishment of the World Wide Web Consortium (W3C)[11] in October 1994 was a turning point within the IT industry; after this date, consortia were the logical place to develop joint specifications, whereas before they had been the alternative place. One of the reasons for this shift was that the IT practitioners who are now leading much of the IT development are part of a generation largely focused on Internet technologies; these practitioners have had little interaction with ANSI and ISO and do not believe the SDOs can develop standards quickly and efficiently.

---

[11] See World Wide Web Consortium (2006) at http://www.w3.org/Consortium for a detailed description of both the creation of the underlying vision of the Web by Tim Berners-Lee and the initiation of the W3C by MIT, INRIA, and Keio University.

Their world is largely bound by consortia, such as W3C and the IETF. They see little or no need for ANSI or ISO standardization – a message they carry to their companies.[12] With the maturity of the Web, an increasing number of consortia have been created to standardize Web-based technology. (Nearly all specifications that relate to the Web or to the Internet are created in arenas that are either consortia or consortia-like.)

The reason behind using consortia lies not so much in the speed of technical development but rather in the willingness of the consortia to use expedited (and hence, user-responsive) processes. The archetypal consortium is the Internet Engineering Task Force (IETF), the group that manages the Internet. The success of this group in both keeping the Internet a cutting-edge technical architecture leader as well as clear of greed, parochialism, and lethargy is a significant accomplishment.[13] The IETF has been using the Internet to communicate among interested parties, post specifications, achieve rough consensus on technical features and functions, and then move forward on standardization. The specifications the IETF adopts are usually based on extant practice, with at least two implementations required for specifications on the standards track, and are available for widespread public review and comment.

---

[12] In the case of HTML 3.2 (a specification developed and promulgated by W3C), ISO/IEC JTC1 SC 18 (the committee charged with standardization of this technology) tried to standardize HTML 3.2 with "JTC1 improvements," but only after W3C had standardized HTML 3.2 and the users had implemented it in millions of websites. After serious negotiations by W3C and major users and providers, SC 18 agreed not to make their standard different from the W3C standard, which was in widespread use.

[13] The IETF describes itself in the following way (IETF 2006): "The Internet Engineering Task Force (IETF) is a large open international community of network designers, operators, vendors, and researchers concerned with the evolution of the Internet architecture and the smooth operation of the Internet. It is open to any interested individual. The actual technical work of the IETF is done in its working groups, which are organized by topic into several areas (e.g., routing, transport, security, etc.). Much of the work is handled via mailing lists. The IETF holds meetings three times per year. The IETF working groups are grouped into areas, and managed by Area Directors, or ADs. The ADs are members of the Internet Engineering Steering Group (IESG). Providing architectural oversight is the Internet Architecture Board (IAB). The IAB also adjudicates appeals when someone complains that the IESG has failed. The IAB and IESG are chartered by the Internet Society (ISOC) for these purposes. The General Area Director also serves as the chair of the IESG and of the IETF, and is an ex-officio member of the IAB" (see http://www.ietf.org).

This practice – using its own technology to permit faster standardization of follow-on technology – is another step that sets the IETF apart from its contemporary organizations of the 1980s. The use of its technologies as a basis for its standardization practices ensures workable specifications that can actually be implemented, but more importantly allows the IETF to develop into a truly international organization. When a specification is complete, it is posted on the IETF website with free access for all.

The W3C operates in a similar, though somewhat more formal, manner and is a good model for the operation of many other consortia. These consortia realize that the key elements are speed and specification accessibility – accessibility to those who are concerned about the consortium's work. As *The Economist* (Anonymous 2001) has pointed out,

[T]he Internet has turned out to be a formidable promoter of open standards that actually work, for two reasons. First, the [W]eb is the ideal medium for creating standards; it allows groups to collaborate at almost no cost, and makes the decision-making more transparent. Second, the ubiquitous network ensures that standards spread much faster. Moreover, the Internet has spawned institutions, such as the Internet Engineering Task Force (IETF) and the World Wide Web Consortium (W3C), which have shown that it is possible to develop robust common technical rules.

These features have made the ICT community turn to consortia and similar structures for their standardization needs in both hardware and software. The creation of highly open, highly visible specifications – widespread in their adoption and use – is essential to the continuing evolution of the ICT sector and ICT industry.

Another aspect of consortia that separates them from the traditional SDOs is their dependence on the market, rather than on institutions, for relevance. A consortium succeeds or fails by its ability to attract members to accomplish its technical agenda. It receives little or no funding other than what its membership is willing to pay; money received from the government is rare and is usually in return for some exact service that the consortium renders to a specific government agency in the role of a contractor.[14] While this dependence on its members for financing can be seen as a limitation on the consortium's freedom of action, it reflects

---

[14] See Spring and Weiss (1995) for a discussion regarding the problems of private sector funding of formal standards organizations.

the state of the market in formal SDOs as well, except that formal SDOs do not shut down if all of the commercially important members (i.e., those who would implement the specification) walk away. There is a delicate balance between an independence that leads to an unused standard and a financial dependency that produces a constrained specification. (For more on consortia and alliances, see the appendix.) The newest wrinkle in consortia are "Commercial Joint Ventures," which may be described as "ur-consortia." They have many of the features of consortia, but have a contractually defined governance body (hence, a joint venture of sponsor companies who usually qualify by paying large membership dues). They usually morph into consortia once the sponsors have achieved their initial specification-product goals.

1.4 Open Source movement

The latest trend in standardization is the open source movement, which shies away from using any formal organization, preferring to create its own analogs of the existing infrastructure. Open Source is the attempt to use the Internet to create better (less buggy) and more open (not proprietary) code in a cooperative environment.

Open Source is probably the most expensive type of standardization in which an organization can engage, since participation and use of Open Source code may require that an organization change its fundamental licensing principles with respect to its intellectual property (IP).[15] Open Source does not disbelieve in IP rights – it merely makes the rights of the property holder the same as the rights of anyone else. In all of the other organizational types, the contributing organization can choose the terms and conditions of its giving, as long as the terms are reasonable and non-discriminatory. The difference is that with Open Source the terms and conditions of the grant are mandated in the particular licensing agreement chosen by the group. This is acceptable to some; to many large organizations (including large academic institutions, the sources of intellectual freedom) it is anathema, since these

---

[15] The most popular types of licenses (Mozilla, General Public License, and Berkeley) do not require the IP owner to give up the IP rights. Rather, these licenses require that the IP owner grant broad, perpetual, and non-restrictive rights to use the IP, in effect making all of the users equal. The broad nature of the grant – in which the IP owner reserves few or no rights – is what has given many the impression that Open Source can be equated with forfeiting IP rights.

organizations have patents on nearly every aspect of technology, granted by a forgiving (or forgetting) US Patent Office. This battle, which we do not directly address here, bids fair to completely destroy standardization. The reason for the allure of Open Source is contained in writings by the philosopher and activist of the Open Source movement – Eric Raymond, in *The Cathedral and the Bazaar* (1999), and Jamie Zawinski (formerly of Netscape, who convinced Netscape's management to make the source for Netscape's browser into Open Source and call it Mozilla). Linus Torvalds led the creation of the popular Linux Operating System in the same philosophical frame – which is open for all to use without exception or restriction, other than the requirement to act as part of the community. The movement has caught mindshare and market share, and many large corporations are embracing the Linux phenomena, hoping that later they can find the method to profit (for more on Open Source licensing, please see the appendix).

1.5 Evolution serves as the business rationale for change

The essential element in all of these groups lies in their responses to differing market requirements. Consortia replaced SDOs as a preferred venue because they responded better to the needs of business; commercial joint ventures (a variant form of consortia) emerged to compete with the older, larger, multidiscipline consortia, and the Open Source movement reflected yet another market requirement, the desire for a more cooperative environment with a better and more open code. The need for legislative protection given by the SDO rules was mitigated by the creation of the National Technology Transfer and Advancement Act of 1995, which allowed collaborative research and development. The need for speed and ease of creation led to the various forms of consortia (from those described as heavy-weight to those that are very light-weight). The confusion about IPR helped drive the Open Source movement. Throughout all of this, however, logical evolution served as the business rationale for the creation of various types of organization. This is not the problem, but it is the basis of the problem.

2 The problem

Standardization is economically significant, as we previously noted. The major providers of ICT equipment have realized this and have initiated actions accordingly. When a constituted standardization organization blocks activities, or when it fails to meet necessary[16] expectations, it is the work of a moment to create another consortium, alliance, technical committee, or similar standardization activity that is "more in tune with the expectations of the market," which is a euphemism for an organization that produces specifications that more exactly meet the needs of the creating organization(s). The key item here is that the needs that are being met are not technical needs, but rather are the providers' market-positioning requirements.[17] This, in and of itself, is not unexpected market behavior, nor is it antithetical to the good of the market. The rationale for standardization activities is based on meeting user requirements, and in many cases, users believe that the products of these organizations serve a purpose.[18] Absent user rejection of a specification produced by any of these organizations, the organizations will continue to produce specifications at the behest of their members, who are almost always major providers with substantial market position.

It is here that the real problem with standardization emerges – at least as practiced in the ICT industry within the United States. The proliferation of specifications, coupled with the lack of understanding about what a standard truly is, has led to an explosion of SSOs. As a result, standardization is failing to serve the interests of the sponsoring

---

[16] Egyedi (2001) provides an interesting and factual account of why companies tend to specification shop.

[17] An interesting phenomenon is that there are very few SSOs created by users. The major attempt to create one of which we are aware is the User Alliance for Open Systems, which was created in the late 1980s and was captured by providers within six months of its creation. The capture was effected very simply – the users, who originally wanted to discuss user requirements, were convinced that they had to "talk technology" with the vendors. For the vendors, it was merely a case of "My rules, my cards, my game, my house, and your money." There is no gambler on earth who would pass up those odds.

[18] An interesting discussion can be developed from the concept of "let the buyer beware – because the buyer should know what he is buying." (The second half of this proverb is usually forgotten when it is used.) The problem is that, due to the paucity of education professionally available about standardization, most people have no idea what standardization really is. This then bifurcates the discussion into whether it is the responsibility of the providers to use the term standardization correctly and educate the market or whether it is acceptable for the providers only to pander to the understanding of their users. The problem is probably intractable.

organizations, the public, the industry, and the nation. Its failure (as a useful management tool) has complex and far-reaching consequences for all of the participants. We will look at each part of the problem independently, starting with the phenomenal growth of SSOs.

2.1 Explosion of SSOs

During the technology boom, SSOs rose in popularity, thriving on both the membership dues of new market entrants – that saw standardization as a way to compete with major ICT companies – and the expanding revenues of large ICT companies. These companies could suddenly afford to upgrade their current SSO membership levels while joining additional SSOs and even create their own competing SSOs to serve their company's needs better. The SSOs thrived in this new economy, and the standardization market grew and prospered.

When the boom ended, so did the almost unmitigated investments in SSOs. Companies became more strategic in their investments, and those SSOs that did not respond to market needs began to wither. Instead of dying, however, as was the fate of many technology companies unable to compete in the changed market, SSOs that did not have responsive business models continued to limp along. They were bolstered by a few loyal members that chose familiarity over market viability or were propped up by fortunate ownership of industry brands or essential standards. Market mechanisms that culled the weaker businesses in the rest of the ICT industry were dampened in the standardization arena, and many failing SSOs – which should have responded to conditions by revising their business models to meet market demands – continued to operate as usual, struggling for survival by grasping any revenue opportunity regardless of the long-term health of the organization, the ICT industry, or user needs.

Simultaneously, new SSOs arose that purported to meet market needs better, often in direct – and intentional – competition to existing SSOs. While some of these organizations were truly created to fulfill unmet market and user needs, others were developed and substantially supported by ICT vendors that viewed them as an easy mechanism for influencing market development and growth in a more beneficial direction than the existing SSOs could or would offer. In addition, we believe that companies that were in danger of losing market share if *any* standard was successfully developed in a given area started and/or funded SSOs with the sole purpose of producing competing standards and fragmenting the market.

2.2 Proliferation of specifications

Today, we are in a situation in which all of these SSOs produce specifications, and few, if any of them, interoperate with specifications produced by other SSOs. They have lost sight of two fundamental principles of standardization: (1) the purpose of standardization is to facilitate interoperability, giving users more and better product choices while expanding the overall market for vendors; and (2) the only way to achieve this goal is through cooperation and collaboration with other market players who are often competitors. In essence, we believe SSOs are taking a "do as I say, not as I do" approach, encouraging their members to cooperate to increase the growth and the health of a given market while simultaneously grasping for pieces of the standardization market with little regard for the market's growth or long-term health.

If this unmitigated output of standards, especially competing standards, continues, the market will fragment to the point where interoperability will become impossible. In the past, the ICT industry has responded to changing market conditions by creating new types of SSOs. However, if the standards industry itself undermines interoperability by exceeding the carrying capacity of the market to accommodate not only the number of standards as a whole, but also the number of competing standards, the ICT industry will likely respond by turning to alternative models for cooperation and collaboration. Indeed, this is already starting to happen as is evinced in the rise of commercial joint ventures.

The SSOs and their members are facing the dilemma of "the tragedy of the commons" (Hardin 1968). In the classic example, farmers share a common grazing ground. Each must decide whether he will add another cow to his holdings, increasing his short-term profits while ultimately destroying the pasture due to overuse, or whether to refrain from additional purchases in the hopes that the neighbors will also do the same and the pasture will continue to flourish. In the case of standards, an SSO must decide if it will seize short-term revenue opportunities and possibly push the market past its standards carrying capacity[19] – thus fragmenting the standardization industry and delaying progress in achieving interoperability. The other choice is to work toward a solution in which SSOs operate within the carrying capacity and interoperate with each other to produce standards that improve the overall market. While this growing problem may not yet be readily apparent to many, the trials and tribulations of the Department of Homeland Security in merging disparate systems data can be seen as a leading indicator of problems to come. Henry David Thoreau could pine for his little hand-built cabin by Walden Pond and moan for the days of individualism, but a complex, interworking, mutually interdependent, and technologically advanced society needs tightly coupled interoperation to survive and prosper. Things that are actively constructed to either defeat or oppose the necessary interoperation of society lead to one of two possible endings – either chaotic breakdown or a despotic dictatorship, which (despite the best efforts of everyone from Aristotle to Beckett to Moore) is how those who achieve monopoly positions usually end up.

2.3 Lack of a definition

Contributing to the overall problem in standardization is the lack of definition of the term *standard*. It is consistently abused by those who write about it. So, for the purpose of clarity and as a basis for presenting our solution, we define it for the ICT environment in the following way:

A standard is a technical specification that codifies a set of interfaces which describe the necessary methodology to achieve interoperation between disparate programs. The standard does not say how the interfaces are to be met, only that the interfaces must be open (that is, not proprietary), accessible, and fall within the realm of reality. It would also be nice if the interface recognizes that there are global requirements. This specification is the result of action by an SSO.

---

[19] The carrying capacity of an industry, nation, or the world to absorb standards at any one time or at what rate has not been established. The authors encourage research in this area and would like to extend special thanks to John Hill for posing this question in the first place.

3 A possible solution

We believe that the solution to the problem lies within the public, as opposed to the private, sector. This belief is derived from the observation that:

Other goods, like education and *standards*, are impure public goods. These combine aspects of both public and private goods. Although they serve a private function, there are also public benefits associated with them. Impure public goods may be produced and distributed in the market or collectively through government. *How they are produced is a societal choice of significant consequence.* (*Global standards* 1992, 14, footnote 23, emphasis added)

The private sector within the United States has largely failed in managing the public good that is standardization. Because of the inability to cooperate, the standards being produced are leading to either chaos or monopoly positioning. Either one, in the long run, is not good for the market in general and the ICT industry in particular.

The intervention necessary by the government is reasonably benign. To begin, the attributes of an SSO are not clearly defined. Currently, any group claiming to be a consortium or an alliance can seek protection under the National Technology Transfer and Advancement Act of 1995.

However, in *Circular A119*, the Office of Management Budget (1998, see http://www.whitehouse.gov/omb/circulars/a119/a119.html#4) has defined voluntary consensus standards bodies (with respect to procurement of goods and services for the Federal Government) in the following fashion:

a. For purposes of this policy, "voluntary consensus standards" are standards developed or adopted by voluntary consensus standards bodies, both domestic and international. These standards include provisions requiring that owners of relevant intellectual property have agreed to make that intellectual property available on a non-discriminatory, royalty-free or reasonable royalty basis to all interested parties. For purposes of this Circular, "technical standards that are developed or adopted by voluntary consensus standard bodies" is an equivalent term.

(1) "Voluntary consensus standards" bodies are domestic or international organizations which plan, develop, establish, or coordinate voluntary consensus standards using agreed-upon procedures. For purposes of this Circular, "voluntary, private sector, consensus standards bodies," as cited in Act, is

an equivalent term. The Act and the Circular encourage the participation of federal representatives in these bodies to increase the likelihood that the standards they develop will meet both public and private sector needs. A voluntary consensus standards body is defined by the following attributes:

i) Openness.

ii) Balance of interest.

iii) Due process.

iv) An appeals process.

v) Consensus, which is defined as general agreement, but not necessarily unanimity, and includes a process for attempting to resolve objections by interested parties, as long as all comments have been fairly considered, each objector is advised of the disposition of his or her objection(s) and the reasons why, and the consensus body members are given an opportunity to change their votes after reviewing the comments.

These attributes, of course, are no longer relevant, given the Federal Trade Commission–Rambus hearings. *Openness* is a vacuous term with no legitimacy in a court; defending the concept of *consensus* – as described above – would face serious problems in a hearing. We propose a new set of criteria, which could be written into OMB *Circular A119* that derives its authority from Section 12(d) of Public Law 104-113, the National Technology Transfer and Advancement Act of 1995. (By expanding the scope of Public Law 104-113, Congress can define the attributes of a "legitimate" SSO.) The new criteria would be as follows:

1. The SSO must develop technical specifications.

2. The SSO must be some type of legal entity.

3. The SSO must have a well-defined, legally acceptable set of procedures and processes.

4. The SSO must have a clear and legitimate IPR policy that requires, at a minimum, RAND licensing of all IPR included in its specifications.

5. The technical specifications created by the organization must be implemented by two or more competing entities prior to specification release, following widespread, web-based public review of the specification.

6. There should be reference implementations, competing implementations, and test methods to validate conformance as appropriate.

These attributes focus not on the SSO and the process of the SSO, but rather on the production of potentially interoperable specifications.

The process (item 3) needs only to preclude the ability of the providers to gather to work mischief (apologies to Adam Smith). The key to this entire definition (and the public good component) lies in item 5, which requires that the output, not the input, of the SSO be examined. If only one company (due to say, restrictive licensing or technological capability) can implement a standard, then the standard may not really be open, no matter how many people worked on creating it. Item 5 also begins to address the real danger of exceeding the carrying capacity for standards, since standardization output will be tempered by the capacity and willingness of organizations to produce competing implementations. It is hoped that this item will encourage SSOs to look at the results, or expected results, of a standardization activity – that is, how many implementations there are for a produced standard and whether or not these standards increase user choice or decrease use risk. Using a cartel to create a standard to capture a market is not too farfetched; however, IP restrictions are probably a lot safer to use.[20]

This type of activity would not be groundbreaking. ANSI currently runs a certification program for "legitimate SDOs," and there are numerous test and certification organizations that could be called upon to review and legitimize SSOs. The new criteria would not need to be mandatory; it would merely require a bill such as the Standards Development Organization Advancement Act of 2003 (HR 1086), which limited antitrust penalties for SDOs to single, not treble, damages, to give limited immunity from antitrust (similar to that currently enjoyed by SDOs) to certified organizations. Those who wished to remain outside the pale could do so, depending on their assessment of the economic risk. It would be the market at work.

It would also be not too difficult to begin to create a mapping of those SSOs who register to examine their scope and extent of work. By making available a list of new SSOs that are created on a monthly basis, it would be possible for business people (and the consultants who service them) to begin to understand the activities of the SSOs. If the SSOs could be convinced – as part of the registration – to list their

[20] It is far easier to use cross-licensing of IP rights as an effective barrier. The cellular phone contains up to 137 essential pieces of technology – each of them is owned by a large corporation, which usually has cross-licensing terms with its large competitors. A small company trying to enter the market would find that licensing the 137 patents would pose a formidable barrier to entry that would not be encountered by its larger competition.

standards, the scope of work, and the potential audience, the creation of a systems approach (with its attendant discipline) would be only that much closer. This list would potentially facilitate interoperation and cooperation among SSOs, since it would be easier to identify potential collaborative opportunities.

These criteria offer a more palatable and realistic solution than one requiring stronger government intervention to the tragedy of the commons situation now plaguing SSOs and standardization. Since market mechanisms have not been successful and standards are an impure public good, it is feasible that government may eventually see the need to limit standardization output. This could be accomplished by limiting the number of SSOs that are certified each year and requiring recertification on a regular basis. However, this solution presents several obstacles. First, since the carrying capacity for standardization is unknown, it would be difficult to determine the optimal number of SSOs. Second, the solution would only be effective if it were implemented internationally. Currently, there is no international standards body that would be trusted by all parties and nations with this task. Finally, private industry, especially in the United States, traditionally favors self-policing and market mechanisms over government intervention. While this type of government intervention is an impractical solution at this time, it would be wise for SSOs and their members to actively and cooperatively work towards an alternative solution to the problem rather than become subjected to government regulations such as those experienced by other industries that exceeded carrying capacity (e.g., limits to polluting emissions by oil refineries, manufacturers, etc.).

We believe these proposed changes would help manage – or at least provide insight into – the proliferation of competing, non-interoperable specifications that are limiting the public benefits of standardization and undermining the progression of the ICT industry. In doing so, the United States would facilitate the tightly coupled interoperation essential for the growth and prosperity of a society that relies on advanced technologies.

4 Conclusion

The reforms we have proposed would serve standardization well and are reasonably benign – all are being done now in various fora. What is needed is the belief that standards are important enough to US industry (or to the European Union industry, or Chinese industry) for this approach to be initiated. We believe that objections to it will come from the SSOs that will have to change and cooperate, and from industry, which will see yet another "managerial freedom" being removed. The reforms are a very light set of guidelines that can be implemented in a largely voluntary fashion. Compliance is not mandatory; there is a risk associated with non-compliance (increased risk of antitrust), but that is a business decision left to the organizations and their sponsors.

We also believe that this approach, with its reasonably light touch, will be far preferable to a more draconian measure to which governments will be pushed if the current situation continues. If standards are an impure public good (as we believe they are), then the government has not only the right but also the duty to intervene when the private sector fails. We believe that the beginnings of this failure – as evinced by either chaos or monopoly – are already beginning to be seen. So the question really comes down to whether or not the private sector, with help from the government, can correct itself, or whether it is willing to risk that no one will notice until the entire system collapses. It is a bet that we will see played out over the next five years.

References

Addamax Corporation v. *Open Software Foundation, Inc., Digital Equipment Corporation, and Hewlett-Packard Company, Inc.* 1995. 888 F. Supp. 274; 1995–1 Trade Case, (CCH) P71,036, at ConsortiumInfo.org, http://www.consortiuminfo.org/antitrust/ados.shtml.

Allied Tube and Conduit v. *Indian Head* 1988. 486 US 492, http://www.stolaf.edu/people/becker/antitrust/summaries/486us492.html.

American National Standards Institute (ANSI) 2000. "National standards strategy for the United States," http://public.ansi.org/ansionline/Documents/News%20and%20Publications/Brochures/national_strategy.pdf.

2006. "About ANSI," http://www.ansi.org/about_ansi/introduction/introduction.aspx?menuid=1.

American Society of Mechanical Engineers v. *Hydrolevel Corporation* 1982. 456 US 556 http://www.stolaf.edu/people/becker/antitrust/summaries/456us556.html.

American Society for Testing and Materials (ASTM) 2005. "Mission statement," http://www.astm.org/NEWS/Mission2.html.

Anonymous. 1993. "Survey of information technology," *Economist* February 23, 1993.

2001. "The age of the cloud, survey of software," *Economist* April 14–20, 2001: Special Supplement.

Cargill, Carl F. 1989. *Information technology standardization: Theory, process, and organizations.* Bedford, MA: Digital Press.

Egyedi, Tineke M. 2001. "Why Java™ was – not – standardized twice," *IEEE Proceedings of the 34th Hawaii International Conference on System Sciences,* January 3–6, 2001.

European Committee for Standardization (CEN) 2004. "About us – generalities, structure, information," http://www.cenorm.be/cenorm/aboutus/index.asp.

Global standards: Building blocks for the future, TCT-512, 1992. Washington, DC: Congress of the United States, Office of Technology Assessment, http://caselaw.lp.findlaw.com/casecode/uscodes/15/chapters/69/sections/section_4301.html.

Hardin, Garrett 1968. "The tragedy of the commons," *Science* 162: 1243–8.

Hecker, Frank 2000. "Setting up shop: The business of open-source software," June 20, Revision 0.8 DRAFT, http://www.hecker.org/writings/setting-up-shop.html.

International Electrotechnical Commission (IEC) 2006. "Industry Technical Agreements (ITAs)," http://www.iec.ch/tctools/ita-e.htm.

International Organization for Standardization (ISO) 2006, "International Workshop Agreement (IWA)," http://www.iso.org/iso/en/stdsdevelopment/whowhenhow/proc/deliverables/iwa.html.

The Internet Engineering Task Force (IETF) 2006. "Overview of the IETF," http://www.ietf.org/overview.html.

Leech, David P., Albert N. Link, John T. Scott, and Leon S. Reed 1998. *The economics of a technology-based service sector,* A planning report for National Institute of Standards and Technology, 98–2, Arlington, VA: TASC, Inc., http://www.nist.gov/director/prog-ofc/report98-2.pdf.

Libicki, Martin C., James Schneider, Dave Frelinger, and Anna Slomovic 2000. *Scaffolding the new web: Standards and standards policy for the digital economy.* Santa Monica, CA: Rand Corporation, http://www.rand.org/publications/MR/MR1215/.

National Cooperative Research and Production Act of 1993, US Code §§4301, et seq. http://caselaw.lp.findlaw.com/casecode/uscodes/15/chapters/69/sections/section_4301_notes.html.

National Technology Transfer and Advancement Act of 1995, Public Law 104–13, http://ts.nist.gov/ts/htdocs/210/nttaa/113.htm.

Office of Management and Budget 1998. *Federal participation in the development and use of voluntary consensus standards and in conformity assessment activities.* Final Revision of Circular A-119, http://www.whitehouse.gov/omb/circulars/a119/a119.html.

Raymond, Eric 1999. *The Cathedral and the Bazaar: Musings on Linux and open source by an accidental revolutionary.* Cambridge, MA: O'Reilly, http://www.tuxedo.org/~esr/writings/cathedral-bazaar/.

Spring, Michael, and Martin Weiss 1995. "Financing the standards development process," in *Standards Policy for Information Infrastructure*, Brian Kahin and Janet Abbate (eds.), Cambridge, MA: MIT Press, 289–320.

Standards Development Organization Advancement Act of 2003, HR 1086, 108th Congress, 1st sess., http://thomas.loc.gov/cgi-bin/query/z?c108: h1086:.

Updegrove, Andrew 1995. "Standard setting and consortium structures," *StandardView* 3 (December), http://www.gesmer.com/publications/ consortium/6.php.

Vittet-Philippe, Patrick 2002. "Europe in the e-economy: Challenges for EU enterprises and policies," *Computer Law & Security Report* 18: 24–8.

World Wide Web Consortium (W3C) 2006. "About the World Wide Web Consortium," http://www.w3.org/Consortium/.

Appendix: The evolution and history of standard setting organizations

Formal standards-developing organizations and ANSI

A brief examination of the history of standardization within the United States is necessary to put an organization like ANSI into its proper perspective. Following the First World War, there was a national standardization initiative sponsored by Herbert Hoover to make sense of the chaotic state of standards in the United States. Voluntary cooperation between the organizations was a goal; it was initiated in the twenties and then stopped as the Depression began. However, following the Second World War, the initiative took off again and eventually the organization that was to become ANSI came into prominence.[21] While not a governmental entity, ANSI was meant to

---

[21] The following is a description of ANSI from its website (ANSI 2006):

The American National Standards Institute (ANSI) has served in its capacity as administrator and coordinator of the United States private sector voluntary standardization system for more than 80 years. Founded in 1918 by five engineering societies and three government agencies, the Institute remains a private, nonprofit membership organization supported by a diverse constituency of private and public sector organizations. (http://www.ansi.org/about_ansi/introduction/ introduction.aspx?menuid=1)

regularize standardization in the United States. Several serendipitous legal incidents happened to strengthen ANSI's hand (an antitrust case and a Congressional investigation), and eventually ANSI came out as the first among equals in US formal standardization. It alone (of the myriad of standards organizations in the United States) has the right to publish standards that bear the appellation *American National Standard*. ANSI does itself not create standards; it acts as a publishing arm for the more than 175 organizations which have sought ANSI accreditation.[22] At the same time, other nations (especially Germany, France, the United Kingdom, and Japan) began to strengthen their nationally chartered bodies to pursue standards as a part of their national industrial policies.

A European-style national standards body makes sense in the context of the post-World War II industrial environment. Nations were trying to strengthen their individual industrial capacity; many were rebuilding after a devastating war. The creation of standards allowed an industrial policy that could be controlled (to varying degrees) by the nation. The United States, however, did not create a government-run standards organization. Instead, as was previously mentioned, it encouraged the private sector to enter into standards partnerships, which allowed trade associations to act as standards organizations and encouraged the formation of new organizations. As national and regional economies became more interdependent, however, it was necessary to establish an international standardization authority. Following World War II, and with the growth of the internationalism, the ISO was established and the IEC and ITU had more credence given them, so that there could be truly international standards. There was a cultural sensitivity that was overlooked at times, however; the concept of "international" did not necessarily mean "good" to a country, unless it was that country's specification being carried forward. And since the basis of the international formal activity was the national body, the biases of the various national bodies were brought forward. Within the IT industry, the balance of power turned to the United States, because

---

[22] ANSI ensures that its guiding principles – consensus, due process, and openness – are followed by the more than 175 distinct entities currently accredited under one of its three methods of accreditation (organization, committee, or canvass). (See http://public.ansi.org/ansionline/Documents/Standards%20Activities/American %20National%20Standards/Procedures,%20Guides,%20and%20Forms/ANS% 20Procedures%20-%20Historical/ANSIPRO1987.pdf.)

American-based IT companies were more successful than their counterparts worldwide. This was due in some part to the larger size and homogeneity of the US market, which made economies of scale possible for US firms. With the economies of scale came the ability to innovate more quickly, which in turn fed the need and use requirements of users, which led to more innovation, an increased market, and increased sales.

By 1985, the US dominance in IT – in market share, IP, research and development, and deployed base – was firmly established. Because of this market ascendancy, the dominance of the US in formal standards was also established; a majority of IT standards were those proposed or initiated by US companies, either through the US standardization bodies (e.g., ASC X3 or the IEEE Computer Society) or through US company representatives acting in foreign standards bodies (e.g., the Deutsches Institut für Normung [DIN], the German national body where US subsidiaries exercised heavy influence).

In the early 1990s, the European Community began to coalesce. One of the favored methods of creating a single European market was to require the various nations to abandon unique national standards in favor of pan-European (or regional) standards. By eliminating a multitude of competing and conflicting standards, a British manufacturer, for example, would not have to make multiple separate products or go through national conformance test regimes. By adhering to a single pan-European standardization regime, it was felt that European providers could begin to realize economies of scale, similar to those of the US manufacturers. To further this purpose, the European Union (EU) recognized (or created) three regional standards organizations – the European Committee for Standardization (CEN), the European Committee for Electrotechnical Standardization (CENELEC), and the European Telecommunications Standards Institute (ETSI).[23] The mission for all of these groups was to "promote voluntary technical harmonization in Europe in conjunction with worldwide bodies and its partners in Europe" (CEN http://www.cenorm.be/cenorm/idex.htm).[24] The key to understanding the activities of the EU is to remember that

[23] Websites for these organizations are www.cenorm.be, www.cenelec.org, and www.etsi.org, respectively.
[24] Between 1983 and 1989, the EU began to focus on its internal market and the plethora of standards available within Europe. As a result, the *Council Resolution of 7 May 1985 on a New Approach to Technical Harmonization*

European National Body standardization activities were often a barrier to the unification of European economic activity. By requiring the unification of standards (and a common acceptance of a single standard), the EU was seeking to unify its markets and provide for economic growth as a unified Europe.

This was not, however, the way that the activity was seen in the United States. The unfortunate appearance of the ISO 9000 Quality Management series of standards in 1989 gave the impression that the Europeans were creating a "Fortress Europe" by using standards and certification schemes as non-tariff trade barriers.[25] The debate was exacerbated by the use of common standards phrases with substantially different meanings, depending upon which side of the Atlantic Ocean you lived.

At the behest of some of its members, ANSI began a long, torturous, and losing battle to stop the pan-European standardization activity. The requirement that the European national standardization bodies must accept a CEN standard, and that CEN has a "special" relationship with ISO,[26] gave rise to US concerns that the vote in ISO could be rigged in favor of the Europeans, since the Europeans might vote in concert with one another.

The accusations by ANSI that the Europeans were block voting became (and remains) shrill.[27] While this may be necessary for national

and Standards was passed establishing the principles of European standardization. The essential outcome of all of these activities was to gain a national commitment, where "formal adoption of European Standards is decided by a weighted majority vote of all CEN National Members and is binding on all of them" (see http://www.cenorm.be/cenorm/aboutus/generalities/how+we+work/index.asp).

[25] ISO 9000 is an entirely problematic standard. It was originally started as a US Air Force standard in the 1960s, adopted by the British in the 1970s, and then sent to ISO in the 1980s. It is a management standard, which means that it does not tell you how to do quality, but rather "how to manage a quality program, including the necessary paperwork and records retention." The appearance of this standard and its rapid acceptance and "mandatory use" (including third-party certification) in many European companies and government procurements left a bitter legacy with US companies who were "forced" to comply with third-party testing.

[26] See http://www.cenorm.be/boss/production/production+processes+-+index/cen+enquiry/vaguidelines2004finalversion.pdf for the complete text, recognizing the Vienna Treaty and the common European norms.

[27] At a presentation at the American Academy for the Advancement of Science (February 17, 2001, San Francisco, CA), ANSI President and CEO Mark Hurwitz stated that he believed that the Europeans engaged in block voting to stop American SDO initiatives. From a national point of view, this has

positioning, it is not helpful to the IT industry, which has a substantial international market for its products. The appearance of ANSI's *National Standards Strategy for the United States* has placed IT companies with a significant presence in European standardization bodies in an awkward position – they must either accept the concept of an overriding US national position or they must be willing to dismiss the statements of an organization in which many of them are members.

At the same time, the lack of clarity within the US standardization regime has made many of its counterparts in ISO uneasy with ANSI.[28] ANSI has no absolute mandate as the sole international representative of the US at ISO. ANSI sits at ISO and the IEC because it is the single "most representative" body on all standardization, and because it has the singular right to grant the title of an American National Standards to a specification. Ensuring that those who wish to publish an American National Standard follow the ANSI procedures for creating standards enforces this right. As noted above, ANSI's only contribution to standardization is the process and coordination between groups. Its mission statement reads "ANSI does not itself develop American National Standards (ANSs); rather it facilitates development by establishing consensus among qualified groups." The way that a group becomes "qualified" is to embrace ANSI's development rules – which are the "formal process rules."[29]

It is this formal process which is the value of the "formal organization," whether a trade association doing standards, ANSI, any of the

significance; from an international point of view (that normally taken by multinational companies), the existence of a standard that is meant to satisfy a large potential market (325 million people) is of substantial interest and is worth investigating and possibly implementing.

[28] See Global Standards (1992) prepared by US Congress, Office of Technology for a view of the US standardization process which haunts the United States to this day in Europe.

[29] It is interesting to note that both major international standardization organizations – the ISO and the IEC – have, within the past four years, adopted processes to recognize industry technical agreements (ITAs), which allow any organization as "open" to advance a common industry practice through a lightweight process to achieve the appellation of either an ISO or IEC ITA. The senior organizations have recognized the need within their primary markets for a quicker and faster way to gain widespread recognition of a specification that is widely accepted, but possibly does not need the rigor of their full process. For a description of the IEC program, see IEC (2006, http://www.iec.ch/tctools/ita-e.htm); and for a description of the program at ISO, see ISO (2006, http://www.iso.org/iso/en/stdsdevelopment/whowhenhow/proc/deliverables/iwa.html).

ANSI-accredited Committees, or the international organizations of ISO. The process is specified; variations are not allowed. The mantra of ANSI is:

- Decisions are reached through consensus among those affected.
- Participation is open to all affected interests.
- Balance is maintained among competing interests.
- The process is transparent – information on the process and progress is directly available.
- Due process ensures that all views will be considered and that appeals are possible.

Absent any of these conditions, an organization cannot become accredited. And because their fundamental rationale for existence may not meet the ANSI conditions, consortia have always been outside of the pale of formally accepted standards.

Consortia and alliances

The legal basis of the organizational style known as consortia or alliances is found in the *National Cooperative Research and Production Act of 1993* (US Code 15. §§ 4301, et seq. See http://caselaw. lp.findlaw.com/casecode/uscodes/15/chapters/69/sections/section_4301_ notes.html), which has as its purpose "to promote innovation, facilitate trade, and strengthen the competitiveness of the United States in world markets by clarifying the applicability of the rule of reason standard and establishing a procedure under which businesses may notify the Department of Justice and Federal Trade Commission of their cooperative ventures and thereby qualify for a single-damages limitation on civil antitrust liability." The Act lists a lengthy series of activities that are prohibited if an organization wishes to take advantage of the Act; in many cases, the charter of an organization specifically writes these prohibitions into their charter to make sure that participants understand the purpose of the organization is to encourage innovation and commercialization of technology (two purposes of the Act.).[30]

---

[30] A typical statement, taken from the proposed sponsor agreement of one consortium, is "Nothing in this Agreement shall be construed to require or permit conduct that violates any applicable Antitrust Law. A Sponsoring Member consents to the disclosure of its name as a member of the Corporation, for the purpose of permitting the Corporation to invoke the protection of the National Cooperative Research and Production Act of 1993 (15 USC §§4301, et seq.), if

As was previously mentioned, although the speed at which consortia arrive at standards has been the focus of much attention, it is the process that consortia use to achieve this speed that is most integral to the way consortia differ from the formal standardization process. In most of the cases, the consortia modified the traditional standardization process in several ways. First, they formally imposed some limitation on participation. The limitation usually took the form of dues – that is, there is a requirement to "pay to play."[31] The payment could be modest or significant (from approximately $3,000 per year to the $50,000 that large corporations are often taxed). Second, the consortia announced their intentions – when you have like-minded companies, you can announce and drive to a solution with a greater degree of freedom than can a formal SDO, which usually has no way of controlling where its efforts will lead. Third, the consortia do not need to be broad spectrum – that is, a consortium can focus on and solve only those problems that it wishes to solve. There is no requirement for it to create committees to solve all problems; rather it should (by definition) be working on problems that its members need to have solved in order to produce products.

Finally, and perhaps most damaging to the formal standardization process, consortia specifications are usually immediately turned into product offerings by the participating companies. The rationale for playing (and paying) within a consortium is to create and then market a technology. To participate in a consortium (paying both dues and committing scarce human resources) and then not to implement the specification when it appears is definitely foolish and possibly irresponsible, and is the exception more than the rule. Additionally, depending upon the cohesiveness of the consortia, the specification usually has one or more implementations that validate the specification.

There are two schools of thought on when and what to standardize. The "current practice school" believes that standardizing current

---

the Corporation decides to invoke such protection." Private communication from unnamed consortium and Carl Cargill.

[31] It has been argued by several members of consortia that the travel and meeting requirements of formal organizations constitute a membership limitation, as very few private citizens have the ability to travel to all of the meetings of an international technical committee where the technology is decided. Some of the consortia with Internet-based processes claim that their consortia dues are less than a participant would pay in travel costs.

practice – that is, abstracting an interface specification from existing products – is the preferred method. The other "future technology" school revolves around standardizing future technology in its predeployment phase. The current practice school rewards the innovator by allowing a time-to-market and market-share advantage, while embracing stability in the market and rapid deployment of technology. The future technology school of thought permits a group design, combining the best of the breed (at times), but is usually slower and can produce a specification that is filled with compromise. Both have been used successfully within consortia, but the first, in which the innovator opens a proprietary specification in return for a possibly transient market advantage, is usually the most preferred.[32]

On the one hand, the classic case used to argue for current practice standardization is the failure of OSI (Open Systems Interconnect), which involved standardizing technology that was not deployed and which was being created in committee. On the other hand, there is a reluctance to take a widely deployed but nonstandard technology to the formal organizations, since there have been instances when formal organizations have attempted to change the technology once it arrived in their committees. When this occurs, the worst case results – a standard emerges that does not reflect the installed base usage of the specification. As a result, either the original nonstandard technology or the new specification is declared invalid. With either outcome, both sides lose.

Consortia are also slightly more informal in the coordination of their efforts. Unlike the formal world, where all of the players are known to one another and tracked, the consortia/alliance arena has no central clearing house or authority to coordinate activities. There are efforts made to track consortia, but new consortia appear in the ICT arena at the rate of about one every other week.[33] There is

---

[32] The business case behind this type of decision is usually very complex and filled with enough vagaries to make the prediction of success purely Brownian. Normally, it comes down to a senior executive being willing to take a chance and go forward with opening a technology to the market.

[33] The IT sectorial organization under CEN (CEN/ISSS) undertakes to maintain a list and description of consortia. It currently lists/links to approximately 260 consortia working in the areas of IT, either publishing specifications or specifying requirements. It is available at http://www.cenorm.be/isss/Consortia/Surveyshort.htm.

nothing to prevent multiple organizations from tackling the same general topic (i.e., wireless Internet communications). This is encouraged by the organizations that fund the consortia and alliances, since having multiple solutions sometimes mitigates the impact of catastrophic technical change. What the industry does not like is two SSOs solving the same problem using the same specifications (dueling specifications) or a specification being bifurcated and modified. This is where much of the concern about standardization comes in – and the old tired rubric of "the nice thing about standards is that there are so many of them" is brought up.[34] It is duplicative standards – not duplicative standardization efforts – that are the bane of the industry.

The consortia processes are rigorous, since they must comply with the provisions contained in the National Cooperative Research and Production Act of 1993, under which many of them are chartered. There is an area of expertise on the legal implications of the creation of consortia, and nearly every consortium that is created requires the services of at least one lawyer (for a discussion of the nature of the rules that apply when establishing a consortium, see Updegrove 1995). Consortia operate as strictly under their rules as formal SDOs operate under theirs. If they fail to keep their processes legitimate, they risk all of their members and their own existence. The emphasis that consortia place upon following their rules is illustrated by the fact that, as of this writing, there has never been a successful suit brought against a consortium for antitrust activities.[35]

Consortia and alliances (their more short-lived brethren) serve a need of the ICT industry as a way to stabilize the market in a time of shortened product life cycles and rapid market change. By providing processes that are open, and by providing the market with multiple implementations of the consortia specification, they have increased competition and ensured that the standardization of the high-technology industry can continue.

---

[34] This statement amplifies the contention that there is a lack of education about standards and standardization.

[35] The closest successful suit was *Addamax Corporation* v. *Open Software Foundation, Inc., Digital Equipment Corporation, and Hewlett-Packard Company, Inc.* (888 F. Supp. 274; 1995–1 Trade Case, (CCH) P71,036), which lost and lost again on appeal.

Open Source

The key to understanding the Open Source community is understanding the license. The licensing itself is complex; there are at least five variants (Hecker 2000):

1. No license at all (i.e., releasing software into the public domain)
2. Licenses like the BSD (Berkeley Software Distribution) License that place relatively few constraints on what a developer may do (including creating proprietary versions of Open Source products)
3. The GNU General Public License (GPL) and variants which attempt to constrain developers from hoarding code (i.e., making changes to Open Source products and then not contributing those changes back to the developer community, but rather attempting to keep them proprietary for commercial purposes or other reasons)
4. The Artistic License, which modifies several of the more controversial aspects of the GPL
5. The Mozilla Public License and variants (including the Netscape Public License), which go further than the BSD and similar licenses in discouraging software hoarding, but still allow developers to create proprietary add-ons if they wish.

The intent of these various forms of licenses is to ensure that the code remains open for all to use, validate, modify, and improve. These license forms, more than anything else, are the core of the Open Source standards movement. They encourage the community to act together, and they act as a re-enforcing mechanism for Open Source behavior (which is a larger good to which all standards organizations must subscribe). By tying their unique behavior to licensing activities, they are then freed to espouse rules that re-enforce the benefits of Open Source licensing – including rules on how to write, publish, and correct code, and so on.

The positive aspect of Open Source is that there are multiple implementations of the code – anyone who wishes may take the source code and write an implementation. The difficult aspect of Open Source is that there is never a stabilized standard set of source code to specify, since by its very nature, Open Source constantly and incrementally improves its code base. However, the creators and purveyors of Linux are working on this, and are attempting to create a Linux standard that will solve this problem. If this problem is solved (basically, a version control problem), then the Open Source organization will also be a viable candidate for procurement.

Conclusion

All of the various forms of standardization can and do serve a purpose in the ICT sector. There is the need for stability (provided by the formal arena), a need for defined and structured faster change (provided by consortia and alliances), and the need for complete community involvement (provided by Open Source). The groups within each arena have not learned to work together for the good of open systems. Rather than considering proprietary and closed systems to be the force to be changed, they have dissipated their energies by arguing about which form of standardization is best, forgetting that the answer is that "Standardization is best, and non-standardization is less than optimal." ANSI is a necessary, but not sufficient, standardization component for the needs of the IT sector. Consortia are central to ICT standardization success, but they need the stability that the formal process can offer. And for long-term change (to both the technical and legal fabric of IT and ICT sector standardization), Open Source provides an interesting direction – and may lead to an entirely different standardization environment in the future.

Standardization is a complex discipline that is constantly changing as the industry underneath it evolves. The past decade in the ICT industry has seen massive change as the very nature of information use and sharing by customers has changed. The state and changes in the ICT industry in the United States reflects the state and changes of its consumers – US society, both commercial and private. The ICT sector has been credited with making the US economy much more productive, and this has aroused admiration throughout the world.[36] Uniting the various forms of standardization by allowing equivalency – in legal as well as in economic settings – would only enhance the industry. It is a rare situation that has no negative consequences to the industry or society.

---

[36] As Vittet-Philippe (1999, 2) states, "Despite the relatively modest share of ICT [Information and Communication Technologies] manufacturing in total US production – 8% of total – the remarkable acceleration of productivity in that specific sector has contributed a disproportionately high 0.6% a year to total US labour productivity growth."

10 | *Standards battles and public policy*

LUÍS M. B. CABRAL AND
TOBIAS KRETSCHMER

Abstract

We examine the effectiveness of public policy in a context of competing standards with network externalities. We show that, if the policymaker is very impatient, then it is optimal to support the leading standard; whereas, if the policymaker is very patient, then it is optimal to support the lagging standard. We also consider the timing for optimal intervention and provide sufficient conditions under which it is optimal to delay or not to delay intervention.

Keywords: standards, network externalities, public policy.

JEL Code Nos.: L13, L51, O33

1 Introduction

VHS vs. Betamax VCRs; Apple MacIntosh vs. PC DOS microcomputers; discrete vs. matrix quadraphonic systems. These are three of a long list of examples from recent history where two (or more) alternative versions of a new standard battled for market dominance. One aspect common to most of these standards is the importance of network effects: the fact that many users buy a DOS-based microcomputer increases the utility of buying a DOS-based microcomputer (among other reasons because the amount of software, technical support, etc., available for DOS users will be better and more widely available).

Given the importance of network industries, it is surprising that little attention has been paid to the role of public policy in standards battles.[1] Consider the cases of high-definition television (HDTV) and mobile

We are grateful to Lorenz Schneider and various seminar participants for comments and suggestions. The usual disclaimer applies.
[1] Exceptions include David (1986), Stoneman and David (1986), Katz and Shapiro (1986), Cowan (1991), and Choi (1994).

329

telecommunications. Public policy in these industries differed greatly between Europe and the US: Whereas the European Commission (EC) was primarily concerned with early standardization, the US's Federal Communications Commission (FCC) adopted the more patient approach of letting market forces decide the winning standard. At first sight, the European approach seems preferable in that it takes better advantage of network effects. The US approach, in turn, is more likely to lead to a higher-quality standard.

Our purpose in this paper is to analyze the different trade-offs involved in the policymaker's decisions with respect to standardization in network industries. Specifically, there are at least two questions that a policymaker should address. First, the decision of which standard to support, if any. Second, the decision of when to intervene. Regarding the first question, we show that, if the policymaker is sufficiently patient, then it is optimal to favor the lagging standard. Conversely, if the policymaker is sufficiently impatient, then it is optimal to favor the leading standard. Regarding the second question, we show that, if the policymaker is sufficiently patient, then it is optimal to delay intervention. Conversely, if the policymaker is sufficiently impatient, then it is optimal not to delay intervention.

In our analysis, we consider the extreme cases of an infinitely patient and an infinitely impatient policymaker. An infinitely patient policymaker is one who cares exclusively about the welfare of future adopters, whereas an infinitely impatient policymaker cares exclusively about current adopters. We consider these extremes for illustrative purposes only; reality is likely to fall somewhere in between. There are two factors that determine the degree of policymaker "patience" in each particular case. One is the policymaker's preferences: witness, for example, the contrast between Europe and the US in wireless telecommunications, or the contrast between Japan and the US in HDTV.

More importantly, the degree of patience is likely to reflect the nature of the technology in question. Take for example the case of color television in the 1950s. Given the success of monochrome TV and the absence of a likely substitute for TV, a policymaker should take a long-term view of the standardization process. Whatever solution is achieved, it is likely to stay for a long time and be used by a great number of future adopters. Our infinitely patient policymaker assumption tries to capture this feature.

By contrast, digital audio tape (DAT) is a good example of a technology with a relatively short expected life span, considering the rapid advancements in storage and recording devices such as CDs. In such a situation, a policymaker is more likely to concentrate on the existing set of adopters and the standardization problems they face.[2] Our infinitely impatient policymaker assumption tries to capture this situation.

In addition to issues of time horizon and patience, our model treats the policymaker's actions in a stylized way. Specifically, we assume that the policymaker has the option to "tilt" the system in favor of one standard or the other. In reality, this may come about through a variety of mechanisms such as direct subsidies (e.g., HDTV in Japan), government regulations (e.g., wireless in Europe), or direct adoption decisions by the policymaker when the latter is a "large" user (e.g., nuclear reactors in the US).

Other papers, such as Mitchell and Skrzypacz (2004), develop a model similar to ours and derive outcomes as a function of the agents' discount factor. However, their policy analysis is limited to comparing the welfare-maximizing and the unregulated solutions. Our approach to modeling public policy, while certainly very stylized, is a useful first step toward a more complete treatment of policymakers' options under imperfect information about the quality of emerging standards. In recent years, "heavy-handed" regulation which picks one winner from several standards has increasingly been abandoned in favor of "softer" intervention of the form modeled in our paper. Especially in situations where a mistake would carry significant costs, helping the market to make the efficient choice rather than making the decision itself may be the policymaker's best strategy.

The paper is organized as follows. In the following section, we extend Arthur's (1989) model of standard adoption to consider the possibility of public policy intervention. Next we consider the direction of optimal intervention in the case when the policymaker is very impatient (Section 3) or patient (Section 4). In Section 5, we look at the optimal timing for intervention. Section 6 includes a discussion of some of the results in the context of several recent standards battles. Section 7 concludes the paper.

---

[2] In the case of DAT, there were two different standards, DDS and DataDAT.

2 Basic model

Our analysis departs from Arthur's (1989) seminal model of standard adoption.[3] Suppose there are two unsponsored standards, A and B, available to consumers at constant marginal cost (which we normalize to zero). In each period, one new consumer arrives in the market and buys one unit of one of the standards. Some consumers favor standard A, some standard B; all benefit from the size of the network they link into. Specifically, by choosing standard i, a consumer receives, at time t, utility $v_i + w\, n_{it}$, where v_i is stand-alone utility, w is a measure of the strength of network effects, and n_{it} standard i's network size at time t. We assume that $v_i \in \{0, 1\}$ and that $v_j = 1 - v_i$.

Following Arthur, we assume that, in each period, consumers make adoption decisions based on that period's utility levels. Under this assumption, it can be shown that, if standard i is chosen sufficiently more often than standard j, then all future adoptions are directed to i, even by consumers who, absent network effects, would prefer standard j ($v_j > v_i$). Arthur et al. (1983) have shown that the above stochastic process of technology adoption ends up in one of these absorbing barriers in finite time with probability one. The specific condition for lock-in to standard i is $n_i\, w > n_j\, w + 1$, or $\Delta_i > N \equiv \frac{1}{w}$, where $\Delta_i \equiv n_i - n_j$ is the difference in installed bases. The values $-N, N$ are called absorbing barriers since, once crossed ($\Delta_i < -N$, $\Delta_i > N$), they are never crossed again. Arthur et al.'s result can then be rephrased as: lock-in to one technology occurs in finite time with probability one.

Consider now the following extension of Arthur's model: suppose that consumers are unevenly distributed: a fraction $p > \frac{1}{2}$ prefers one of the standards. Since standards are otherwise symmetric, it follows that the standard with $p > \frac{1}{2}$ "fans" is the better standard.[4] A crucial assumption in our analysis is that the policymaker knows the above information as well as the prior distribution of p, which we assume is

---

[3] Callaner (2003) develops a model similar to ours in a voting context to illustrate the formation of bandwagons.

[4] Standardization, i.e., lock-in to one standard, is optimal in our model as it is in Arthur's (1989), a result that depends on the assumption of a linear utility function. Farrell and Saloner (1986) and Bassanini and Dosi (1998) develop models where this assumption is relaxed and find that standardization need not be optimal.

symmetric around $\frac{1}{2}$. However, the policymaker does not know the exact value of p.

Consider now the problem faced by a welfare maximizing policymaker. Since marginal cost is constant and identical for both standards, a sufficient statistic for social welfare is discounted consumer surplus:

$$W = \sum_{t=1}^{\infty} \sum_{\tau=1}^{t} \delta^t u(\tau, t),$$

where $u(\tau, t)$ is period t utility of the consumer who joined the network at time τ, and δ the discount factor.

We will consider the following policy instrument: At a given point in time, the policymaker has the option of forcing the next s_i adoptions of standard i. These "forced" adoptions can be interpreted in various ways. One is to assume the policymaker subsidizes adoption by private agents. An alternative interpretation is that the policymaker is itself a large adopter (see Section 6 for examples). As we will see, the direction of the optimal policy depends crucially on the policymaker's discount factor. We will consider two extreme cases: a very impatient, or myopic, policymaker; and a very patient policymaker.

3 The case of an impatient policymaker

We start with the case of a very impatient policymaker. Our main result is that such a policymaker should favor the leading standard.

Proposition 1

If δ is close to zero, and given that policy intervention takes place in state Δ_i, it is optimal to favor standard i if Δ_i is sufficiently greater than zero.

Proof

If δ is close to zero, then all periods after the next are of second-order importance. The network benefits added to the current base of users are given by wn_i. The difference between the two standards is thus $w\Delta_i$. If Δ_i is sufficiently high, then the benefits on the existing users outweigh the benefits received by the new user, and the result follows. ∎

An alternative version of the result is as follows. Suppose that the policymaker has the option of offering a subsidy to the new user at time t. Then the subsidy to standard i is positive if and only if $\Delta_i > 0$.

This result corresponds to the "classical" case of an externality. Since the discount factor is close to zero, there is no informational issue; that is, the policymaker is not concerned with the value of p and how it will influence the expected pattern of future adoptions (beyond the next period). The main thing the policymaker is concerned with is how the next adopter will affect the previous adopters. If the i installed base is greater than the j installed base, then the externality is greater when an i adoption takes place, and thus the policymaker is better off subsidizing this standard.

4 The case of a patient policymaker

Consider now the opposite case with respect to the previous section, namely that of a very patient policymaker. From an optimization point of view, this is the rather more interesting case. The policymaker's problem is that, while knowing that one of the standards is superior (higher p), it does not know which one is which. All that the policymaker knows is the prior distribution on p, which we assume is symmetric around $\frac{1}{2}$. In other words, the two standards look the same at the start of the process. Naturally, as the adoption process unfolds, the policymaker acquires more information, specifically, the number of adoptions of each standard.

Our main result is that the policymaker's optimal policy is to favor the lagging standard:

Proposition 2
If δ is close to one, and given that policy intervention takes place in state Δ_i, it is optimal to favor standard j by $s^* = \frac{1}{2}\Delta_i$.

Proof
See the appendix. ∎

This result states that the optimal intervention intensity is to pull the leading standard halfway back to the symmetric state ($\Delta_i = 0$). Intuitively, moving the process halfway back takes into account the trade-off between keeping the process away from the absorbing barriers for some more time (which implies supporting the lagging standard) and making use of the information gained from the process prior to intervention (which suggests that the leading standard is leading for a reason: it is more likely that it is indeed the right one). Notice that the result does not depend on the particular distribution of p; the only restriction is that the distribution is symmetric, i.e., the two standards have a priori an equal chance of being the optimal standard.

Specifically, consider the extreme case of a binomial distribution and suppose that p is very close to 1. In other words, suppose that each of the standards is equally likely to be favored by a fraction p of the population, where p is close to one. Even then, the optimal policy would be to delay the lock-in process. This may at first seem counterintuitive: if so many adopters have chosen standard i previously, then it is very likely that this is the right standard. But precisely because p is close to one and the policymaker is very patient, favoring the lagging standard is an optimal policy: in the (likely) event that the leading standard is the right standard, then favoring the lagging standard won't do much harm; most likely, the leading standard will eventually win anyway.

Broadly speaking then, Proposition 2 seems consistent with David's (1987) prescription that "one thing that public policy could do is to try to delay the market from committing."

5 Optimal timing for public intervention

So far, we have addressed the question: given that the policymaker must make a decision at time t, which standard should the policymaker favor? The natural next step is to ask when the policymaker should intervene. We will address a somewhat more specific question: given that the policymaker must choose a single time at which to intervene, what is the optimal time t^*?

The main result in this section states that a patient policymaker should wait, whereas an impatient one should act soon.

Proposition 3

Suppose that the policymaker must choose a single time at which to intervene. If the discount factor δ is close to one, then it is optimal to wait until $\Delta_i = N$. If δ is close to zero and Δ_i is large, then it is optimal to intervene right away.

> **Proof**
> See the appendix. ∎

The intuition for the impatient policymaker case is similar to that of Proposition 1. Regarding the patient policymaker case, the question might be asked: Why should a patient policymaker wait until $\Delta_i = N$? The answer is, the closer to N we are the more information the policymaker has. Since N is achieved in finite time with probability one, and the policymaker is infinitely patient, there is no cost of waiting. Waiting for longer than $\Delta_i = N$ does the policymaker no good: once we hit an absorbing barrier, no additional information is gained.

6 Examples

The results presented in the previous sections are as tentative as the model they are based on is stylized. Real world examples are far more complicated than simple models. Still, we believe the theoretical analysis allows us to make some qualitative points about public policy. In this section, we present a few examples of public policy in industries with strong network effects. These examples illustrate the structure and assumptions of our model.

6.1 Second generation mobile telephony

Second generation wireless standard setting provides an interesting testing ground for the economic theory of public policy. The US and the EU took very different approaches to the problem. Whereas in the US the Federal Communications Commission (FCC) followed a "hands-off" approach, in Europe the European Commission (EC) mandated a standard from very early on.[5] Standard-setting in Europe was regarded as a success story, especially in the early stages of 2G technology: early diffusion was faster in European countries than in the

---

[5] For a qualitative assessment of US and European decisions, see Gandal et al. (2003). Toivanen (2002) uses a decision-theoretic framework to analyze 1G standard choice in eighty-five countries.

US at roughly comparable prices,[6] and roaming (i.e., using one's cell-phone outside the provider's coverage area) was clearly better in Europe early on. As the technology matured however, these differences became less relevant. Currently, diffusion is at similar levels and roaming is virtually seamless in both markets. Finally, as third-generation technology enters the picture, it is interesting to note that the competing standards are both based on CDMA, the standard that survived the battle for supremacy in the policy-neutral US ground.

Our theoretical analysis (Propositions 1–3) suggests that a very patient policymaker should wait and favor the lagging technology before the market sets onto a particular standard; whereas a very impatient policymaker should favor the leading technology early on. Moreover, by continuity, Propositions 1 and 2 suggest that, for intermediate values of δ, the optimal government policy is not to favor any of the technologies. This result is strengthened if we consider additional sources of uncertainty (for example, uncertainty regarding payoff levels), or if we consider more than two types of adopters. In other words, the best policy may in fact be not to have a policy.

The contrasting approaches taken by the US and the EC suggest that either one of them made the wrong decision, or else that they started from different "utility" functions. The latter may be accounted for by different perceived time horizons or different weights placed on early adopters.

6.2 Wide-body aircraft: DC-10 vs. B-747

Over a period of time during the mid-1970s, the US Air Force ordered about sixty military cargo and tanker aircraft. It was seen as a "no brainer that the USAF would select the Boeing proposal" on the grounds of the technical specifications of their planes. As it turned out, the McDonnell Douglas KC-10 was selected. The KC-10 is the military version of the DC-10 and shares many features with the latter. The Air Force decision thus had the effect of keeping the DC-10 program alive for a while longer. In the end, the indirect network effect

---

[6] See, e.g. Gruber and Verboven (2001) or Koski and Kretschmer (2005) for empirical studies of the effect of standardization on the evolution of mobile telephony markets.

created by the learning curve, as well as a series of DC-10 crashes in the late 1970s, led to a sharp decline in orders for the McDonnell Douglas plane; production was discontinued in 1980.[7] This example illustrates how the policymaker can intervene as a "large" adopter.

6.3 Nuclear power reactors

By the late 1950s, there were about a dozen relevant technologies for nuclear power reactors. Of these, the main contenders were light water, heavy water, and gas graphite. None of the technologies was perceived as clearly superior, and early adoption figures indicated that consumers were divided in their preferences. Due to strong learning and network effects, experts predicted that one of the technologies would eventually dominate. One important event in the race was the US Navy's decision to adopt the light water technology in their nuclear submarines. Eventually, when a market for civilian nuclear power emerged, the light water "absorbing barrier" had been crossed and the industry was locked-in to this technology. According to Cowan (1990), "light water is considered inferior to other technologies, yet it dominates the market for nuclear reactors." This example thus illustrates, among other things, how suboptimal outcomes may take place in the standard setting process with public intervention.

6.4 Pest control technology

For a limited period of time, the US Department of Agriculture sponsored one of the alternative technologies for pest control: Integrated Pest Management (IPM). Individual farmers have little incentive to deviate from the common practice in the vicinity, which implies a network effect similar to the one we consider in our theoretical model. For this reason, while the government intervention was temporary, its effects were permanent: the industry got locked-in to IPM, which, according to Cowan and Gunby (1996), was the welfare maximizing outcome. This examples illustrates that early public intervention may have a determinant effect even if limited in its extent and duration.

---

[7] For more on McDonnell Douglas, see http://www.angelfire.com/dc/douglasjets.

6.5 Linux vs. Windows

Recently, several government agencies in the US, Europe and Asia have decided to adopt the Linux operating system at various levels.[8] Acting as large and influential customers, governments may support the lagging technology with the aim of delaying the outcome of the standards battle, or simply to lower the dependency on single software vendors.

7 Conclusion

The above examples illustrate the variety of situations where standards battles take place and government intervention is a possibility. Sometimes the policymaker acts by law, sometimes by offering adoption incentives, sometimes by acting as a lead adopter. Notwithstanding the specificities of each situation, one thing is common to all cases: the policymaker faces the dilemma of which standard to favor, if any, and when. We thus think that our model, stylized as it is, addresses an important set of public policy issues.

Appendix

Proof of Proposition 2: We begin by assuming that the prior distribution of p takes two values, and later generalize to the case of a symmetric distribution. In other words, the policymaker knows that one of the standards is preferred by a majority $p > \frac{1}{2}$ of the population, knows the value of p, but does not know which standard is which.

Suppose that at time t the system is in state $\Delta_i > 0$. Let $P(\Delta_i)$ be the probability that the system will eventually get locked-in to i. Let $\Pi(\Delta_i)$ be the probability that standard i is the right standard, that is, the standard associated to $p > \frac{1}{2}$. Then the unconditional probability that the system gets locked-in to the right standard is simply

$$\pi(\Delta_i) = \Pi(\Delta_i)P(\Delta_i) + \Pi(-\Delta_i)P(-\Delta_i). \tag{1}$$

---

[8] The list includes: in the US, the Air Force, the Federal Aviation Administration, the Postal Service, and the Departments of Defense, Agriculture, and Energy; in Europe, the European Commission, various government offices in Germany, and France's Ministries of Culture, Defense, and Education; and China's Post Office. Sources: http://www.ZDNet.com on 04/06/2002; http://www.usatoday.com on 30/05/2002.

The policymaker's goal is to maximize the probability that the right absorbing barrier is hit. Absent any intervention, that probability is given by $\pi(\Delta_i)$. We assume that the policymaker has the option of starting at time t and over a period of time forcing adoptions in favor of one of the standards. Define $\hat{\pi}(\Delta_i, s)$ as the probability that the right standard is chosen given that, starting in state Δ_i, the next s adopters are forced to adopt standard i.

■ *Derivation of $P(\Delta_i)$ and $\Pi(\Delta_i)$*

Given the stationarity of the process, the probability that the system in state Δ_i will get locked-in to A satisfies the difference equation

$$P(\Delta_i) = pP(\Delta_i + 1) + (1 - p)P(\Delta_i - 1).$$

Let N be the necessary lead for one of the standards to lock in (so that the distance between barriers is $2N$). The boundary conditions are then given by $P(0) = 1$ and $P(2N) = 0$. We thus get

$$P(\Delta_i) = \frac{p^{2N} - p^{N-\Delta_i}(1 - p)^{N+\Delta_i}}{p^{2N} - (1 - p)^{2N}}.$$

The probability that A is the right standard, $\Pi(\Delta_i)$, is defined by the probability that the current state is reached given that A is associated with $p > \frac{1}{2}$. If there have been t adoptions and the probability of adopting A is p, then the likelihood that state Δ_i is reached is

$$mp^{\frac{t+\Delta_i}{2}}(1 - p)^{\frac{t-\Delta_i}{2}},$$

where m is the number of possible combinations of "ups" and "downs" which lead to state Δ_i. On the other hand, the probability of reaching state Δ_i given that A is associated with $(1 - p)$ is given by

$$mp^{\frac{t-\Delta_i}{2}}(1 - p)^{\frac{t+\Delta_i}{2}}.$$

The posterior probability that A is associated with p is therefore given by

$$\frac{mp^{\frac{t+\Delta_i}{2}}(1 - p)^{\frac{t-\Delta_i}{2}}}{mp^{\frac{t+\Delta_i}{2}}(1 - p)^{\frac{t-\Delta_i}{2}} + mp^{\frac{t-\Delta_i}{2}}(1 - p)^{\frac{t+\Delta_i}{2}}} = \frac{p^{\Delta_i}}{p^{\Delta_i} + (1 - p)^{\Delta_i}}.$$

Finally, substituting for P and Π in (1), we get the unconditional probability that the system, $Y(t)$, will hit the right barrier:

$$\pi(\Delta_i) = \frac{p^{\Delta_i}\left(p^{2N} - p^{N-\Delta_i}(1-p)^{N+\Delta_i}\right)}{\left(p^{\Delta_i} + (1-p)^{\Delta_i}\right)\left(p^{2N} - (1-p)^{2N}\right)}$$

$$+ \frac{p^{-\Delta_i}\left(p^{2N} - p^{N+\Delta_i}(1-p)^{N-\Delta_i}\right)}{\left(p^{-\Delta_i} + (1-p)^{-\Delta_i}\right)\left(p^{2N} - (1-p)^{2N}\right)}.$$

■ Optimal intervention for specific p

A policymaker will maximize the probability that the right barrier is hit by forcing s adopters to adopt either the leading or the lagging standard. Let $s > 0$ denote forced adoptions of the lagging standard and $s < 0$ adoptions of the leading one. Note that $s \neq 0$ influences only $P(\Delta_i)$. That is, the probability that a given barrier is the right one is not affected. We can now see that the new probability of achieving a desired outcome is

$$\hat{\pi}(\Delta_i) = \frac{p^{\Delta_i}\left(p^{2N} - p^{N-\Delta_i+s}(1-p)^{N+\Delta_i-s}\right)}{\left(p^{\Delta_i} + (1-p)^{\Delta_i}\right)\left(p^{2N} - (1-p)^{2N}\right)}$$

$$+ \frac{p^{-\Delta_i}\left(p^{2N} - p^{N+\Delta_i-s}(1-p)^{N-\Delta_i+s}\right)}{\left(p^{-\Delta_i} + (1-p)^{-\Delta_i}\right)\left(p^{2N} - (1-p)^{2N}\right)}.$$

We now maximize $\hat{\pi}$ with respect to s:

$$\frac{\partial\hat{\pi}(\Delta_i)}{\partial s} =$$

$$-\frac{p^{\Delta_i}\left(-p^{N-\Delta_i+s}\ln(p)(1-p)^{N+\Delta_i-s} + p^{N-\Delta_i+s}(1-p)^{N+\Delta_i-s}\ln(1-p)\right)}{\left(p^{\Delta_i} + (1-p)^{\Delta_i}\right)\left(p^{2N} - (1-p)^{2N}\right)}$$

$$+\frac{p^{-\Delta_i}\left(p^{N-\Delta_i+s}\ln(p)(1-p)^{N-\Delta_i+s} - p^{N+\Delta_i-s}(1-p)^{N-\Delta_i+s}\ln(1-p)\right)}{\left(p^{-\Delta_i} + (1-p)^{-\Delta_i}\right)\left(p^{2N} - (1-p)^{2N}\right)},$$

or simply

$$\frac{\partial\hat{\pi}(\Delta_i)}{\partial s} = -\left(\psi(-\Delta_i)\left(p^{\Delta_i} + (1-p)^{\Delta_i}\right) + \psi(\Delta_i)\left(p^{-\Delta_i} + (1-p)^{-\Delta_i}\right)\right) \cdot$$

$$\frac{\left(\ln(1-p) - \ln(p)\right)}{\left(p^{-\Delta_i} + (1-p)^{-\Delta_i}\right)\left(p^{\Delta_i} + (1-p)^{\Delta_i}\right)\left(p^{2N} - (1-p)^{2N}\right)},$$

where

$$\psi(\Delta_i) = p^{\Delta_i} p^{N-\Delta_i+s}(1-p)^{N+\Delta_i-s}.$$

The denominator is different from zero, and so is $\ln(1-p) - \ln(p)$ (for $p \neq \frac{1}{2}$). A necessary condition for maximizing $\pi(\Delta_i, s)$ is therefore that

$$\psi(-\Delta_i)\left(p^{\Delta_i} + (1-p)^{\Delta_i}\right) + \psi(\Delta_i)\left(p^{-\Delta_i} + (1-p)^{-\Delta_i}\right) = 0.$$

which implies $s^* = -\Delta_i/2$. We take the second derivative to determine whether s^* is a maximum:

$$\frac{\partial^2 \hat{\pi}(\Delta_i)}{\partial s^2} = -\left(\psi(-\Delta_i)\left(p^{\Delta_i} + (1-p)^{\Delta_i}\right) + \psi(\Delta_i)\left(p^{-\Delta_i} + (1-p)^{-\Delta_i}\right)\right) \cdot$$
$$\frac{\left(\ln(1-p) - \ln(p)\right)^2}{\left(p^{-\Delta_i} + (1-p)^{-\Delta_i}\right)\left(p^{\Delta_i} + (1-p)^{\Delta_i}\right)\left(p^{2N} - (1-p)^{2N}\right)}.$$

Observe that all of the bracketed expressions on the right-hand side are positive. It follows then that the second derivative is negative and s^* is a global maximum.

■ Generalization to any symmetric distribution

The above results readily generalize to any symmetric distribution of p. The idea is that any distribution symmetric about $\frac{1}{2}$ is the integral of a series of binomial distributions like the one we considered above. Since the optimal solution does not depend on p, it follows that the same solution holds for any distribution of p that is symmetric around $\frac{1}{2}$. ■

Proof of Proposition 3: The case when δ is close to zero is straightforward: anything that takes place after the current period is of second-order importance; and an intervention in the current period has a positive effect on welfare.

When δ is close to one, discounting is irrelevant (or close to irrelevant). We need to find out in which period the impact of public policy is greatest. Define $\rho \equiv \frac{1-p}{p}$. Notice that, given our assumption that $p > \frac{1}{2}$, it follows that $0 < \rho < 1$. With this change in variables, we can simplify various previous expressions as follows:

$$\Pi(\Delta_i) = \frac{1}{1 + \rho^{\Delta_i}}$$

$$P(i) = \frac{1 - \rho^{N+\Delta_i}}{1 - \rho^{2N}}.$$

Substituting in the expression for $\pi(\Delta_i)$ and simplifying, we get

$$\Phi \equiv (1 - \rho^{2N})\pi(\Delta_i) = 1 - \rho^N. \tag{2}$$

Moreover, since by Proposition 2 we have $s^* = \frac{1}{2}\Delta_i$, it follows that

$$P(\Delta_i + s^*) = \frac{1 - \rho^{N+\frac{1}{2}\Delta_i}}{1 - \rho^{2N}}.$$

Substituting in the expression of $\hat{\pi}(\Delta_i, s)$ and simplifying, we get

$$\Psi \equiv (1 - \rho^{2N})\hat{\pi}(\Delta_i) = 1 + \rho^{N-\frac{1}{2}\Delta_i}\left(\frac{\rho^{N-\Delta_i} - \rho^N}{\rho^{N-\Delta_i} + \rho^N} - 1\right). \tag{3}$$

Comparing (2) and (3), we conclude that: (a) expected value without policy is independent of Δ_i; (b) expected value with policy is increasing in Δ_i. We conclude that the expected incremental value from implementing the optimal policy is increasing in Δ_i.∎

References

Arthur, W. Brian 1989. "Competing standards, increasing returns, and lock-in by historical events," *Economic Journal* 99: 116–31.

Arthur, W. Brian, Yu Ermoliev, and Yu Kaniovski 1983. "On generalized urn schemes of the polya kind," *Kybernetics* 19: 49–56.

Bassanini, Andrea, and Giovanni Dosi 1998. "Competing technologies, international diffusion and the rate of convergence to a stable market structure," IIASA Interim Report IR-98-012.

Callander, Steven 2003. "Bandwagons and momentum in sequential voting," Unpublished Draft, Northwestern University, December.

Choi, Jay Pil 1994. "Irreversible choice of uncertain technologies with network externalities," *Rand Journal of Economics* 25: 382–401.

Cowan, Robin 1990. "Nuclear power reactors: A study in technological lock-in," *Journal of Economic History* 50: 541–67.

1991. "Tortoises and hares: Choice among technologies of unknown merit," *Economic Journal* 101: 801–14.

Cowan, Robin, and Philip Gunby 1996. "Sprayed to death: Path dependence, lock-in and pest control strategies," *Economic Journal* 106: 521–42.

David, Paul 1986. "Narrow windows, blind giants, and angry orphans: The dynamics of systems rivalries and dilemmas of technology policy,"

Technological Innovation Project Working Paper no. 10 (CEPR, Stanford University).
1987. "Some new standards for the economics of standardization in the information age," Ch. 8 in *Economic policy and technological performance*, P. Dasgupta and P. Stoneman (eds.), Cambridge: Cambridge University Press, 206–39.
Farrell, Joseph, and Garth Saloner 1986. "Standardization and variety," *Economics Letters* 20: 71–4.
Gandal, Neil, David Salant, and Leonard Waverman 2003. "Standards in wireless telephone networks," *Telecommunications Policy* 27: 325–32.
Gruber, Harald, and Frank Verboven 2001. "The evolution of markets under entry and standards regulation – the case of Global Mobile Telecommunication," *International Journal of Industrial Organization* 19: 1189–212.
Katz, Michael, and Carl Shapiro 1986. "Technology adoption in the presence of network externalities," *Journal of Political Economy* 94: 822–41.
Koski, Heli, and Tobias Kretschmer 2005. "Entry, standards and competition: Firm strategies and the Diffusion of Mobile Telephony," *Review of Industrial Organization* 26: 89–113.
Mitchell, Matthew, and Andrzej Skrzypacz 2004. "Network externalities and long-run market shares," Unpublished Draft, Stanford GSB, April.
Stoneman, Paul, and Paul David 1986. "Adoption subsidies vs. information provision as instruments of technology policy," *Economic Journal* 96: 142–50.
Toivanen, Otto 2002. "Choosing standards," Unpublished Draft, Helsinki School of Economics, April.

11 | Switching to digital television: business and public policy issues

NORBERT MAIER AND
MARCO OTTAVIANI

Abstract

This paper investigates the incentives of broadcasters to use subsidies and sunset dates to affect the viewers' decisions to switch from analog to digital television. It is shown that when viewers have identical preferences for digital television, it is never optimal for the broadcaster to subsidize just a fraction of viewers. When instead viewers have different valuations, broadcasters might want to induce viewers to switch gradually. Implications for welfare and effects of universal service requirements on equilibrium outcomes are also discussed.

1 Introduction

Television is currently undergoing a major transformation. The old analog standards are being replaced by new digital standards, widely perceived to be technologically superior. Digital television (DTV) makes possible the delivery of a signal virtually free of interference, with better image and audio quality and improved interactivity. In addition, data compression technologies allow for a more efficient use of bandwidth.[1] Not only does DTV provide the flexibility of increasing the quality and number of channels, but it also frees up bandwidth for alternative uses.[2]

We thank Victor Stango for guidance, Jozsef Molnar for research assistance, and the UK Economic and Social Research Council for financial support (research grant: RES-000-22-0385).

[1] With the same bandwidth required for a single analog channel, the new digital technology is capable of transmitting five to ten digital channels of comparable ("standard") quality. Alternatively, that bandwidth can be used to deliver high definition television with movie-quality picture and sound.

[2] We do not discuss the different standards for digital television. We refer to Farrell and Shapiro (1992) for an early account of the development of the Advanced Television Systems Committee (ATSC) standard in the United States, and to Grimme (2002) for a discussion of the development of the digital video

These benefits can be realized only if broadcasters as well as viewers are willing to invest in the new technology. On the supply side of the market, broadcasters need to invest in digital transmission equipment and make content available on the digital platform. On the demand side, viewers must be able to receive the digital signal either with a decoder (also called a *set top box*) or an integrated DTV set. In addition, costs and benefits are unevenly distributed across viewers and broadcasters and vary depending on the television delivery platform.

Policymakers in the United States and Europe have taken a keen interest in the transition process.[3] In this paper, we explore the main challenges to the transition process to DTV. In particular, we investigate viewers' incentives for switching to DTV, and how these incentives depend on the actions of broadcasters and policymakers.

1.1 Television market

In most industrialized countries, viewers can opt for free-to-air (FTA) television or pay television. Traditionally, FTA television is an analog technology that is transmitted terrestrially by radio waves and can be received through a rooftop aerial. For technical reasons, the part of the radio spectrum used for terrestrial transmission is limited, so only a small number of channels can be broadcast with the analog technology.[4]

In most countries, almost the entire population has access to FTA television, with the exception of those living in very remote areas. In most European countries, FTA public channels are mainly financed by

broadcasting (DVB) standard in Europe. According to Hart (2004) and Galperin (2004), the transition to DTV so far is the result of the interplay of economic and political factors. In this paper, we take the political factors as given and focus mostly on the normative economic implications.

[3] For information on the US policies, see Congressional Budget Office (1999); and for information on the EU policies, see Commission of the European Communities (2002, 2003).

[4] Terrestrial television employs part of the very high frequency (VHF, between 30 and 300 megahertz [MHz]) and ultra high frequency (UHF, between 300 MHz and 3.0 gigahertz [GHz]) bands. In North America, terrestrial television operates on channels 2 through 6, which use the VHF-low band (54–88 MHz); on channels 7 through 13, which use the VHF-high band (174–216 MHz); and on channels 14 through 69, which use the UHF television band (470–806 MHz). In the United Kingdom, terrestrial television operates exclusively on the UHF band, since VHF transmission was discontinued in 1985.

a special tax (the "license fee") on the ownership of a television set. In addition, there are FTA commercial channels, financed mostly through advertising revenues. In the United States, there are no publicly owned channels and no license fee, and local FTA commercial broadcasting stations are typically affiliated to national networks.[5] Although often licensed to broadcasters, the terrestrial spectrum is owned mostly by governments.[6]

Pay television operators mainly broadcast through cable and satellite.[7] Cable operators transmit their signals through a physical network of underground cables, directly connecting to viewers' homes. Satellite broadcasters send the signal to viewers through a satellite. Viewers equipped with a parabolic antenna (or dish) can then receive the signal provided there is a clear line of sight from the dish to the broadcast satellite. Cable and satellite technology can be used to broadcast many more channels than traditional terrestrial technology.

In addition to the FTA channels, pay television platforms typically offer a large number of other channels bundled in a menu of packages sold at different monthly subscription fees.[8] Platforms compete in the

---

[5] US broadcasting stations use radio spectrum frequencies licensed by the Federal Communications Commission in exchange for the promise to deliver socially valuable content. In addition, there are some public broadcasting stations financed by viewers' contributions and public subsidies. See Owen and Wildman (1992) for an overview of the US television industry and Levy et al. (2002) for a discussion of terrestrial television in the United States.

[6] Since Coase (1959), economists have argued in favor of privatization of the radio spectrum, without restrictions for its use. See Cramton et al. (1998) for how the terrestrial spectrum could be privatized, even if encumbered by terrestrial broadcasters. See Rosston and Hazlett (2001) for the advantages of eliminating barriers to the development of secondary markets for spectrum.

[7] In addition, digital subscriber line technology allows high-bandwidth data transmission on a conventional residential telephone line. Despite its limited penetration to date, this technology has a bright future. Both digital subscriber line technology and fiber optics to the home allow for one-to-one transmission of programs and therefore the delivery of video on demand. See Hazlett (2001) for a discussion of the superiority of wired to wireless television in the long term. We refer to Katz (2003) for a discussion of the likely impact of Internet television on the broadcasting industry.

[8] Pay television broadcasters typically offer packages of basic programs that must be taken by all subscribers as well as premium programs (such as major sport events and latest Hollywood films) for a supplementary fee. See Cave and Crandall (2001) on the importance of sports rights for television.

market for channels,[9] and channels compete in the market for television content as well as for advertising.[10]

Viewers make long-term decisions of which platform and package to adopt, depending on the corresponding one-off cost of the equipment and the monthly subscription fees. Using their remote control, viewers can then choose to watch a program from the channels to which they subscribe.

The transition to digital technology applies to all three transmission platforms (terrestrial, cable, and satellite).[11] In this paper, we focus on the viewers' long-term decisions of which platform to adopt, and in particular on their incentives to migrate from the analog to the corresponding digital version of any given platform.

1.2 Digital transition

The costs and benefits of DTV are unevenly distributed among the different market participants. This makes the transition process difficult, especially in the absence of transfers among the parties involved. The transition to DTV is further complicated by the interplay of two peculiar features of television, one economic and the other political.

First, television is "nonrival" in consumption, that is, a viewer receiving the television signal on any platform (be it terrestrial, cable, or satellite) does not preclude other viewers from receiving the same signal. The nonrival nature of broadcasting means that broadcasting has only a fixed cost component, and, as a result, serving only one viewer or all the viewers imposes the same costs on the broadcaster for each specific technology (analog and digital). This means that operating both analog and digital technology at the same time duplicates the

---

[9] Some platform operators (e.g., the UK satellite operator BSkyB) are vertically integrated and act as producers as well as distributors of some television channels, especially those with premium programs. Competition among platforms and broadcasters then takes place in a number of stages. First, the content is obtained and the channels are produced in the upstream market. Second, access to the channels is resold to competing platform operators. Third, platform operators compete for viewers' subscriptions. See Armstrong (1999) and Harbord and Ottaviani (2001).

[10] See Anderson and Coate (2005) for the two-sided nature of the television market, and, more generally, Rochet and Tirole (2003) and Armstrong (2004) for the economics of two-sided markets.

[11] Adda and Ottaviani's (2005) Table 2 reports the progress of digitization by platform across EU countries.

costs of broadcasting. To implement the smoothest transition to digital, platform operators must address the following business policy question: *Given the nonrival nature of broadcasting, which technology should be operated at any period and which subsidy system can most effectively support this choice?*

Second, governments consider access to information through television the right of every citizen. This universal access requirement represents a constraint, especially for terrestrial television used for FTA broadcasting.[12] Due to this constraint, the terrestrial analog signal cannot be switched off unilaterally. In particular, the US and the UK governments have announced that they do not intend to switch off the analog terrestrial signal until a sufficiently high (respectively, 85% and 95%) fraction of viewers have already switched to digital. Therefore, the government, as a platform operator, is facing the following public policy question: *Given the nonrival nature of broadcasting technology, as well as the universal service requirement, which technology should be operated at any period and which subsidy system can most effectively support this choice?*

The paper proceeds as follows. In the remainder of this section, we describe our approach to analyzing the effects of the nonrival nature of broadcasting technology and the universal access requirement for the transition to digital television. Next, in Section 2, we introduce the basic static model and present our results. We investigate viewers' optimal choice of platforms as a function of their preference parameters for digital service and derive our main insights for business policy. In Section 3, we present the dynamic extension of our model and discuss the timing issue. In Section 4, we conclude by identifying the main challenge imposed by the universal service obligation.

1.3 Our approach

To illustrate the simple economics of the effects of the nonrival nature of broadcasting technology and the universal access requirement for the transition to digital television, we consider the case of a *single*

---

[12] Serving residents of remote areas is often not commercially viable for private operators. Governments have indirectly subsidized terrestrial broadcasters in a number of ways, such as the license fee and the allocation of spectrum at subsidized rates. In the telephone sector, governments have instead used incentive schemes to create competition among universal service providers (see Laffont and Tirole 2000 and Riordan 2002).

platform in isolation. In our stylized model, the platform can broadcast a given content by analog and/or by digital technology, while the viewers can choose which standard to adopt among those available. Within the model, we analyze the viewers' responses to different policies chosen by the platform.

As previously explained, in reality, many platforms compete with each other and face different costs and benefits of switching to digital broadcasting. Nevertheless, our model ignores the interaction between different platforms. This simplification allows us to concentrate on each platform's decision of which standards and subsidies to offer and consequently on their effect on viewers' incentives to migrate to digital.[13]

Due to the nonrival nature of broadcasting technology, transmission of each technology involves only a fixed cost. This cost is lower for the digital than for the analog technology, because of the reduced bandwidth requirement for digital transmission. We assume that the platform collects revenues from advertisers only and that the amount of these revenues is proportional to the number of viewers.[14] For a given number of viewers, the platform's only concern is to minimize the cost of transmission. The platform operator has the following choices at any period: (1) operate the analog signal only, (2) launch the digital signal without switching off the analog, and (3) launch the digital while switching off the analog.

We are interested in analyzing the incentives for viewers to migrate from analog to digital. Viewers derive a positive utility from the analog service and obtain an additional utility from DTV. To capture the heterogeneity of viewers' preferences, we allow for two types of viewers, depending on how much they value the benefits of DTV. *High-type viewers* have a higher valuation of the benefits of DTV than *low-type viewers*.

Viewers initially have access to the analog signal and must decide whether to stay with analog, migrate to digital, or opt out of television altogether. To switch to the digital service, both types of viewers must incur the same switching cost, which is comprised of the cost of the digital set top box and the inconvenience of installing it. The choice of each viewer clearly depends on the switching cost, as well as his or her preferences for the different options available.

---

[13] We refer to Adda and Ottaviani (2005) for an empirical analysis of viewers' adoption choices in the presence of coexisting platforms.

[14] Our model mainly captures the features of FTA terrestrial broadcasting, but can be extended to cover the case of pay television.

1.4 *Our findings*

We use a static version of the model both to analyze the platform operator's decision regarding which technology to use and to derive the basic features of the optimal subsidies used to induce the viewers to switch.

Subsidies

Since viewers derive a higher utility from analog than from no television, they need to be offered a higher subsidy to switch to digital if analog is also available. Therefore, it is always optimal for the platform operator to switch off the analog when it launches the digital signal, as this reduces the size of the subsidies that must be offered to the viewers.

To encourage the viewers to switch to digital, the platform operator may decide to offer subsidies to the viewers. The platform operator may decide to offer a subsidy to a group of viewers only. In this case, however, subsidized viewers would switch to digital, while unsubsidized viewers would stay with analog (if it is not switched off) or opt out of television altogether.

If the unsubsidized viewers stay with analog, the two technologies are operated simultaneously, and the platform operator would be better off by not giving a subsidy to anyone at all in order to save on both the cost of transmission and the amount spent on subsidies.

If, instead, unsubsidized viewers opt out of television, the net profit per viewer switched to digital (advertising revenue minus the amount of subsidy paid) is positive, so it is profitable to induce all the viewers to switch to digital by the same subsidy. As a result, it is never optimal to offer a subsidy to a group of viewers only.

Welfare

We compare the switching pattern resulting under laissez faire with the first best and find that both excess and insufficient switching can occur in equilibrium. On the one hand, excess switching results from the fact that the platform operator cannot charge viewers for the television services but can subsidize the switch to digital. Note that the platform operator cannot extract all the viewers' surplus under analog broadcasting, but it can extract their entire surplus by switching off the analog signal and subsidizing their switch to digital. As a result, in some cases the platform operator might induce a forced migration to digital more often than would be socially efficient.

On the other hand, private information about viewer's types might lead to insufficient switching. Assume that in the first-best setting both the low and the high-type viewers switch to digital. In a world of incomplete information, however, the high subsidy offered to low-type viewers must also be given to the high-type viewers. This raises the platform operator's costs of switching to digital so much that the platform operator may decide to stick to analog broadcasting, even if switching to digital would be socially efficient.

Sunset date

To address the optimal timing of the switch to digital, we extend the model to a simple dynamic framework with two periods. We allow the platform operator to commit *ex ante* to any policy. A late subsidy seems undesirable since it might induce some viewers who otherwise would have adopted early to delay adoption and cash in on the subsidy.

We show that the platform operator may find it optimal to offer a late subsidy that will be taken only by the low-type viewers. High-type viewers will switch earlier without waiting for a subsidy. This extension provides some discrimination among viewers and might alleviate the problem of insufficient switching described in the static model. The equilibrium outcome explains why analog and digital technologies are sometimes operated jointly during the transition phase, with viewers choosing to switch to digital at different times. Although the operator prefers a swift transition to digital if viewers are homogeneous, delays in the transition can be optimal for the operator if viewers have heterogeneous preferences for DTV.

Universal access

Returning to the static version of the model, we then investigate the implications for public policy of the universal access requirement. As the analog signal can be switched off only if a sufficiently high fraction of viewers migrate, viewers' expectations about the actions of the other viewers become relevant for the equilibrium outcome. Depending on these expectations, multiple equilibria can arise.

Consider the case in which each individual viewer thinks that only a few of the others intend to switch so that the criterion for switching off will not be met. With such pessimistic expectations about the others' switching behavior, it is indeed optimal for the individual viewer not to switch. As a result, the viewers will not switch, the criterion will not be met, and the platform operator will not switch off the analog service, thereby confirming the initial expectations. A similar logic applies for the case when each viewer has optimistic expectations about the others' switching. In this second equilibrium, all viewers switch to digital and the platform operator can successfully switch off the analog service. We give conditions for multiple equilibria to arise.

2 Business policy

In this section, we build a simple static model to analyze viewers' incentives to switch to digital service. We derive the policy adopted by the platform operator and evaluate the resulting switching patterns from the social point of view.

2.1 Static model

There is one platform operator and N viewers. The platform can broadcast a given content by analog and/or digital technology. The viewers can choose to adopt either standard or opt out of television.

Broadcasting involves a fixed transmission cost, equal to C_A for analog and C_D for digital signal. Due to the nonrival nature of broadcasting, this cost is independent of the number of viewers reached by a particular technology. Because of the smaller spectrum requirement of digital broadcasting, we assume that $C_D < C_A$.

The platform derives revenues only from advertising, in proportion to the number of viewers. In particular, r units of advertising revenue are collected for each viewer. For a given number of viewers, the platform then aims at minimizing the transmission cost.

The preferences of a given viewer are described as follows: The utility of no television is normalized to zero. The utility of viewing analog television is equal to $a > 0$. The utility of viewing DTV is $a + b$, so the incremental utility derived from DTV is equal to b.[15] To switch to digital, the viewer must pay the switching cost s.

Initially, viewers receive the analog signal and the platform operator has the following choices: (1) operate the analog signal only, (2) launch

---

[15] In the case of pay television, b would instead denote the valuation net of the subscription fee.

the digital signal without switching off the analog, and (3) launch the digital while switching off the analog.

In the rest of the section, we shortly review the viewers' decisions when the analog signal is and is not switched off. We then analyze the platform operator's optimal policy and evaluate it from the welfare perspective.

2.2 Viewers' switching decisions

Suppose that analog, digital, and no television are made available. Since utility from analog television is positive, it is never optimal for the viewer to opt for no television. Staying with analog results in payoff $u_A = a$, while migrating to digital yields $u_D = a + b - s$. Viewers prefer to switch to digital whenever the benefit from digital exceeds the switching cost, that is, when $b \geq s$.

If, instead, the platform operator switches off the analog signal when launching the digital, the viewer can choose only between digital service and no television. Not migrating to digital television gives a payoff equal to 0, instead of a, while migrating to digital gives the same payoff. Therefore, viewers will switch to digital broadcasting whenever $a + b - s \geq 0$, or equivalently, when $b \geq s - a$. Clearly, the threshold for switching to digital is lower in this second case.

Next, what is the impact of a subsidy equal to S on the viewers who switch to digital? Such a subsidy makes viewers more willing to switch by increasing the utility from switching to digital to $u_D = a + b - s + S$. The condition for switching then becomes $a + b - s + S \geq a$, or $b \geq s - S$.

2.3 Operator's policy

We now address the problem of the platform operator's technology choice and the business policy supporting that choice. As was previously discussed, the platform operator must decide which technology to operate and which subsidization policy to adopt. The optimal business policy then includes a pricing and a subsidy strategy.[16]

Assume that the viewers differ in their incremental valuation of the digital service. In particular, a fraction ρ of the population has a low valuation, b^L, while the remaining fraction $(1 - \rho)$ has a high valuation, $b^H > b^L$.

---

[16] While we focus on FTA broadcasting, subsidies alter the viewers' valuations. This suggests that our analysis can be extended to the case of pay television.

The platform operator knows the distribution of viewers' preferences in the population, but cannot observe the type of each particular viewer. (Alternatively, if the platform operator can observe each individual viewer's type, then it cannot discriminate directly among the viewers.) Note that in this incomplete information environment, the platform operator cannot use subsidies to discriminate even indirectly among the different types of viewers.[17]

The objective of the platform operator is to select which technologies to operate and to design a subsidy scheme to support this choice when necessary. Observe that the lower operating costs make digital broadcasting more attractive for the platform operator. Therefore, the platform operator may want to offer subsidies to encourage the viewers to switch to DTV.

In two extreme cases, subsidies are irrelevant. First, viewers are willing to switch to digital even without a subsidy when they have a strong preference for digital (i.e., the value of b is relatively large compared to the value of s), so that the platform operator can switch off the analog signal without subsidies. Second, when viewers' preferences for digital are extremely weak and the costs of switching are very high, the platform operator must stay with the analog signal because the subsidies inducing viewers to switch would be too expensive.

Therefore, it is more interesting to focus on the intermediate case between these two extremes, namely, the one in which viewers would not switch by themselves but can be induced to switch by a subsidy. Will the platform operator offer a subsidy to all the viewers or to only a fraction of them? Should the operator switch off the analog signal once it launches digital broadcasting or not? The following proposition answers these questions:

Proposition 1
The optimal policy adopted by the platform operator has the following features:
a. It is never optimal to subsidize only a fraction of a particular type of viewers.
b. Once digital broadcasting is launched, it is optimal to switch off the analog signal.

---

[17] In the dynamic framework of Section 3, intertemporal discrimination becomes possible instead.

To present the intuition for Proposition 1a, we consider two cases in turn. In the first case, assume that the platform operator cannot switch off the analog signal when some of the viewers would prefer it to the digital signal. If the platform operator chooses to offer a subsidy to only a part of the viewers, these viewers are induced to switch to digital, so that both digital and analog technologies must be operated at the same time. Compared to using only analog, this choice increases the platform operator's costs by two items, namely, the operating cost of the digital technology and the amount of subsidies paid. As a result, the platform operator will never choose this option.

Second, consider what happens when the platform operator can unilaterally switch off the analog signal once it has launched the digital signal. In particular, the platform operator can implement two subsidization policies: one is to offer subsidies that would induce only the high-type viewers to switch, and another one that would induce low-type viewers to switch as well.[18] For such plans to be profitable, the advertising revenues generated by the number of viewers having chosen digital to no television after being offered a subsidy must be larger than the cost of these subsidies. Because both these revenues and costs are the same for each targeted viewer, if their difference is positive, it is optimal to extend that subsidy to the entire target group. If the difference is negative, offering no subsidies at all becomes optimal. Therefore, offering a subsidy to only a subset of the viewers of a particular type is never optimal.

The optimality of switching off the analog signal once the digital is launched is due to the following two facts. First, if it is in the platform operator's interest to offer a subsidy to viewers, switching off the analog signal allows the operator to induce viewers to switch with a smaller subsidy, as the viewers' threshold for switching is reduced when the analog signal is not available. Second, the platform operator may find it optimal to operate both technologies and not give any subsidy, because, in this case, high-type viewers would switch to digital and low-type viewers would stay with analog. Yet, operating both technologies without any subsidy is more expensive than not launching digital at all.

---

[18] Depending on the value of viewers' preference parameter, any of these subsidies can be equal to zero.

2.4 Welfare

The most important question from the welfare point of view is whether excessive or insufficient switching occurs in equilibrium.[19] To answer this question, it is enough to look at the case when $b^L > s - a - r$ and $\rho r \geq (C_A - C_D)/N$. As is shown in the appendix, switching everybody to digital is optimal for the platform operator whenever $b^L \geq s - a - (C_A - C_D)/N$.

The efficient allocation can be derived from maximizing the joint surplus of the platform operator and the viewers. It can be shown (see appendix) that everybody switching to digital is efficient whenever $b^L \geq b^H - (1/\rho)(b^H - s + (C_A - C_D)/N)$. The following proposition summarizes our welfare result:

Proposition 2
Both excessive and insufficient switching to digital service can occur in equilibrium.

There are two forces that drive the decentralized outcome away from the first-best outcome. First, there is a tendency toward excessive switching, because the platform operator is unable to extract all the viewers' surplus (equal to a) if they choose the analog service. The operator can, however, extract all the viewers' surplus when inducing a switch to digital, because the optimal subsidy in that case leaves the viewers indifferent between switching and opting out of television (with consumer surplus equal to zero). As a result, switching to digital allows the operator to get closer to full rent extraction, so that switching results in some cases when it would not be optimal from the social point of view. Obviously, the magnitude of this distortion rises as the level of a rises.

Second, the fact that the platform operator does not know each viewer's type points in the direction of socially insufficient switching. The reason is that the operator cannot discriminate among viewers and must pay the same amount of subsidy to the low-type and to the high-type viewers. Hence, the operator can extract only part of the benefits

---

[19] We assume here that the platform operator has the option to unilaterally switch off the analog signal.

of switching. If the fraction of high-type viewers is large, the subsidies intended for the few low-cost viewers are very costly for the operator, so that less switching results compared to the first best level.

3 Timing

To address the optimal switching time of the platform operator, we need to extend our model to multiple periods. To keep the analysis simple, we extend our model to two periods only and assume that the platform operator cannot announce a switching-off of the analog signal.

3.1 Dynamic model

Consider again a single platform operator that can broadcast a given content by analog and/or digital technology for two periods, $t = 1,2$. In each period, the viewers can choose to adopt either standard or opt out of television altogether.

As in the static version of our model, broadcasting involves only a fixed cost in each period, equal to C_A for the analog and $C_D < C_A$ for the digital signal. The platform collects r units of revenue from advertisers for each viewer in each period. For a given number of viewers, the platform's only concern is to minimize discounted transmission costs.

The preferences of a given viewer can be described as follows. The utility of no television is normalized to zero, whereas the utility of viewing analog television is equal to $a > 0$ in each period. Viewing digital television in period t gives utility $a + b_t$, where b_t represents the incremental utility derived from digital television. To switch to digital in period t, the viewer must pay the one-off switching cost s_t. Second-period payoffs are discounted according to the factor δ.

Initially, viewers receive the analog signal. We assume that the platform operator cannot switch off the analog signal unless all viewers have migrated to digital.[20] The platform operator has three choices: Introduce digital broadcasting in the first period, in the second period, or in neither period.

---

[20] This is the case when no unilateral termination of the analog signal is possible. Even though a more general version of the model should incorporate the unilateral termination of the analog signal, we ignore this option to keep our analysis simple. The case considered here fits the case of the terrestrial platform well.

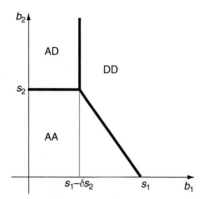

Figure 11.1 Dependence of viewers' choices on preference parameters.

We begin by deriving the viewers' optimal choice of technology, and then turn to the platform operator's dynamic decision.

3.2 Viewers' switching

In each period, the viewers decide whether to stay with analog or migrate to digital. Once migrated to digital service, the viewer cannot return to analog service. Staying with analog for both periods (choosing AA, where the capital letters denote the choices in the corresponding period) results in payoff $u_{AA} = a + \delta a$. Migrating to digital in the first period (choosing DD) results in a payoff of $u_{DD} = a + b_1 - s_1 + \delta(a + b_2)$. Finally, staying with analog in the first period and migrating to digital in the second period (choosing AD) results in a payoff of $u_{AD} = a + \delta(a + b_2 - s_2)$.

Figure 11.1 illustrates the dependence of the viewers' choice on their preference parameters for digital in the two periods. In the graph, b_1 is plotted on the horizontal axis and b_2 is plotted on the vertical axis.[21] To understand this graph, we now compare the viewers' utility for each of the three scenarios identified above.

A viewer chooses DD over AA if and only if $a + b_1 - s_1 + \delta(a + b_2)$ $a + \delta a$, or equivalently, when $b_1 + \delta b_2 \geq s_1$. This is the case for the

---

[21] The preference for analog service can be neglected in the graphical illustration, since the decision depends only on the incremental preference for digital over analog television.

preferences represented by points to the northeast of the diagonal line between areas AA and DD in Figure 11.1. Intuitively, a viewer will choose to switch to digital in the first period rather than remain with analog technology forever, whenever the present value of the benefits from switching is greater than the switching cost incurred in the first period. Note that an increase in the discount factor increases the present value of the benefits from switching.

A viewer chooses DD over AD if and only if $a + b_1 - s_1 + \delta(a + b_2) \geq a + \delta(a + b_2 - s_2)$. This reduces to $b_1 \geq s_1 - \delta s_2$, which is satisfied in the area to the right of the vertical line in Figure 11.1. Intuitively, the viewer switches in period 1 rather than in period 2, if the benefit from digital in the first period is larger than the rental cost of switching.[22] So, DD is the most preferred option for a particular viewer if the two inequality conditions above are simultaneously satisfied, that is, if the viewer's preference parameters for digital service in both periods are high and can be represented by a point in the DD area.

The boundary between the AA and AD areas can be identified in the same way. In particular, a viewer chooses AD over AA if and only if $a + \delta(a + b_2 - s_2) \geq a + \delta a$, or $b_2 \geq s_2$, which is satisfied for the points above the horizontal line in Figure 11.1. Intuitively, a viewer would choose to switch to digital service in period 2 if the benefit from digital more than offsets the cost of switching. It can be seen that AD is the most preferred option for a particular viewer if $b_1 \leq s_1 - \delta s_2$ and $b_2 \geq s_2$, that is, if the viewer has high preferences for digital service in period 2 and low preferences for digital service in period 1. Similarly, AA is the most preferred option for someone with low preferences for digital in both periods. In addition, note that someone with a high preference in the first period and a low preference in the second period will also switch in the first period.

The impact of subsidies on viewers' optimal choice can easily be analyzed in this framework. If a subsidy is offered in the first period (see Figure 11.2), the switching costs of viewers in period 1 decreases, which shifts to the left the borderlines between both the AA and DD areas (defined by $b_1 + \delta b_2 = s_1$) and the AD and DD areas (defined by

---

[22] The difference of the present values of switching costs in the two periods is $s_1 - \delta s_2$. If s is the price of a digital decoder, this difference is equal to the rental cost of such an equipment, as it is the difference between the price for which the equipment can be bought in period 1 and the present value of the price for which it can be sold in period 2.

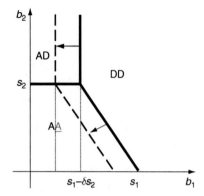

Figure 11.2. Impact of a subsidy in the first period on viewers' choices.

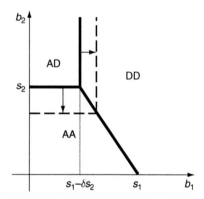

Figure 11.3. Impact of a subsidy in the second period on viewers' choices.

$b_1 = s_1 - \delta s_2$). The impact of a subsidy in period 2 is illustrated in Figure 11.3. As we have already seen in the static model, subsidies can be used to induce users to switch to digital service in cases when they would otherwise prefer to remain with the analog service. In the following section, we analyze the platform operator's choice of when to launch digital broadcasting and the subsidy policy supporting this decision.

3.3 Subsidization policy

We now analyze the platform operator's optimal subsidy policy. Solving for the optimal subsidy policy in general involves deriving the optimal timing for launching the digital signal. In this two-stage game, the viewers take into account the subsidies offered by the platform. In the first period, the platform operator commits to a dynamic subsidization policy. In the second stage, the viewers make their two-period service choice. Since each player moves only once, credibility is not an issue here.

As in the static model, viewers have heterogeneous preferences for digital service. We denote type-i viewer's ($i \in \{L,H\}$) preferences for digital service in period t by b_t^i and assume that $b_t^L < b_t^H$, that is, the high-type viewer has a higher valuation for digital in both periods.

In this dynamic setting, the platform operator may decide to discriminate among viewers, thereby inducing them to switch to digital technology in different periods. Operation costs are higher, however, when viewers do not switch simultaneously, as both technologies must be operated in the same period.[23] Consequently, the platform operator will only choose to discriminate among viewers if the benefits from discrimination more than offset the extra costs imposed by the simultaneous operation of the two technologies.[24] The following proposition formalizes this idea:

Proposition 3

When analog and digital broadcasting technologies can be operated at the same time, the platform operator may induce viewers to switch to the digital service in different periods. In particular, if digital broadcasting is much cheaper to operate than analog, and the surplus of low-type viewers from digital is very low in the first period, the platform operator might offer a subsidy only in the second period. Low-type viewers will take this subsidy and switch in the second period, whereas high-type viewers switch in the first period without benefiting from the subsidy.

The intuition for this "asymmetric" switching pattern is the following: Suppose that the low-type benefit, b_1^L, is much lower than s_1. A subsidy offered to low-type viewers in the first period should be very high. In addition, since the platform operator cannot observe the viewers' type, high-type viewers also would take this high subsidy.

---

[23] We assumed that there is no unilateral switch-off of the analog signal.

[24] Note that we cannot have both technologies operated at the same time in the static version of our model, as that scenario would be dominated by operating the digital signal only (see Section 2).

Therefore, such a high first-period subsidy would be costly for the platform operator and would not necessarily be offset by the savings incurred by switching off the analog signal in the first period.

With low-type viewers having a higher benefit from digital in the second period (or equivalently when the evolution of technology lowers switching costs), their subsidization may become cheaper in the second period. High-type viewers would switch to digital early on in the first period and would not wait for a moderate subsidy in the second period. Therefore, the costs imposed by the second-period subsidies on the platform operator will be of moderate magnitude and will be more than offset by the savings generated by switching off the analog signal in the second period. As a result, it would be profitable for the platform operator to offer a second period subsidy of a moderate amount targeting low-type viewers.

Even though the operator can now intertemporally discriminate among viewers, the full benefits of screening cannot be realized because of two reasons. First, since we are considering FTA television, viewers do not pay for either type of the service. As a result, the platform operator has no means to extract all the viewers' surplus, which weakens its incentives to discriminate. Second, as broadcasting is an excludable public good, the cost of providing it is constant and does not depend on the number of viewers served. This necessarily leads to a duplication of costs if the platform operator discriminates among viewers – and, therefore, it discourages discrimination.

4 Public policy

In this section, we analyze the problems raised by the universal service requirement. The universal service obligation requires that all viewers be assured access to some kind of broadcasting. Therefore, the platform operator cannot unilaterally switch off the analog signal. The analog signal can only be switched off if a sufficiently high fraction of viewers has already migrated to the digital service.

To keep the analysis simple, we return to the static version of our model. We also assume that viewers are identical. Because of the universal service requirement, the platform operator has the option to switch off the analog signal only if a sufficiently high fraction of viewers has already migrated to digital. The effects of a conditional switch-off are summarized below:

Proposition 4

Suppose that it is announced that analog broadcasting is to be switched off, conditional on a given and arbitrary fraction of the population of viewers taking up digital. If $s - a \leq b \leq s$, there are two equilibrium outcomes, one in which the entire population of viewers switches to digital and the other in which the entire population stays with analog.

Condition $b \geq s - a$ implies that viewers prefer switching to digital if the choice is between digital television and no television. Condition $b \leq s$ implies that viewers prefer staying with analog television if both analog and digital are available.

In the first equilibrium, individual viewers expect all the other viewers to switch to digital, so the critical mass required by the "take-up criterion" will be achieved. The analog service will then be switched off, so it is in the interest of individual viewers to switch to digital as $s \leq a + b$, and the initial expectation is fulfilled.

In the second equilibrium, each individual viewer expects that no other viewer will switch to digital service. Given this expectation, it is in the best interest of each viewer not to switch to digital, as $b \leq s$. All viewers will then remain with analog service, so the critical mass for switching is not achieved, and the analog signal is not switched off, which confirms the original expectation.

Note that if viewers' preferences are different from those described in the proposition, there are no multiple equilibria. Nevertheless, this result can be generalized to the case with heterogeneous viewers, and it can be shown that it is reasonable to expect multiple equilibria in empirically plausible scenarios (see Adda and Ottaviani 2005). Expectation management then becomes important.

In future research, it would be interesting to extend the model to allow for competition among platforms, which has proven essential in the UK experience. In particular, we believe that governments should seriously consider market solutions to the universal service obligations.[25]

---

[25] Governments could create competition among different platform operators to obtain subsidies to provide television in remote areas. These areas are often less costly to serve by satellite than terrestrial technology.

References

Adda, J., and M. Ottaviani 2005. "The transition to digital television," *Economic Policy* 41: 160–209.

Anderson, S., and S. Coate 2005. "Market provision of broadcasting: A welfare analysis," *Review of Economic Studies* 72: 947–72.

Armstrong, M. 1999. "Competition in the pay-TV market," *Journal of the Japanese and International Economies* 13: 257–80.

2004. "*Competition in two-sided markets,*" mimeo, London: University College London.

Cave, M., and R. Crandall 2001. "Sports rights and the broadcast industry," *Economic Journal* 111: F4–26.

Coase, R. 1959. "The Federal Communications Commission," *Journal of Law & Economics* 2: 1–40.

Commission of the European Communities 2002. "eEurope 2005: An information society for all," COM (2002) 263 final, Brussels.

2003. "Communication from the Commission to the Council, the European Parliament, the European Economic and Social Committee and the Committee of the Regions on the transition from analogue to digital broadcasting (from digital 'switchover' to analogue 'switch-off')," COM (2003) 541 final, Brussels.

Congressional Budget Office of the United States 1999. "Completing the transition to digital television," Washington, DC: Government Printing Office.

Cramton, P., E. Kwerel, and J. Williams 1998. "Efficient relocation of spectrum incumbents," *Journal of Law & Economics* 41: 647–75.

Farrell, J., and C. Shapiro 1992. "Standard setting in high-definition television," *Brookings Papers on Economic Activity: Microeconomics* 1–77.

Galperin, H. 2004. *New television, old politics: The transition to digital TV in the United States and Britain.* Cambridge: Cambridge University Press.

Grimme, K. 2002. *Digital television: Standardization and strategies.* Norwood, MA: Artech House.

Harbord, D., and M. Ottaviani 2001. "Contracts and competition in the UK pay-TV market," Discussion Paper 01-5, London Business School.

Hart, J. 2004. *Technology, television and competition: The politics of digital TV.* Cambridge: Cambridge University Press.

Hazlett, T. 2001. "The US digital TV transition: Time to toss the Negroponte Switch," Working Paper 01–15, Washington, DC: AEI-Brookings Joint Centre for Regulatory Studies.

Katz, M. 2003. "Television over the Internet: Industry structure and competition absent distribution bottlenecks," in *Internet television*, E. Noam,

J. Groebel, and D. Gerbarg (eds.), Mawah, NJ: Lawrence Erlbaum Associates, 31–59.

Laffont, J. J., and J. Tirole 2000. *Competition in telecommunications.* Cambridge, MA: MIT Press.

Levy, J., M. Ford-Levy, and A. Levine 2002. "Broadcast television: Survivor in a sea of competition," OPP Working Paper Series 37, Washington, DC: Federal Communications Commission.

Owen, B., and S. Wildman 1992. *Video economics.* Cambridge, MA: Harvard University Press.

Riordan, M. 2002. "Universal residential telephone service," in *Handbook of telecommunications economics*, M. Cave (ed.), Amsterdam: Elsevier Science, 423–73.

Rochet, J. C., and J. Tirole 2003. "Platform competition in two-sided markets," *Journal of the European Economic Association* 1: 990–1029.

Rosston, G. L., and T. W. Hazlett 2001. "Comments of 37 concerned economists [on] promoting efficient use of spectrum through elimination of barriers to the development of secondary markets," WT Docket No. 00–230, Federal Communications Commission, Washington, DC: AEI-Brookings Joint Center for Regulatory Studies.

Appendix: *Proofs*

Proof of Proposition 1

There are six cases to be considered separately depending on the magnitude of b^L and b^H, relative to $s - a$ and s:

(i) $b^L < b^H < s - a$;

(ii) $b^L < s - a < b^H < s$;

(iii) $b^L < s - a < s < b^H$;

(iv) $s - a < b^L < b^H < s$;

(v) $s - a < b^L < s < b^H$;

(vi) $s - b^L < b^H$.

We present the proof only for case (i), which is the one that best illustrates the logic of the result. In this case, the level of the subsidy required to make either type of viewer switch depends on whether or not analog is available in addition to digital. If only digital is available, the platform operator can design two types of subsidies, a "high subsidy" equal to $s - a - b^L$ with an impact on the choice of all viewers, and a "low subsidy" equal to $s - a - b^H$, which affects only the choice of high-type viewers. Note that the low subsidy is not enough to induce the low-type viewers to switch, and so is paid only to the high-type viewers. Similarly, if both analog and digital are available, the high subsidy is equal to $s - b^L$ and the low subsidy is equal to $s - b^H$.

The surplus of the platform operator for each option is:

(1) Offer analog only and no subsidy: $Nr - C_A$;
(2) Offer digital only and a number $K \leq (1 - \rho)N$ of low subsidies: $Kr - K(s - a - b^H) - C_D$;
(3) Offer digital only and a number $K \leq N$ of high subsidies: $Kr - K(s - a - b^L) - C_D$;
(4) Offer digital only and no subsidy: $- C_D$;
(5) Offer analog and digital and a number K of low subsidies: $Nr - K(s - b^H) - C_A - C_D$;
(6) Offer analog and digital and a number K of high subsidies: $Nr - K(s - b^L) - C_A - C_D$;
(7) Offer analog and digital and no subsidy: $Nr - C_A - C_D$;
(8) Offer neither analog nor digital and no subsidy: 0.

It can be seen that option (1) dominates option (7). Since $b^L < b^H$, option (5) dominates option (6). Option (5) is dominated by option (1) because of its extra second and fourth term. Also, option (8) dominates option (4). In turn, option (1) dominates option (8) if analog is profitable in the first place. The only remaining options are (1), (2), and (3), which proves claim (ii), namely, that it is not optimal to simulcast analog and digital signal.

In option (3), it is in the platform operator's interest to set the value of K equal to N whenever $r - (s - a - b^L) > 0$, and $K = 0$ (the case of no subsidies at all) otherwise. Similarly, in option (2) the platform operator should set $K = (1 - \rho)N$ if $r - (s - a - b^H) > 0$, and $K = 0$ otherwise. This shows that it is never optimal to subsidize a fraction of the viewers targeted by a subsidy, the first claim of the proposition. This completes the proof of Proposition 1 for case (i), with $b^L < b^H < s - a$.

Cases (ii) through (vi) can be analyzed in a similar way. For the second part of the proposition, note that in cases (i), (ii), and (iii) the platform operator can reach the low-type viewer with the analog signal and save the cost of the subsidy needed to induce the low-type viewer to switch to digital by simulcasting the analog and digital signal. This cannot be optimal for the operator, however, because transmitting the analog signal only would save the digital transmission cost and the eventual subsidy to the high-type viewer.

Proof of Proposition 2

We first derive the platform operator's optimal choice for the case presented in the proof of Proposition 1. Assume that $r - (s - a - b^L) > 0$, or equivalently, that $b^L > s - a - r$. This implies that $r - (s - a - b^H) > 0$; therefore, only the following options must be compared (see proof of Proposition 1):

(1) Offer analog only and no subsidy: $Nr - C_A$;
(2) Offer digital only and low subsidy: $(1 - \rho)N[r - (s - a - b^H)] - C_D$;
(3) Offer digital only and high subsidy: $N[r - (s - a - b^L)] - C_D$.

It can be seen that whenever $b^H < s - a + \frac{\rho}{1-\rho}r - \frac{1}{1-\rho}\frac{C_A - C_D}{N}$, option (1) dominates option (2). If we assume $\rho r \geq (C_A - C_D)/N$, then condition $b^H < s - a + \frac{\rho}{1-\rho}r - \frac{1}{1-\rho}\frac{C_A - C_D}{N}$ is satisfied automatically if $b^H < s - a$.

The platform operator chooses option (3) over option (1) whenever $b^L > s - a - (C_A - C_D)/N$. Note that $\rho r \geq (C_A - C_D)/N$ also implies $r \geq (C_A - C_D)/N$, which in turn implies $s - a - (C_A - C_D)/N \geq s - a - r$, or equivalently, that it is sometimes optimal to choose analog. In particular, the platform operator chooses analog whenever $s - a - r < b^L < s - a - (C_A - C_D)/N$ and chooses digital whenever $s - a - (C_A - C_D)/N < b^L < s - a$.

We now turn to the first-best outcomes. The joint surplus of the viewers and the platform operator for the four possible allocations are:

(I)   All view analog: $Na + Nr - C_A$;
(II) High-type viewers use digital and low-type viewers use analog: $N[a + (1 - \rho)(b^H - s)] + Nr - C_A - C_D$;
(III) All viewers use digital: $N[a + \rho b^L + (1 - \rho)b^H - s] + Nr - C_D$;
(IV) High-type viewers use digital and low-type viewers use no television: $(1 - \rho)N(a + b^H - s) + (1 - \rho)Nr - C_D$.

Since we are considering the case with $b^L < b^H < s - a$, we also have $b^H < s + \frac{1}{1-\rho}\frac{C_D}{N}$, so that outcome (II) is dominated by outcome (I). In addition, outcome (IV) is dominated by outcome (III), since $b^L \geq s - a - r$.

Consequently, it is efficient for everyone to switch to digital whenever the joint surplus in outcome (III) is higher than in outcome (I), that is, whenever $b^L \geq b^H - \frac{1}{\rho}\left(b^H - s + \frac{C_A - C_D}{N}\right)$. Since $s - a - r < b^L <$

$b^H < s - a$, we also need condition $\frac{C_A - C_D}{N} > a > \frac{C_A - C_D}{N} - r$ for having both cases in which analog or digital is socially efficient. In particular, analog is socially efficient whenever $s - a - r$ and digital is socially efficient whenever $s - \frac{C_A - C_D}{N} < \rho b^L + (1 - \rho) b^H < s - a$.

Excessive switching occurs whenever the threshold for the decentralized outcome is lower than the corresponding threshold for the first-best outcome. In other words, $b^H - \frac{1}{\rho} \left(b^H - s + \frac{C_A - C_D}{N} \right) > s - a - \frac{C_A - C_D}{N}$, or equivalently $b^H < s - \frac{C_A - C_D}{N} + \frac{\rho}{1-\rho} a$. By taking into account that $s - a - r < b^H$, we also need to have $\frac{1}{1-\rho} a + r > \frac{C_A - C_D}{N}$. For example, excessive switching occurs when $b^H = \min \left\{ s - \frac{C_A - C_D}{N} + \frac{\rho}{1-\rho} a, s - a \right\} - \varepsilon$ and $b^L = s - a - \frac{1}{N}(C_A - C_D) + \varepsilon$.

Similarly, insufficient switching occurs whenever $b^H > s - \frac{C_A - C_D}{N} + \frac{\rho}{1-\rho} a$. Yet, since $b^H < s - a$, we also need to have $\frac{C_A - C_D}{N} > \frac{1}{1-\rho} a$. For example, insufficient switching occurs when $b^H = \max \left\{ s - \frac{C_A - C_D}{N} + \frac{\rho}{1 - \rho} a, s - a - r \right\} + 2\varepsilon$ and $b^L = s - a - r + \varepsilon$.

Proof of Proposition 3

For the purpose of this proof, it is enough to concentrate on the case in which the preference parameters of the low-type viewer are located in area AA of Figure 11.1 and the preferences of the high-type viewer are in DD area. In the absence of subsidies, the low-type viewer would then remain with analog service in both periods, while the high-type viewer would switch to digital in the first period. We also make an additional assumption that $b_1^H + \delta b_2^L > s_1$. This assumption requires that the high-type viewer prefers DD to AD even when offered a subsidy equal to $s_2 - b_2^L$ for switching in the second period.

Providing the two types of viewers with the previous choices presented requires operating both technologies in both periods. The platform operator might find such a solution costly and decide instead to offer a subsidy to the viewers to induce them to change their decision.

Nine final scenarios can be envisaged, as each type of viewer might potentially end up in either one of the three areas AA, AD, and DD. The platform operator's problem aims at the cheapest among these nine scenarios.

We now compute the costs associated with each of these nine scenarios. Let $C_{ij,IJ}$ denote the present value of the costs incurred by the platform operator when the low-type (high-type) viewer chooses technology i (I) in the first period and technology j (J) in the second period, while taking offered subsidies as given. Obviously each cost $C_{ij,IJ}$ has two components: the cost of operating the given technology (coexistence of technologies is allowed) and the cost of subsidies that induce viewers to switch to that technology. For example, $C_{AD,DD}$ is the present value of the cost the platform operator incurs when the subsidies induce the low-type viewer to choose analog in the first period and digital in the second, and the high-type viewer to choose digital technology in both periods.

Depending on the final position taken by the two types of viewers, the platform operator's costs are:

(i) $C_{AA,AA} = C_A + \delta C_A$;

(ii) $C_{AA,AD} = C_A + \delta C_A + \delta C_D$;

(iii) $C_{AA,DD} = C_A + C_D + \delta C_A + \delta C_D$;

(iv) (AD, AA) – not feasible;

(v) $C_{AD,AD} = C_A + \delta C_D + \delta(s_2 - b_2^L)$;

(vi) $C_{AD,DD} = C_A + C_D + \delta C_D + \delta \rho(s_2 - b_2^L)$;

(vii) (DD,AA) – not feasible;

(viii)(DD,AD) – not feasible;

(ix) $C_{DD,DD} = C_D + \delta C_D + (s_1 - b_1^L - \delta b_2^L)$.

In this list, the cost $C_{AD,DD} = C_A + C_D + \delta C_D + \delta \rho(s_2 - b_2^L)$ in (vi) should be read as follows: The first two terms represent the transmission cost for analog and digital in the first period. The third term represents the present value of the cost of operating digital technology only in the second period. The last term denotes the subsidy given to the low-type viewers that induces them to switch to digital in the second period. High-type viewers prefer to switch early and not wait for the late subsidy in this case. The last term of $C_{AD,DD}$ denotes the present value of the costs associated with this subsidy policy. The other costs in the list can be interpreted in a similar manner.

Note that there is no subsidy policy implementing cases (AD,AA), (DD,AA), and (DD,AD) as any subsidy designed for low-type viewers would be taken by high-type viewers too, who would never switch to digital later than low-type viewers, since choices are monotonic in preferences.

In its cost minimization problem, the platform compares the values in (i) to (ix). It can be seen that technology patterns (AA,AD) and (AA,DD) are not profitable, as they are dominated by the pattern (AA,AA). We are interested under which conditions pattern (AD,DD) is optimal. By comparing costs (i), (v), (vi), and (ix), we conclude that pattern (AD,DD) is optimal if the following conditions are satisfied:

$$\frac{C_D}{\delta(1-\rho)} \leq s_2 - b_2^L \leq \frac{\delta C_A - C_D - \delta C_D}{\delta\rho}, \qquad (1)$$

and

$$s_2 - b_2^L \leq \frac{s_1 - b_1^L - \delta b_2^L - C_A}{\delta\rho}. \qquad (2)$$

The first inequality is only feasible if

$$\frac{C_A}{C_D} \geq 1 + \frac{1}{\delta(1-\rho)}, \qquad (3)$$

and inequalities (1) and (2) can be satisfied simultaneously if and only if

$$s_1 - b_1^L - \delta b_2^L \geq C_A + \frac{\rho}{1-\rho} C_D. \qquad (4)$$

So, whenever conditions (1) through (4) hold, it is in the platform operator's interest to induce asynchronous switching by viewers. This can be the case when δ and s_1 are large, but ρ, b_1^L, and b_2^L are small.

12 | Should competition policy favor compatibility?

JOSEPH FARRELL

Abstract

A widespread "pro-standards view" holds that compatibility standards and modularity are beneficial but are under-supplied by imperfect markets. The author stresses that this view is not unambiguously proven by economic logic, but tentatively concludes that it is more right than wrong, especially where it affects horizontal competition.

1 Introduction

Standards mavens often think that compatible competition is more competitive, more efficient, and more salubrious than incompatible competition; and they worry that private interests do not reliably reflect these social advantages. Such a view suggests that policy should seek compatibility and should guard against sabotage by special interests that gain from incompatibility.

Economists know that this pro-standards view (PSV) is not always right: It depends. Yet, stressing "on the one hand versus on the other hand" may give policymakers the wrong idea. As a step toward averting that problem, I undertake the uncomfortable project of going beyond "it depends" – even though it does. At a rigorous level, any such attempt must fail, but if I push myself to decide anyway, I make the judgment call that policy probably should thoughtfully encourage compatibility, especially in horizontal contexts. The PSV channels the

These views are mine alone, but my thinking draws on joint work with Michael Katz, Garth Saloner, Carl Shapiro, and Phil Weiser. Paul Klemperer urged me to go beyond "it depends," and our joint work (Farrell and Klemperer, in press) takes a similar view. The present paper grew (painfully and very slowly) out of a presentation at the Federal Reserve Board's Chicago conference in May 2004; I thank Shane Greenstein and Victor Stango for patience and helpful comments, Joel West for recording my oral presentation, and Kathleen Foley for transcribing it.

spirit of much sound economic analysis: The standards mavens are more right than wrong.

Outside the horizontal context, the key question is, How does competition deal with complementarities? Ambivalence on that question infests telecommunications policy and a wide swath of antitrust, including tying, aftermarket competition, essential facilities, intrabrand competition, and bundling. These questions understandably make many observers uncomfortable, and the PSV seems less strong, but still well worth taking seriously.

2 Horizontal and vertical forms of the pro-standards view

I start by drawing a (not watertight) distinction between what I call the horizontal and vertical questions. Suppose Firm M offers a product or platform P for which systems issues arise, by which we mean that the supply of complements to P is important and potentially problematic.[1] Two broad questions about openness then arise:

The vertical question: If another firm N wants to offer a complement to P, can it just do so, or must it get M's permission? If the latter, permission might be given, denied, or conditioned on payments (access charges) that may be clear in advance (i.e., transparent) or not. If N can offer a complement, perhaps with transparent access charges, we call this *vertically open*. If it has to get permission, especially if permission is often refused or is subject to burdensome or competitively worrying conditions, we call this *vertically closed*. Some platforms are clearly open, some clearly closed, and some in a gray area.

The horizontal question: If someone offers a substitute Q for platform P, can consumers of Q automatically use the complements that consumers of P can use? (Note that much may be buried in the adverb *automatically*.) Again, there is a matter of degree: If it is easy to port complements, then the platform may be fairly open. This formulation applies most readily to indirect network effects, where there is a clear division between consumers and complementors, who interact via P or via Q. With direct network effects the complements may *be* the consumers, or be hard to separate from them, as happens with communications networks.

---

[1] Importance alone is not enough – napkins are an important complement to McDonald's hamburgers, but we need not worry too much about systems issues, because the supply of napkins is not much affected by what they do.

The vertical/horizontal distinction helps clarify the often murky term *open standard*. For instance, Microsoft's Windows platform is normally vertically open – independent complements are allowed and even solicited (this is called *evangelism*). Yet, Windows is horizontally closed: A Windows application does not also run on competing operating systems unless the applications provider or the competing operating systems vendor incurs real costs to make it do so. Indeed, the famous *United States* v. *Microsoft* (2001) antitrust case can be viewed as saying that Microsoft was not entitled to withdraw vertical openness (to Netscape Navigator in particular) when that might indirectly enhance horizontal openness and weaken the "applications barrier to entry" that protected Microsoft's platform dominance.

As another illustration, in the America Online (AOL)–Time Warner merger, the Federal Trade Commission focused largely on vertical openness: Could other Internet Service Providers get nondiscriminatory access to Time Warner's cable? Meanwhile the Federal Communications Commission focused on horizontal openness: Could users of non-AOL instant messaging systems communicate with their AOL friends?[2]

2.1 Horizontal compatibility

Does competition work better when each seller M manages its own separate supply of complements (as in closed organization or with horizontal incompatibility) or when they are shared (as in open organization or with horizontal compatibility)? In the end, overall, I tend to favor the latter view, the horizontal PSV, but there are sensible arguments in the other direction; the balance, of course, depends on the specific case.

Incentives for building networks: Each M has a stronger incentive to optimize its supply of complements when that supply is proprietary, and there will be a free-rider problem if it is shared (see Kristiansen and Thum 1997). That is, network size becomes a public good among compatible rivals. Of course, the force of this argument depends inter alia on the extent to which an efficient supply of complements requires active "evangelism."

---

[2] See Faulhaber (2004).

Price competition: Incompatibility can either blunt or sharpen price competition; it is more likely to sharpen it if adopters collectively are very good at choosing the collective best deal, meaning that both coordination and (if necessary) side payments among adopters work well. Suppose that competing products are horizontally differentiated: some customers prefer one, some the other. If the products are compatible, any horizontal differentiation confers some market power in the usual way. If they are incompatible, competition for the market will be fierce and reasonably efficient if collective adoption decisions maximize collective adoption value by "tipping" the market to one product or the other. Incompatibility then requires that some adopters have the wrong product for their needs or tastes, but that sacrifice may be worthwhile for the gain in incentives and for the sharpened competition.

Few consumers would seek to maximize the number of markets that look like traditional franchised monopolies such as cable television (Williamson 1976). But there are real-world cases where buyers seem to like winner-take-all competition for the field. Dana (2005) has explored buyers' (notably hospitals') groups, which often adopt a strategy of buying all, or nearly all, their products from a single vendor. By *adopt a strategy*, I mean more than just that one vendor ultimately supplies all or most of the customer's requirements: the strategy is a commitment to such a lopsided outcome, even if bids are close enough that, ex post, the buyers would be better off each choosing based on product differentiation.

The buyer group has thus shifted the locus of competition among vendors from the individual product to the range of requirements, strategically replacing competition in the market with competition for the market. This shift can benefit buyers by weakening differentiation in two ways. First, by a law of large numbers, more customers will be near the middle of a Hotelling line in terms of aggregate tastes for a whole range of goods, than will be near the middle for each particular good. Second, because a hospital can be a buying agent for many doctors, nurses, and janitors, decentralized procurement would allow each staff member to pay more for his or her preferred brand, but if different staff members prefer different brands then central procurement is a commitment to ignore such preferences.

While it may be suspicious when *vendors* tie or bundle, we would expect it to be pro-buyer on balance when *buyers* voluntarily commit to (indeed, insist on) this. Yet some discomfort remains: Even if the hospital's choices reflect final consumers' price/quality trade-offs, might not this strategic overweighting of price (relative to product differentiation) inefficiently encourage cheap-and-crummy rather than innovative products?[3] And if it works well there, it is probably because those buyer groups do a fairly good job of choosing among bids, and this not only helps directly but also encourages vendors to offer their best bids.

It is not so clear that "the market" does so well with decentralized choice and proprietary network effects; this makes the PSV more pessimistic about incompatible competition. The market may tip to a product that does not offer the most surplus, either because coordination is difficult and can seize on ad hoc focal points, or because strategic players manipulate the market's techniques of coordination. In particular, expectations may focus on an incumbent, a powerful firm, or the historic status quo, rather than responding sharply to small changes in surplus actually offered. Even if the surplus-maximizing product is adopted in the end, competition will be softened if sellers do not perceive that small improvements in relative surplus offered would *reliably* drive shifts in coordination. Technically, incompatible competition sharpens competition for pivotal adopters and weakens competition for non-pivotal adopters; if adopters make a well-coordinated surplus-driven collective choice then they are all pivotal, while, for instance, if each expects most others to stick to the status quo (e.g., buy from Microsoft because that is what people do), then none is pivotal.

Moreover, if the market fails to tip, then incompatibility sacrifices network effects; and this can happen through Pareto-inefficient "splintering" as well as through tolerably well-functioning trade-offs between variety and economies of scale as in Dixit-Stiglitz-Spence.

My judgment is that large-numbers coordination problems are seldom beautifully solved. They may remain unsolved for long periods (splintering); perhaps more often, they are solved in imperfect ways – by

---

[3] Some years ago the *San Francisco Chronicle* ran a series of articles about how innovators in "safety needles," less likely to jab nurses accidentally, had trouble selling to hospitals. Blame was laid in part on hospitals' contracts to procure a large percentage of their needs from specified distributors; not all these distributors offered safety needles, and some nurses contracted diseases when accidentally jabbed by non-safety needles that had been used on infected patients (Carlsen 1999).

convention, authority, clumsy agreement, or chaotic (in the nontechnical as well as technical senses) dynamics whose outcomes may look more like those in Arthur (1989) than in Farrell and Saloner (1985), even if participants seek to apply foresight. I am not proposing a policy to improve the market's coordination processes. Rather, my point is that those coordination problems are difficult, making it wise to avoid them if we can, by facilitating compatible competition. Under compatible competition, the coordination problem does not arise.

In addition to "inherent" coordination problems (broadly construed), incompatible competition makes gradual entry (which is the usual kind) hard. Conditional on incompatibility, it may or may not make it too hard, but that's not the comparison I'm making here. Moreover, this in turn makes predation more rewarding. Should policy respond by being more alert to the dangers of predation where there are incompatible network effects? Perhaps, yet the complex dynamics of proprietary-network markets makes good predation policy extremely difficult (Farrell and Katz 2005). Similarly, proprietary network effects can set up incentives for anticompetitive product preannouncements (Farrell and Saloner 1986). Limiting (truthful) preannouncements would be risky, and I am not advocating that policy should do so; rather, the point is that, given incompatible competition, any policy on preannouncements, as on predation, risks leaving anticompetitive opportunities, banning legitimate behavior, or both. If we can avoid this problem by steering toward compatible competition, it would seem wise.

For reasons such as these, after many years of thinking about incompatible competition, I believe that unless adopters coordinate very well (both on initial choices and on subsequent switches), incompatible competition is apt to work poorly. Will compatible competition work better? I believe on average it will, but of course the real question is how well it will work if it is imposed when it does not emerge "naturally" in the market. This distinction matters in two ways: the market's choice may signal or reflect efficiency, and imposition of compatibility might create its own problems.

The first of these points can be restated as the idea that failings of incompatible competition will create incentives for compatibility. Thus, Katz and Shapiro (1986) analyze a dynamic version of the Einhorn (1992) compatibility-enables-specialization model,[4] and find

---

[4] Matutes and Regibeau (1988) combined this idea with horizontal differentiation.

Joseph Farrell

that firms' incentives to choose compatibility are ample, indeed excessive, when incompatibility will induce splintering and (with or without compatibility) there will be fierce competition in surplus. Another kind of evidence is that competitors often gather in standards organizations to set voluntary consensus standards, a process whose main role, arguably, is to avert splintering. As those illustrations might suggest, the point seems more compelling if incompatible competition would lead to splintering, and less likely if it would reinforce a dominant incumbent's position.[5] Meanwhile, Einhorn's results often are reversed when we move from duopoly to vertically differentiated oligopoly (Palfrey 1983; Farrell et al. 1998).

Does policy-mandated compatibility involve severe problems? One such problem might be lock-in on the compatibility standard itself. For this reason it seems worth considering giving people rights to ensure compatibility (even going against intellectual property rights) rather than letting governments or committees set binding compatibility standards. The strongest case for mandated compatibility is when there is an important interface that is an unlikely locus of technological progress, and private control of which would lead to a great deal of market power generated by adopter coordination problems rather than by true superiority. Compulsory standards on which side of the road to drive and on telephone jacks are nice (but it's good that the latter didn't stop the development of Ethernet jacks); a government-mandated computer operating system standard would be unwise.

2.2 Vertical compatibility

Modularity is an important technique for both product design and project management. Surely there are big gains from modularity in competition also: This is what vertical openness is about. Complementors to a vertically open platform P do not need to worry about their relationships with M, about M confiscating their quasi-rents, etc. They just need to make better and cheaper complements than others. There is a lot of good to that system.

---

[5] Farrell and Klemperer (in press) argue that *splintering* means equilibria that are not coalition-proof, and that voluntary consensus standards can be interpreted as the formation of voluntary coalitions that block splintering equilibria.

Modularity also implements specialization, or division of the market (in the positive Adam Smith sense, not the antitrust sense). Someone with an idea for an Internet-based application or a website need not worry about stringing wires all over the place, nor about reaching a deal with those who have done so. He may have to pay the latter for the use of its wires, but in a predictable, transparent, non-discriminatory way. Specialization is important, not least because the corporate cultures, competences, and skills that make a firm good at stringing wires may not make it good at dreaming up off-the-wall applications. This is closely linked to the classic antitrust "two-level entry" concern: If an incumbent can force an entrant to do many things at once, entry gets harder.

Given this praise for modularity, the PSV seems very natural: Why wouldn't we want to protect these benefits of modularity? As above, I start by rehearsing the main arguments against. First, it is not always clear what interfaces should be protected. One might talk about "wires" versus "applications," but the Internet has more than just two layers. This is just an updated classic antitrust question about tying: To protect the independent competitiveness of markets for accessories to cars, should car manufacturers not pre-install radios? How about tires? How about fuel gauges? The same inevitable arbitrariness came up in the classic "protect modular competition" case, namely, the breakup of AT&T. Courts had to define *long-distance* telephone service, which cannot be done really well.

While this can be a real issue, I do not think it is the core concern. Often, we can more or less tell what (at least some of) the modularity boundaries should be, and the fact that there are inevitable gray areas need not force us to abandon the whole notion.

Another concern is that – especially in innovative markets – openness can be allergic to vertical integration ("competing with one's custo-mers"). The Justice Department took this view in the AT&T breakup and insisted that requiring the Bell system be open to independent long-distance providers would not work if Bell were providing long-distance service itself (as the Bell companies now do, following implementation of Section 271 of the 1996 Telecommunications Act). Proponents sometimes argue that "parity pricing" can yield the best of both worlds, but there are reasons to doubt this claim.[6] Even when manufacturer M is vividly aware of the benefits of modularity, it may have a hard

---

[6] See the regulatory literature on vertical separation, and recently Farrell (2003).

time sustaining those benefits if it also integrates.[7] Thus, modularity may require a sacrifice of some otherwise efficient vertical integration. And vertical integration also facilitates price discrimination, which generally improves M's payoff. Thus, one view is that modularity, while efficient ex post, hinders M's attempts to collect the surplus created by building platform P, with bad *ex ante* consequences.

Both of these concerns suggest that policymakers perhaps should not take the PSV at face value but may need to do a thorough cost/benefit analysis of modularity, or of protecting a particular interface. The third argument against mandated modularity, in contrast, advises them to do no cost/benefit analysis themselves but to delegate it to M. The argument claims that when modularity is efficient, M will implement it voluntarily, so no cost/benefit analysis is called for (except for M's own). According to this argument, while modularity may be valuable 99.44 percent of the time, *mandated* modularity is bad because the mandate only binds when M dislikes modularity, and that fact signals its inefficiency.

Phil Weiser and I call this claim (an extension of the Chicago School's "one monopoly rent" argument) ICE, or internalization of complementary efficiencies.[8] When more and better complements for P are available at lower prices, demand for P rises – by a vertical shift equal to the resulting increase in surplus available to those who have P. Ideally, this prospect induces M to internalize the complementary efficiencies (efficiencies in the complements to P), and therefore to pick an efficient policy governing the supply of those complements.

That efficient policy often will be openness, because complements for P (like goods generally) are often best supplied by open competition. Nevertheless, it is not true that competition at all imaginable layers is always efficient. Indeed, firms exist largely because sometimes open competition is better, sometimes hand-in-glove integration is better, and sometimes some intermediate approach is best.[9] Even

---

[7] See Gawer and Henderson (2003) on Intel's practices in this area, and Farrell and Katz (2000) for economic theory.

[8] Farrell and Weiser (2003) explain ICE and its link to the Chicago School's "one monopoly rent theorem."

[9] Thus, for example, modularity may come at the cost of finger-pointing when something goes wrong, as was argued in the Kodak case (see *Eastman Kodak* v. *Image Technical Services* [1992]). In telecommunications, rhetoric and policy have vacillated between the appeal of modularity and the appeal of integration or one system.

when the efficient policy is not openness, the ICE argument suggests that (efficiency-oriented) competition policy should not intervene.[10] If M internalizes efficiencies and inefficiencies in the market(s) for complements to P, this argues for vertical laissez faire. If one accepts this argument, it lets us delegate (to the presumably better informed M) the subtle trade-offs that otherwise policy might have to address. Likewise, it relieves us of having to fight M's many techniques for controlling would-be complementors' access to P, if M decides to do so.[11]

Unfortunately, ICE can break in many ways. For instance, it breaks if M's price or profits in P are bindingly regulated; if control of complements helps M to price discriminate; if the presence of independent complements might aid a competitor to P; if there is a large installed base of platform owners, etc. We do not altogether know how often and how badly ICE breaks: Is it a pretty good guiding principle with some exceptions, or is it a Swiss cheese, a fishing net, a mass of holes? Views differ widely.

Sometimes we can reliably assess ICE in a particular case, and then we do not need to know how it does on average. This is the spirit of rule-of-reason treatment of vertical issues. Unfortunately, it is not always easy to assess ICE in a specific case, either. Some of the ways ICE *can* break – notably the incentive for price discrimination – are pervasive, so one often cannot trust ICE fully, but this does not imply that it actually breaks, let alone that specific real-world policies in response will help.

Thus this way of understanding vertical complementarity issues is helpful but sometimes seems to raise as many questions as it answers. The grayness of this intellectual guidance is a recipe for intellectual discomfort, inconsistencies, and debates that feature more heat than light. How far to trust firms in their dealings with complementors, and what to do about it if we cannot, is among the hardest and most

---

[10] In antitrust, some use the term *competition* or its cognates to mean economic efficiency and/or consumer welfare, making it a semantic challenge to distinguish (1) the substantive claim that competition usually serves those ends from (2) a tautology.

[11] See, for instance, the article by MacKie-Mason and Netz in this volume. Legal controversies over leveraging supply a list of ways in which M can achieve this. For instance, it can assert intellectual property over the interface; or it can strategically change the interface without much warning (see *ILC Peripherals* v. *IBM* [1978]; *Transamerica Computer* v. *IBM* [1979]; *Berkey Photo* v. *Eastman Kodak* [1980]; and *C. R. Bard* v. *M3 Systems* [1998]).

controversial questions in antitrust and telecommunications policy. In the subsequent sections, I provide a few examples.

Aftermarkets

When a manufacturer M sells a product P, should policy seek to protect competition in spare parts, service, etc., for M's product P? For some reason the question has been especially prominent for photocopiers: The most famous aftermarket case (in the United States) is *Image Technical Services* v. *Eastman Kodak* (1990), and the Federal Circuit more recently heard a case against Xerox.[12] But it arises in many markets including computers, automobile parts, and medical equipment.

In terms of the ICE argument, the question is whether exclusion of independent service in the aftermarket can both harm consumers and be profitable for M, or whether any markup or performance problem in the aftermarket amply feeds through into lower demand in the foremarket (for photocopiers, say) and is therefore unprofitable whenever it is inefficient. That is, can we trust M to organize the provision of parts and service efficiently?

ICE was much discussed in the Kodak case, under the name *the systems theory*. The Supreme Court instructed courts not to be awed by this theory but to examine the facts. Arguably (see, e.g., Shapiro 1995; Borenstein et al. 2000) the systems theory did not apply fully to Kodak, perhaps especially because it had an incentive to exploit its installed base ex post. We should, however, beware of rejecting ICE in all-or-nothing fashion. If (discounted) future sales are large compared to the installed base, one might reasonably argue that ICE "almost" applied. Of course, if one thought that aftermarket monopolization could not be efficient (and could see a good remedy), one might ask why society should put up with *any* such harm. Or, by analogy with modern policy on horizontal mergers, some might suggest that when the consumer harm and (a fortiori) excess profits are small, perhaps there is an efficiency explanation.

Finally, much discussion has focused on competition in the foremarket and the idea that this will rebate to consumers any aftermarket profits. From an ICE perspective this seems odd: after all, ICE applies to a monopoly M. The argument, however, seems to be that if a monopoly mismanages its value chain (by failing to commit efficiently

---

[12] See MacKie-Mason and Metzler (2004) and Shapiro (1995).

to aftermarket openness, for instance), consumers suffer, while if a firm in a "competitive" market does so, it is its own problem. Thus, competitiveness of the foremarket is a partial backstop if ICE breaks down, although this is not as simple as it may sound.[13]

Intrabrand competition

When M is a manufacturer of P, and the relevant complements are distributors (or perhaps other complementors), the vertical openness question is whether there is free intrabrand competition. Should M be expected to set a wholesale price and let all comers buy (in appropriate quantity) at wholesale, or is it acceptable for M to impose conditions, especially conditions that look like restrictions on competition? This issue has arisen, for instance, in resale price maintenance. In *Albrecht* v. *Herald Company* (1968), the Supreme Court held that resale price maintenance was per se illegal, a category supposed to indicate that there is no room for further debate about effects. In *State Oil* v. *Khan* (1997), Judge Posner pointed out that this was wrong for maximum resale price maintenance (the retailer promises to charge no more than $X). The more worrying "minimum RPM," or agreement that the retailer will not charge less than $Y, remains illegal despite the ICE argument that it may be efficient if M voluntarily engages in it.

Telecommunications

Physical telecommunications networks are costly and few; so how should the provision of services over those networks be organized? On the one hand, coordination (plausibly through integration) might avert network harm, facilitate priority routing, or limit destructive services such as spam. Even aside from such ex post efficiency gains, allowing integration boosts the incentive to build a network. On the other hand, we may well gain immensely (as the history of the Internet suggests) from untrammeled open innovation.

Starting with *Hush-a-Phone* v. *United States* (1957) and the AT&T breakup, modern telecommunications policy in the US and increasingly worldwide sought to protect competition in complements to network

---

[13] Shapiro (1995) shows that if foremarket competition holds overall profits to zero whether or not aftermarket competition is protected, then consumers' gains from an antitrust rule that protects aftermarket competition are (in a parameterized example) often substantially lower than one would think looking only at the aftermarket.

bottlenecks. This approach may have peaked in the 1996 Telecommunications Act, which required incumbents to unbundle a wide range of things that rivals could not readily *provide* but that they might want to *complement*. In that respect, the Act was essential-facilities on steroids.

As William Baxter, President Reagan's assistant attorney general for antitrust, stressed in the AT&T case, ICE predictably breaks when regulation constrains returns in the platform but not in its complements, because then the downward vertical shift in platform demand translates into only a small horizontal inward shift at the regulated price. Moreover, the price discrimination exception to ICE applies not only in the "old, regulated" telecom world but also in the "new, unregulated" worlds of wireless and broadband. But, of course, the failure of ICE tells us only that we cannot expect vertical laissez faire to get the right modularity boundaries; it does not tell us what those boundaries should be.

One answer, arguably as in the breakup of AT&T, the *Kodak* case, and the Telecommunications Act, is that policy should enforce competition in every layer where it is sustainable. Yet, this answer is too extreme: There may well be layers where competition would be sustainable but not particularly valuable. An equally undiscriminating opposite answer is to eschew unbundling mandates, as if we trusted ICE despite the reasons not to. A case-by-case treatment is difficult and can look (or be) inconsistent.

This has led to sustained discomfort among thoughtful people, and a retreat to dogma and rhetoric among others. Those favoring unbundling mandates stress the benefits of competition, often without noting the inherent limitations of intrabrand competition. Those opposed stress the costs of regulation and the gains from one-system integration, often without noting how weak ICE tends to be in this context.

In telecommunications, rejection of ICE has sometimes been taken to suggest not only mandating that independent complementors be allowed, but (since an integrated M often has incentives to exclude them) also "quarantining" M away from the market for complements to P. But this has generated discomfort and policy reversals. For instance, the 1984 breakup of AT&T quarantined the Bells from long-distance and equipment; the 1996 Telecommunications Act let them back in (with conditions). The Bells were sometimes quarantined, sometimes not, from enhanced/information services in the Federal Communication Commission's back-and-forth rules in *Computer Inquiries I, II, III*. Possibly these policy shifts reflected changed circumstances, but I suspect a greener-grass syndrome produced by the fundamental vertical discomfort and ambivalence.

Current US telecommunications policy, especially in broadband, seems to be shifting away from the PSV and toward a laissez-faire approach, or possibly even back toward the pre-*Hush-A-Phone* "one system" view that stressed the (real) advantages of vertical integration and/or vertical laissez faire. This shift is to the consternation of those, such as Stanford Law Professor Lawrence Lessig, who believe that vertical compatibility, or modularity, has great advantages and that we cannot (ICE-style) count on M to recognize and be persuaded by those advantages. Brennan (2005) suggests that the Supreme Court's *Trinko* ruling reverses Baxter's understanding of the relationship between regulation and antitrust. As in the aftermarket context, some argue against vertical modularity based on an increase (sometimes overstated) in horizontal competition against the core bottleneck.

3 Where does this leave us?

I have said elsewhere that the difference between an economist and a non-economist is that the economist understands why ICE is true, while the difference between an economist and a good economist is that the good economist *also* understands why it is false. In broad terms, a firm has an incentive to make sure its complements are efficiently supplied; but there can be important exceptions to this; and some of the exceptions can be hard to diagnose.

Given what we know now, I think it probably would be wise to protect the modularity of the Internet, as discussed in Farrell (2006); yet I cannot come as close to endorsing the vertical PSV as I can to endorsing its horizontal form. Competition within a bottleneck, let alone within a non-bottleneck platform, tends to be a lower policy priority than making real competition against a bottleneck feasible, and when M is a residual claimant, ICE can have real power.

In the end, it depends on the case, though this will disappoint readers who have come this far and expect a ringing conclusion. I have heard attributed to Judge Posner the slogan that vertical antitrust claims should be approached with skepticism but not incredulity. Let me close with the equally true opposite slogan:[14] A firm's dealings with its complementors should be approached with sympathy, since it wants its value chain to work efficiently. But those dealings can readily affect rivalry and efficiency in other ways, and so the sympathy should not soften into credulity.

References

Albrecht v. *Herald Co.* 1968. 390 US 145.

Arthur, W. Brian 1989. "Competing technologies, increasing returns, and lock-in by historical events," *Economic Journal* 99: 116–31.

Berkey Photo, Inc. v. *Eastman Kodak Co.* 1980. 444 US 1093.

Borenstein, Severin, Jeffrey MacKie-Mason, and Janet Netz 2000. "Exercising market power in proprietary aftermarkets," *Journal of Economics and Management Strategy* 9: 157–88.

Brennan, Tim 2005. "*Trinko* v. *Baxter*: The demise of *US* v. *AT&T*," *Antitrust Bulletin* 50, http://ssrn.com/abstract=831870.

Carlsen, William 1999. "Hospitals, clinics tell of needle sticks; in reports, many ask that OSHA require the use of safety devices," *San Francisco Chronicle*, March 17.

C. R. Bard, Inc. v. *M3 Systems, Inc.* 1998. 157 F.3d 1340 (Fed. Cir. 1998).

Dana, James 2005. "Buyer groups as strategic commitments," CSIO Working Paper 0067. Evanston, IL: Northwestern University.

Eastman Kodak Company v. *Image Technical Services, Inc.* 1992. 504 US 451.

Einhorn, Michael 1992. "Mix and match compatibility with vertical product dimensions," *RAND Journal of Economics* 23: 535–47.

Farrell, Joseph 2003. "Integration and independent innovation on a network," *American Economic Review* 93: 420–4.

   2006. "Open access arguments," in *Net neutrality or net neutering: Should broadband services be regulated?* Thomas Lenard and Randolph May (eds.), Amsterdam: Kluwer.

Farrell, Joseph, and Michael Katz 2000. "Innovation, rent extraction, and integration in systems markets," *Journal of Industrial Economics* 48: 413–32.

---

[14] Supposedly it was physicist Niels Bohr who said that the opposite of a deep truth is also a deep truth, although this one may be more a rephrasing than an opposite.

2005. "Competition or predation? Consumer coordination, strategic pricing, and price floors in network markets," *Journal of Industrial Economics* 53: 203–31.

Farrell, Joseph, and Paul Klemperer, in press. "Coordination and lock-in: Competition with switching costs and network effects," in *Handbook of industrial organization*, Vol. III, Mark Armstrong and Robert Porter (eds.), Amsterdam: Elsevier.

Farrell, Joseph, Hunter Monroe, and Garth Saloner 1998. "The vertical structure of industry: Systems competition versus component competition," *Journal of Economics and Management Strategy* 7: 143–82.

Farrell, Joseph, and Garth Saloner 1985. "Standardization, compatibility, and innovation," *RAND Journal of Economics* 6: 70–83.

1986. "Installed base and compatibility: Innovation, product preannouncements and predation," *American Economic Review* 76: 940–55.

Farrell, Joseph, and Philip Weiser 2003. "Modularity, vertical integration, and open access policies: Towards a convergence of antitrust and regulation in the information age," *Harvard Journal of Law and Technology* 17: 85–135.

Faulhaber, Gerald 2004. "Access and network effects in the 'New Economy': AOL-Time Warner (2000)," in *The antitrust revolution*, John Kwoka and Lawrence White (eds.), New York: Oxford University Press, 453–75.

Gawer, Annabelle, and Rebecca Henderson 2003. "Organizational capability and entry into complementary markets: Evidence from Intel," mimeo, Boston: Sloan School, MIT.

Hush-A-Phone Corporation v. *United States of America* 1957. 238 F.2d 266, 268 (DC Cir. 1956), on remand, 22 FCC 112 (1957).

ILC Peripherals Leasing Corporation v. *International Business Machines Corporation* 1978. 458 F. Supp. 423 (ND Cal.).

Image Technical Service [sic], *Inc.* v. *Eastman Kodak Co.* 1990. 903 F.2d 612 (9th Cir. 1990).

Katz, Michael, and Carl Shapiro 1986. "Product compatibility choice in a market with technological progress," *Oxford Economic Papers* 38 (Supplement: Strategic Behaviour and Industrial Competition): 146–65.

Kristiansen, Eirik, and Marcel Thum 1997. "R&D incentives in compatible networks," *Journal of Economics* 65: 55–78.

MacKie-Mason, Jeffrey, and John Metzler 2004. "Links between markets and aftermarkets: *Kodak* (1997)," in *The antitrust revolution*, John Kwoka and Lawrence White (eds.), New York: Oxford University Press, 428–52.

Matutes, Carmen, and Pierre Regibeau 1988. " 'Mix and match': Product compatibility without network externalities," *RAND Journal of Economics* 19: 221–34.

Palfrey, Thomas 1983. "Bundling decisions by a multi-product monopolist with incomplete information," *Econometrica* 51: 463–83.

Shapiro, Carl 1995. "Aftermarkets and consumer welfare: Making sense of *Kodak*," *Antitrust Law Journal* 63: 483–511.

State Oil Company v. *Barkat U. Khan and Khan & Associates, Inc.* 1997. 522 US 3.

Transamerica Computer Company v. *International Business Machines Corporation* 1979. 481 F. Supp. 965 (ND Cal.).

United States of America v. *Microsoft Corporation* 2001. 253 F.3d 34 (DC Cir. 2001).

Williamson, Oliver 1976. "Franchise bidding for natural monopolies: In general and with respect to CATV," *Bell Journal of Economics* 7: 73–104.

Index

389